CHILD DEVELOPMENT 0–5

Holmes McDougall
SEMINARS

Child Development 0-5

Margaret Roberts (0−2 years)
Joan Tamburrini (2−5 years)

General Editor:
Michael Morgan

 Holmes McDougall

© 1981 Selection and Editorial M. Roberts and J. Tamburrini

Printed and Published by
Holmes McDougall Ltd.
Allander House
137-141 Leith Walk
Edinburgh EH6 8NS

ISBN 0 7157 1966-1

Compiled and Edited by
Margaret Roberts and Joan Tamburrini

Foreword

This *Child Development Seminar* is intended to involve students in activities, some of which include observations of children, as well as reading. If one is to acquire any depth of understanding of this field neither observing children nor reading about their development is adequate on its own; both are necessary and interrelated.

Observation of children is insufficient by itself for two main reasons. First, one may fail to notice items of behaviour that are of considerable significance. In Module 2, some basic principles of how we perceive are discussed. It is shown that our perceptions are seldom faithful copies of reality. On the contrary, they are frequently modifications of reality resulting from our selecting some aspects and ignoring others. Indeed, sometimes our perceptions are distortions of reality and we are convinced that we have 'seen' something that is not there: a rich and much studied field in the psychology of perception has been, and continues to be, visual illusions. What we perceive is influenced by our expectations which, in turn, depend on what we already know or have experienced. The more one knows of the theory of child development the less likely one is to fail to notice significant items in children's behaviour.

The second reason for not confining a study of child development to observation is that we need to interpret and explain behaviour, not merely describe it. Sometimes at the beginning of their studies students we have taught have confessed that they believe interpreting and explaining children's behaviour is simply a matter of 'common sense'. It is not long before their reading of child development theory disabuses them of this notion. There are numerous examples in the papers in this book of common-sense interpretations clearly being incorrect. Two examples will suffice. Common sense suggests that children acquire language simply by imitating what adults say. Modul 6, on language development, describes a much more complex process in which children often compose phrases they cannot have heard and, thus, cannot have imitated, and, by contrast, are sometimes incapable of imitating phrases correctly even when carefully repeated several times by a patient and sympathetic adult. Explaining young children's drawings is another example where common sense is incorrect. The most frequent common-sense explanation of the strange characteristics of young children's drawings is in terms of their poor manual control. This common-sense explanation fails to take into account the universality of some of their features, for example that all young children at some time draw tadpole figures of human beings, that is figures with no apparent trunk, or that they frequently draw these figures with legs but no arms, but seldom with arms and no legs. No more manual conrol would seem to be necessary to draw a circular trunk than a circular head, or, when limbs are represented as stick-like appendages, to draw arms as well as legs. As Unit 2 of Module 5 shows, the ways in which psychologists have explained these universal features in young children's drawings are much more complex than the common-sense interpretation.

Some of the findings concerning children's development are dramatically surprising and quite at variance with common-sense suppositions. For example, the work of Bower reported in Unit 2 of Module 3 shows that the very young baby is more competent than we have hitherto supposed. Such findings have emerged not only from naturalistic observations of babies but also from highly original experimental situations such as those in which the baby's response is observed to 'virtual' objects, to objects that are made to appear and disappear, and to objects that are made to move in different directions and then become stationary. Experimental situations such as these have been devised to test hypotheses that have been generated as a result of questioning research findings and the theories explaining them. In sum, there is a close interrelationship between theory and observation in which theory leads an experimenter to observe behaviour he might otherwise not have noticed, and observations, in turn, serve to verify, refute, or elaborate theoretical notions.

The activities in this book that involve students in observing and working with children are essential to a proper understanding of the theoretical issues involved. In some cases observations precede the reading of a particular paper and are intended to give students first-hand experiences that will help them make more sense of issues discussed in it. In other cases, observation follows the reading of a paper so that students may be helped to see in practice the behaviour they have read about.

Other activities require students to isolate principles or draw conclusions from something they have read. These activities are an important part of the book. One of the most recurrent principles to emerge from studies of human learning is that it is most successful when the individual is actively engaged rather than being a passive recipient of information.

The reader will not proceed far with the papers in this book before discovering that sometimes there is not a right or wrong answer. Child development is a field of study where we often do not have clear unambiguous answers and where there are sometimes theories that appear to conflict. In some cases when this happens one theory seems, in the light of the evidence, more adequate than others. In other cases the conflict is spurious: the theories are complementary rather than contradictory, either explaining different facets of behaviour or each being a partial explanation of the same behaviour.

It can be argued that such a state of affairs indicates that child development is in good health, for science deals in relative, not absolute, truths, and good theories are ones that, in the light of empirical evidence, continually undergo modifications as well as elaboration. It means that students must be prepared to forego firm conclusions and to tolerate ambiguities. This is important to keep in mind with respect to the discussions which follow the study of each unit. Where conclusions can be drawn the discussions should make them clear, but where our knowledge is still in a relatively ambiguous or inconclusive state they are intended to clarify issues rather than reach firm conclusions.

Because many issues in child development theory are unresolved no student should think that at the end of a course of study he knows the field and needs to study no further. For anyone interested in the subject for its own sake, and for anyone concerned with its implications for professional practice, such as teaching or social work, child development should be a continuing study. This book is only an introduction to some of the major issues at this point in time, but we hope it will give students sufficient understanding to enable them subsequently to continue their studies independently. The suggestions for further reading should be of some help in this respect.

Perhaps, finally, something needs to be said about technical terms. We have tried to avoid these whenever they would be unnecessary jargonese. Where we have used technical terms it has been necessary because they have special meanings within a theory which are not quite the same as those of their counterparts in layman's language. We have tried to spell out the meanings of technical terms as much as possible in the text; where this has not been possible they should appear in the glossary.

Margaret Roberts
Joan Tamburrini

London, August 1981

Contents

The Seminar Series

An introduction by the General Editor.

The Holmes McDougall Seminar Series has been designed specifically for professional studies courses in initial teacher education and training and as resource material for in-service teacher training programmes. Further Seminars are being produced for study relevant to other professions.

The Seminars are produced either as *Study Kits,* packaged in a box containing sufficient resource material for four or five students, or as single *Seminar Books.*

1. What prompted the idea of the Seminar Series?

When compared with a properly planned and conducted small group situation the collective lecture method is not the most effective way of teaching. The idea of the Holmes McDougall Seminars is based on the knowledge that in courses of study in institutions of higher education, as well as in in-service education and training, seminar and other small group learning situations are key learning strategies.

It is widely known that students in training and practising teachers have shown a marked preference for this approach, which they see as a technique offering practical involvement in their studies not associated with the more usual practice of lectures followed by tutor-led group discussions. Indeed, the Seminar Series makes use of the objectives and methods that both trainee and experienced teachers are urged to adopt in their own teaching.

2. How, and in what professional settings, will the Seminars be used?

The concept of the Seminars is clearly in keeping with the most effective way in which adults learn and with the latest developments in teacher education and related professional training. They are designed to be used in a flexible way; the learning materials can provide the basis for a directed course of study in a college or they can be used in a variety of locations, in schools and elsewhere, by those groups of individuals who wish to control their own programme of work. Opportunities exist for tutors to play different roles, (eg. organiser/administrator; initiator/motivator; director/co-ordinator; evaluator) and the Seminars provide maximum scope for students to be given full responsibility for their own learning.

We visualise the Seminars being used in two distinctive but related situations:

(a)   in a college setting where the students using them will be following initial training courses and will have, in a seminar or tutorial group, access to a tutor who will organise the work of the group;

(b)   with qualified teachers following in-service programmes in their own schools, teachers' centres or in colleges where the Seminars can be studied by individuals or groups without, necessarily, having access to tutorial support.

Such a context is widely envisaged by the Editorial Board who have paid particular attention to the needs of the individual teacher or the unstructured self-supporting group who will make use of the material.

3. What kind of resource material is included in a typical Seminar?

Aims and objectives:

The student will find a statement of aims which governed the compilers' selection of topics and supporting material. The material is arranged in a series of *Modules* and *Units* of work, and a statement of the objectives for the student studying the material is set out. These objectives help the student to evaluate for himself what he is intended to gain from the study and provide key questions which he should be able to answer after study of the Seminar is concluded.

Resource Material:

Each Seminar includes a detailed *Study Guide* prepared by the compilers which refers to the different components contained in the material and guides the student's work.

The Seminar will contain a variety of papers, which will include the compilers' own summaries, lead articles, explanatory material and comment.

Many viewpoints are represented so that the student, and tutor, can make reasonable judgements. Actual comments and statements by authors are included as originally published.

Assignments and activities:

A wide variety of group and individual *Activities* engage the student in solving problems posed by the material, requiring his comprehension, his ability to evaluate the material and to make deductions and apply his knowledge. The assignments involve the student in search skills, observation, experiment, group interaction and co-operation as well as individual study. The activities include work experience with children in schools and elsewhere. In this book *Activity Guides* are printed as masters with permission to photocopy.

Discussion Guides introduce topics related to the work of the Seminar.

Style of presentation:

The compilers adopt throughout the Seminar the general posture of addressing readers directly and avoid impersonal passive modes.

The different components within the Seminar are selected for particular purposes and care has been taken to ensure that these are clearly indicated. For example, where materials can be adapted for in-school group studies these are made clear as are those materials best suited for individual work.

The construction of questions and suggestions for assignments and activities are so worded as to ensure the maximum response from the students.

Further reading and Seminar extensions:

The Seminars introduce central issues and the compilers enrich the material for the more able student by offering an indication of further reading and activity.

4. How is the work with the Seminars organised?

The material in this Seminar book is consulted by an individual or a group with or without a tutor or discussion leader present. In those situations where trainee teachers are using the material, practical work in homes, schools and playgroups is suggested as part of the experience. The Seminar material may be supplemented, where appropriate, by a lead lecture, but its basic design is that of a self-contained unit comprising careful instructions on how the group or individual might approach the material in order to gain the most from it. Student-led sessions, individual work and tutor-led sessions are all facilitated by such a structure.

The material is neither prescriptive nor exhaustive but forms the nucleus of a course of study, raising topics which lead to worthwhile activity on the part of the student. The Seminars focus on problems which link theory with practice and, as indicated, are appropriate for both individual and group use. Where appropriate, available teaching strength may support and supplement the published material in order to make the best use of all the resources available in the setting where the Seminar is being used.

Careful attention has been given to these organisational aspects of learning and it is hoped that the clear instructions and approximate timings given for readings and activities will enable users of the Seminars to gain maximum value from their use.

5. What seminars have been published or are being developed?

The first seminar, published in Study Kit form in 1978, was devoted to *Teaching Reading,* one of the most important and fundamental processes in the education of children. The compiler was Donald Moyle, the well-known writer and researcher in this field, who is also a member of the Editorial Board.

At the same time, a Series of Seminar Books has been developed. The first of these was the Seminar Book on *Language Skills through the Secondary Curriculum* by W. A. Gatherer and R. Jeffs. This present Seminar Book, *Child Development* (0—2 years and 2—5 years), is the second and two others will follow it; *Teaching History* by John Fines and *Teaching Mathematics* by Edith Biggs and Sheila Roberts.

It will be seen that this *Child Development* Seminar is not merely another book. It uses the strategies of the Study Kit by including a carefully arranged sequence of studies, discussions and activity assignments. In deciding on the topic for this second Seminar, the Editorial Board has recognised its value in courses of study other than those associated with teacher education, such as the training of nursery nurses, nurses and social workers.

The compilers are Margaret Roberts, formerly Senior Lecturer in Child Development at the University of London Institute of Education, who is a member of the Editorial Board, and Joan Tamburrini of the Froebel Institute, each of whom has an international reputation in the field of child development studies.

I am grateful to them both for compiling such a challenging compendium of papers and activities to launch this further Seminar Book in the Series.

Nicolas Morgan.

General Editor
Holmes McDougall Seminars
November 1981

Study Guide

- Although most of the activities suggested in the Seminar are based on practical experience, the times suggested for various items can only be approximate. It is impossible to estimate the exact times different persons will need to read or discuss different topics. **You must work out your time scale for yourself.**

- Since there are many more Activities suggested than any one person or group could possibly undertake within a reasonable time scale, **you should select projects to suit your own needs.**

- It is, of course, quite possible for two or three groups to work through the Seminar together, joining up for Discussions; or for a group to subdivide and take different projects.

- A guide to the work in each Unit appears on the title page for that unit.

- The Discussion Guides are at the end of each unit.

- The sheets required for the Activities are at the end of the book. These pages should be photocopied to provide worksheets for the participants in the seminar.

- The sequence of colour photographs referred to in Module One is on the back fold-out cover.

Module One

Pre-Natal
Development

Birth, the Impact of Change

- Read Paper 1 focussing attention on birth as an incident in development
- Complete Activity 1 studying photograph 1 and answering the questions
- Read Paper 2A to check your answers
- Complete Activity 2 checking answers with Paper 2B
- Complete Activity 3
- Read Paper 3 checking your answers to Activity 3
- Work through questions in Discussion Guide A with a group of colleagues
- Read Paper 4

Reading	35 mins.
Activities	40 mins.
Discussion	30 mins.
Total	105 mins.
	= 1 hr. 45 mins.

Before I was born . . .
Margaret Roberts

We celebrate a child's first birthday a year after his birth although he has been a 'living being' normally for one year and nine months. We tend to overlook the fact that complex and important developments take place out of sight during the nine months before birth; it is only comparatively recently that our knowledge has been extended to include this stage of development.

In a sense we start this module with the 'finished product' at the dramatic moment of birth and consider the impact of this event on the parents and on the child. After briefly considering the survival kit of the baby at seven months and the need for maximum care and attention, we turn to the main focus of this module: life before birth.

Before I was born out of my mother generations guided me . . . (Walt Whitman).

This is the poet's way of saying that in a sense each individual new life has no specific beginning. Its existence is inherent in the preceding parent cells. The united parent cells bring together a blend of the inherited characteristics from both sets of ancestors. The inherited material from father and mother is in the nucleus of each parent cell. The father's nucleus is in the head of the sperm; the mother's in the middle of the egg (ovum). In each nucleus there are at least fifteen thousand genes, these are the packages of chemical 'instructions' for the design of each and every part of the new baby. As you will see in Paper 4 it is the father's sperm that will contribute the sex of the child.

When the sperm nucleus reaches the egg nucleus the two nuclei lie side by side and, following synthesis, two new nuclei arise. The genetic make-up of these two new nuclei differs from either parent: it is a blend of both. When the now fertilized egg divides in two the life of a new individual has begun. Together the two parent cells initiate the assembly of a living body out of single molecules of protein, carbohydrates and other biochemicals.

With the exception of identical twins (formed from a single fertilized ovum) each new baby is a unique individual, never entirely like either parent or any ancestor.

The metamorphosis of a cell into a human being normally takes place in the mother's womb but it is no longer the mystery it was two decades ago. The Swedish photographer, Lennart Nilsson, spent a number of years photographing stages of embryonic growth in Stockholm hospitals where the embryos were removed for various medical reasons.

The sequential stages of the birth process emphasize the symbiotic relationship of mother and child (Paper 8), while the supporting role of the father is not forgotten. It is hoped that you will be able to start your own first-hand observations of the baby's behaviour soon after birth.

Commentary on the birth of a baby
Margaret Roberts

Use this commentary in conjunction with Activity 1.

Part A   Commentary on Photograph 1

Photograph 1 depicts an important moment in time in the life of a new-born baby, the parents and the doctor. The doctor holds up the new-born for the mother and father, if present, to see: the culmination of nine months of waiting for the parents, the effort of labour for the mother, and nine months of growth and development for the baby.

The baby has not yet been cleaned up and appears rather 'messy' from his journey through the mother's birth passage. Note his life-line cord to the mother via the placenta is still attached. Attention is focussed in this activity on the possible emotions experienced by the parents and the events which normally follow the birth.

What emotions are the parents likely to be experiencing at this first appearance of their baby? What questions are likely to be in their minds? Consider the possibility of disappointment over the sex of the child. Consider also the possibility of a less happy event in the birth of a handicapped child and the likely emotional reactions of the parents. The two most urgent questions in the minds of parents at this time are the sex of the child and whether or not the child is 'normal'.

The first cry

The baby, after being thrust out of the dark warmth of the mother's womb, where his supply of oxygen came from the placenta, emits a cry following the inhalation of his first breath. The first breaths of air require great efforts to expand the thousands of tiny uninflated air sacs of the lungs. For the parents it is a reassuring sound which immediately rivets their attention.

Cutting the cord

The cutting of the cord takes place soon after birth. Blood stops flowing through the umbilical cord as soon as the child is born; circulation is cut off when it is exposed to air. The cutting of the cord is practically bloodless and is done for convenience.

The placenta

The placenta, or after-birth, is usually born very soon after the cord is cut. Through the nine months of pregnancy it has supplied the baby with all its needs and is now no longer required. As a substitute lung it extracted oxygen from the mother's blood and deposited it in the blood of the embryo. Now the baby is capable of independent breathing.

You will read more about this important organ in Unit 2 when we trace the sequence of human development from conception to birth, that is, the period of pre-natal development.

Part B   Events following a birth

Birth as a happening

J. M. Tanner writes in *Foetus into Man* of birth as 'a happening' which signifies upheaval and change for some physiological functions, such as the respiratory and cardio-vascular systems, while for very many other physiological functions birth is an incident without much significance in a steadily changing and maturing programme of events.

After birth

The following few paragraphs from *The Everyday Miracle* by L. Nilsson, A. Ingelman-Sundberg and C. Wirsen, provide a succinct description of some of the important changes affecting the baby after birth and should be read in conjunction with Activity 2.*

It is an immense change to come from the warm closeness of the womb out into a wide world with changes of temperature, to exchange the constant flow of nourishment through the placenta for six meals a day. After floating weightlessly in the fetal waters, it is rather hard to keep one's head upright out in this ocean of air.

The baby gets hungry. This is a new sensation for someone who has never been without food for a single minute. Now he has to work hard for food. The baby fills its lungs with air, cries, and cries some more. Fortunately this is all that is needed. Soon the nourishment from his mother's blood will stream once again into the baby via the warm milk from her breast.

Except for the fact that the baby has difficulty getting around during the first months, he is actually rather well equipped. He has his own way of letting others know when he is dissatisfied or hungry; he can grip and cling; he can suck and swallow. All these things have been practised for months; none of them needs to be learned all at once when he comes into the world.

* Nilsson, L., Ingelman-Sundberg, A. and Wirsen, C. (1967) *The Everyday Miracle. A Child is Born*, Penguin (1967).

Every day his skills increase. The jerky and erratic waving of arms and legs turns into deliberate, controlled motions. The baby will soon follow things with his eyes, and then begin the endless, persevering exercises of trying to look at a thing and grasp it at the same time. It won't be long before he is strong enough to sit nicely upright on his mother's knee.

The seventh, eighth and ninth months

Geraldine Lux Flanagan

In these three months the baby gains most of his birthweight and outgrows his home in the womb. He usually puts on more than a pound in the seventh month and will probably gain four more pounds in the following six weeks.

In the seventh month the hair on the baby's head may grow long and most of the downy lanugo is shed from his body. He may begin to practise sucking and may already suck his thumb. Some babies are actually born with a callus on the thumb from sucking it in the womb.

In the eighth month he gains at least two pounds, mostly in a protective padding of fat that will help to keep his body warm after birth. He may even become quite chubby if his mother overeats at this time. Even with a normal weight gain, he fits so snugly into the womb towards the end of the month that he can only turn from side to side and can no longer turn somersaults. It is likely that he will now settle into a head-down position. Most babies do, probably because the head is the heaviest part of the body and is best accommodated in the bottom contour of the uterus.

In the ninth month his quarters become even more cramped. When he moves, the contours of his arms and legs make moving bulges on the abdomen of his mother. A kick from the baby in the womb has been known to almost knock a book off the mother's lap.

When the mother lacks the resources to fill the increasing needs of the baby, he may be born ahead of his time. Statistics show that this happens most frequently for reasons that are social and economic. Poor nourishment, poor health and very hard work are some of the main causes of premature birth. Twins are also often born early. This is thought to be simply the result of lack of space. When the uterus can expand no more, the babies are born.

Late in the seventh month most babies reach a weight of two and a quarter pounds and in medical language become viable, which means 'with organs sufficiently formed to enable them to live if born'. These babies still lack the important heat-insulating layer of fat mentioned earlier and acquired in the eighth month. They must always be cared for in a heated incubator, to shelter them from temperature change and protect them from infection.

Even with the best medical attention, the baby that is already so strong and lively in the womb is set back by premature birth. He will be a frail creature in an incubator. His existence is often precarious, for he may still have great difficulty in breathing. Even if he can maintain breathing, his lung tissues may not yet be sufficiently formed to absorb the necessary quantity of oxygen. His digestive system may not function well and he will inevitably lose weight at first. He will also be extremely vulnerable to infections.

The baby mothered in the womb gets a good deal more than warm, sterile accommodation and a well regulated supply of oxygen and predigested groceries. In these last three months in the womb he also gets one of the most essential ingredients for survival. From his mother's blood, from the placenta, and also perhaps from the amniotic fluid which he swallows, he receives substances that will endow him with immunity to a wide variety of diseases.

By the ninth month the baby is hardy because many immunities are transferred to him in the last three months before birth. From the blood of his mother he receives the special disease-combating proteins called antibodies. She has specific antibodies in her blood against all those diseases (but only those diseases) which she has had and to which she has acquired some immunity. Among them may be measles, chicken pox, mumps, whooping cough, scarlet fever, the common cold, some strains of streptococci and influenza and also poliomyelitis. If the mother has been effectively vaccinated against smallpox or poliomyelitis, she will carry antibodies against these diseases and her baby will be protected against them as well. His protection is good but not perfect. It may be helped by the mother's antibodies that will be in her milk, especially in the watery colostrum that comes in before the milk. But it has not been established whether antibodies can be absorbed through a baby's stomach, as we know they are in many domestic animals. The immunities a baby acquires from the mother before birth will gradually wear off and disappear within about six months. By that time the baby's own system can cope better with infections and can begin to build up its own permanent immunities. A girl baby will in time be able to pass these on to the next generation.

While the baby generally benefits from his mother's antibodies, there is at least one kind that can cause trouble — those related to the Rh factor. This Rh factor is so named for the *Rh*esus monkeys that were used in the studies of the problem. The problem can, but does not always, arise when an Rh-negative mother, one who has no Rh factors in her blood, carries an Rh-positive baby — one who has inherited these Rh factors, from an Rh-positive father. In such a case, antibodies may be formed in the mother to combat the Rh substance that the baby has introduced into her body. These antibodies may cause trouble for both mother and baby. The same principle can apply to some other blood incompatibilities between mother and baby. We are today learning more about these and how to treat them effectively.

In addition to antibodies, the baby receives another substance that is very effective in combating diseases. This is gamma globulin. Some comes from the mother. Most of it is produced by the placenta and it is shared by baby and mother. It probably helps to make the mother more immune to diseases during the last three months of pregnancy.

In the last month before birth, the baby will have a level of antibodies and gamma globulin in his blood which at least equals his mother's. In this and all other aspects, he is coming to the point where he has reaped the full benefit of this totally dependent way of life. Nature begins to make preparations for birth. The mother feels the 'lightening', as her expanded uterus sinks about two inches downwards in her body. When this happens, the 'presenting part' of the baby becomes engaged in the tight-fitting circle of pelvic bones. The head (or buttocks) from then on remains firmly wedged at the entrance of this bone tunnel through which he must make his exit. Now he is really pinned down.

The baby usually stops growing by his two hundred and sixtieth day, about a week before birth, probably because the placenta ages and loses much of its efficiency. The ageing of the placenta also brings about the change in the maternal hormone balance which aids in setting off the mechanism of labour. The mechanism works so well that 75 per cent of all babies are born within eleven days of the appointed 266 in the womb. The number of days is small compared to the extent of change. In quantity the change involves numbers so large as to be almost meaningless. One cell has become two hundred million cells before birth, and these cells weigh six billion times more than the fertilized egg. Although the initial pace of growth slows down long before birth, the baby, if he continued to grow even at the slowed rate of his ninth prenatal month, might weigh one hundred and sixty pounds on his first birthday. Fortunately, man increases his weight only about twenty times from birth to adulthood.

Chromosomes
Lennart Nilsson, Axel Ingelman-Sundberg and Claes Wirsen

These figures, which look like a swimming party in a prehistoric cave painting, are human chromosomes. Normally the chromosomes lie extended in the cell's nucleus as thin threads, but when the cell is going to divide, they contract into short rods, easily visible under a microscope.

Along the length of the chromosomes lie the hereditary units, or genes, arranged in a certain order. Each chromosome, during cell division, is split into two identical halves so that the genetic material can be equally distributed between daughter cells. Until division occurs the halves are held together at one single point. In the human being there are 46 chromosomes, or 23 pairs at the time the cell divides. When each pair is arranged according to size, one of the 23 pairs doesn't match. This odd pair is the sex chromosomes, which in this individual consist of one big X chromosome and one small Y chromosome, that is, the chromosomes belonging to a male individual. The female has two X chromosomes in the 23rd pair.

It is natural, and correct, to conclude that one chromosome in each of the pairs comes from the mother and the other one from the father.

An ordinary cell division as seen in one of the chromosome pairs could be pictured as follows:

Figure 4.1

Each daughter cell gets a set of 'half' chromosomes. Before the next cell division can take place, new halves must be made so that the chromosomes may split again. This is accomplished by duplicating the genetic material:

Figure 4.2

In this way the same genetic setup will prevail from one generation to another of new cells. We remain the same individuals throughout our lives, although a great many of our body cells wear out and are replaced by new ones.

But to our children we give only one of the chromosomes in each pair — they are to have one of each pair from their mother and one from their father. This is why the cells which are to give rise to sperm or ova must pass through their two special divisions.

Figure 4.3

Before the first division the chromosome pairs celebrate a kind of delayed wedding. Since each chromosome — except in the XY pair of a male individual — has a mate of the same size and with a similar arrangement of genes, a pairing may occur. During this pairing, whole sequences of genes may be exchanged before the chromosomes separate again at the first division. At the next division four different combinations may result from one pair.

As there are thousands of genes in each chromosome and thus thousands of exchange possibilities, and as chance seems to determine the results of this exchange in all pairs, an almost endless number of combinations is possible in the production of sperm and ova. Every individual (except mono-

vular twins, triplets, etc.) is unique. At the same time, of course, this individual resembles his or her parents, for it is their genes that have been mixed. Also the children are born to be human beings, that is, their genes are arranged within 46 human chromosomes.

Now what about the sex chromosomes? Why is the child a boy? Or a girl?

That depends on the sperm. Since there are two X chromosomes in female cells, all ova contain one X chromosome. But male cells have a Y chromosome instead of one X, and so the maturing sperm will be of two kinds: some containing a Y chromosome, some not. There has been much discussion as to whether this is reflected in the form and function of the individual sperm, but no definite conclusions have yet been reached. As it happens, more male babies are born than female, and judging from miscarriage and abortion statistics, still more appear to be conceived. It may well be that the proportion of X and Y sperm is not always 50-50. Some scientists maintain that the relationship in time between coitus and ovulation may be an important factor in determining the sex of the child. Whatever remains to be learned about the composition of human families, we may safely assume that sex is not determined at random.

Discussion Guide A

Impact of birth on parents and baby

You should allow at least 30 minutes for this discussion. Activities 1, 2 and 3 may have seemed somewhat 'off-target' for this module entitled as it is 'Pre-Natal Development' but, as you will now realize, the birth of the baby is the focusing event that leads to questions about pre-natal development. Before embarking on this it is relevant (to our later study) to spend some time on the impact of the new baby on his parents, and the effect of this sudden change in his environment on the baby.

It will be useful to discuss the following points systematically and to exchange views with a group of colleagues. Make a note of any consensus view, and also note minority viewpoints that appear important to the discussion.

1 Consider different emotions and reactions likely to be experienced by the mother and, if present, the father following the birth of their child. Discuss likely emotional reactions:
   (a) in relation to the sex of the child;
   (b) in the case of an apparently physically handicapped child;
   (c) in the situation of an unplanned or unwanted child.

2 Consider the implications of the baby's first cry:
   (a) biologically – what is happening to the baby;
   (b) socially – the effect of hearing his first cry on the parents.

3 Discuss the special needs of a baby born at seven months. Consider the likely effect of the birth of a premature baby on the mother and the father.

Unit Two

The Embryo

- Complete Activities 4 to 7 by examining Photographs 2 to 10
- Answer questions with reference to Paper 5
- Complete Activity 8 by examining Photograph 11
- Read Paper 6 checking your answers to Activity 8
- Work through Discussion Guide B with your colleagues to clarify the sequence of events covered in Activities 4 to 8

Reading	30 mins.
Activities	40 mins.
Discussion	30 mins.
Total	100 mins.
	= 1 hr. 40 mins.

Module One   Paper 5

Description of Photographs 2-11
Margaret Roberts

This paper describes Photographs 2-11; it relates directly to Activities 4–8 involving the use of this material. This approach aims to sharpen your viewing of the photographs and to expand your knowledge of development from the very beginning of human life. The material dealing with the encounter of male and female sex cells – Photographs 2, 3 and 4 – relates to Activity 4.

Ovum (Photograph 2)

The ovum is a female sex cell and must be fertilized by the male sperm before a baby can be produced. It is the coming together of the male and female germ cells that starts another life. The ovum is one of the largest cells in the body, measuring about 0.1 mm in diameter; barely visible to the naked eye. One ovum is produced every four weeks in the ovaries – an important stage in the menstrual cycle. If the ovum is not fertilized, the lining of the uterus is shed in the process of menstruation.

Sperm (Photograph 3)

The sperm that find their way to the ova must be delivered inside the female's body. In the subsequent long journey via the vagina, through the uterus to the oviduct many die on the way. The fusion of only one sperm and one ovum is needed for the creation of a new individual. Photograph 3 shows an army of sperm swimming towards the ovum. The heads show the direction of movement as they swim through the glassy, fluid, cervical mucus. (However, a technical difficulty in making the slides has resulted in some sperm facing in different directions.)

Sperm encountering ovum (Photograph 4)

A single sperm can be seen penetrating the gelatinous coating which envelops the ovum in Paragraph 4, the last of many to start out on the long journey. A number of sperm may explore the surface of the ovum at any one time, but when the strongest and liveliest has bored its way through the ovum nucleus following sperm are turned away. The sperm nucleus and the ovum nucleus lie side by side as their contents are combined. The fusion of the two nuclei is called fertilization and it is this vital event that initiates the new life. This normally takes place in the sheltered confines of the mother's body.

Cell division (Photographs 5-7)

This material relates to Activity 5 dealing with what happens after fertilization. The first two cells increase, two by two, to more than a hundred cells in the first week. The cells get smaller and smaller but the volume remains constant inside the original envelope . . . together they are smaller than a full-stop.

Implantation in the uterus (Photographs 8-10)

Activity 6 is concerned with what happens next to the fertilized ovum and you will find Photographs 8 and 9 helpful in formulating answers to the questions posed together with this commentary. The new creature floats down from the oviduct and enters the uterus where rapidly dividing cells will eventually submerge the fertilized ovum in the uterine lining. Further cell division takes place during the journey from the oviduct to the uterus.

Photograph 9 depicts the early stages of implantation. This important process generally occurs about seven days after fertilization, near the twenty-first day of the menstrual cycle. But, of course, events are not as straightforward as this. Professor Tanner describes this as a 'hazardous period' when 'many more ova are fertilized than come to fruition. Some 10 per cent fail to implant and of those that implant and become embryos about 50 per cent are spontaneously aborted, usually without the mother knowing anything about it' (Tanner, 1978).

As can be seen cells have not only divided steadily (about 150 cells at the time of implantation) but differentiation has occurred. Changes in the outer layer culminate in the formation of the placenta and a small proportion of the inner layer develops into the embryo.

The speed of development at this stage is demonstrated by Photograph 10 showing an embryo at 33 days. Activity 7 will help you to identify important organs in their embryonic state. Between two and eight weeks after fertilization the embryo develops recognizable human arms and legs, a heart that beats, and a nervous system that shows the beginning of reflex responses to tactile stimulus and is now called a foetus. No further fundamental changes will occur; everything is present that will be found in the full-term baby.

Placenta (Photograph 11)

Before we look at development at the foetal stage (Unit 3) there is the important matter of the baby's life-line with the mother to be considered – the vital connection providing nourishment and protection from infection.

Activity 8 poses some important questions some of which can be answered by studying Photograph 11 and this commentary; further information is presented in

Paper 6.

The baby in Photograph 11 is now a tiny plump being approximately 17 mm long with short arms and legs, floating in its amniotic sac, well moored to the placenta by the umbilical cord. The large dark shadow in front is all the blood streaming through its liver and heart. The yolk sac can be seen sailing like a balloon fastened to its thin stalk; fresh blood corpuscles are delivered from it to the circulation in the early stages. The main part of the circulatory system is outside the embryo in the large placenta where the blood is oxygenated and gets nourishment and where carbon dioxide and waste products are filtered out (L. Nilsson *et al.*, 1967). Note that the baby does not use its lungs for obtaining oxygen until after birth so he is not in danger of drowning!

See Paper 6 to find out more about the varied service the placenta performs for the baby before birth, its role and function, its successes and failures.

References
Nilsson, L., Ingleman-Sundberg, A. and Wirsen, C. (1967) *The Everyday Miracle. A Child is Born*, Penguin.
Tanner, J. M. (1978) *Foetus Into Man*, Open Books.

The placenta —
life-line for a precious parasite
Albert Rosenfeld

After the baby has spent his appointed 266 or so days in the tranquillity of his mother's womb, he is abruptly shoved out — by a 100 lb. propulsive force.

Soon after birth the umbilical cord is cut, and after this the last thing to come out — which is why it is called the afterbirth — is the placenta. It is now just a pound or so of left-over material to be discarded and forgotten.

But it is an extraordinary organ, one of the most potent and versatile nature ever devised. Only lately have scientists begun to appreciate its remarkable abilities.

The placenta supplies the embryo with all its needs, carries off all its wastes, protects it in a variety of ways from harmful invaders. It does all this through the baby's pipeline to life, the umbilical cord. Contrary to popular belief, there is no direct connection whatever between the mother's circulation and the baby's. In the placenta there are two separate sets of vessels. One set goes to and from the mother; the other goes to and from the embryo. They are side by side but are entirely closed off from one another. The blood vessel walls, however, are permeable. An exchange of ingredients — oxygen, dissolved food, waste matter and so on — is constantly taking place through the walls.

This may seem a peculiarly indirect and inefficient way of effecting the exchanges between mother and embryo, but it is the only way it can be done, for the baby is a parasite.

From the day of fertilisation, the embryo is foreign material. If the circulatory system of the embryo was directly hooked to the mother's system, the mother's body would reject the embryo. The body, through its immunological system, always tries to reject foreign material — and this is the great stumbling block in all recent attempts to transplant organs from one body to another. In fact, after the baby is born, if a piece of its skin is transplanted to the mother, the mother does reject it.

Yet she tolerates this entire foreign body in her system for nine whole months. She tolerates it only because of the placenta's unique ability to subvert her immunological defences.

This little-understood ability is getting considerable attention these days from researchers interested in the surgical transplanting of organs. If they can figure out the placenta's secret, they may be able to keep transplanted organs from being rejected.

The fertilised egg cell contains in its tiny nucleus not only all the genetic instructions for building a human body, but also a complete manual on how to construct the complex protective armour — amnion, umbilical cord, placenta and all — that makes possible the embryo's existence in the womb. In the egg cell's very earliest days in the uterus it already contains nutrition cells called trophoblasts which are the primitive precursors of the placenta.

One of the first things these cells do is invade the wall of the uterus, usually near the top of it, to build for the embryo what amounts to a little nest. In fact, this invading process is called nidation, or nesting.

The wall of the uterus is a thick, spongy material. The trophoblast cells dig right into it, destroying the uterine cells, taking nourishment from the blood and passing it along to sustain the first embryonic cells.

Then they use the scar tissue from the healing wound as a temporary protective capsule for the still microscopic parasite.

The uterus must protect itself against the further incursions of the aggressive trophoblast cells. Exactly how it does this is a mystery because no other part of the body can do it. A trophoblast implanted anywhere else in the body will eat away whatever tissue it comes in contact with. It was recently discovered that the trophoblast would even eat away cancer cells — a lead that is being hotly pursued by cancer researchers.

Once the egg cell is firmly implanted, it starts secreting a hormone that helps keep the uterine lining in place for the rest of the embryo's stay. Without this hormone, menstruation would occur and the embryo would not survive.

Over the course of days, weeks and months, the embryo becomes firmly rooted in the uterine wall, and the trophoblast cells develop into the placenta. A dynamic organ, the placenta changes constantly along with the embryo's changing requirements. It can perform tasks which are normally reserved for the lungs, liver, kidneys, intestines and endocrine glands, among its other miscellaneous accomplishments. Yet the placenta is basically no more than an intricate filigree of blood vessels and membranes.

There is a lot of it, to be sure — it ultimately grows to a diameter of some eight inches — but no one, as yet, quite understands how a structure like this can possibly acquire such a gamut of biochemical capabilities.

As a substitute lung, the placenta extracts oxygen from the mother's blood and deposits it in the blood of the embryo. The placenta brings in nutrients of all kinds from the mother's blood, often predigesting the dissolved food for the embryo en route. The placenta is so efficient that within an hour or two after the mother takes nourishment the embryo gets some too. If the mother drinks or smokes heavily, some of the alcohol or nicotine will also reach the embryo.

In addition to trading off oxygen from carbon dioxide and food for wastes, the placenta safeguards the embryo by keeping out bacteria and bringing in antibodies that bestow immunity to a variety of diseases. The placenta also manufactures vital hormones for the mother to make up for some of the things it takes away.

But the placenta is not perfect. It cannot always screen out everything that might be injurious to the embryo. Viruses — like the German measles virus — sometimes slip through to cause deformities. Certain damaging drugs manage to breach the barrier too.

When its prodigious tasks are done, the placenta dies. But even after it is dead, some of its effects linger awhile. The baby is born with its external sex organs swollen, a temporary effect of the special hormones long shared with the mother — hormones brought in by the placenta. Because some of these same hormones produce the mother's milk, the new baby also has milk in its breasts known as 'witches' milk'.

Sometimes it is so plentiful that it drips from the baby's nipples, and it makes no difference whether the baby is a boy or a girl.

But in a few days all these effects are gone, and the one thing left over by the placenta is a set of immunities. Whatever diseases the mother was immune to, the baby will also be immune to. These immunities last for about six months, the most vulnerable months of a child's life. By the time these immunities wear off, the baby will have gained some strength and will have been sufficiently exposed to the world to start building up immunities of its own. This is the placenta's final and most precious legacy.

From: Women's Mirror Sept. 18 1965 (Australia)
A Fleetway Magazine, Fleetway House, Farringdon Street, London EC4.

Discussion Guide B

Important changes in the first eight weeks of life

Allow at least 30 minutes for this work. Arrange to meet with a group of colleagues after studying Photographs 2–11 and after you have all read Papers 5 and 6. This Discussion Guide aims to clarify your knowledge of the sequence of events from conception to the end of the embryonic stage.

Important changes occur in the development of a human embryo in the first eight weeks of pre-natal life. After this period no further fundamental changes of structure will occur: everything present will be found in the full-term baby.

Bring your activity records, diagrams etc. and have Papers 5 and 6 ready for reference. Focus the discussion on the sequence of development and the processes involved at the embryonic stage.

Consider what is involved in each of these processes:

(a) fertilization of the ovum;
(b) cell division and differentiation;
(c) implantation;
(d) the completion of the embryo stage.

To understand some of the hazards of this stage you are recommended to read J. M. Tanner's book *Foetus into Man*, chapter 3, 'Growth before birth' (London: Open Books, 1978).

Discuss with your colleagues the role and function of the placenta.

1 Consider how far it is true to describe the placenta as 'the other half of the story of life before birth'.
2 List the placenta's functions and possible failures.

Use Paper 6 as a reference for points 1 and 2.

Embryo to Foetus

- Complete Activity 9 by examining Photographs 12 to 17 and answering questions on the development of the face at the foetal stage
- Read Paper 7 to check your answers
- Complete Activity 10 by examining Photographs 18 to 28 and answering questions on the development of the hands and feet
- Check your answers with Paper 7
- Read Paper 8 dealing with events prior to the baby's birth
- Carry out Activity 11 involving visit to mother and new-born
- Meet for Discussion C to exchange observations and information from parents
- Review work done as a preparation for observation of new-born

Reading	25 mins.
Activities	125 mins.
Discussion	30 mins.
Total	180 mins.
	= 3 hrs.

Description of Photographs 12–28
Margaret Roberts

As in Unit 2 this paper complements the photographs and relates directly to the activities for Unit 3. It aims to focus your attention on the differential rate of growth of parts of the body at the foetal stage and to anticipate their later functions while keeping in mind the essential unity of the developing human being.

Photograph 12 depicts an embryo of seven weeks showing clearly the domination of the trunk by the head, the lack of neck and the tiny limbs barely more than outgrowths from the trunk. Note the lidless eye is dark because of the pigment in the retina; the eyelids are already beginning to form.

Photograph 13 shows the baby at eight weeks – now called a foetus. His basic structure has been laid down, he is fully formed, everything is present that will be found in the new-born baby. Now the baby must grow and develop.

Different parts of the body grow at different speeds. The head grows faster than the rest of the body and it is already much bigger at eight weeks. The liver clearly dominates the scene at first, receiving the flow of oxygenated blood from the placenta, but gradually the heart receives most of the blood from the umbilical vein and pumps it round the body. The heart has already been beating for a month at this stage.

Photograph 14 shows a new feature – the closed eye. In the ninth week the upper and lower lids meet, fuse and do not re-open until the seventh month in order to protect the developing eye. The ear appears at first rather low in the region of the neck due to the slower development of the lower part of the face. Note overall proportions and the continued dominance of the head.

Photograph 15 depicts the foetus at sixteen weeks. It is important to think of the baby growing and developing within a supporting and protective environment within the mother's body. He floats about supported by the fluid in the amniotic sac, secured by his umbilical cord. This life-line which allows him to move as freely as the space permits, secures him to the placenta from which he obtains oxygenated blood, nourishment and immunity and which also deals with waste products via the mother's system.

Photograph 16 is a close-up of the closed eye of the twenty-week-old foetus. The baby conveys the impression of being in a deep, calm sleep but he cannot open his eyes at this stage. The eyelids meet at the beginning of the third month when the cells fuse at their edges. The eyeballs bulge under the eyelids. The lids are closed to ensure protection during the critical development of the eye as a visual organ with its complex structure and neural connection with the brain. But human babies open their eyes well before birth. Note the fine downy hairs at the eyebrows indicating that the skin is beginning to be fully developed.

Photograph 17 is of a full-term thirty-six week foetus; it is included here to demonstrate the unity of growth and development and the potential readiness of the baby for birth and life in the world. But this baby's potential was, of course, never realized and so the nine months of waiting by the parents and the potential energy for further growth, development and learning was, apparently, wasted. Still too many babies die, for varied reasons, within the first few months of life in this country. In this case, there may have been a breathing difficulty, incompatibility of blood or a serious heart defect.

Hands and feet

Photographs 18–24 deal with the growth and development of the hands and feet.

Photograph 18 (five to six weeks) is a close-up showing the tiny hand forming. The hand is the part of the arm that appears first and grows most rapidly. The fingers can be seen protruding beyond the 'webs' which remain as folds of skin between the fingers in the adult hand; there are no joints at this stage. Note the edges of the opened amniotic sac in this photograph.

Photograph 19 at seven weeks shows the slow development of the upper limbs in the early stages. Although the hands can reach the face they cannot yet meet; note flexion at the elbow and wrist.

Photograph 20 at ten weeks depicts the arm, flexed at the elbow; it has lengthened sufficiently to allow the hands to meet. The fingers have lengthened and the joints are more pronounced. The dark shadows indicate the cartilaginous skeleton that will be transformed soon into bony tissue. Growth takes place in the ossification centres which grow towards the ends of the bones preceded by growth in the cartilage.

Photograph 21 at eighteen weeks shows the hand already shaping up as a 'precision tool' practising grasping. The baby is holding its umbilical cord which can take vigorous squeezing. The reflex grasp of the hand appears to be well developed before birth.

Photograph 22 at twenty weeks shows the kind of contact the baby is beginning to have with his own body. The hand passes near the most sensitive organ, the mouth, and touches the lips. Many babies gain comfort from sucking their fingers and thumbs but Lennart Nilsson (1967) was the first to secure a photograph of a baby of 4½ months clearly sucking his thumb in utero. Photographs 22 and 23 were the nearest we could get to this situation and we think he *is* sucking his thumb. If so, it would be a reflex action set off by the thumb coming into contact with the sensitive lips – practice sucking!

Photograph 24 again at twenty weeks shows a relaxed hand with lines on the palm, flexed finger and thumb joints and the beginning of nails which often grow quite long. But the most important characteristic is the potential for finger–thumb opposition in terms of later use of the hand as a precision tool (see the work of Piaget and Bower in later modules).

Photographs 25–27 indicate the development of the feet and legs. Photograph 25 at five to six weeks shows the foot as a rounded plate from which can be seen emerging the buds of future toes. The knee is barely visible; the umbilical cord dominates the lower trunk which is relatively undeveloped at this stage.

Photograph 26 shows the foetus at twenty weeks. Here we see the lengthening limbs and the still thin and slender lower part of the body, though the thighs are developing with good flexion indicated here and at the knees and ankles.

Photograph 27 at twenty-four weeks shows a typical kicking display or 'treading the waters' which the baby practises while he has space, turning round and round and floating head down or heels down bumping against the walls of the uterus as he does so. His mother may have her cup of tea upset if she holds it too near to the baby! As full-term approaches the baby takes up all the available space in the amniotic sac and normally the head slips down into the pelvic cavity ready for the delivery; he is now firmly anchored and this prevents further acrobatics.

It is difficult to hold in mind even the barest indication of what is involved (as shown by these photographs) in the miraculous changes which take place between the fertilization of the ovum and the birth of a full-term, healthy baby nine months later.

Reference
Nilsson, L., Ingelman-Sundberg, A. and Wirsen C. (1967) *The Everyday Miracle. A Child is Born*, Penguin.

Birth

Lennart Nilsson, Axel Ingelman-Sundberg and Claes Wirsen

The last months seem very long. Everything is ready now, the baby has only to grow. From the seventh month until term it increases its length from 13 to 20 inches and nearly triples its weight. A thick layer of adipose tissue develops under the skin. This layer serves both as insulation and food supply and confers on the newborn infant its characteristic chubbiness. The finger and toe nails grow, eventually reaching beyond the fingertips. Often the fingernails have to be cut immediately after birth to avoid scratching. The lanugo hairs are shed together with the vernix. The baby swallows part of them together with fetal fluid and they come out on the first nappies. Much of the vernix sticks on the head, and the nurse carefully washes it off so that the little tuft of hair will be clean and shiny when brushed for the first time.

As far as we know it is not the baby who decides the time of delivery, but the placenta and the uterine musculature. Once the baby's head has slipped down into the pelvic cavity everything is ready for the delivery. Now delivery is due any day. During the last weeks the womb has been active; now and then it contracts and gets hard, and sometimes causes an ache in the back. It is preparing for the real labor. Now the cervical canal, which has been closed during the whole pregnancy, must dilate so that the baby can pass through. The uterus is firmly anchored to the bottom of the pelvis; each contraction will therefore press the upper wall of the uterus down toward the cervix. But the fetal fluid — like all other fluids — is not compressible. It will expand the membranes toward the point of least resistance. A bulging of the membranes will result, pressing down through the cervical canal. The baby's head then follows and dilates it further.

At each contraction the muscle fibers of the uterine wall compress the cavity further and the baby will have very little space for a while. But each time there is a pause, fresh blood streams into the placenta, and the baby's heartbeats, which slow down and even become a little irregular during the contractions, resume their normal frequency and are strong and regular again.

The mother rests. She must save her strength until the expulsive stage, when she is both allowed and encouraged to assist. Now there is not much she can do, only relax and try to remember what they told her during the prenatal classes about bending, curving her back, breathing with the whole abdomen, and trying not to strain during the contractions.

The father feels rather awkward, out of place. But he can do much to help his wife — rub her back as the pains grow stronger, cool her face with a nice wet towel when she feels hot and sweaty, console her when things get tedious. Above all, he's the one she wants near her, the one she feels safe with.

The baby's head has come down through the wide-open cervix and stands in the pelvic outlet; one sees it appear at each contraction. In the vaginal opening, more and more of the baby's crown with its black hair is coming into sight.

She feels like pushing out her whole abdomen. Now something has to happen. It has to get out, out, out . . .

Discussion Guide C

Observations of a new-born baby

You should allow at least 45 minutes for this discussion. Following Activity 11 arrange to meet your colleagues to discuss your experiences; a small group of 3 or 4 would be helpful. Bring your observation records to the discussion group so that you may exchange observations and so increase your knowledge of other people's experiences and reactions.

Consider first any difficulties experienced by individuals:

(a) in finding a new-born baby with a mother willing for you to visit;
(b) observing the baby;
(c) talking to the mother and/or father, if present.

Present your observations in *age–order*, the youngest baby first.

1 Give name, age and position in family.
2 Report from observation checklist.
3 Report information provided by mother/father including any special information concerning birth, health, feeding (frequency and amount), aspects of development.

State:

(a) in what way the visit was useful to you;
(b) how the earlier work in this module prepared you for the observation of a new-born baby, for example, the pre-natal development of the face, hands and feet.

Consider how far your observations could be said to be:

(a) objective;
(b) subjective.

We will be considering this last matter in the next module.

Module Two

Perceptual Discrimination and the Growth of Sociability

General guidance for first-hand observations of young children related to activities for Modules 2–4

In the home

It would be most helpful if you could visit a mother with a young baby (later, a toddler) already known to you who would be interested to hear about your study. Clearly you will have to observe some different children for the relevant age-levels, because of the time factor on the course, but one child observed over a year would be a valuable extension to your experience.

Meet the mother and arrange your visits well ahead of time, checking by telephone, if possible, the day before that it is still convenient for you to come.

If there are siblings at home at the time of your visit you may have to adapt your programme to include them, or provide interesting activities for them, but these modules are concerned primarily with the child under two years of age.

At the Health Clinic

If you are unable to make arrangements to visit a mother and baby in their home, link up with your local Health and Baby Welfare Clinic. Ask the matron whether she can help you by introducing you to mothers with young babies of the age you plan to work with, in order to observe different aspects of behaviour when the babies are with their mothers.

Enquire whether there is any small room, or other quiet place, where the observations could be made where the baby would not be unduly distracted. Explain that your records will be kept anonymous using only the first name of the baby.

At a Mothers' and Toddlers' Club

The person in charge of the local Mothers' and Toddlers' Club attached to a playgroup, nursery school/class, or infants' school may be able to help you to contact co-operative mothers with babies of the ages you need. A quiet corner may be available where you and the mother and baby will not be disturbed.

General Guidance

Observe the baby when he is happily settled and the mother or other care-giver is present or nearby. It is important that the baby is not hungry, tired or fretful, or uncomfortable in any way, and is not disturbed by your presence. If the baby seems happy with your being there then proceed sensitively with your programme of observations and other activities as set out in the relevant Activities.

Be sure not to outstay your welcome! Your visit should last between 30 and 45 minutes overall. Do not forget to leave your thanks for the co-operation you have received.

Module Two   Unit One

Seeing is Believing

- Carry out Activities 12, 13 and 14 dealing with visual perception. Complete these individually before discussion
- Read Paper 9 dealing with factors operating in visual perception
- Take part in Discussion D focussing on individual differences in perception

Reading	15 mins.
Activities	30 mins.
Discussion	30 mins.
Total	75 mins.
	= 1 hr. 15 mins.

Figure-ground segregation
R. N. Haber and M. Hershenson

It may seem strange to start a module on the development of perceptual discrimination and the growth of sociability in young babies by presenting somewhat disturbing experiences demonstrating the uncertainty of adult visual perceptions. Can we rely on what we see? Is what the brain recognizes really a fact, or fantasy? Do people see the same things differently? Do individuals see things differently at different times?

What message has this complex situation for students who set out to try to observe children's behaviour objectively? If two people are unable to agree on an object both are looking at how can they agree when the object of their observation is a small, lively child? Clearly there are marked limitations to our objectivity in such situations. We must be on our guard against generalizing from our own individual experiences in observing children; hence the inclusion of discussion groups to consider our own experiences in relation to those of our colleagues and to examine relevant research.

Haber and Hershenson's paper helps us to understand some of the theories underlying the complex subject of visual discrimination, for example, the theory of figure-ground organization first studied by Rubin and later developed by Hebb. But we are primarily concerned with the early development of these potentially very important skills and maybe Hochberg's idea that information is picked up from several glances is central to visual search and particularly so to young babies' visual search for interest, novelty, pattern and movement. In the second year of life visual discrimination becomes even more important as visual experience is stored, retrieved and reconstructed in symbolic form available for the young child's individual purposes.

If a perceiver naively attends to his perceptual experience, he describes that experience as one of objects seen on surfaces or as figures against background. This phenomenal appearance occurs regardless of the complexity or simplicity of the stimulation in the retinal projection. It is considered so basic that this segregation has usually been taken as the starting point of organized perception. Thus, any inhomogeneity in the retinal projection leads to a perceptual segregation of the field into one part called a figure and another part called a ground. These parts are usually separated by a contour which may be said to divide figure from ground, although the contour seems to belong to the figure. Generally, only one of two homogeneous parts of a field may be seen as the figure and the other as the ground; it is the rare case where both would be experienced as figure on ground. Thus, figure-ground segregation may be said to be immediate and self-evident.

The features of figure-ground organization were first studied by Rubin (1921); see Figure 9.1. He noted that the figure has form or shape, whereas the ground is formless. The ground may have form properties but those properties are weaker and less definite. Thus the figure has thinglike qualities whereas the ground appears uniform. The figure appears to be nearer than the ground, and the ground appears to be extended unbroken behind the figure, even though all of the ground cannot be seen. The figure is more easily identified; its color is more impressive; it is more easily connected with meaning, feeling, and aesthetic values. The reason camouflage works is that it breaks down the figure-ground relationships which carry the meaning.

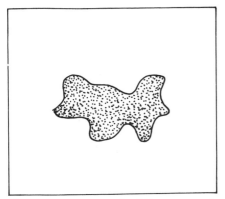

Figure 9.1   An example of figure-ground segregation.

In his neurological theory of perceptual and psychological development, Hebb (1949) noted three aspects of figure-ground segregation: a primitive, sensorially determined unity; a nonsensory unity, affected by experience; and the identity of a perceived figure, affected by experience. By primitive unity Hebb meant that segregation from the background which is seen as a direct product of the pattern of sensory excitation and the coding strategies of the visual nervous system. It is an area of homogeneous color and intensity within a sharp boundary which is seen as one, unified, and distinct from its surroundings. As Hebb points out, this segregation is necessary and inevitable for perception.

The nonsensory figure was viewed as one in which the boundaries of a figure are not determined by luminosity discontinuities in the visual field. For Hebb this occurred whenever a perceiver responded selectively to a limited portion of a homogeneous area in the visual field. Hebb's example was that of looking at the middle part of a rope as distinct from the rest of it when one is interested in tying a knot; or when one perceives a foreground in an unbroken landscape. In these cases, no sensory or physical delimitation of figure from ground could be made, and yet there is a segregation of sorts in perceptual experience.

For Hebb the wife-and-mother-in-law reversible figure illustrated a combination of sensory and nonsensory figures (see Figure 9.2). Clearly the figural outlines are sensory in nature. Nevertheless, perceptual organization is controlled by experience and expectation, which involves nonsensory organization. A similar case may be made for looking through a microscope to read neurological sections of brain tissue. Here perceptual organizations are made only after experience with the objects. In some figure-ground organization there is an inevitable component determined by the stimulus structure; in other cases, organization also requires prolonged experience. Thus the properties of nonsensory figures may be affected by experience and other nonsensory factors. In this sense they are not inevitable or necessary for perception.

Figure 9.2   The wife-and-mother-in-law reversible figure (from Boring, 1930).

The third aspect of figural organization which Hebb described is identity. This represents the properties of association or memory inherent in perception. For example, a figure is seen immediately as similar to some figures and dissimilar to others; it falls at once into certain categories and not into others. Thus, identity may be thought of as spontaneous association, since it may occur on the first exposure to an object. An object with identity or thingness is capable of being associated readily with other objects or with some action. A figure which does not possess identity is recalled with great difficulty, or not at all, and may not be recognized or named easily. Moreover, identity is a matter of degree; it depends to a large extent on past experience. Identity can be observed to grow, as in situations which have been described by Gibson (1969): the tea taster learning to discriminate taste, or the researcher learning to discriminate among chimpanzees. First, all chimps appear to look alike, and to have similar features, but later one can select among them and call each by name.

Figure-ground unity may not be a primitive and primary process, however. Unless we are quite distant from the figure-ground pattern, a perceiver will not be able to see all of the figure clearly in a single glance. Instead, he will make a number of eye movements to explore the pattern visually. Can there be a primitive segregation of figure from ground if it takes several eye movements to achieve it? Hochberg (1968, 1971a, 1971b) suggests that, in viewing large figures, figure-ground segregation may not result in the perception of a unified figure until the information in several glances has been combined and integrated. The information in each glance would be stored until integration could be achieved. Further, the content in the first glance may determine the direction of the eye movement to get the second glance. In addition, eye movements have to be programmed prior to their execution. Thus a decision, probably based on information seen in peripheral vision is made about where to look next.* This determines what information will be brought into foveal view. This pattern of information acquisition suggests a derived segregation of figure from ground as a result of successive views of the stimulus pattern. The process does not in itself imply a learned activity, but it certainly cannot be primitive in the sense of an automatic outcome of the structure of the stimulus pattern.

Figure 9.3 provides an illustration of some of these points. The 'impossible figures' show how the function of a contour changes when one looks from one place to another in the pattern. The stimulus components of organization and depth are not specified by the entire configuration, but only by specific features — local depth cues — which exert their control over small regions. However, form perception must result from an integration of these separate glances into an abstract structure, a construction of what Hochberg calls a schematic map.

Some interesting support for this notion comes from King (1971), who has developed a computer simulation of figure-ground segregation. The program organizes any pattern of two-dimensional line-drawing elements into figures against backgrounds, including properties of 'in front of'. His program does not have to know the shapes beforehand, nor have any prior experience with the figures, to be able to resolve discontinuities in the two-dimensional visual field into separate figures. It arrives at virtually

*See chapter 9 in the original source.

the same figures that human perceivers describe when shown the same patterns. The principal component of King's model is a shifting center of attention or eye position. If the first look is centered near a discontinuity, this 'edge' is tried out as part of the figure. If not, the center of attention shifts until it maps out the contours and interprets them from successive looks.

Hochberg has emphasized this distinction between what is registered in a single glance or fixation and what is represented or integrated from successive glances. He is not arguing that figure-ground segregation cannot occur within a single glance, but rather that in many circumstances perceptual organization, including figures against backgrounds, must depend on the information picked up from several glances. In this sense, figure-ground segregation cannot be primitive, as Hebb thought.

Hochberg's distinction is central to visual search, to selection and recognition, and especially to the perception of space. Visual image representation must be more than a representation of the luminance discontinuities contained in the current fixation of the eye. Rather, it has to be an integration of the information from several fixations, in just the way Hochberg argues that the accumulation of information from successive glances is needed to segregate figure from ground.

Although a segregation of figure from ground, as Rubin described it, represents a perceptual organization, it is only the very first of far more complex aspects of the perception of form.

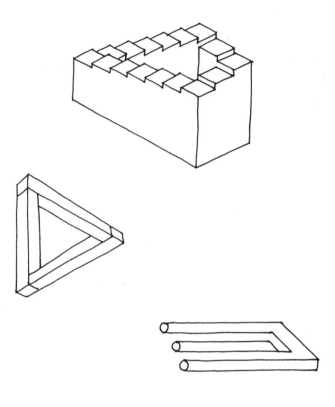

Figure 9.3 Several examples of two-dimensional drawings of impossible three-dimensional forms.

References
Boring, E. G. (1930) 'Apparatus note. A new ambiguous figure', *American Journal of Psychology*, 42, 444.
Gibson, E. J. (1969) *Principles of perceptual learning and development*, New York: Appleton-Century-Crofts.
Hebb, D. O. (1949) *The Organization of Behaviour*, New York: John Wiley.
Hochberg, J. (1968) 'In the mind's eye' in Haber, R. N. (ed.) *Contemporary theory and research in visual perception*, New York: Holt, Rinehart & Winston, 303–31.
Hochberg, J. (1971a), 'Perception: I Colour and shape' in Kling, J. A. and Riggs, L. A. (eds.) *Woodworth and Schlosberg's Experimental Psychology* (3rd edn), New York: Holt, Rinehart & Winston, 395–474.
Hochberg, J. (1971b) 'Perception: II Space and movement' in Kling, J. A. and Riggs, L. A. (eds.) *Woodworth and Schlosberg's Experimental Psychology* (3rd edn), New York: Holt, Rinehart & Winston, 475–550.
King, S. J. (1971) 'A system for separating objects from the background in automatic picture processing', unpublished doctoral dissertation, Cornell University.
Rubin, E. (1921) *Visuell Wahrgenommene Figuren*, Copenhagen: Glydendalske.

Discussion Guide D

What do you see?

You should spend at least 30 minutes considering these items. Arrange a meeting with your group to discuss the results of Activities 12, 13 and 14. Add any qualifications or comments you wish to make in relation to the question put in Activity 12. Report your decision to the group, together with your reasons, qualifications etc. Report your answers to questions in Activities 13 and 14.

Which is the dominant view, that is, the view that comes spontaneously into focus, for the group for each of the pictures presented? Give numbers for each view and total number in the group.

Picture (1)   Greek vase

Two profiles

Picture (2)   Old woman

Young woman

1 What are possible reasons for one 'view' dominating?
2 Do any members of the group have difficulty in shifting from one view to the other in either or both pictures?
3 Check whether people are aware of eye movements particularly at the time of shift.
4 What part do edges play in identifying figure/ground?
5 Is there an 'aha' experience when people suddenly 'see' at the time of first identity and/or at the time of shift?
6 Check whether there is agreement (consensus) that the perceiver can see things in different ways at different times.
7 Is it possible to see both 'views' at the same time?
8 Make a list of factors you think may be involved in visual perception. Compare your list with those of your colleagues. Add to this list after reading Paper 9.

Unit Two

Early stages of perceptual development

- Read Paper 10 introducing the development of visual perception in young babies and reporting Fantz' study of visual discrimination in infancy
- Carry out Activities 15A and 15B involving experimental work with babies' visual attention and smiling response
- Read Paper 11 on infant perceptual activity
- Read Paper 12 on further research findings
- Take part in Discussion E considering questions arising from Activities and reading on visual perception and social behaviour in young babies.

Reading	30 mins.
Activities	25 mins.
Discussion	30 mins.
Total	85 mins.
	= 1 hr. 25 mins.

Aspects of visual perception in young babies
Margaret Roberts

The study of early visual behaviour through the investigation of visual interest and visual preference is significant in terms of the baby's developing knowledge of his environment both social and physical, that is, his growing awareness of, and response to, people and things. The child attends to what he sees; if his eyes fixate on something we say the object holds his attention, or that he is interested in the object. If he looks longer at certain things he appears to be not only attending but selecting what he will attend to. Later he behaves as if he recognizes objects he has seen earlier; he may respond by smiling and making pleasure noises, for example, to familiar faces, to his toys, and very soon to pictures. There appear to be developmental sequences linking the structure and function of the eye and the brain with the visual experience (stimulus) provided by the baby's environment. As Gesell put it 'the eyes lead'.

Earlier writers assumed that the baby had to learn from scratch how to make meaning of his world. William James, for example, described the baby's early perceptual experience as a 'buzzing, booming confusion'. Even after it was known that young babies can see light, colour and movement it was thought that they could not respond to form, that is, shape, pattern, size or solidity. The pioneer work of Robert Fantz in the 1950s at the University of Chicago provided the foundation for later investigations into the perceptual competencies of the very young baby as shown in the work of H. R. Schaffer, T. G. R. Bower and C. Trevarthen.

Fantz asked the question, does the baby perceive and differentiate among distinctive forms? He was interested in the nature/nurture controversy, that is, whether the baby started with a 'blank slate' or whether he had from birth visual competencies which permitted him to attend selectively to visual stimulus.

In the first instance Fantz carried out experiments on newly hatched chicks to ascertain that their visual pattern preferences in terms of pecking (for certain shapes that were associated with things likely to be edible) were innate. From here he studied the visual object preferences of baby chimpanzees before turning to experimental work with human babies. The baby lying comfortably on his back in a 'looking chamber' was stimulated by objects hung from the ceiling of the crib. An observer was able to note reflections in the baby's eyes, and the length of each fixation on the displayed objects was recorded electrically.

The results of tests on 30 infants, aged between one and fifteen weeks, at weekly intervals revealed that the more complex pairs received the greater attention. Four main pairs of test patterns were presented in random sequence as shown in Activity 15 (horizontal stripes and bull's eye design; a checkboard and two sizes of plain square; a cross and a circle; two identical triangles). He found that the relative attractiveness of the two members of a pair depended on the presence of a pattern difference. 'The differential response to pattern was shown at all ages tested, indicating that it was not the result of a learning process.' However, Fantz found that visual acuity, that is, the ability to distinguish detail, improved with age. By six months babies could distinguish stripes $\frac{1}{64}$ inch wide at a distance of 10 inches when paired with a grey square of equal brightness. He inferred that improvement with age resulted from the process of maturation.

Fantz next turned his attention to the problem of learning in visual perception. He experimented with monkeys reared in darkness for varying periods from one to eleven weeks. He found that visual performances were affected in relation to the period they were kept in darkness. The older infant monkeys were, for all practical purposes, blind when first brought into the light. However, after some weeks they 'learnt to see'.

Fantz concluded that visual behaviour in the early months of life was affected by a complex interplay of innate ability, maturation and learning. He thought there was 'a critical age for the development of a given visual response when the visual, mental and motor capacities are ready to be used and under normal circumstances will be used together'.

He then returned to his earlier question as to whether or not the infant's innate capacity for form perception introduced a measure of order and meaning into what would otherwise be a chaotic jumble of sensations. He inferred that an active selection process was necessary to sort out sensations and make use of them in behaviour. He then conjectured that as people have an importance to babies perhaps the human face might bring out selective perception in an infant even as pieces of grain did so for the chicks.

He used three flat objects the size and shape of a head. One was painted with a stylized face in black on a pink background; on the second the features were re-arranged in a scrambled pattern, and on the third was painted a solid patch of black at one end equal in area to that covered by all the features. The three objects paired in all possible combinations were shown to 49 infants aged from four days to six months old. These results did not differentiate the age-levels: all the infants looked mostly at the 'real' face, less often at the scrambled face and largely ignored the control pattern. Fantz suggested that there was an unlearned, primitive meaning in the form perception of infants as well as of chicks.

He showed by further experimentation, giving the young infants a choice between a solid sphere and a flat circle of the same diameter, that a solid form was the more interesting to infants from one to six months, particularly when the solid was different in texture and shading from the flat circle. Fantz concluded that the selection of a pattern associated with a solid object was an unlearned activity which provides a basis for perceiving depth.

Fantz concludes that the young infant's interest in pattern is related to the uses of vision for child and adult. We need to recognize objects under varying conditions, such as changing colour and light conditions, apparent changes in size with distance, changes in outline with orientation and so on. The human face with its changing expression, movement of eyes and mouth, together with the varying tones of the human voice is inevitably intrinsically interesting to the young baby and becomes increasingly so as he is introduced to a wider circle of family and friends. As he becomes aware of the detailed character of individual faces, using hands as well as eyes, he can discriminate the strange from the familiar and will express his anxiety when confronted by a stranger around the age of seven months. This appears to be an important component in the process of identification of a baby with his mother, or other regular care-giver, and in the resulting proximity he maintains as he becomes mobile and increasingly independent and, at the same time, increasingly vulnerable to environmental dangers. Fantz concludes that the young baby has an innate knowledge of the environment demonstrated by his interest in the kinds of form 'that will later aid in object recognition, social responsiveness and spatial orientation. This primitive knowledge provides a foundation for the vast accumulation of knowledge through experience.'

Reference
Fantz, R. L. (1961) 'The Origin of Form Perception' in *Scientific American*, no. 459.
Gibson, J. J. (1950) *The Perception of the Visual World,* Boston: Houghton Mifflin.

Infant perceptual activity – young babies using their eyes
Margaret Roberts

Following the pioneering work of Fantz on infant perception (see Paper 10), Salapatek and Kessen concentrated their attention on perceptual activity in very young babies. They presented a sample of ten new-born babies with a black triangle on a white field whilst a control group of ten new-born babies were shown a homogeneous black visual field (black card). From photographs of eye positions taken at a rate of one second during each exposure the investigators found that infants exposed to the triangle showed much less dispersion of scanning (range of eye movements) and tended to focus on a single feature of the triangle, usually a vertex (meeting points of lines), and to exercise slight mainly horizontal movements about this point. These findings obtained regardless of the orientation of the triangle.

Salapatek found that between one month and two and a half months of age infants showed a shift from fixation of only a limited portion of a visual stimulus towards scanning a more substantial area. As the infant grows older he actively scans more and more extensive portions of figures presented.

In summary, evidence indicates that the human infant actively seeks visual stimulation rather than passively receiving it. He is thus in a position as he matures to receive more and more information about his environment.

From seeing to smiling
Margaret Roberts

Gesell, one of the pioneers in the study of child development, tells us that the child takes up the world with his eyes long before he takes it up with his hands. Fantz studied visual interest in very young babies by noting reflections in his subjects' eyes as they lay in a 'looking chamber'. He found that more complex patterns drew the most interest, a bull's-eye pattern and a checker-board pattern receiving the most attention. His experiments provided evidence that some degree of form perception is innate, that is, unlearned. Fantz went on to ask whether or not the infant's innate capacity for form perception introduces a measure of order and meaning into 'what would otherwise be a chaotic jumble of sensations'. In view of the importance of people to infants he thought a face-like pattern might be expected to bring out selective perception in an infant if anything could. He tested infants with three flat objects the size and shape of a head (see Activity 15B). He found that the infants looked mostly at the 'real' face, somewhat less often at the scrambled face, and largely ignored the control pattern. In a further experiment the face pattern was overwhelmingly the most interesting followed by printing and the bull's-eye; three brightly coloured plain circles trailing far behind.

Wolff found that infants would look for much longer at an actual human face than at any other object at four weeks of age. The eyes appear to be the focal point of interest between six weeks and three months. By four months other facial details such as nose and mouth have to be present in any representation of the human face in order to elicit smiling. After seven months smiling is no longer indiscriminately elicited by all faces but by certain specific faces only (see Schaffer, *The Growth of Sociability*, chapter 3 'Social signalling systems').

Early visual perceptual development appears to progress from the reflex physical level to the level of functioning that involves experience, both personal and social experience. It seems that the infant soon after birth is able to extract and make use of complex information from the environment. Gewirtz (1969) suggested a three-stage developmental framework to encompass the progressive changes found in the development of smiling:

(a) a phase of reflex smiling in which smiles occur in the absence of readily definable visual stimuli;

(b) a phase of 'social' smiling in which human faces in general represent the necessary stimuli;

(c) a phase of 'selective' social smiling when the infant no longer reacts indiscriminately to all social objects and only selected individuals continue to evoke the response.

From a wide range of varied experiments, for example, Schaffer, Haber and Hershenson, it would seem that the baby obtains a great deal of information from the human face and he becomes able to discriminate between those he knows and strangers to him around seven months. This is an important aspect of his development and learning which appears to be related to the social environment in which he is reared. For example, Ambrose (1961) found that for family-reared infants smiling was first observed within the six- to ten-week period range compared to the nine- to fourteen-week range for institution infants. This could be explained by the availability of people to reinforce the smiling response.

Smiling is an example of a social signalling device of which there are others, for example, crying, cooing, babbling, which, though part of the baby's genetic equipment, are dependent on the social environment for their further functional development. Knowledge of these social signalling devices are important for our understanding of the development of 'attachment' between the baby and his mother or other care-giver in the first year of life. The baby seems to be predisposed to interact with people in quite a different way than with any other object. 'From an early age the baby learns to communicate with people and to do things with objects.'

References
Ambrose, J. A. (1961) 'The development of the smiling response in early infancy' in Foss, B. M. (ed.) *Determinants of infant behaviour*, New York: Wiley.
Gewirtz, J. L. (1968) 'The course of social learning: some roles of stimulation and behaviour in early development' in Goslin, D. A. (ed.) *Handbook of Socialization Theory and Research*, Chicago: Rand McNally.

Discussion Guide E

A buzzing booming confusion?

You should spend at least 30 minutes considering these points. Arrange a meeting with your group to discuss Activity 15 in relation to Paper 10.

1 What can be inferred from the Fantz experiments?
2 Why do you think more time was spent by the babies looking at the more complicated patterns?
3 Is it simply a question of the length of time it takes for the baby's eye to explore the boundaries/edges?
4 Would Hebb's perceptual experience be operating with babies of one to fifteen weeks of age? Refer to Paper 9.

Focus on the baby's reaction to a representation of the human face in an experimental situation such as that used by Fantz. Reporting on the 'face' experiments Fantz states: 'The experiment suggested that there is an unlearned primitive meaning in the form perceptions of infants.'

1 Discuss the view that Fantz is going beyond the evidence in this statement. Can 'primitive meaning' be inferred from the baby's behaviour? List points for and against Fantz's view.
2 Consider factors likely to be involved in the young baby looking longer at an actual human face at four weeks as recorded by Wolff (see Paper 10). Why are the eyes so important?
3 How important is the adult's response to the young baby?
4 What are some of the other aspects of the baby's behaviour that contribute to his growing interest in familiar adults?

Unit Three

To smile or not to smile

- Check that you have read the Guidance Paper for visits (see page 37)
- Arrange visit for first-hand observation of young babies and carry out Activity 16
- Study observation schedule before visit
- Read Paper 13; this will help you understand what is involved in starting to be a person
- Carry out Activity 17. Arrange second visit extending observations
- Take part in Discussion F comparing your observation records and exchanging ideas with colleagues

Reading	20 mins.
Activities	120 mins.
Discussion	30 mins.
Total	170 mins.
	= 2 hrs. 50 mins.

Starting to be a person
Penelope Leach

In the very earliest weeks of a baby's life it is easy to write about him, and indeed to handle him, as if he were a precious object rather than a person. There is so much to learn about his physical appearance, his feeding, his elimination, his crying and his general physiological reactions to the world, and he is so unpredictable, that his mother can easily find herself caught up in his physical care to the exclusion of everything else.

Yet with every day that passes, the infant is developing all those qualities and capacities which mean that he is indeed a human being, and not just an especially precious little animal for whom the mother is uniquely responsible. At this stage, the infant does not react to people as one person reacts to another. But a detailed study of his reactions to the world around him show that he is *predisposed* to interact with people in quite a different way than with any other object. If a study is made of the sights which interest the infant most, the sounds which get his attention, the sensations he enjoys most and seeks to repeat, they all turn out to be most readily available in the form of an adult care-taking human.

Bowlby (1971) puts it like this: 'Newborns do not respond to people as people, nevertheless (as we have seen) their perceptual equipment is well designed to pick up and process stimuli emanating from people and their reactive equipment is biased to respond to such stimuli in certain typical ways.'

Physical contact

Infants are usually at their most contented when they are held by the mother in one of the positions which simulates clinging. Unlike infant monkeys and apes, human babies cannot cling until they are several months old. Indeed the 4–5-month infant may be very much easier for his mother to carry than is the lighter newborn, just because he holds on so efficiently by this later stage.

There is some evidence of an instinctive tendency to cling, left over from earlier evolution. In 1918, Moro, a German pediatrician, described a reflex by which newborns reacted to any sudden change of position, and especially to any change which made them feel they were about to be dropped, and which caused their overheavy heads to fall back on their unsteady necks. Put down carelessly in his cot, so that he does not feel the security of the firm mattress before his mother's hands start to release him, the infant throws out and then bends both his arms and his legs, he gives the impression of being violently startled, and he usually cries. This reflex — called the 'Moro response' — puzzled research workers, who could not see what function it could serve in evolutionary or survival terms. In 1965 Prechtl showed that the Moro response takes a very different and far more comprehensible form if it is evoked while the infant's hands are being gently pulled. In these circumstances his palmar grasp reflex is also brought into play, and the Moro response takes a form which clearly suggests a sudden gripping, with hands, arms and legs. It is now thought that this response is, in fact, a leftover from a time when the infant habitually clung to his furry mother, and that it would have been evoked by any sudden movement on her part that made the infant feel he was going to be dislodged.

The instinctive desire to cling probably explains the discomfort which infants display when they are held in positions which prevent them from making full body contact with the mother. Few, for example, are happy if they are carried in a cradled position, with the mother's hands under their heads and shoulders, thighs and knees. Few like to be laid across the mother's lap, or to be held with their backs to her.

Being firmly wrapped in soft textured material often comforts distressed infants who cannot be carried. Similarly, physical exposure in open space usually alarms this age group. Even if the infant's clothes are not removed, he is likely to appear worried and tense if he is put down on a hard flat surface, or if he is held in space. He needs, all the time, to feel the kind of contact which he would feel if he were clinging to warm fur. Modern baby-aids are a great help to *mothers*, but many of them directly contradict the needs of infants. Weighing a baby provides a composite example. He is undressed — which he may well find frightening — he is then placed in a hard plastic or wicker basket, suspended in space. The basket descends suddenly under his weight, and makes a sharp sudden sound as it reaches the bottom of its travel. To weigh a baby without tears takes real understanding, foresight and skill.

Seeing

If the infant is predisposed to remain in close physical contact with human beings, so he is innately predisposed to look at their faces rather than at anything else. From birth an infant will focus his gaze for about two seconds on any new sight which is brought before his eyes. This brief focus shows that he has 'noticed' the object. The length of his gaze thereafter can be taken as a measure of his actual interest in it, and some very interesting research has been carried out into the kind of object which newborns look at for longest.

Fantz (1966) found that at 48 hours of age infants looked for longer at a coloured pattern than at a plain block of colour, and for longer at a circle with eyes, nose and a mouth sketched in than a plain circle. Most interest of all was always elicited by a face-pattern which also moved. These very new infants were therefore selecting for visual inspection objects which had the qualities of a human face.

Studying 4-week-old infants, Wolff (1963) found that infants would look for much longer at an actual human face than at any other object, however garish the alternative objects were. This scientific finding is regularly confirmed in ordinary homes. A mother, striving to get her infant to look at a new toy, finds that the infant continually disregards it and returns his gaze to her own face.

Hearing

The human voice also seems to be innately attractive to new babies. Infants are almost always startled by loud sudden sounds, and usually seem soothed and pleased by music or by gentle rhythmic continuous noise. But a human voice elicits a special response from the baby. If he is crying, he is likely to stop when his mother talks to him, remain quietly alert as long as she goes on talking and cry again as soon as she stops. If he is content when she starts talking, her voice may elicit a very brief, fleeting smile, even as early as the third week of life. By the time the baby is 5 weeks old he may always smile when his mother talks to him. From this time on, he may also babble in response to her voice, although he does not yet babble in reaction to any other sound.

Language

At the beginning a new infant has no language other than crying. Various types of cry can be distinguished, by means of sound spectrographs. These do form a 'language' in the sense that all infants' hunger cries have one typical pattern, all

pain cries another and so on. Mothers have to learn to interpret their infant's cries by experience. Most maintain that they would not recognize their own child's cry from those of other babies of similar age, but various experiments have shown that in fact mothers are extremely good at recognizing the cries of their own newborns. Formby (1967) showed that of 23 mothers in one maternity ward, 12 successfully recognized the tape-recorded cry of their own child at 48 hours old, and all were successful during the next few days. Furthermore in the first three nights after they had given birth, 15 mothers woke only when their own babies cried; on subsequent nights only one mother ever woke to the cry of another woman's baby. Wolff found that mothers' reactions to different cries in their babies were extremely variable: they might, or might not, go at once in answer to the basic, hunger cry. But the mothers in his experiment all reacted with extreme speed to their babies' pain cries — and were both furious and relieved when they found that these were tape-recorded rather than immediate.

Until about 3 weeks old, babies usually have a repertory of cries consisting of the basic or hunger cry, the distinctive pain cry and what is often described as an 'anger' cry, which mothers often call 'trying it on'. It is a grumbly, grizzly cry which often lasts for some minutes, and which turns into the basic hunger cry if the mother does not intervene.

By about 4 weeks old, the first non-crying sounds usually appear. Not distinct separate sounds at this stage, but gurgly googly noises. Often they occur first of all when the infant is just beginning to feel fretful. They may give way to grumbling and thence to basic crying, in a regular sequence.

By 6 weeks there will probably be some phonetic syllables among the gurgles. Sound-making tends to become differentiated from feeling fretful at this point. The infant probably now 'talks' most when he is talked to. Some babies will even 'talk back' by this age, making a sound, listening to the mother make the sound back, and then making it again themselves.

Smiling

Smiling is a vital social accomplishment. It is the means whereby infants ensure that adults will interact socially with them, will pay them the personal attention they must have for full human development. Such a bald statement is justifiable because for any normal adult a new baby's smile is irresistible. The bored visitor may bend dutifully over the cot, and make some trite remark to the mother about the occupant's beauty. But if that occupant smiles at him, he will almost certainly drop his guard and smile and talk directly and spontaneously to the baby.

However much mothers know, intellectually, about the early development of infants, and the importance of treating them personally, looking at them directly, talking to them by name from the beginning, all these things cease to be intellectually governed once the infants respond and reward them with smiles. Of 120 mothers whom the author saw over two years, all but one made some spontaneous remark during the week when her child began to smile, along the lines of 'Now he really knows me' or 'Now she's really getting to be fun.'

The actual dating of smiling varies wildly according to different authorities. No doubt this is partly because it varies wildly according to different babies. Most smile fleetingly, in response to a variety of stimuli, almost from birth. These fleeting pseudo-smiles used to be put down to wind. It is now thought that they are actual practice smiles.

By about 4 weeks these pseudo-smiles tend to occur most often in response to the human voice, and they begin to have some social effect — they *look* more smiley. A little after this, the baby seems transfixed by the human face. He gazes at it, often for a minute at a time, slowly exploring its contour from hairline to chin; returning always to the eyes. By 6 weeks, about 50 per cent of babies complete their detailed examination of the face by returning their gaze to the eyes, and smiling. The other half of any given group of babies will reach this stage in a diminishing scatter over the next 2½ months. Only a very few — probably including those who were born prematurely — will fail to smile by four months.

In a way an infant's smiling, gurgling responses are the mother's reward for her devoted care while he got himself settled into life. Earlier on, the baby could give his parents pleasure by his very existence, by his contentment, his growth, his obvious 'all rightness'. But once he begins to react to being handled in this brilliantly social, enchanting way, he gives them pleasure of quite a different sort. His smiles and his 'talk' are an immediate reward to the mother who has torn herself out of deep sleep to feed him in the night, an irresistible compensation for yet another nappy needing changing in the middle of her favourite television programme. Even from these very early weeks, the infant whose social responses start early and are frequent and easily evoked is likely to get more attention than the one whose social development is slower. All human beings like to be liked. The mother whose baby smiles at her has no doubt of his affection or of his humanness.

References
Bowlby, J. (1971) *Attachment,* Penguin.
Fantz, R. L. (1966) 'Pattern discrimination and selective attention as determinants of perceptual development from birth' in Aline, J., Kidd, J. and Rivoire, J. L. (eds.) *Perceptual Development in Children,* University of London Press.
Formby, D. (1967) 'Maternal recognition of the infant's cry', *Developmental Medicine and Child Neurology,* 9.
Prechtl, H. F. R. (1965) 'Problems of behavioural studies in the newborn infant' in Lehrman, D. S. and Hinde, R. A. (eds.) *Advances in the Study of Behaviour,* Vol. 1, Academic Press.
Wolff, P. H. (1963) 'Observations on the early development of smiling' in Foss, B. (ed.) *Determinants of Infant Behaviour,* Vol. 11, Methuen.

Discussion Guide F

Comparison of observation records

Allow at least 30 minutes for comparing your records. Read Paper 13 before meeting for discussion. Bring all observation records from Activities 16 and 17 with you. The aims of discussion with colleagues are:

1 to compare experiences;
2 to compare the baby's behaviour with relation to age, sex, position in family, attitude of mother and/or father, total situation;
3 to note similarities and differences in the records of the baby's behaviour and situation;
4 to relate your reading to first-hand experience of a mother/father and baby and to note any incompatibilities.

Present the observations of your first visit in age-order. When reporting to your group give a few introductory remarks regarding the contextual situation and the atmosphere. Then focus on the baby and mother/father or other care-giver, using your observation records, plus basic data and comments.

Report on your second visit in the same way as above. The value of making a second visit about four weeks later is seen in:

(a) your more relaxed approach;
(b) changes in behaviour of baby;
(c) the baby's likely greater interest in you;
(d) the fact that the baby is four weeks older and is likely to be larger, stronger and more alert.

It will be helpful to make a note of similarities and differences in terms of other students' observations and experiences. List changes noted on the second visit by yourself and others. List similarities and differences in terms of other students' observations during the second visit. Why is it likely that there will be more variations noted in the second series of observations?

Discuss what you could do to make your observations more scientifically accurate, remembering the personal element in perception discussed in Unit 1 of this module. Would two observers working together provide a reasonable check?

Module Three

Social/Cognitive and Motor Development

Mother–Child Interaction

- Read Paper 14; this paper prepares for first-hand observation of mother and baby interacting with one another
- Carry out Activity 18 arranging visit and completing observations
- Read Paper 15 focussing on reaching and grasping behaviour
- Work through Discussion Guide G; this will help you to compare observations and consider the baby's capacity for learning about people and objects

Reading	30 mins.
Activities	60 mins.
Discussion	30 mins.
Total	120 mins.
	= 2 hrs.

Module Three   Paper 14

Mother and baby partnership
Margaret Roberts

Video-taping, with its additional slow-motion device, has provided evidence of the intricate nature of early mother–child communication. We have seen from first-hand observations in Module 2 that the young baby is already making sense of the environment by means of his sensory equipment. He can react to moving objects and visual stimulation from an early age and soon shows a preference for complex and varied visual patterns such as the human face. He can also discriminate sounds and soon responds to the human voice.

The coming and going of his mother or other care-giver with regular satisfying experiences of holding, feeding, bathing and talking stimulates a response to these forms of human behaviour and the development of expectation that certain happenings will occur in familiar sequence. The young baby of three months is already established in patterns of behaviour which provide the foundation for later learning.

Sleep is as important as stimulation to the young baby. The central nervous system develops further neural connections during sleep and all systems of the body increase their competence and co-ordination. Babies vary a great deal in their sleeping and their waking from sleep behaviour. Some take a considerable time to become fully awake and responsive even to familiar adults.

Video-recordings of mothers and young babies interacting with one another demonstrate the sensitive nature of the mother's response to her baby's state and his developing social skills. Given the baby's capacity to observe visual similarities and differences, as we have seen from the work of Fantz, and early sensitivity to the human voice together with the mother's awareness of her baby's needs, it is not surprising that the baby gradually develops the ability to discriminate between familiar adults and strangers. About the age of seven months babies usually demonstrate an attachment to a specific person. This behaviour is accompanied by expressions of distress when this special person goes away and a reluctance to accept comfort from other people. Gradually multiple attachments are formed but from about five months to fifteen months 'stranger-anxiety' is likely to be expressed especially in unfamiliar surroundings.

Rutter (1978) looked closely at early social development and attachment behaviour and noted several important research findings. He emphasized that much has still to be learned about the factors which influence the develop-ment of attachment but research shows that neither feeding nor care-taking is an essential feature. 'Moreover,' he states, 'bonds do not necessarily develop to the person who spends most time with the child. The intensity of interaction probably has more effect than duration. Attachment tends to be strongest when someone plays with the child and gives him a lot of attention, especially if this is associated with responsiveness and sensitivity to the baby's signals. Probably sensitive responsiveness is the one quality in any interaction which is the most likely to foster attachment. However, a baby's tendency to seek attachment is increased by anxiety and fear, and also by illness and fatigue (Bowlby, 1969). Attachments are particularly likely to develop to the person who brings comfort at such times.'

In Module 3 we shall be observing the young baby's increasing social and cognitive skills within the setting of his first personal relations. Schaffer (1971) makes the point that cognition and social behaviour are not separate categories of behaviour. 'It is essential,' he says, 'to bear in mind that social behaviour does not constitute a class apart from all other forms of behaviour: the responses that an individual makes to the social part of his environment are based on the same fundamental processes of attention and perception, learning and retention, as the responses he makes to inanimate objects.' The baby's behaviour in responding and in initiating contact increases his mother's interest in him, so enhancing the partnership.

We will try to observe first the mother's responsiveness and sensitivity to the baby's signals, to his smiles, his cries and other vocal communications, and to his interests in objects in his environment: noting how her behaviour varies in response to him. Secondly, we will observe his activity with objects, his reaching and grasping behaviour, and his later attempts to do things with objects that interest him. Reaching and grasping behaviour brings the baby into direct contact with objects in his world and are important aspects of developing cognitive development. But as Schaffer points out they are not separate categories of behaviour from social development. They are probably closely related to what Rutter calls 'early sources of security and competence', arising from the child's confidence in the adult's concern and interest. Deeply distressed babies do not show interest in reaching and grasping objects in their environment around five to six months. They tend to become increasingly withdrawn and retarded in development.

Interest shown by the care-giver in the child's activity with objects he can hold, suck, bang etc. stimulates the baby's urge to investigate the world around him and to share his activities with the adults; he enjoys their interest in him and his activities. We will be observing how the mother facilitates reciprocal activities and engages in dialogue with the baby, and also the baby's patterns of response, sometimes imitating and sometimes initiating his own activities. Schaffer (1977) describes the mother's relationship as that of a partner – 'though a senior partner by virtue of being more experienced, more powerful, and more likely to have consciously formulated ideas about the purpose and direction of the interaction. She rarely does anything without being aware of her child's precise requirements or without adapting her behaviour in their light; the younger the child the greater her need to adapt in this way . . . Whether we observe a baby feeding, playing, being bathed, changed and put to bed, or merely being bounced on his mother's knee, we find a highly intricate pattern of interaction – a pattern that is based on the intrinsic organization of social behaviour but that subsequently develops through the sheer experience of mutual contact.'

Schaffer sees socialization as a two-way, not a one-way, business: like education, he says, it is essentially a joint venture. He goes on to look at factors involved in inadequate, indifferent and rejecting mothering in a variety of cultures and the effect of institutional upbringing. In view of the sensitive nature of the earliest reciprocal relationships he is cautious in his reaction to the idea that separations before around seven months are of no consequence. What is required, he concludes, are studies that examine at a much more microscopic level the effects of changing the mother-figure.

In order to become aware of some aspects of this early mother–baby partnership you will need to visit a mother and baby, if possible in their own home. It will be easier for you if you are already known to the mother. Ask to see the mother and baby together at a relaxed period of the day. Perhaps after the mid-day meal, or when well awake from morning or afternoon nap. Ask the mother to chat and play normally with the baby. Notice the time the baby spends actually looking at the mother and she at him. Notice if the baby turns his head away and back again. Note vocal sounds exchanged between mother and baby. If possible see the baby bathed and fed, concentrating on how mother and baby communicate.

Some babies will be interested in you as a different person from the mother and may look from her to you. Under the age of four or five months babies will be unlikely to show distress at the presence of a newcomer in their home. This, of course, depends on whether there are frequent visitors to the mother and baby. In any case you are advised to approach gradually and to talk to the mother before making contact with the baby.

References

Bowlby, J. (1969) *Attachment and Loss* Vol. 1, Hogarth Press.
Rutter, M. (1978) in Bruner, J. and Garton, A. (eds.) *Human Growth and Development*, Clarendon Press, ch. 2.
Schaffer, H. R. (1971) *The Growth of Sociability*, Penguin, ch. 1.
Schaffer, H. R. (1977) *Mothering*, Fontana/Open Books.

Learning how to grasp the world of objects
Margaret Roberts

Have you ever stopped to think how often and on how many occasions during a day you use your hands? Have you noticed how you adjust your hands according to the size, shape and/or weight of the object you are preparing to handle? We only have to injure our thumb or fore-finger slightly to realize how essential they are to our manual activities. To lose the smallest degree of function from our hands is enough to cause us anxiety. And yet for the first months of life the only activity of the hands is a reflex grasp which you can test out at any time by inserting your finger into the curled fist of a very young baby. A new-born baby can support his own weight in this manner, a reflex from bygone days when the baby's ability to grasp his parent's fur was essential for survival. This early reflex gradually disappears to be replaced by a purposive grasp. It takes four or five months to develop an intentional grasp and longer still to learn to let go intentionally! But a young baby of a few weeks will wave his arms and hands in the direction of an attractive object he has fastened his eyes on. Trevarthen (1975) made a film study of a three-week-old baby which indicated rudimentary reaching movements even though the reach was too short to actually touch the object. Trevarthen studied the difference in behaviour of the baby from birth until six months old, (a) in response to the mother 'chatting' with the baby and (b) in response to a suspended object. He noted two different kinds of response, one for the object and one for the mother. Most different were the expressions of face, voice and hands, as if the baby knew that different actions were required for communicating with persons and 'doing' with objects.

You will notice from observations over a period of time that there is a sequential pattern in the development of manual dexterity. In the early stages of grasping the baby uses a 'palmar scoop' grasping the object with the whole hand, fingers flattened towards the palm – the thumb is not brought into use at this early stage (four to five months). Finger–thumb opposition develops about ten months when the baby delights in picking up very small objects between the tips of thumb and first finger. The first finger is often used as a probing tool, and also as an indicator from about ten months. Either hand is used according to which is the more convenient for the first eighteen months or so.

The development of hand and eye co-ordination, which permits the baby not only to 'pick up the world with his

eyes', as Gesell put it, but actually to pick objects up with his hands, develops gradually towards the fifth month of the first year of life. It continues to improve through childhood and forms the basis for many highly skilled activities in adult life.

The act of sitting up stimulates the baby's interest in graspable objects and frees his arms and hands from assisting in maintaining his position when reclining. At first both hands are activated and brought to the mid-line without co-ordination, or, if the object is lying to right or left of the mid-line, they may be used separately. When the object is secured it is invariably brought to the mouth for sucking – the mouth will be shaped up in anticipation for this activity. Bruner (1974) sees the mouth playing an important role 'as the terminus of guided reaching activity'. He carried out observations of babies from six weeks to eight weeks (sitting with adequate support) and on to six months (later eighteen months) examining the sequence of reach-grasp-retrieve-mouth with visual inspection. He noted that loss of visual contact at seven months (he covered the object with a light cloth just as the child grasped it) led to a withdrawal of the hand empty. Whereas at nine months loss of visual contact did not interrupt the act of grasping, 'the infant's hand emerged from under the masking cloth with the object firmly in hand'.

During development Bruner notes that the sequential acts of reaching and grasping 'seem to require cessation of all other enterprises . . . involving total commitment'. The complex activity gradually gets smoothed out in terms of close attention, anticipation of direction, smoothness and speed. The baby by eight months can begin a reach without tensing the whole torso. He is less likely to bring the object to his mouth and will begin to explore tactually, or visually, or use the object for rhythmic banging.

Bruner describes a film of a seven-month-old baby 'trying to get hold of a moderately heavy drinking mug and literally shutting his eyes while bringing his hands together on the cup, as if to free the task from constant visual supervision'. It is as if the child trusts his anticipatory schema and turns to attend to further action to be carried out with the object he has grasped. Reaching, grasping and retrieving now become sub-routines as Bruner describes them 'able to fit into a variety of other activities with which they can become integrated'. Objects can now be used in productive relationship with one another. However, Bruner makes the point that this picture of development is too task-directed, too play-less to be characteristic of the first year of life. In order to understand how the child achieves his growing competence we must consider early play, what Gesell identified as 'the joy of being the cause!' There is much behaviour, notes Bruner, that seems to be 'without clear-cut means–ends structure, where the activity seems more playful, where ends are changed to fit available means, and means and ends become admixed'. He writes of play which precedes the symbolic play in late infancy and early childhood, an earlier type of play which is crucial for development during the first year or year and a half.

'I shall call it mastery-play, and its form is playful means–ends matching.' He notes examples drawn from his Harvard studies which appear to be 'pleasure-giving variations of newly acquired routines'. The six-month-old infant, having learned to hold on to an object and get it easily into his mouth, then begins a programme of variation. When he takes the object after mastery has been achieved, he holds it to look at, he shakes it, he bangs it on his high chair, he drops it over the edge, and before long he manages to fit the object into every activity into which it can be put. Inversely . . . when he can hold an object steady in one hand while exploring it with the fingers of the other, he very soon uses this new act on any object that has a 'loose end' or 'pick-at-able' property. In the first case, a new object is fitted into as many routines as available; in the second, a newly mastered act is addressed to as many different objects as possible. Both are absorbing work (play) for the child. Bruner expressed surprise at the length of time young infants will stay with such variation of activity — a six to eight month up to half an hour.

Running parallel to this exploratory type of work/play you will see the baby's pleasure in repetition. Sensory-motor skills need practice and the baby works hard at this but there comes a time when repetition appears to be serving another purpose, as if the baby is assuring himself that the result will be the same. A baby of ten months on one occasion tipped cowrie shells from a container into my lap and then on to the floor, again and again for over half an hour. Each time he scrabbled the shells back into the container and proceeded to repeat the whole operation until, when exhaustion was setting in, he allowed himself to be distracted by the smell of his favourite supper dish! Although barely able to balance himself, alternating between standing at my lap and crouching to tip the shells onto the floor, he concentrated on his self-chosen activity as if determined to convince himself that *he* could make these things happen!

It is essential to keep in mind the unity of the child's growth, development and learning when observing particular aspects of his behaviour. Social exchange, hand–eye co-ordination, anticipation of events, awareness of routines, repetition and imitation are not separate categories of behaviour but expressions of the developing mind of the child resulting from complex interaction of innate potential and a range of environmental experiences.

References
Bruner, J. (1974) *Beyond the Information Given*, Allen & Unwin.
Trevarthen, C. (1975) 'Early attempts at speech' in Lewin, R. (ed.) *Child Alive*, Temple Smith.

Discussion Guide G

Interaction with people and things

Allow at least 30 minutes for this discussion. Bring the observation records with you from Activity 18. You will find it helpful to work in small groups. This discussion should help you to see the value of interaction with people and objects in the young child's early development and learning. The exchange of observation records and comparison of findings will help you to realize the range and variety of behaviour within the framework of an agreed schedule of observations. Later we will consider the influence of deprivation on the young baby's development at this time.

Report observations in age-order (youngest first). Give first name and basic data first, followed by a brief description of the contextual situation and atmosphere. Proceed with your observation record over ten to fifteen minutes. Conclude your report with any further information or comments from the mother. Follow the reporting session with discussion on differences in behaviour:

(a) between the children;
(b) with persons and with objects.

Use the following questions to focus on the young baby's capacity for learning (a) about people, and (b) about objects. Make brief notes on the main points of the discussion.

1 Do babies communicate with persons and 'do' things with objects?
2 Do your observations confirm or contradict Trevarthen's findings regarding the baby's expressions of face, voice and hands during these two activities (Paper 15)?
3 Did you see the baby spontaneously seek companionship during his activity? If so, how did he do this?
4 Did you see any difference in the baby's behaviour towards you as compared with his behaviour towards his mother? If so, what reasons would you suggest for this?
5 Do you think the baby is capable of learning from his experiences at this young age? If so, what is the basis for this in your view?

Behaviour with Objects and Persons

- Read Paper 16; this paper presents the Piaget/Bower controversy regarding the development of 'object/concept'
- Carry out Activity 19 replicating Piaget's 'object-concept' test
- Work through Discussion Guide H; this will help you to focus on mental processes involved in 'object-concept'
- Read Paper 17 dealing with differences in behaviour with persons and with objects
- Carry out Activity 20, Tasks 1 to 5, replicating Bower's test with moving objects
- Work through Discussion Guide I comparing observations and considering implications of Bower's challenge
- Discussion Guide J considers whether Piaget and Bower are testing the same thing or different aspects of complex behaviour

Reading	40 mins.
Activities	120 mins.
Discussion	90 mins.
Total	250 mins.
	= 4 hrs. 10 mins.

—C

Cognitive development
T. G. R. Bower

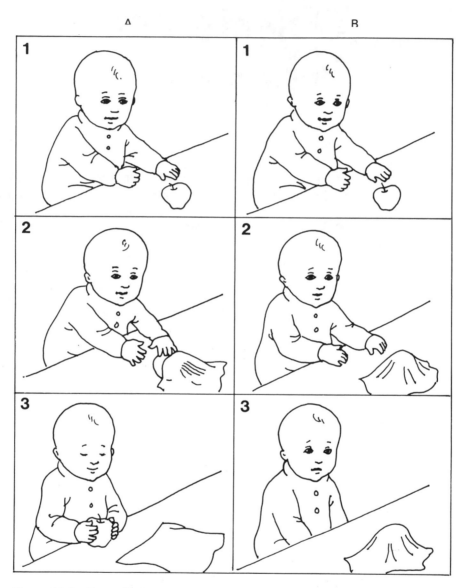

Figure 16.1   Stage III. A stage-III infant (A) will reach out and take a partially covered object, but he is unable to obtain an object that has been completely covered by a cloth (B).

There comes a stage in development when the infant ignores perceptual information and relies on other kinds of information, such as that supplied by memory, consistency, or other non-perceptual processes. A behaviour may develop to a peak of perfection without development necessarily being over; but the rules for the application of the behaviour must still be elaborated. In development, there is thus a progression away from dependence on immediate stimulus input toward dependence on rules that combine perceptual information with information from memory. This progression – *cognitive* development – is the subject of this paper.

Piaget has described the processes and details of infant cognitive development in his famous trilogy, *The Origins of Intelligence in Children* (1936), *The Construction of Reality in the Child* (1937), and *Play, Dreams and Imitation in Childhood* (1946). The breadth and originality of these works dwarfs all the other essays in this field. It would be impossible to summarize these books within the compass of the present work. Indeed they depend on an interplay between observation and theory that defies summarization. Instead of attempting a summary of the whole trilogy, I shall select one or two topics to describe in full; hopefully, a detailed analysis of selected topics will illuminate the processes at work in cognitive development.

The choice of a topic is not an easy one for the whole range of topics is fascinating and important. There is one topic that stands out, however, and that is the development of the *object concept.* Piaget refers to this segment of development as the prototype of cognitive development; he describes the attainment of the object concept as the most precocious expression of processes that will eventually generate mathematical reasoning and logical thinking in adults. Other authors are equally convinced of the importance of the object concept. Elkind and Sameroff (1970) refer to it as Piaget's most significant discovery — no mean attribution when one considers how many revolutionary discoveries Piaget has made.

What then is the object concept and how does it develop? According to Piaget, the main milestones of the development are best seen by studying how the infant reacts to objects that have vanished or been hidden. To begin with, according to Piaget, there is no special behaviour toward vanished objects. This description, however, as we shall see, must be qualified. In terms of gross searching behaviour, there is nothing to be seen at this early stage. The infants do not reach out or crawl after objects that have left their field of view; this, perhaps, is not a surprising result since the infants we are discussing are under four months of age. Infants in the second half of this period (two to four months) will look after objects that have moved out of their field of view. Infants in the first half (zero to two months — referred to as *stage I*) do not even do this. During *stage II*, head and eye tracking and looking after objects that have moved out of view does occur. By *stage III*, infants can reach out to pick up objects that they see. If presented with a partially covered object, they can reach out and take it (see Figure 16.1). If the object is completely covered with a cloth or a cup, the *stage III* infants make no attempt whatsoever to get the object. They withdraw from the object and its cover and make no attempt at all to remove the cover. Indeed, they act as if the object no longer exists. Many authors have taken this behaviour to be evidence that infants of this age (four to six months) in fact believe that an object no longer exists when it is out of sight.

When the infant can recover an object that has been hidden under a cloth this third stage ends. The *stage IV* infant, though, still seems to have a peculiar

concept of objects. The infant will look for an object if the object is hidden under a cloth. If, however, the infant is allowed to find an object under the same cloth two or more times and then the object is hidden within the infant's view but under a different cloth in a different place, the infant will look for the object in its original place under the first cloth — totally ignoring where the object actually is. This happens even if the hidden object is quite large; the infant will still pick up the flat cloth that had previously covered the object (see Figure 16.2). This error implies that the infant does not yet really understand that an object which has been covered by a cloth is under that cloth. The infants seem to think that an object that has been hidden will always be found in the same place. This place error is characteristic of the *stage IV* baby and is usually overcome around the age of ten to twelve months.

By the age of ten months, we might think that the object concept was fully developed. However, infants of this age can still be confused by some methods of hiding objects. Suppose we place two cloths on a table; we put an object under one of them and then switch the position of the cloths, as shown in Figure 16.3A. The *stage V* infant will pick up the cloth on the side where the object was first placed, ignoring the cloth that is actually hiding the object. At this point, infants seem to believe that an object will be found where it was hidden; they do not take into account invisible displacements of the object even when the displacements of the cover on the objects are fully visible. Figure 16.3B illustrates a similar failure in a related task. Eventually infants succeed in even these tasks; this normally occurs somewhere around eighteen months of age. These stages are summarized in Table 16.1.

These then are the main behavioural landmarks in the development of the object concept. But how much does this tell us about the meaning of the infant's failures and successes? Our interpretation of the behaviour is critical, and many different interpretations have been made. Consider the behaviour of the infant in *stage III*. If an infant is presented with a desirable toy that is then covered while the infant is watching, the infant will make no attempt to remove the cover. The standard interpretation is that the infant thinks that the object no longer exists when it is under the cover. According to this interpretation, once the object is out of sight, the infant thinks it is no longer to be found anywhere and, consequently, makes no attempt to search for it.

This explanation certainly accounts for the observed behaviour. If the infant thinks the object no longer exists, we could hardly expect him to pick up the cover. However, other possible alternative explanations do exist. One is that the infant does not pick up the cloth simply because he cannot. It is quite possible that the infant knows that the object is

Table 16.1 Stages of development

Stage	Age (in Months)*	Success	Fail
I	0–2	No particular behaviour shown in response to hiding event.	
II	2–4	Infant will track a moving object that goes behind a screen. Infants can learn to track an object from place to place.	Infant continues to track a moving object after it has stopped. Infant will look for an object in its familiar place even when sees object moving to new place.
III	4–6	Infant no longer makes tracking errors of Stage II. Infant recovers an object which has been partially covered by a cloth.	Infant cannot recover an object which has been fully covered by a cloth.
IV	6–12	Infant can now recover an object which has been completely hidden under a cloth.	Infant searches for an object in place where previously found, ignoring the place where seen hidden.
V	12–15	Infant no longer makes place error of Stage IV.	Infant cannot cope with invisible displacements of an object.
VI	15–18	Complete success — infant can find object no matter where or how hidden.	

* These ages are approximate; there may be considerable individual differences.

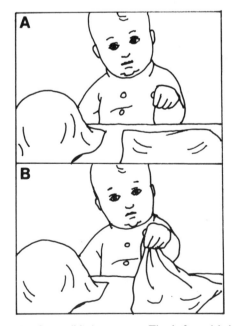

Figure 16.2 Stage IV place error. The infant thinks that an object which has been hidden will always be found in the same place. Even when the hidden object is quite large, the infant will still go to the place where the object was previously hidden.

under the cloth but does not know how to remove the cloth; in this case, of course, the same lack of behaviour would ensue. These two explanations are obviously quite different ways of accounting for the same behaviour. Nothing we have said so far allows us to decide between these explanations; however, the relevant sorts of experiments are not too hard to do. What we need is some alternative to search behaviour as a measure of whether an infant thinks that an out-of-sight object still exists. Startle measures could obviously be useful in this account.

One thing we can do is present an infant with an object and then drop a screen over the object so as to make it vanish. We then remove the screen, either revealing the object or revealing an empty place where the object had been (see Figure 16.4). What responses would be predicted by the two alternative explanations? If infants indeed think that an object

4 ... removes hand, leaving object under cloth.

1 Object is in experimenter's hand.

5 Child looks in experimenter's hand.

2 Experimenter closes hand ...

6 Obviously upset, child quits

3 ... puts hand under cloth ...

B

Figure 16.3B Stage V switching error. The child is unable to infer that if the object is not in the experimenter's hand, it must be under the cloth.

4

1 Object in view

5

2 Object under cloth

3 Cloths transposed

A

Figure 16.3A Stage V switching error. The infant cannot yet cope with invisible displacements of the object.

69

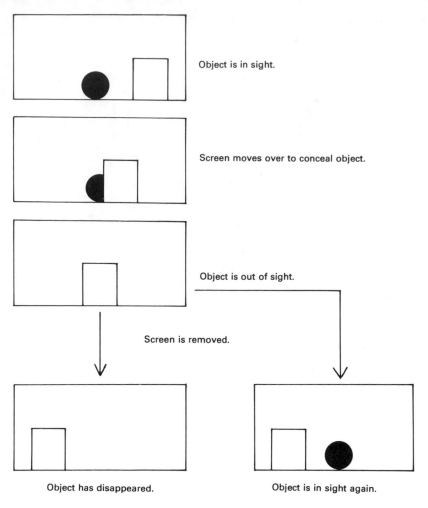

Object is in sight.

Screen moves over to conceal object.

Object is out of sight.

Screen is removed.

Object has disappeared.

Object is in sight again.

Figure 16.4   How will a stage-III infant respond to these two events?

no longer exists when it is out of sight, they should hardly expect to see the object again when the screen is removed. In other words, they should be more surprised by the reappearance sequence than by the non-reappearance sequence. On the contrary, if infants believe the object is still there, hidden behind the screen, then they should be more surprised by non-reappearance than by reappearance. Experiments of this kind have been done by Bower (1966) and Charlesworth (1966).

In my own experiment, change in heart-rate was used as a measure of surprise. I found that infants too young to be able to pick up a cloth were more surprised by non-reappearance than by reappearance. This suggests that the infants did believe that the hidden object still existed even though it was out of sight. If heart-rate change can be taken as a fair measure of cognitive upset, it would seem that this is a clear disproof of the standard explanation of *stage III* behaviour.

If infant subjects actually do believe that an object still exists after it has been covered by a screen, then their belief should also manifest itself in other behaviours. If presented with a moving object which they can track, the infants should be able to track the

object and anticipate its reappearance when the object goes behind a screen. In other words, if an infant sees an object move behind a screen, he should expect the object to come out on the other side of the screen − provided he really believes the object continues to exist when out of sight. Experiments like this have also been done (Gardner, 1971; Bower, Broughton and Moore, 1971). The results indicate quite clearly that infants as young as eight weeks of age will anticipate the reappearance of an object that has gone behind a screen. That is to say, they will turn their eyes to reach the exit side of the screen just before, or just as, the moving object emerges from behind the screen. It is not the case that the object is looked at after it emerges. Rather, the infants' eyes are at the exit point just as, or just before, the object appears. This indicates anticipation of emergence rather than reaction to emergence.

This result, together with the results of infants' surprise at non-reappearance, would seem to be conclusive proof that quite young infants − infants still in the age-range of Piaget's *stage II* − know that objects continue to exist after they have been occluded by a screen. They can demonstrate this knowledge in their eye movements but not in hand and arm movements. Clearly, the implication is that the *stage III* deficit is really a deficit in the motor system – not a deficit in the infant's knowledge of the world.

References
Bower, T. G. R. (1966) 'Object permanence and short-term memory in the human infant', unpublished manuscript.
Bower, T. G. R., Broughton, J. M. and Moore, M. K. (1971) 'The development of the object concept as manifested by changes in the tracking behaviour of infants between 7 and 20 weeks of age', *Journal of Experimental Child Psychology,* 11 (1).
Charlesworth, W. R. (1966) 'Persistence of orienting and attending behaviour in infants as a function of stimulus-locus uncertainty', *Child Development,* 37.
Elkind, D. and Sameroff, A. (1970) 'Developmental psychology', *Annual Review of Psychology,* 21, 191–238.
Gardner, J. K. (1971) Unpublished doctoral dissertation, Harvard University.

A commentary on Bower's findings
Margaret Roberts

Bower investigated further the behaviour of young babies in relation to moving objects and concluded that babies under five months seem to think that a single object, seen in different places, is in fact a number of different objects. This was demonstrated by training the baby to watch a train with a flashing light move between point A and point B staying stationary for 10 seconds at each point. After this training session the train was moved from A to a new point at C. The baby continued to look to point B where the train had stopped on all previous trials. 'The infants ignore the clearly visible object at location C and look steadfastly at B – often looking surprised and puzzled that the object is not to be seen at B.' (Bower, 1974.)

Bower asks: 'Is it the case, then, that an infant thinks an object is the same as long as it stays in the same place? And similarly, does he think an object is the same as long as it continues on the same path of movement?' It appears that infants between twelve and twenty weeks do not seem to be aware that place and movement are linked – that a single object can move from place to place without becoming a whole series of different objects. Around twenty weeks the infant's behaviour has changed. When presented with a stationary object that proceeds to move, the twenty-week-old can follow it no matter where it moves or has moved. These infants seem to be aware that an object can go from place to place along movement paths; place and movement are co-ordinated. They also seem to know that movement links spatially disparate places.

This knowledge has been demonstrated through visual perception experiments and suggests that conceptual development is ahead of sensory-motor co-ordination. If this is so it would throw light on the apparently more advanced social behaviour towards the mother-figure. Bower found that an infant less than five months of age was not disturbed at all by multiple mirror images of his mother, in fact interacted with all three mothers in turn. However, past the age of five months (after co-ordination of place and movement) the sight of three mothers becomes very disturbing to the child. Bower contends that the young infant (less than five months) thinks that he has a multiplicity of mothers whereas the older child knows he has but one. Piaget has argued that conceptual knowledge may have to be reformulated at a different level in the sequence of development. What is known at the perceptual–social level may have to be reformulated in relation to inanimate objects in space and time. This is a possible explanation of Bower's findings.

Looking at Bower's experimental work in terms of development prior to full 'object-concept' he is seen to be exploring Piaget-type ideas from a different point of view. His questions and the nature of his investigations have contributed to our knowledge of the complexity of perceptual/conceptual development in relation to the young child's knowledge about persons and objects.

His discovery of the difficulties the child has over the perception of movement of objects in relation to their identity is important. It is possible that the baby understands about the permanence of persons earlier than the permanence of objects as shown by expressions of distress at the disappearance or non-appearance of the mother-figure from an early age. This behaviour suggests that the baby believes that he can effect the reappearance of his mother if he protests loudly enough. The vigorous protests of a nine or ten month baby can go on for a long time at maximum capacity as baby-sitters will testify!

The far greater complexity of the mother's behaviour towards the baby in terms of coming and going and the quality of human interaction is likely to be a factor in the baby's earlier awareness of the continuity of existence of the mother compared with inanimate objects. Movement is clearly part of the problem of appearance/disappearance, and non-appearance, and the co-ordination of identity, movement and place is an important dimension of 'object-concept' in relation to persons and inanimate objects.

Bower's study can be further linked with Piaget's developmental sequence in terms of experiments involving 'displacements'. When Piaget introduced 'displacements', that is, placing objects under a cover and withdrawing them, without letting the child see, to hide them under another cover, he was putting considerable stress on the child's developing capacity for constructing a hypothesis about movement and the identity of objects. The hypothesis that an object which is no longer in its original place of concealment has been moved to another place requires knowledge that objects can be moved from one place to another *and remain the same object*. It follows that movements from one place to another and changes in line of movement without changing identity have to be mentally grasped *before* Piaget's difficult 'displacements' can be coped with. The child's activity with objects, moving them himself from place to place and back again, putting them in and out of containers, will help in this development. In addition the support and interest of familiar adults will add to his delight in newly found skills and strengthen his developing self-image and the growth of self-confidence.

We are dealing here with the early stages of the development of mental representation. It appears that perceptual knowledge develops first in terms of personal relations involving attachment to one person – the mother-figure. Perceptual knowledge of the world of things develops as a result of the child's own action in reaching, grasping and manipulating objects from around five months of age. During the second half of the first year he develops knowledge of objects as existing in space and time even when he cannot see them. The notion of 'object permanence' is more clearly formulated as he begins to manipulate objects and becomes himself mobile, exploring movement in space and time and increasingly becoming an 'active-agent' in his own learning.

By fifteen to eighteen months the child is capable of searching for, and finding, objects hidden with several displacements, providing his interest is maintained and he is not fatigued! His knowledge about objects has been considerably extended; he now acts on a working hypothesis, based on expectation about the nature and behaviour of objects, and, aided by his developing language skills, he is on the verge of new imaginative discoveries. These will be taken up again in Module 4.

Reference
Bower, T. G. R. (1974) *Development in Infancy*, San Francisco: W. H. Freeman, ch. 7, fig. 7.5.

Discussion Guide H

What is involved in 'object-concept'?

Allow at least 30 minutes to exchange observations with colleagues following Activity 19 and to consider the development of the 'object-concept', that is, the notion of the permanence of objects.

Bring with you to the discussion: checklists and comments from Activity 19; additional data; comparative summary charts for different ages.

1 Arrange to report your observations in chronological order noting any sequences of behaviour in terms of age-levels. Notice differences of behaviour:

   (a) at the same age(s);
   (b) different ages.

2 Following the exchange of observations consider the following questions.

   (a) What is involved in the act of searching for an object no longer present in the visual field?
   (b) How do *you* go about this?
   (c) Is it necessary to assume a mental image (picture) of the object?

3 Translating this activity to the social realm, consider behaviour relating to persons who appear and disappear from view.

   (a) How do we hold in mind persons no longer present in the visual field?
   (b) Can you recall a person well-known to you? What mental processes are involved? Do you see this person in your 'mind's eye'?

4 Consider the possibility that the young baby may develop the capacity for holding persons in mind some time earlier than the capacity to hold objects in mind? What evidence is there to support this view?

5 Consider 'stranger anxiety' which develops around seven months in most babies; how does this relate to the child's developing notion of the permanence of objects, both people and things?

Discussion Guide I

Does the baby know that objects can move and remain the same?

You should spend at least 30 minutes considering these points. Bring your observation records and additional information with you from Activity 20. Work in small groups, if possible, and present your observations in chronological order, noting any difference in age-level.

Consider the following points after presenting observations.

Tasks 1 and 2: Did the younger babies continue to look for the toy at B where they had seen it several times before? If they were thinking of the toy as a single object they should have tracked it to C eventually. If not, they appear to see the toy in the new position as a different object. They may not look at it at all! They don't seem to realize that a single object can move and stop in a different position and remain the same object. Do you agree with this interpretation (see Paper 16)?

Task 3: The fact that babies can track an object behind a screen and out the other side, or, if it doesn't re-appear, try to get it from behind the screen, suggests that they are aware of its continued existence. Do you agree? Is 'behind something' easier to understand than 'under something' at this age? Why might this be so?

Tasks 4 and 5: If the younger babies are *not* upset by a switch in toys behind the screen, when the same line of movement is maintained, we might assume that they think it is the same object emerging. It appears as if the younger babies, under five months, think the object is the same on the same line of movement. They appear to equate objects with their path of movement at this stage. They do not appear at this time to pay attention to changes in the appearance of the object. Later, after about five months, behaviour changes and the baby shows that he expects the object to retain its appearance when it moves. He appears to realize the object is the same whether it moves or is stationary. He can co-ordinate appearance (identity), place and movement. This topic will be taken further in Unit 3 relating to motor development.

Discussion Guide J

Is Bower's challenge valid in relation to Piaget's 'object-concept'?

Allow at least 30 minutes for this discussion, the aim of which is to clarify the argument put forward by Bower in relation to Piaget's findings on the development of 'object-concept' and to consider the viability of Bower's challenge. Relate your discussion to your reading and activities involving first-hand observations and experiments. The main value in replicating these experiments is to enable you to clarify the sequence of events and the main ideas involved.

You are advised to go through these questions in preparation for discussion.

1 In what way does Bower's experiment differ from Piaget's? Is he testing the same thing?

2 What light do Bower's experiments throw on:
   (a) the young infant's knowledge of moving objects?
   (b) the older infant's ability to co-ordinate movement, place and identity of objects?
   Refer to your observation records.

3 Does Piaget's theory regarding the development of 'object-concept' remain viable in the face of Bower's challenge?

4 What evidence did you find that there is a developmental sequence involved in the child's knowledge about the behaviour of objects? If so, can you state the sequence?

5 What evidence is there of discontinuity in terms of the baby's changing pattern of behaviour?

Make brief notes of the main points of the discussion and carry these forward to issues discussed in Unit 3: Learning to Walk.

Learning to Walk

- Read Papers 18 and 19 focussing on the maturation/learning issue in the development of walking
- Complete Activity 21 and check your answers with Paper 20, introducing Sheridan's development scale
- Carry out Activities 22, 23 and 24 involving visits and first-hand observations of walking behaviour
- Complete Activity 25 comparing babies' performances
- Work through Discussion Guide K exchanging and comparing observations
- Read Paper 21 commenting on Bower's views on learning to walk
- Work through Discussion Guide L, clarifying your ideas on maturation and learning and focussing on the role of the care-giver as the baby learns to walk

Reading	55 mins.
Activities	115 mins.
Discussion	105 mins.
Total	275 mins.
	= 4 hrs. 35 mins.

Can new-born babies walk?
Margaret Roberts

The answer to this question depends, of course, on what is meant by the word 'walk'. New-born infants will 'walk', after a fashion, if provided with the maximum support (see Figure 19.4 in Paper 19). Bower notes: 'This behaviour normally disappears, and true walking begins many months later.' He then poses the question: 'Is the early walking an ancestor of later walking?' Consider what sort of evidence would be necessary in order to be in a position to answer this question. You will find the report of one experiment by André-Thomas and St. A. Dargassies which provided an answer in Paper 19. This study demonstrates that primary walking, as this reflex walking is called, *is* the ancestor of later or secondary walking, but the actual relationship is not clear.

This leads us to the question of the relationship of maturation and learning. Maturation is a concept relating to development largely unaffected by environmental influences, other than extreme malnutrition. Bower writes in Paper 19:

A number of ingenious studies have been carried out to support the general hypothesis that motor behaviour develops as a result of maturational processes. By 'maturation' we mean the growth of nerve circuits, unfolding inevitably, requiring no specific intervention.

The question arises: What is the role of learning in the achievement of the skill of walking? Does the baby in fact learn to walk, or does walking simply develop as the result of growth processes, that is, from maturation? To search for answers to these questions we need to look more closely at the child's early motor development in relation to posture and large movements.

In the early months the baby is dependent on adults for mobility, the development of walking is an important achievement which rapidly alters his perception of the world and of himself as an autonomous being among other beings. The day that a baby takes his first step without support is hailed as a red-letter day in his family.

But a great deal of practice in balancing, co-ordinating and controlling speed and direction is necessary before the baby can be said to be a walker – the term 'toddler' is perhaps fitting to describe him during this learning period.

Most babies go through the classical sequence of head lifting, rolling over, sitting, crawling, standing, walking with help and finally walking alone; others may omit the crawling stage or develop a variant of it. Babies commonly learn to walk before they learn to talk but some will use single words before they walk alone (see Figure 19.1, Paper 19).

In this unit you will carry out observations of babies learning to walk, and consider the effect of this on aspects of mental development, for example, the development of 'object-concept'. You will relate the development of walking to the general theoretical argument concerning the role of maturation in development and learning. The notion of maturation relates to the part played in development by the genetic 'blue-print' laid down at conception in the genes, which ensures the development of universal characteristics of the species. It is significant here to note that the human species normally 'learns' to walk between 49 and 73 weeks (see: M. M. Shirley, *The First Two Years* (1931), Schedule of motor development). Environmental variations such as the cradle board of the Hopi Indian mothers produces little variation in the onset of walking (Paper 19). However, as soon as the baby can walk alone and begins to explore and investigate his environment the quality of the social/physical environment provided will affect his learning experiences. Vitally important is the attitude of the adults to the child's desire to be mobile and their response to his efforts and his subsequent exploratory, investigating behaviour. This is a time when frustrating experiences frequently dominate the toddler's day.

The development of motor behaviour – walking

T. G. R. Bower

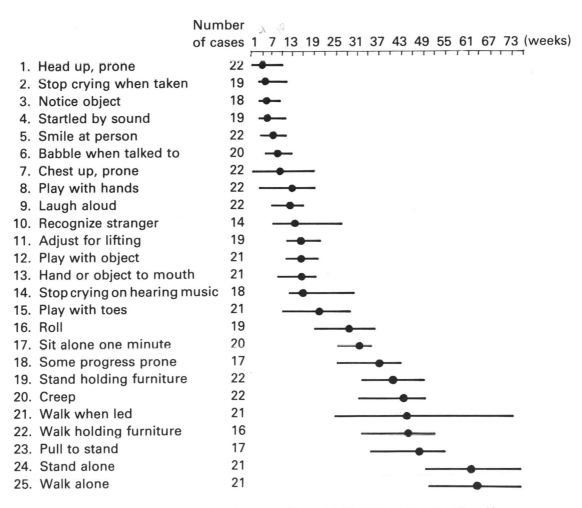

Figure 19.1   A schedule of motor development. (From M. M. Shirley, *The First Two Years, Vol. 1: Postural and Locomotor Developments.* University of Minnesota Press, © 1931, 1959 University of Minnesota.)

Motor behaviour is the easiest component of development to study. In studying motor behaviour, the subject of study is at least clearly visible, even though the mechanisms controlling it are not. Perhaps because of this, there have been many studies of the development of motor behaviours during infancy. Most texts include a schedule of development like that shown in Figure 19.1. Investigators have been concerned both with the details of development and with the general principles that change in a particular behaviour can exemplify. Such studies have contributed a great deal to our understanding of the process of maturation, the role of learning in constructing behaviour, and the way

in which the overall environment affects specific motor skills.

A number of ingenious studies have been carried out to support the general hypothesis that motor behaviour develops as a result of maturational processes. By 'maturation' we mean the simple growth of nerve circuits, unfolding inevitably, requiring no specific intervention. One of the simplest ways of testing this hypothesis is to compare the behaviour of premature infants with that of full-term or post-term babies. The normal infant is born forty weeks after conception: when his chronological age is zero, his conceptual age is forty weeks. Premature infants may survive when born at a conceptual age of twenty-eight weeks; when a premature infant has a chronological age of zero, his conceptual age may be only twenty-eight weeks. At the other extreme, some infants remain in the womb as long as four weeks past term; when a post-term infant has a chronological age of zero, his conceptual age may be forty-four weeks. If behaviour development is determined entirely by experience outside the womb, then chronological age should be our best predictor of the onset of any particular behaviour. Further, we should find no differences between premature, term, and post-term infants of the same chronological age. On the other hand, if behaviour simply 'grows' from conception onwards and is unaffected by events in the environment, then conceptual age should be our best predictor of the onset of a particular behaviour, and we should find no differences between premature, term, and post-term babies of the same conceptual age. The logic of such studies is very clear. It allows us to decide between two extreme theories of the development of motor behaviour.

Smiling is one behaviour that has been studied in this way. Normal infants will smile in response to a visual stimulus – a face in particular – at a chronological age of six weeks, at which time their conceptual age is forty-six weeks. The question is: will premature and post-term babies also smile at a chronological age of six weeks, or will their response begin at a conceptual age of forty-six weeks, regardless of chronological age. The results for smiling are quite unambiguous. Infants smile at a conceptual age of forty-six weeks, regardless of their chronological age. The extra time outside the womb does not accelerate the development of premature infants, nor does the extra time inside the womb retard development of post-term infants. Is it therefore fair to conclude that smiling is primarily determined by processes of maturation? The answer must be no. The study shows that the different environmental histories of premature, term, and post-term infants do not affect the conceptual age at which smiling begins. It is still possible that stimulation from the environment is critical; if so, we know that it is only effective after a conceptual age of forty-four weeks has been reached. Thus the study could indicate that a given level of maturation is required before environmental events could have any effect. Further research is needed to show that *no* environmental event is critical for the development of the behaviour.

An alternative source of information about the effects of environment on development is cross-cultural comparisons. Babies are treated in different ways in different cultures, and a comparison of the rates of motor development under a variety of conditions may give us some clues about the relative contribution of environment to such development. A classic study of this sort was carried out by Wayne

Figure 19.2   An infant secured to a cradle board.

Dennis (1940), who studied the development of walking in Hopi Indian babies. Hopi Indians have traditionally bound their infants to cradle boards during the first months of life (Figure 19.2). Infants are unwrapped only once or twice a day to be cleaned and have their clothes changed. An infant on a cradle board thus has a very restricted range of possible movement. The infant cannot sit up or roll over, and only the slightest arm and leg movements are possible. Even nursing and feeding are carried out on the board. These traditionally reared infants were compared with other Hopi babies whose parents, affected by European practices, did not restrict their infants at all. The results were quite surprising. There was no difference at all between the two groups of infants: both groups walked unaided around the age of fifteen months. This finding seems to lend strong support to the hypothesis that walking is primarily determined by maturational processes and thus is under genetic control.

Taken at face value, this study seems to show that the onset of walking is determined entirely by processes of maturation. But, again, it is not impossible that it is only the case that a critical point in maturation must be reached before environmental factors can have an effect. Another objection that could be raised is that it did not control for possible genetic differences between the two groups. It is possible that the restricted group were simply faster developers than the unrestricted infants and might even have walked *sooner* than the unrestricted infants if they had been allowed freer movement earlier. In any comparison of the effects of environment on development, we always face some uncertainty over whether or not the two groups given the two treatments are genetically equivalent.

There are ways to reduce such uncertainties. One obvious way is to use identical twins as subjects, one twin receiving one environmental exposure, his co-twin the other. Since identical twins are genetically identical, any difference in their rate of development could only result from their different environments. A number of studies of this sort have been carried out.

A typical comparative study of identical twins whose environments differed was that carried out by Arnold Gesell and his co-workers (Gesell and Thompson, 1929). Gesell worked with a pair of identical twin girls. The twins' mother had died shortly after their birth and so they were raised in a nursery home under very similar living conditions. They were given the same food, clothes and sleep schedule. From the published paper it would seem that the twins were virtually identical in appearance and were treated in identical ways by the staff of the nursery home. When the twins reached the age of forty-six weeks, however, one of them was given special training in two motor skills: stair climbing and cube manipulation. The trained twin was identified as T; her sister, the control twin was called C. Prior to the training period the twins were tested thoroughly to ensure that they reached comparable stages of development. The similarity in skill was very striking. Even more striking was the correspondence of their behaviour in free situations. Gesell and Thompson write that when they were each given a spoon to play with 'a chain of four or five behaviour events occurred in almost simultaneous sequence in both children. This kind of correspondence ... takes on a weirdly astonishing aspect.' This observation supports the point made earlier, that identical twins reared in the same environment are virtually two versions of the same individual.

The training programme for the one twin consisted of daily 20-minute sessions, six days a week for six weeks. The 20-minute sessions were equally divided between cube play and locomotor activity, particularly stair climbing. The cube play was free, but if the baby did not play with the cubes the experimenter would attempt to stimulate the activity in a variety of ways, e.g., by giving the baby blocks, building a tower of blocks himself and so on. The stair-climbing training was more stereotyped. The baby was placed at the bottom of the stairs and a toy placed at the top. If T made no attempt to get up the stairs, she was moved by the experimenter from step to step and allowed to play with the toy when she got to the top. When the two twins were compared at the age of fifty-three weeks, one week after the end of T's special training, T could climb the staircase in 17 seconds. C, who had had no practice with the staircase at all, still succeeded in climbing it, although it took her 40 seconds. After this, C was given two weeks of training on the staircase, at the end of which she was as skilled as her sister had been after six weeks of training. At the age of fifty-six weeks there was virtually no difference between the two.

Similarly for cube stacking; after six weeks of training, T did no better in terms of speed or numbers stacked than did C who had no practice whatsoever. The training experience produced no acceleration of development whatsoever. As Gesell and Thompson conclude, these findings 'point consistently to the preponderant importance of maturational factors in the determination of infant behaviour ... The time of appearance is fundamentally determined by the ripeness of the neural structures.' At best, practice produces only fine-tuning of behaviour already established by maturation.

McGraw (1940) came to a similar conclusion at the end of her study of the effects of toilet training. In this study one twin was introduced to toilet training at a relatively early age and given daily training for no less than twenty-three months, after which the child had become effectively toilet trained. The completely untrained twin was then introduced to toilet training and achieved the same level of success right away (Figure 19.3). This result, so contrary to folklore, again seems to point to the primary role of maturation in early development. Or does it?

There are severe difficulties in the way of a straightforward interpretation of such results. Strictly speaking, what do they in fact show? They show that some selective manipulations of the baby's environment do not accelerate or retard the appearance of a certain behaviour. However, they do not provide evidence that *no* environmental event is critical for the emergence of the behaviour in question: they show only that the environmental events that have been *controlled* are not critical. This is a much more tentative conclusion than the experimenters would wish, and some may feel that such caution is unnecessary. Nevertheless, there are many problems in the analysis of development that no studies of the kind so far reviewed have confronted. The question at issue is the *origin* of behaviours that appear to arise all of a sudden throughout infancy. We are really asking whether behaviours have an ancestry, whether they are derived from temporally prior behaviour or experiences.

This problem of defining the antecedents of a behaviour is a considerable one. A possible model for enabling identification of the antecedents of behaviour comes from embryology, the study of the

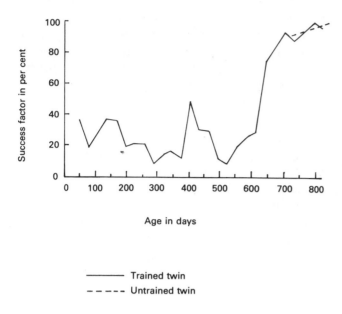

genesis of structure. Embryology attempts, among other things, to trace the *cell lineage* of structures of the mature system, e.g., to discover what cells in the early stages of cell division develop into the eyes. To do so, a cell is stained in the early stages of development; all of its descendants will then carry the stain and thus can be readily identified later. An even more obvious method is possible in the case of mosaic systems; by destroying a cell we can discover its descendants by looking to see what is missing in the developed organism. In studying the genesis of behaviour, however, we have no resource to such direct physical techniques. We cannot stain or ablate behaviours – even less can we stain or ablate experience. The problem of establishing a relation between an environmental event and some later behaviour is even more severe than that of establishing a relation between an early and a later behaviour. The studies cited thus far have all concluded that environment was not involved in the development of a particular behaviour. However, all of the babies studied were open to environmental stimulation at all times. For all we know, some other unsuspected, uncontrolled stimulus may have been critical.

There is one clinical case that avoids this. Wolff (1969) studied an infant who suffered from, in addition to other neural disorders, holotelencephaly (failure of separation of the hemispheres of the brain). A consequence of this condition was that the infant experienced continuous random seizures; in adults this condition is known to prevent the perception of external events. If this infant was similarly affected, then she too would have had no awareness of the events in her environment. None the less, some development did occur: the infant developed the ability to raise her head in a prone position, to support herself on her elbows, and to make co-ordinated creeping movements. Although these behaviours hardly approach successful development, they apparently resulted without any external environmental support.

Although such an extreme example can hardly serve as a paradigm for research, the study of infants with more selective sensory handicaps could obviously provide information about the effects of missing categories of experience on the development of behaviour. Infants who lack one sensory modality can be used to study the development of behaviour in much the same way that experimental organisms subjected to cell destruction are used to study structural development. If infants who lack one or another sensory modality fail to develop certain behaviours, we can argue that the input through that modality is causally linked to the development of the behaviours in question. The causal connection need not be direct, but some causal connection would be hard to deny.

Can we find a marking technique for the study of behavioural development analogous to the technique of cell staining? I think we can. Suppose we have two behaviours we think might be connected. If we introduce some environmental change that alters the earlier behaviour, then, if the two behaviours are connected, there should be some evidence of that change in the later behaviour. We could then conclude that the behaviours are at least ancestrally connected.

Walking is an example of a behaviour whose development can be subjected to the second kind of analysis. Newborn infants will 'walk' after a fashion if supported (see Figure 19.4). This behaviour normally disappears, and true walking begins many months later. Is the early walking an ancestor of the later walking? The two behaviours are separated by many months, yet they are commonly referred to as 'primary' walking and 'secondary' walking. It is argued that primary walking disappears because of an active inhibition that is necessary for secondary walking to appear. This is purely speculative, however; it is quite possible that the two behaviours are independent of one another. What evidence would convince us that the two behaviours are connected? If the earlier behaviour is an ancestor of the later behaviour, surely environmental modifications that affect the first would also affect the later behaviour; this would be comparable to introducing a stain into a primordial cell and tracing the stain in the cell's

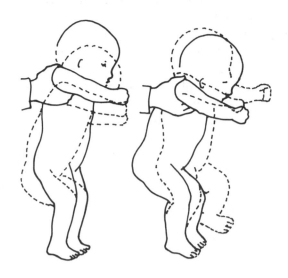

Figure 19.4 Neonate walking. (From M. B. McGraw, *The Neuromuscular Maturation of the Human Infant.* Columbia University Press, 1943.)

descendants. In one experiment the primary walking of a group of infants was exercised on a daily basis rather than being ignored as is commonly done.* As a result, the appearance of secondary walking in these infants was greatly accelerated (André-Thomas and St. A. Dargassies, 1952). Since the early training produced effects on the later behaviour, this study demonstrated that primary walking is indeed the ancestor of secondary walking. If the early training had produced no effects, we would be forced to conclude that the two behaviours were unrelated. If one accepts this criterion for establishing a connection between earlier and later behaviours, then one must assume that studies in which practice of one behaviour has no effect on some later behaviour in fact show that the practised behaviour is unrelated to the criterion behaviour.

This study also is an example of yet another approach to motor development. Numerous other behaviours disappear in the course of development. This fact is quite contrary to common-sense conceptions of development. Common sense tells us that development is a process of cumulative acquisition, with older children having all of the behaviour and capacities of younger children, plus some more. None the less, behaviours do disappear in the course of development. Behaviour loss is as much a development phenomenon as behaviour acquisition, but is more available for study than the latter. While a behaviour may disappear as suddenly as another appears, at least the disappearing behaviour is there until it does disappear, and so is available for study, practice, etc. – a gift to obser-

* It is worth noting that the duration of primary walking was much longer than in normal infants, a fact that rules out the inhibition hypothesis mentioned above.

vation that we should not neglect. The question whether or not the appearance of a new behaviour is primarily determined by maturational or environmental influences could equally apply to the *disappearance* of an existing behaviour.

The development of vocal behaviour is one area where all of these techniques discussed so far are applicable. It is characterized by both the loss of early behaviours and the constant appearance of new behaviours. It is also clearly affected by sensory handicaps, such as deafness and exemplifies some principles of motor development that appear to be quite general. There are two phases of speech development. Normal infants develop highly differentiated babbling behaviour in the first five months. The range of sounds that infants of this age can produce is very wide; some have claimed that it includes the sounds of all human languages. Babbling wanes during the second half of the first year. The next phase of vocalization begins when the infant begins to reproduce the speech sounds of his own particular environment. This involves a loss of many sounds that were produced during the babbling phase. It is noteworthy that these sounds, perfectly available to the child in the first half-year of his life, disappear from his repertory and cannot be reproduced again without considerable training and practice. It is little consolation to those of us who struggle to recreate a French *r* or German *ö* to realize that we could make these noises perfectly when we were babies.

The development of vocalization has been studied in deaf infants. Infants who are profoundly deaf go through the same initial phase of babbling as do hearing infants. At five months their range of sound production is as extensive as that of hearing infants, despite the fact that they have never heard a spoken word and cannot even hear their own babbling. This suggests that the initial phase of vocalization does not require auditory input. The second phase of vocal production, the reproduction of the speech sounds in the child's environment, does not, however, occur in deaf children. This indicates that the second phase does require auditory input for its establishment. In addition, it seems that in order for speech sounds to be maintained and speech to develop, continued auditory input is necessary for some time after the initial onset of this phase of development. The vocal production of children who are deafened during childhood may regress in extreme cases to the level of congenitally deaf children. The later the deafening occurs the less likely this is, however. After the age of six or so deafening has no effect on vocal production; at this point it seems that vocal production has become completely independent of supporting auditory feedback. If children born deaf are given hearing aids at some point in development, they can develop normal vocalization. The earlier the aid is introduced, the better the results; if the introduction of the hearing aid is postponed too long, language may never be acquired (Lenneberg, 1967 and 1969). The critical point again seems to be about age six. There have been a few cases of normal hearing children so criminally neglected that they were never exposed to language, and who thus did not develop vocalization. One exception, Genie, was able to develop language although she was thirteen 'years old before being exposed to it (Curtiss et al., 1974).

Data like these force one to reconsider the relationship between environmental events and development. Learning theory argues that development will not occur without specific environmental intervention; if the specific environmental event does not occur, development does not occur, and neither does anything else. The organism simply stays stationary until the event comes along. Whereas the maturational theorists – Gesell, McGraw, and Dennis – argue that development proceeds successfully in the absence of any particular environmental event. The attainment of successful behaviour through maturational processes is emphasized. We must agree that the learning theorists are wrong in asserting that behaviour will remain stationary in the absence of environmental stimulation. Behaviour, as we have seen, will change regardless; but the change need not be successful. In the absence of relevant input from the environment, behaviour may take a completely aberrant direction, and that direction may become so firmly established that no environmental intervention will be able to redirect the behaviour back to its proper course.

References
André-Thomas, C. and Dargassies, St. A. (1952) *Études neurologiques sur le nouveau-né et le jeune nourrisson,* Paris: Masson.
Curtiss, S., Fromkin, V., Krasken, S., Rigler, D. and Rigler, M. (1974) 'The linguistic development of Genie', *Language,* 50, 528–54.
Dennis, W. (1940) 'The effect of cradling practices upon the onset of walking in Hopi children', *Journal of Genetic Psychology,* 56, 77-86.
Gesell, A. and Thompson, H. (1929) 'Learning and growth in identical infant twins: an experimental study by the method of co-twin control', *Genetic Psychology Monographs,* 6, 1–125.
Lenneberg, E. H. (1967) *Biological Foundations of Language,* New York: Wiley.
Lenneberg, E. H. (1969) 'On explaining language', *Science,* 164, 635–43.
McGraw, M. B. (1940) 'Neural maturation as exemplified by the achievement of bladder control', *Journal of Paediatrics,* 16, 580–90.
Wolff, P. H. (1969) 'Motor development and holotelencephaly' in Robinson, R. J. (ed.) *Brain and Early Behaviour,* Academic Press.

An introduction to the Stycar Schedules by Dr Mary Sheridan

Margaret Roberts

Stands holding on
6 months

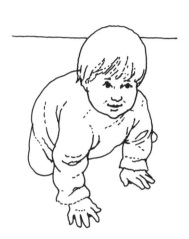

Attempts to crawl
9 months

Walks one hand held
12 months

Writing in her introduction to the Stycar Schedules Dr Sheridan emphasizes that all professional workers who deal with children should be familiar with accepted 'milestones' (or as she prefers to call them 'stepping stones') of development. After reviewing some of the earlier scales by Gesell, Bühler, Illingworth and Ruth Griffiths she describes her own scales based on observations of babies in clinics, nurseries, schools and hospital wards.

The Stycar Schedules consist of four main sections headed:

1. Posture and Large Movements
2. Vision and Fine Movements
3. Hearing and Speech
4. Social Behaviour and Play.

They reflect the four outstanding human biological and social achievements. Sheridan thinks that it is important to note that her scale is not intended to produce a developmental quotient of any sort.

We are not using the full scale, however, but drawing on a selection of data in the area of posture and large movements; social behaviour and play. This material provides guidance in terms of the situation most likely to present us with information regarding the baby's present level of behaviour. In this way a common framework of reference is available for group discussion. It would be worthwhile to obtain the full Developmental Progress Scale and to study Dr Sheridan's introduction where she reviews the origin and history of the schedules noting their limitations and present use.

The following material is taken from the schedule for babies aged one month in relation to Activity 21. The drawings prepared from Dr Sheridan's personal collection of slides will repay careful study.

For guidance on the first hand observation of posture and large movements see page 37.

Age 1 Month – Posture and Large Movements

In supine, lies with head to one side; arm and leg on face side outstretched, or both arms flexed; knees apart, soles of feet turned inwards.

Large jerky movements of limbs, arms more active than legs.

At rest, hands closed and thumb turned in.

Fingers and toes fan out during extensor movements of limbs.

When cheek touched at corner of mouth, turns to same side in attempt to suck finger.

When ear gently rubbed, turns head away.

When lifted from cot, head falls loosely unless supported.

Pulled to sit, head lags until body vertical when head is held momentarily erect before falling forwards.

Held sitting, back is one complete curve.

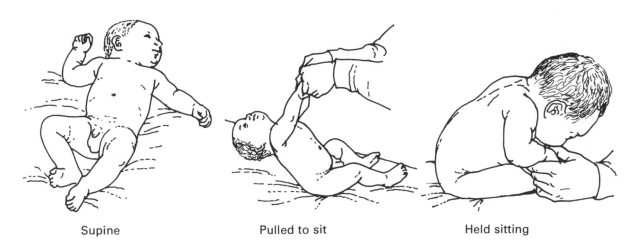

Supine   Pulled to sit   Held sitting

In ventral suspension, head in line with body and hips semi-extended.

Placed in prone, head immediately turns to side; arms and legs flexed, elbows away from body, buttocks moderately high.

Held standing on hard surface, presses down feet, straightens body and (usually) makes a forward reflex 'walking' movement.

Stimulation of dorsum of foot against table edge produces 'stepping up over curb'.

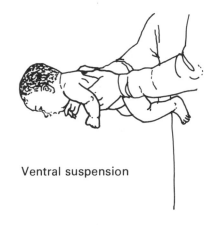

Ventral suspension

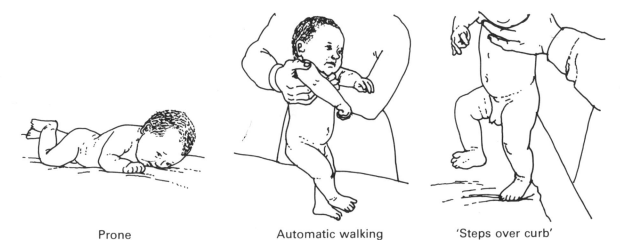

Prone   Automatic walking   'Steps over curb'

What is the role of learning in the achievement of walking?
Margaret Roberts

The question under consideration is how far learning to walk results from growth processes which are inborn, that is, inherent in the genes, and how far environmental opportunity and experience are important.

Bower (see Paper 19) seems to be saying that studies support the general hypothesis that motor behaviour develops as a result of the development of maturational processes, that is, innate growth processes, in interaction with environmental experience. Nevertheless, he is impressed by two experiments that continued the newborn walking pattern and resulted in both cases in the babies concerned walking alone much earlier than usual. He speaks of a tremendous acceleration of development. He sees this as evidence of maturation through environmental interaction which would appear to be putting emphasis on the influence of the environment. Clearly walking is not a sudden development without any relation to earlier development and the baby does appear to be learning from his experience, how to balance, for example, before taking his first step.

Thinking back over your own observations, how do they contribute to your understanding of what is involved in this important event in the life of a young child? You will have noticed that the baby uses his arms which he extends to help him to balance in the early stages of walking. He seems to know that he must stand on a wide base until he can balance more easily; he also runs rather than walks, which appears to be an aid to balancing; rather surprisingly he often runs on his toes in the early stages!

However, efforts to accelerate these and related skills, such as the Gesell and Thompson (1929) twin studies, when experiments were carried out with the twins involving stair climbing, failed to show that these skills can be accelerated by environmental influence. Speed of stair climbing was only minimally affected by training; although Bower's criticism of the type of training involved appears valid. A minimum level of maturation appears to be required before advantage can be taken of helpful environmental experiences in learning to walk. Individual *rate* of maturation is important in terms of ability to make use of environmental opportunities.

If both maturation and learning are necessary for success in learning to walk we need to give some thought to how these two processes relate to one another. For example:

> Is a minimum level of maturation required for learning to be effective?
> Does learning take over when maturation reaches a certain level? Or is there continuous interaction between the two?
> How far is the notion of 'readiness' for learning justified in the case of learning to walk?

Our answers to these questions are likely to influence our behaviour towards a baby in our charge who is learning to walk. Time will be given for consideration of these questions in your discussion group.

Achievement
Having achieved the skill of walking the baby certainly appears to be highly motivated to practise hard to improve his performance and soon puts his new skill to good use. His world is suddenly a much larger place waiting to be explored and investigated. He rapidly improves his skill, he learns to vary it, and to use it more purposefully. His ability to interact with other people and the world of objects is extended.

He can now move himself in relation to objects that move and can be moved. He learns that he can go round some things, for example, to get at an object; also things go underneath things. A ball is a valuable plaything at this time. The idea that objects can move and be moved and remain the same object is gradually clarified. It appears that his ability to hold in mind a sequence of movements develops alongside the development of walking. Later this notion of the permanence of objects (object-concept) will widen to include the permanence of number, no matter how the members of the group are rearranged (see later modules). The important point here is that motor development has implications for mental development. He can investigate and explore where before he was a more passive onlooker. He can now go alone out into the world and will soon do so.

Those responsible for the upbringing of the young child at this time, both his care and education, need to consider some of the likely changes in his daily experience as a result of learning to walk, both positive and negative experiences. Considerable adjustment will be necessary in the attitude and behaviour of the mother, or other caregiver, to the now mobile and exploring, investigating baby.

Reference
Gesell, A. and Thompson, H. (1929) *Learning and Growth in Identical Twins: an experimental study by the method of twin control*, Genetic Psychology Monographs, 6, 1–125.

Discussion Guide K

Observations of walking behaviour at six, twelve and eighteen months

Allow at least one hour for this discussion. You will find it valuable to exchange observations with a small group of colleagues. The first objective of the group is the pooling of information gained from your first-hand observations and the discussion of the behaviour of individual children that indicates major variations from the Sheridan Scale bearing in mind Sheridan's cautionary note and the limitations of your own observations.

Before the meeting you will have completed:

1 first-hand observations of posture and large movements at six months, twelve months, and/or eighteen months (at least two of these);
2 checklist (Sheridan's Scale);
3 personal data for each child;
4 comparative summary chart;
5 Paper 19.

Bring these records and Paper 20 (Sheridan's Scale) to the discussion group.

Arrange the programme so that the records are reported in chronological order, that is, at approximately six, twelve and eighteen months. One person reads out his basic data record and checklist findings for his youngest child after which members of the group contribute any variations from their records *for the same age children* noting any special circumstances in the situation.

A different person reads out the next age-level (twelve months) with group members contributing variations and comments and similarly for the eighteen-month level. Report any difficulties experienced, by you or the baby!

Discuss any apparent wide divergence of behaviour for a particular age. Note changes in behaviour at different age-levels using your summary charts.

Discussion Guide L

Learning to walk

Allow at least 45 minutes for this discussion. The first objective is the consideration of the role of *maturation* and *learning* in the child's achievement of the basic skill of walking. The question under consideration is how far learning to walk results from maturation, that is, growth processes which are inborn and part of the child's heredity, and how far environmental experience coming from outside the child is important.

You will remember the question posed in Paper 21: *'What is the role of learning in the achievement of walking?'* If both maturation and learning are necessary for success in learning to walk we need to consider how these processes relate to one another. Discuss these points with your group making notes of consensus views and any minority views.

Does learning take over where maturation leaves off?

Or is there continuous interaction between the two?

Is a minimum level of maturation required for learning to be effective?

How far is the concept of 'readiness' for learning justified in the case of learning to walk?

The second objective is the consideration of the role of the care-giver. Consider the following questions.

1 Would you feel confident in helping a child who is learning to walk?
2 Would you be happy to let an adept crawler continue to crawl?
3 Is the baby's weight a factor in the onset of walking?
4 How does the baby behave when he loses his balance and falls over? Does he cry, look round for help, or does he get up and go on his way?
5 What would *you* do in these circumstances?
6 Was there any evidence that the babies you observed had learnt to climb stairs? If so, how did they manage this?
7 Is the child more or less difficult to manage when mobile?
8 What are some of the likely environmental hazards?
9 What frustrations are likely to come his way?
10 Under what circumstances would you consider it wise to limit his freedom of movement?

Module Four

Factors affecting early development and learning

Unit One

Communication before words

- Read Paper 22 introducing pre-verbal communication
- Study Observation Guide in preparation for visit
- Carry out Activity 26 using Checklist and tape recorder
- Read Bruner's Paper 23
- Complete Activity 27 listening to and analysing tape
- Take part in Discussion M arising from sharing of taped material

Reading	35 mins.
Activities	90 mins.
Discussion	30 mins.
Total	155 mins.
	= 2 hrs. 35 mins.

Back to people: communicating before words
Margaret Roberts

In Module 3 Unit 1 we saw something of the pattern of the two-way relationship developing between mother and child. We noted how this is based on the mother's sensitivity to the young child's signals and response to his needs, leading to the first secure attachment for the child providing a base from which he will explore the world further.

Unit 2 focused our attention on the baby's increasing awareness of the world of objects in which the adult provides a supporting and, at times, initiating role. The growth of what Piaget calls 'object-concept', that is, the baby's awareness that people and objects exist even when no longer visible to him, signifies an important identifiable change in the baby's cognitive development. He appears to be equipped to deal with persons and objects differently from the beginning: to communicate with persons and to 'do' things with objects.

The toddler of eighteen months knows much more about persons and about objects than he did as a baby of five months. His knowledge includes the ability to *think* about people and objects no longer visually present, that is, the ability to 'hold in mind' absent people and absent objects. The growing ability to reflect on the nature and behaviour of people and objects represents an important change in the young child's intellectual equipment whereby he increases his knowledge of the world around him. This increase of knowledge and understanding will be studied further in later modules.

Here we are concerned with the early beginnings of mental thought, of symbolic representation, of imaginative and sequential thought which will form the foundation for later logical reasoning. An important dimension of this is the child's increasing command of the use of words understood by others, words representing meaningful situations, feelings, relationships, people, objects and eventually ideas. However, long before words, as universally understood, are used the baby communicates with expressive sounds and gestures within a meaningful social context while understanding a good deal more than he can verbalize.

Linguists assure us that babies are equipped from birth to learn to speak any language barring serious damage to speech organs, brain centres for speech and hearing. Gradually they eliminate from their vocal repertoire sounds they do not hear and increasingly practise the sounds they do hear. *But* language acquisition is more than imitation of sounds heard, though clearly this in an important aspect of learning to speak. There is evidence that babies also generate their own sounds, and sequence of sounds, related to meaningful experience, for example, David's 'go-goes' for all moving vehicles used repeatedly before he was two years old, also John's 'bib-bon' for all food that was put before him. Slightly older children generate more complex original sentence structure, for example, Christine, two years three months, referring to her younger sibling who had just bitten and burst her balloon exclaimed: 'Baby bite balloon!' and after a pause and with emphasis: 'Baby other bite balloon, no!' referring apparently to her own balloon which she wished to preserve. More of the generative aspect of language will be examined in later modules.

Baby's early vocalizations and the generating of meaningful sounds have been studied in great detail by Trevarthen and his colleagues in Edinburgh (*Child Alive*, ed. Roger Lewin, 1975). He has identified various activities which he includes under the general heading of pre-speech. He has noted a rudimentary form of 'speaking' 'involving movements of lips and tongue', he writes: 'These distinctive movements are often made by young infants soundlessly. At other times young babies are very vocal, making a variety of cooing sounds as they move mouth and tongue.' He further notes that pre-speech is accompanied by a specific pattern of breathing, even when sounds are not made, and associated with distinctive 'hand-waving'. Trevarthen sees communication activity as much more complex than any other form of activity engaged in by infants at this age, and, as he states, it needs a partner.

Bruner places the acquisition of language firmly within the mother–child partnership. This is based on his exploration of how communication between a mother–child pair is established before language proper comes on the scene and how, gradually, the older modes of communication are replaced by more standard language. In his Wolfson College lecture (1976) entitled: 'Learning how to do things with words' (Paper 23), Bruner notes two uses of communication: for reference, and for carrying out joint action. He sees these two as stemming from quite different roots:

> The one relating to the sharing of attention, the
> other to the management of complementary

intentions. In each of them we shall see the emergence of communication forms that have language-like properties which, at the opportune moment, and with the help of an adult, provide a clue for the child as to how to crack the linguistic code he is encountering.

We will be attempting to capture for ourselves something of the complex sharing of the 'field of attention' and the 'management of complementary intentions' in our observation sessions with mother and baby in Activity 26.

We will endeavour to combine the observation and recording skills so far developed with an awareness of the way the mother follows and supports the baby's interests and the way in which she involves him in new interests. We may also see evidence of the baby initiating new 'fields of attention' and new interests. In addition to observing and recording with your checklist you will have your tape-recorder working in order to record vocalizations and words used by mother and child.

More complex interactions may be observed with older children possibly going beyond the checklist provided. Brief notes on how the mother appears to be responding to the baby's signals, and the baby to the mother will be helpful here.

Learning how to do things with words
Jerome Bruner

Joint attention and reference

We come now to the empirical part of our inquiry. We have been studying children from roughly three months of age to about their second birthday, visiting them in their homes fortnightly, and video-recording a half-hour of ordinary play-interaction between the mother and child, often much enriched by the presence of the experimenter. This has been supplemented by occasional video-recordings made by parents of behaviour they thought we should see and had not (often very valuable indeed) and by diary records. As a preliminary, we looked at six children in this way; more latterly we have concentrated on three, and I shall mostly be telling you about two of them. The object of the exercise was to explore how communication between the pairs was established before language proper came on the scene and how, gradually, the older modes of communication were replaced by more standard language. Our effort, as you may guess from what has already been said, was to explore how language was used, how its forms were made to serve functions. I shall concentrate as noted on two uses of communication: for referring and for carrying out joint action. I choose the two because they may stem from quite different roots, the one relating to the sharing of attention, the other to the management of complementary intentions. In each of them we shall see the emergence of communicative forms that have language-like properties which, at the opportune moment, and with the help of an adult, provide a clue for the child as to how to crack the linguistic code he is encountering. Let me say, before turning to these matters, that I shall not burden you with the dates or milestones at which new forms appear in language, but only with rough indications. It is the order of emergence that matters rather than absolute dates, for some children learn quickly and some less so, with no seeming effect on later performance. Nor is it evident that all children go through precisely the same order, for the literature on the subject and our own data suggest that order is dependent on context in some degree and reflects the individual progress of the mother–infant bond.

So let me turn first to the course of reference. The deep question about reference is how one individual manages to get another to share, attend to, zero in upon a topic that is occupying him. At the start, the child can neither reach nor point toward an object that he wants or is interested in. He can of course cry or fret, he can of course look at what interests him and that, as we shall see, stands him in good stead. As for the mother, her options are almost as limited as the child's: neither her vocalizations nor her gestures are able to accomplish the end of bringing the child's attention to objects or events she wishes to single out. From the mother's side, her first and most useful basis for sharing the child's 'referent' is her power of interference backed by her inevitable theory of what the child is intending. She inevitably interprets the child's actions as related to wants and needs: he cries because he is hungry or wet, stares at something because he wants to take possession of it or, simply, is 'fascinated by it'. She is not the least disturbed by the difficulty of philosophers in establishing communicative intent, how we know that others are attempting to send a message. She simply assumes it, and indeed, Macfarlane's (1974) study of greeting rituals of mothers toward their newborns suggests that, from the start, the maternal theory is premissed on the infant's acts being purposeful and his gestures and vocalizations being attempted communications. It is not surprising, then, that in a recent study by Collis and Schaffer (1975), the mother's line of regard follows the infant's line of regard virtually all the time that the two of them are together in an undistracted situation.

But perhaps more interesting is the infant's behaviour. Dr. Michael Scaife (Scaife and Bruner, 1975) working in my laboratory here at Oxford has demonstrated that infants as young as four months of age will also follow the mother's line of regard outward to the surrounding environment. Some of you who have read about infantile egocentrism may be surprised, since this indicates that the child can use another axis than his own egocentric one to guide his orientation. Scaife now reports that there are indications that such gaze-following may occur even when the child is not interacting directly with the adult involved. If two adults, conversing with each other, now look jointly in a convergent direction, and they are within the infant's range of attention, the infant's line of regard will often converge with theirs, all of this before the infant is much over a year.

Before the child begins his reaching career, his chief focus of attention is his mother's face, eye contact leading to smiles, vocalizations, and a variety of exchange manoeuvres – of which more later. Once the child begins reaching for objects, however, *en face* contact between mother and child drops drastically from about 80 per cent of contact time to roughly 15 per cent. Characteristically at this stage the child either orients to the objects he reaches for, manipulates, and mouths, or he orients to the mother. At 5 months, for example, he never looks to the mother when his attempts to reach or grasp an object fail. He is possessed by the one or the other and does not alternate. At this stage, the chief communicative feature of the child's object-directed activity is his first vocalization in the event of not being able to reach or get hold of something he wants.

Note the infant's typical reach at this stage. It is an effortful gesture reeking with intention to possess the object: hand and arm fully extended, fist opening and closing, body bent forward, mouth often working, eyes fixed on the object. This gestural effort, which gives no indication of being communicatively directed toward the mother, is none the less treated by her as communicatively intended, and the mother often obtains an object the child cannot reach. The child in time comes to expect this support.

By 8 months, usually, the child's reach metamorphoses. It becomes markedly less exigent, and he begins looking toward the mother while he is in the act of reaching for an object. The gesture is changing from an instrumental reach to something more like an indicator – a semi-extended arm, hand held somewhat angled upward, fingers no longer in grasp position, body no longer stretched fully forward. His gaze shifts from object to mother and back. He can now reach-for-real and reach-to-signal.

For a few months after the appearance of indicative reaching, there is a transitional phase. Indicative reaching becomes dissociated from the intention to get an object: it may signal only and the child may not even take an indicated object that is proffered. Indicative reaching increasingly extends outward to objects more remote spatially. And, characteristically, the mother conforms to the change, interpreting reaching as interest rather than as desire, and chatting accordingly to the child's reach.

What emerges next suggests that new forms of communication emerge initially to fulfil old functions, and then bring in new functions with them. It is the pure point, and in no sense is it gesturally like a reach – forefinger extended, the infant not reaching bodily forward. Initially it is used like an indicating reach. But like most new forms, pointing explodes in usage soon after first appearance. At 13 months, for example, six pure points were observed in Richard in a half-hour's play with his mother. At 14 months/3 weeks, in a holiday setting, 29 pure points occurred in the same time, and in a three-hour observation session the next day more than a hundred were observed. The objects selected as targets were governed by the following rules: (a) objects more than a metre distant and either novel or in an unexpected context, (b) neither novel nor unexpected, but a *picture* of a familiar object, (c) neither novel nor pictured, but imaginary or hypothetical, the locus being indicated (as pointing upward to the ceiling, and saying 'bird'). Though Richard had few words, he was working on the hypothesis that his uttered sounds had semanticity. And we should note, finally, that his pointing was typically accompanied by vocalization and by looking back at the interlocutor. Needless to say, his mother interprets his pointing much as she would interpret that of an adult.

I should like to note one thing particularly about the growth of pointing over the next months. It is extended to many things, as in indicating a choice between objects, aiding requests, and so on. But it is also a prime instrument in the children we have studied for exploring the relation between objects and both their loci and possessors. At 15½ months, the turning on of a light evokes in Richard a point toward the ceiling and 'li(ght)'; later the sound of an auto in the drive produces a point towards it and 'Daddy'; a picture of a wine bottle in a book results in a point to the bare dining table, etc. Such instances are invariably shared by glancing back at the adult. I mention this point here to make clear one matter that tends to be swamped by the implicit notion that referencing or indexing is somehow associative. I would urge that however associative it may be, such indicating behaviour also serves for generating and testing hypotheses, bringing objects (even if they are hypothetical) into the realm of discourse.

Again, the mother goes readily along with the new development and begins incorporating the child's pointing and his interest in semantic or naming sounds into dialogue. Indeed, it was the Russian linguist Shvachkin (1948) who noted that the child's interest in the phonemic system of the language coincided with his interest in naming. The mother's new medium for dialogue is 'book reading', and I have no doubt that cultures without picture books find suitable substitutes.

Looking at picture books together concentrates the joint attention of mother and infant upon highly compressed foci of attention.* They are foci of attention, moreover, that by virtue of being representations rather than real things eliminate competition from virtually all other response systems – notably the reaching system. In this sense, the medium is part of the message and it is not surprising that, at the earliest stage, the mother spends hard effort in getting the child into the medium – converting the book from an object to be banged and mauled into a carrier of pictures to be looked at. The end point of that enterprise is the establishment of a dialogue pattern, and that dialogue pattern, we shall see, is crucial to the development of labelling.

There is a period of several months – from a year to about fifteen months – when the mother's strategy seems to be devoted to getting the child to look, to point, and to vocalize at the right junctures in the dialogue exchanges between them. I fully agree with Catherine Snow (in press) that the establishment of such turn-taking, sequenced dialogue is a prerequisite for language acquisition. In Richard's case, the dialogue is controlled by three linguistic devices used by his mother in a highly predictable way. The first is the attentional vocative *Look* or some variant, appropriately accompanied by pointing. The second is what linguists call a 'Wh.. question' and it takes the form of some such question as 'What's that, Richard?' again often with a supporting point. Interrogatives are not novel: they constitute from a third to a half of the mother's utterances during the first year, a matter to which we shall return. The third device is labelling. During this stage and the next, described later, the mother's labels are always nominals – object words or proper names, never attributes or states or actions.

The dialogue exchanges initiated by one mother while she and Richard were looking at pictures together show the following striking regularity. Where there are two or more rounds in the exchange, in eight cases out of ten, the mother says 'Look' before either asking a 'Wh.. question' or proffering a label. If there are only 'Wh.. questions' and labels in the dialogue, the former precede the latter. The almost invariant order was from a vocative through a question to a realization of the label. And each was given in an appropriate context. And so, for example, 'Wh.. questions' follow only upon the child's gesture of pointing, and never upon a vocalization. A wide range of vocalizations are accepted in this first 'dialogue establishing' stage as appropriate responses to either an attentional vocative or a 'Wh.. question', however wide they may be of the standard lexical mark. If Richard responds with a vocalization, his mother's response to him in the great majority of cases is a label. Indeed in mother-initiated dialogues, she responds to Richard's reaction in about 75 per cent of the instances, virtually always giving him full marks for an appropriate communicative intent. A small point adds a sense of the meticulousness of this process. The mother makes a rather sharp distinction between those vocalizations of the child that slot into the dialogue routine of book-reading, and those that are out of place in the exchange. The

---

* The work on 'book-reading' has been done jointly with Dr. Anat Ninio of The Hebrew University of Jerusalem.

latter vocalizations and gestures are treated by the mother as procedural – 'You like this book, don't you, Richard?' or 'Yes, it's very exciting, isn't it?' – such remarks always addressed to him directly and without reference to the book.

You will be quite right if you infer that the child initially is learning as much about the rules of dialogue as he is about lexical labels. But once the dialogue routine is fully established, at about 18 months or earlier, it becomes the scaffold upon which a new routine is established. For now the mother comes more sharply to distinguish between vocalizations that are 'acceptable' and those that are not. They are now in a 'shaping stage'. Mother tightens the criterion of acceptability as soon as there emerges a sign that the child is trying to produce words. I should warn you that my last sentence includes the whole field of developmental phonology, about which I know just enough to know the depth of my ignorance. But it is not the phonologist's theories that interest us here, but the mother's. When Richard slots in a sound that she thinks too wide of the mark, she will now respond not with a label, but with the question, 'What's that, Richard?' or with a highly emphasized label.

But to put it that way may seem to give too much of a role to pure imitation. Rather, what is notable is that the child does not learn his labels by directly and immediately imitating his mother's labellings. Compare the likelihood of Richard uttering a label during the second half of his second year of life under two conditions. One is in response to the mother's just previously uttered label. The other is in response to his mother's 'What's that?' question. The latter produces four times as many labels as the former. A label for the child is something that slots into a position in a dialogue. Indeed, 65 per cent of the labels uttered by Richard during the second half of the second year were said without the mother having uttered the label in that exchange. And an interesting sidelight: Richard responds to 'Wh.. questions' almost invariably on the first time round. Where he responds with a label in response to a mother's label, it almost invariably requires at least one repetition by his mother to get him to do so. We are not, as a species, copy-cats.

One regularity during this shaping phase suggests how crucial is the role of the mother in *teaching* language and its use. She is constantly establishing linguistic distinctions between the given and the new, the familiar and unfamiliar. She is, for example, much more likely to use 'What' questions with special intonation for pictures the child already knows and can label easily. New or less familiar pictures are labelled forthwith. The result is a presuppositional structure about what one asks about and what one tells.

Perhaps a good way to put the mother's pedagogical role in perspective is to look at it as providing a stabilizing scaffold during the two phases of label learning we have been exploring, a stabilizing scaffold with respect to which the child can vary his responses as his mastery permits. And so we find, for example, that the time devoted to dialogue exchanges remains constant over these months. The number of turns in an exchange remains roughly the same. The repetition rate for labelling remains the same. The probability of the mother's reciprocating the child's response remains unchanged. And once the child is in the shaping stage, the mother's rate of confirming correct utterances remains about the same. All of these are controlled by the mother. They are what the child can count on in dialogue with her.

What things change over time, on the other hand, are almost all under the child's control. For one, there is a steady increase in the number of 'book reading' exchanges initiated by the child – from 0 per cent to 40 per cent. There is a steady increase in the child's rate of responding to gestural or verbal overtures initiated by the mother. He even learns to respond to repeated, rhetorical requests, ones he has just answered, suggesting that he is even learning to conform to the arbitrariness of pedagogical exchanges!

So much then for indexing and referencing. It is a very incomplete story as I have told it, but at least it gives a sense of how related acquisition is to use, to the functions of dialogue and exchange.

References

Collis, G. and Schaffer, H. R. (1975) 'Synchronisation of visual attention in mother–infant pairs', *Journal of Child Psychology and Psychiatry*, 16 (4), 315–20.

Macfarlane, A. (1974) 'If a smile is so important', *New Scientist* (25 April 1974), no. 895, 164–6.

Scaife, M. and Bruner, J. (1975) 'The capacity for joint visual attention in the infant', *Nature*, 253 (5489), 265–6.

Shvachkin, N. Kh. (1948) 'The development of phonemic speech perception in early childhood', translated by E. Dernback, and edited by D. I. Slobin in Ferguson, C. A. and Slobin, D. I. (eds.) *Studies of Child Language Development*, New York: Holt, Rinehart & Winston, 91–127.

Snow, Catherine E. 'The development of conversation between mothers and babies', *Journal of Child Language*, Cambridge University Press.

Discussion Guide M

Relating tape-recordings to patterns of interactional behaviour

It will be helpful to work in small groups of 3 or 4 members; you should spend at least 30 minutes on this work. Present material from Activities 26 and 27 in age-order, starting with the youngest. Give personal data and a brief description of the situation in which you observed the child.

Tape-recording: select the most interesting three- to five-minute sequence on your tape. Check that you have to hand the relevant information from your checklist of behaviour. Start the tape; give any relevant information from your checklist to match the verbal sequence, where possible. If there is too much material on the tape to permit this, give the relevant information from the checklist *after* hearing the selected tape-recording. Follow this with additional information from the mother, her comments etc.

Discuss these records in terms of patterns of interacting behaviour between the mother and baby/baby and mother on the following lines.

Baby looks at mother while vocalizing then looks away.
Baby points and looks at objects followed by vocalizing to mother, or, naming object.
Note whether the toy seems to provide a stimulus to the interaction or whether the baby tends to spend more time with the toy to the exclusion of the mother.
Notice if, and when, the mother uses the toy to involve herself further with the child or to get the child to play more on his own.

Try to identify what signals are operating between mother and baby and the importance of timing on the mother's part when she intervenes in the child's play or tries to re-direct his attention.

Consider how far your presence may have distracted the child. Consider possible effects of a change of care-giver in terms of the intimate nature of these early attempts at dialogue between mother and baby and baby and mother.

The social basis of Language Development

- Read Papers 24, 25 and 26 stressing the importance of early interaction/ communication between child and adult
- Complete Activity 28 Tasks 1 to 5 child fifteen months to 2 years Mother/child/observer interaction
- Proceed to Activity 29 transcribing from tape and completing Schedule
- Engage in Discussion N comparing tape recorded material and Discussion O focussing on role of adult in early language

Reading	75 mins.
Activities	100 mins.
Discussion	70 mins.
Total	245 mins.
	= 4 hrs. 5 mins.

Commentary
Margaret Roberts

'A large part of infancy is spent in preparation for the use of language', writes Bower as his opening sentence for Paper 25. He goes on to demonstrate experimentally the young baby's power of discrimination of speech sounds as a prelude to vocalization and the later use of words.

We have made a preliminary study of the preparatory period in Unit 1 of this module and now aim to explore the later part of this early stage involving the use of first words and later two-word sentences, focusing on interaction between child and adult. The adult is seen as an essential factor in the early language environment of the young child. Bower identifies important processes involved in linking the pre-speech with the early stages of verbal behaviour. We will endeavour to focus on some of these important aspects by recording examples on tape and checking sequences of behaviour.

In this unit you will obtain tape-recorded samples of developing verbal expression and communication in infants between fourteen and fifteen months and two years of age in particular social situations familiar to them. In addition you will make a record of associated behaviour and activity emphasizing the importance of the related contextual situation. For preference this will be in the children's own homes with their mother or other normal care-giver.

Those of you who observe and record children approaching their second birthday may obtain examples of two-word sentences relating people (or objects) and place, for example, 'Daddy gone', or less explicit 'sentences' such as, 'Mummy sock', when mother is putting the child's sock on. This structure may also be used on a different occasion, for example, when Kathryn picked up her mother's sock as reported by Roger Brown in *A First Language: The Early Stages*. These examples indicate the importance of noting the contextual situation of these early speech patterns, especially the ongoing activity between the two speakers which frequently enhances the meaning aspect of the verbal exchange. The use of the tape-recorder *and* the behaviour checklist should help you to see the way in which early language is embedded in a meaningful social context.

Through exchange of experiences and discussion of recordings later in small groups you will gain knowledge of the range and variety of contexts in which language is used and of the characteristic features of the young child's use of language. You will become increasingly aware of the importance of the personal–social situation in which communication takes place within a shared background of meaning. The mother's response normally reassures the child that the meaning behind what he has said has been understood. In the examples given earlier the mother would respond differently in each situation, expanding the child's two-word utterance in the first instance perhaps by saying, as Brown suggests: 'That's right, Mummy's putting on your sock', and in the second instance: 'That's right, it's Mummy's sock'. Not only does the mother reassure the child that he is understood but she provides the child with a model of extended linguistic structure. Through this kind of exchange both the meaning and the social function of language are reinforced.

Sometimes, of course, mother and child fail to communicate due to a misunderstanding regarding the shared framework of meaning. This may prove very disconcerting to the child who may become silent, or react with an emotional outburst. Between three and four years of age the child normally learns to deal with this breakdown by prefacing his response with: 'What I mean is . . .', or 'I don't mean . . .', depending on the relationship previously established.

In this unit we will be studying the work of Michael Halliday relating to the developing language system of the young child through analysis of the recorded speech of a number of children, including his son Nigel. See Paper 25 by Bower which includes Halliday's analysis. For Halliday language learning involves learning how to mean. For example, learning one's mother tongue is learning the uses of language *and* the meanings, or rather the meaning potential, associated with this usage. Halliday looks at the relation between the child's linguistic structure and the uses he is putting language to in the social situation of relating to his mother. Awareness by the student of the reciprocal nature of early communication is essential in order to understand how a baby develops his linguistic skills. Examples of such skills being:

(a) the turn-taking nature of conversation;
(b) the messages conveyed by intonation and emphasis and awareness of the importance of a shared field of meaning.

Meaning in the early stages of language development is related normally to the existing situation in which the speakers find themselves, that is, the 'here and now'. It is not very long, however, before the child expands his framework of reference to include past and future happenings again within the shared field of meaning. This development is more likely where the child is given frequent opportunity to engage in this level of conversation.

The question of inadequate 'mothering'

It is important at this juncture to consider how lack of adequate mothering, to use Bowlby's term, or a breakdown in continuity of mothering for whatever reason, is likely to affect adversely the young child's early development and learning with possible retardation of his language development. The child learns the attributes of being human, among them the ability to express himself and communicate his needs and feelings, from his first human relationships. For this experience to be satisfying he needs the sensitive response to his advances of the adult who is caring for him. It is from a secure basis of trust, fulfilled anticipation in relation to the satisfaction of basic needs, enjoyable repetition and a sense of delight in achievement within the personal–social situation of shared meaning, that the young child develops his language potential.

The opposite side of this picture, unfulfilled anticipation; lack of time with familiar adults; or, perhaps worse, a succession of strange adults, resulting in breakdown of his developing framework of meaning, can cause the baby acute distress from around five to six months and if continued may lead to severe and prolonged unhappiness and possible chronic depression, as the work of Bowlby, the Robertsons and Spitz has indicated (see additional Reading List at the end of this book). This, at a time when language development would normally be at the vulnerable preparatory stage, can cause loss of motivation and apparent retardation which, though not necessarily irreversible, as Clarke and Clarke indicate in *Early Experience: Myth and Evidence*, will be difficult to remedy later.

Language learning is clearly vulnerable in the situation of broken personal relationships; even more important for future development and learning may be the damage to the child's emotional life. The loss of warm ongoing affectionate relations providing basic security may cause considerable emotional disturbance between four to five and twelve months. In addition from twelve months to two years the baby/toddler separated from his usual caregiver loses the familiar support of their reasonable control and discipline in terms of his impulses and urgent needs and desires. The working through of the more negative aspects of behaviour, such as, outbursts of temper, night fears, aggressive and destructive behaviour, also needs the continuous, warm, human understanding of known and trusted adults. The child who is separated for short or longer periods from those to whom he has become strongly attached, is likely to be vulnerable in terms of his emotional stability, his potential development and his capacity for learning. The child who has not yet established adequate language patterns for expression and communication of his feelings is most vulnerable to emotional disturbance. The Robertsons's films of children in brief separation, illustrate this point, particularly the film: *John*. This film documents the experiences of a young, not yet speaking, toddler of seventeen months, over a period of nine days in a residential nursery where he was placed by his parents during the period of the mother's second confinement. Film records of other children cared for in the home of a known foster-parent who was aware of their likely unhappiness and took steps to keep the memory of the mother 'alive' suggests that the young child's distress can be mitigated; language development appears to be an important factor in the young child's ability to cope with the situation.

Language development in infancy
T. G. R. Bower

A large part of infancy is spent in preparation for the use of language. In a sense we all know what language is, because we all use language. We produce strings of noises that have meaning for those around us (provided they speak the same language). We on our part understand the strings of noises that they produce. A great deal of developmental research has focused on these two aspects of language, the productive and the receptive aspects. A great amount of time has been expended on describing the sounds that children make at various ages. More recently, some ingenious methods have been used to discover what sounds babies can tell apart at various ages.

A study carried out by Eimas *et al.* (1971) is an example of the fascinating things we are learning about the language capacities of very young babies. Babies, in fact, are capable of making very subtle discriminations between speech sounds. For example, they can discriminate between the sounds *p* and *b*. Although this discrimination might sound trivial, it is actually quite difficult, for there is not much difference between the two sounds, as Figure 25.1 shows. Many adults cannot make this distinction reliably. Adults whose first language is not English, even after becoming fluent in English, may have difficulty in telling these two sounds apart. Native speakers of Gaelic are particularly prone to this confusion.

The experimental technique used in this case was a most ingenious variant of the habituation method. Two groups of four-week-old babies were given pacifiers to suck on. The pacifiers were connected up in such a way that hard sucks would switch on a tape-recorder connected to a loudspeaker through which one group of babies heard a *pa-pa-pa* sound

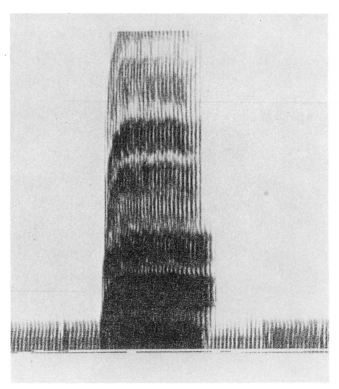

'Pa'

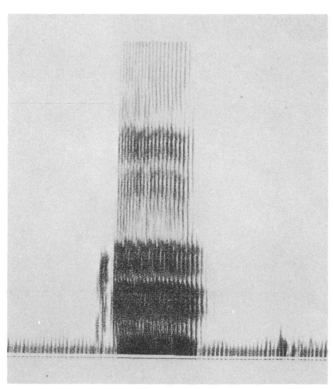

'Ba'

Figure 25.1   A spectrographical recording of the sounds *pa* and *ba*. There is little discernible difference between the *p* and *b* sounds. (From Speech and Communication Laboratory, University of Edinburgh.)

while the other group heard a *ba-ba-ba* noise. At first these noises were interesting to the babies; they gave vigorous sucks at a fast enough rate to keep the sound on continuously. However, as we would expect, the rate of vigorous sucking declined quite rapidly as the sounds became boring.

At this point the experimenters changed things around so that the babies who had been hearing the *ba-ba-ba* sound could now hear *pa-pa-pa* instead, and vice versa. It was argued that if the babies could hear this new sound as a new sound — a different sound — their interest would be reawakened and vigorous sucking would begin again. That is just what happened. The new sound produced a high rate of sucking, high enough that the babies, at first, were listening to the noise continuously.

Clearly the infants in this experiment could make the very subtle distinction between the sounds *p* and *b*. The same technique has recently been used to show that Japanese babies can discriminate the sounds *l* and *r*, as in the words *fly* and *fry*. This discrimination, easily made by Japanese babies, is virtually impossible for Japanese adults.

The most striking experiment on speech perception in babies is usually put in context with the social behaviour of newborns. Condon and Sander (1974) demonstrated that newborn babies will move in precise rhythm with the segments of human speech, a response they called interactional synchrony. In fact, speech is a more or less continuous flow of stimulation, with the units marked by minuscule variations in stimulation (Figure 25.2). We adults usually experience a foreign language as a meaningless flow of sound. If the linguistic base is different from that of our native tongue, we are hard put to pick out words, much less the units that make up words. Young babies suffer no such limitation. The babies in this study showed interactional synchrony whether they were addressed in English or in Chinese, in Korean or French They could pick out the units of speech that they had never heard before, something the adults around them certainly could not do.

This demonstrates an astounding ability to segment language. It supports a hypothesis put forward by many people that babies are born ready to take their place in any language community, ready to make any speech discriminations that this community demands of them.

The same hypothesis has been offered in connection with the vocal productions of young babies. Vocalizing has two distinct developmental phases. During the first six months, babies develop a repertoire of vocalizations which is very large, larger than that of any adult. It has been claimed that the repertoire of the babbling baby in the first half-year contains all the sounds of all the languages of man. This vast repertoire does not persist. By the second half-year of life the baby is uttering only the sounds of the language used by the adults around him. If the language of the adults around him is English, he produces the sounds that characterize English; if it is French, he produces the sounds of French; if it is Russian, he produces the sounds of Russian, and so on. It seems that the baby retains only those sounds that he hears from others in his environment.

It is puzzling to us that young babies can with ease produce sounds which are completely beyond us when we, as adults, struggle to learn a second language. It is small consolation to know that as infants we could easily make all the noises we have such difficulty in producing now. It seems that the baby comes into the world ready to participate in any possible language community. Apparently he is able to produce the sounds of any language while he is small. Then, with increasing age, the range of sounds he can articulate gradually becomes limited to the sounds produced by the adults around him. It

Then   the   North   Wind   blew   as   hard   as   he   could

Figure 25.2 The flow of sound in a sentence. (From Speech and Communication Laboratory, University of Edinburgh.)

seems plausible that the range of sounds he can distinguish is similarly restricted.

Restriction of this sort may seem a sad loss. However, the restriction serves an important function. It does so because our information-handling capacity is limited. In general, the ease with which one detects a stimulus depends more on the number of stimuli that *might* occur than on the characteristics of a specific stimulus. Similarly, the speed and ease with which one can make a response depends on the number of responses one might have to make, rather than on the characteristics of the specific response. By restricting the range of sounds he is prepared to hear, the baby becomes able to process those he does attend to with greater ease. He is able to pay more attention to sound sequences, the chains of sounds that make up the words of a particular language. Similarly, by cutting down on the range of sounds he produces, he becomes better able to integrate these sounds to produce words.

We do not have a clear understanding of the developmental processes by which the baby changes from a state of being ready for any language to the point of producing the words of a specific language. We do know that the experience of hearing language is necessary for this transformation. The consequences of not hearing language may be a permanent infancy. In some mysterious way, the developing child gradually loses the capacity to acquire language. The reason for this loss is simply not known at present.

It is widely asserted that the experience of hearing a spoken language is enough to ensure that a child will come to speak that language. The language heard, apparently, need not be embedded in any kind of reward context. The late Eric Lenneberg (1969) maintained that the sound of a radio turned to a talk show was a sufficient stimulus for normal linguistic development. He based this conclusion on studies of the children of deaf—mute parents. The parents could not talk to one another or to their child. The children none the less developed language skills at a normal rate in the normal way, provided there was some source of speech input around them, even one as unresponsive as a radio.

While explanations such as Lenneberg's may hold for the productive and receptive aspects of language, I must confess that I have my doubts about their validity as an account of the development of language as a system of communication. The noise-making aspects of language have preoccupied psychologists to such an extent that, until recently, the development of communication was totally ignored. This is a deplorable oversight, for the essence of language is not noise, but communication, and obviously, communication is possible without words. The newborn baby communicates. By engaging in synchronic interaction with adults, the baby is communicating something—

that he is one of us, for example, that he is with us. Interpersonal communion of this kind can also be conveyed in words, but it need not be. 'Togetherness' seems to be the main message communicated in non-verbal exchanges between mother and baby. The linguist Halliday (1975) refers to this as the *interpersonal* function of language. For Halliday there are seven basic functions in language:

1. The *instrumental* function is the function that language serves of satisfying the child's material needs, of enabling him to obtain the goods and services that he wants. This is the 'I want' function of language; and it is likely to include a general expression of desire, some element meaning simply 'I want that object there (present in the context)', as well as perhaps other expressions relating to specific desires, responses to questions 'Do you want . . .?' and so on.

2. The *regulatory* function is related to this, but it is also distinct. It is the function of language as controlling the behaviour of others, something which the child recognizes very easily because language is used on him in this way: language is used to control his own behaviour and he soon learns that he can turn the tables and use it to control others. The regulatory is the 'do as I tell you' function of language. The difference between this and the instrumental is that in the instrumental the focus is on the goods or services required and it does not matter who provides them, whereas regulatory utterances are directed towards a particular individual, and it is the behaviour of that individual that is to be influenced. Typically, therefore, this function includes meanings such as, again, a generalized request 'Do that' meaning 'Do what you have just been doing (in this context)', 'Do that again', as well as various specific demands, particularly in the form of suggestions 'Let's do . . .' such as 'Let's go for a walk', 'Let's play this game', 'Let's sing a song' and so forth.

3. The *interpersonal* function is what we might class as the 'me and you' function of language. This is language used by the child to interact with those around him, particularly his mother and others that are important to him, and it includes meanings such as generalized greetings, 'Hello', 'Pleased to see you', and also responses to calls, 'Yes?' as well as more specific forms. For example, the first names of particular individuals that the child learns are typically used with a purely interactional function; and there may be other specific meanings of an interactional kind involving the focusing of attention on particular objects in the environment, some favourite objects of the child which are used as channels for interacting with those around him.

4. Fourthly, there is the *personal* function. This is language used to express the child's own uniqueness; to express his awareness of himself, in contradistinction to his environment, and then to mould that self — ultimately, language in the development of the personality. This includes, therefore, expressions of personal feelings, of participation and withdrawal, of interest, pleasure, disgust, and so forth, and extends later on to more specific intrusion of the child as a personality into the speech situation. We might call this the 'here I come' function of language.

5. Fifthly, once the boundary between the child himself and his environment is beginning to be recognized, then the child can turn towards the exploration of the environment; this is the *heuristic* function of language, the 'tell me why' function, that which later on develops into the whole range of questioning forms that the young child uses. At this

very early stage, in its most elementary form the heuristic use of language is the demand for a name, which is the child's way of categorizing the objects of the physical world; but it soon expands into a variety of more specific meanings.

6. Finally we have the *imaginative* function, which is the function of language whereby the child creates an environment of his own. As well as moving into, taking over and exploring the universe which he finds around him, the child also uses language for creating a universe of his own, a world initially of pure sound, but which gradually turns into one of story and make-believe and let's pretend, and ultimately into the realm of poetry and imaginative writing. This we may call the 'let's pretend' function of language.

There is in fact a seventh to be added to the list; . . . this is the one that we can call the *informative* function of language, the 'I've got something to tell you' function . . .

Halliday has described the development of one child's ability to use these functions. At ten-and-a-half months his subject had the language repertoire shown in Table 25.1. This is really a very large repertoire. It is noteworthy that it bears very little relationship to the sounds made by adults. The meaning of the sounds the baby makes must be inferred from gestures and context, a deduction, according to Halliday, that is not especially difficult. Parents seem able to work out what their baby wants with fairly high reliability, although strangers cannot cope anything like so well.

Halliday has not published a systematic study of the development that went on before the stage he describes. This is unfortunate. Although the newborn cannot communicate as extensively as the ten-month-old, newborns do communicate. They communicate togetherness, the interpersonal function, in their synchronous response to human speech. Crying, which newborns certainly can do, might seem to be a clear instance of the instrumental function. However, very careful observational studies indicate that early crying is a response to discomfort rather than the request for attention it later becomes. Wolff (1969) places the onset of the latter kind of crying in the third week of life. Rather unkindly, he calls it 'fake crying', describing this cry as:

> of a low pitch and intensity; it consists of long drawn out moans which occasionally rise to more explicit cries, and then revert to poorly articulated moans. A mother will respond to the fake cry in one of various ways which largely depend on her general style and momentary disposition. More often than not she ignores such sounds until they become full-fledged rhythmical cries; at other times she picks the baby up to comfort him, or else changes his position so that he can see her while she works.

Wolff makes the interesting observation that non-crying vocalization appears at about the same time as these fake cries and in the same context, seemingly functioning as calls for attention, perhaps subserving the instrumental and personal functions simultaneously.

By the eighth week babies are using sounds for the personal and the interpersonal function. Wolff describes the behaviour thus:

> The baby's non-cry vocalizations diversify rapidly between the sixth and eighth week, and now novel sounds are no longer discovered in a context of fussiness. The baby invents new noises while he is playing alone, including 'Bronx cheers', gurgling, and tongue games and then practises them in circular fashion. On the sound spectrogram these sounds are more complex, and to the ear the individual types of vocalizations are more discrete. Exercise of new vocalizations is more prolific when the baby is not distracted by persons moving about in the room, so that the best recording of novel sounds are obtained from behind a screen. The baby's private conversations can be interrupted by silent visual contact; at the same time one can initiate 'conversation' with the baby by imitating his vocalizations and encouraging him to talk when he was previously silent. I have tested this effect by alternately nodding my head *silently* for five minutes, then *babbling* and nodding for five minutes, then nodding silently for another five minutes, etc., recording the session, and comparing the amount of baby vocalizations under the two conditions (whole sequence can be reversed systematically). In this way it is possible to demonstrate a significantly greater amount of vocalizations when the partner talks than when he is silent. A spectrographic comparison of the sounds made by the experimenter and the baby show that an adult cannot in any strict sense imitate the baby's voice pattern, and that baby vocalizations are not direct copies of the sounds adults made (see Lenneberg, 1964). But once the baby has several discrete sounds at his disposal which he has practised in circular fashion, one can demonstrate that the infant makes some effort to imitate the sounds he hears. When the observer, for example, introduces low-pitched *da-da* sounds which are a part of the infant's repertory, while the infant is making high-pitched squeals, the baby stops squealing and produces his own version of the low-pitched *da-da* sounds. When the observer then imitates the earlier high-pitched squeals the infant resumes his own version of squealing. Even at this stage it seems legitimate within limits, to speak of vocal imitations, not in the sense of direct copies, but as an active 'accommodation' of vocal patterns which are already at the infant's disposal; the baby acts as if the adult's sound was sufficiently like his own to make him want to 'perpetuate' what he has heard.

Some time after the fourth month pointing begins. This gesture is designed to attract the attention of another person to an object or event of interest. If a four-month-old baby is shown a desirable toy that is out of reach, the baby will typically do nothing. An older baby will extend his hand toward the object. This hand gesture is different from reaching; the hand is quite limp, and there is no finger—thumb opposition for grasping (Figure 25.3). The extension of the hand is often accompanied by 'gimme' noises. It is, in fact, a form of pointing. It may be accompanied by 'what's that?' noises, too, if the event is novel to the baby. Pointing may also be used to subserve interpersonal needs. Looking at things together is something that babies seem to enjoy. Trevarthen (1975) has labelled this phase secondary intersubjectivity and sees it as crucial for cognitive and linguistic development.

It is striking that throughout this phase of development, up to the age of nine or ten months, babies are using sounds and gestures in a communicational way, but relying on private sounds. By and large, the sounds they use are not the sounds used by adults. The privacy of this early language was most forcibly brought home to me by two pairs of twins, one of them my own twin daughters. Each twin developed a 'gimme' noise that would accompany pointing. However, each child produced a unique noise. Not even the pair of identical twins (not my own) made the same noise for the same purpose. We must ask how does this private vocal language become shaped into the public language of the child's community? It is hard to believe that listening to a radio is enough. What seems more likely is that adults decode the meaning of the baby's utterances by looking at the specific non-verbal behaviours, non-verbal gestures, and so on that accompany them. The adults may then utter the correct sound. As a result of processes of association, the baby may come to grasp that he will be more efficient in getting the things he wants if he uses the sounds or words that adults already use. Halliday relates one fascinating instance of a child trying, as he puts it, 'very patiently', to explain what a particular noise meant. The child repeated the noise slowly and carefully, accompanied by a wealth of gestures, and so on, but his father simply could not understand what the child wanted. Pretty much instantaneously, this sound apparently dropped out of the baby's repertoire.

It seems possible that reinforcement processes of this sort are necessary for the child to acquire the sounds used by adults. Babies in institutions, it is often claimed, will develop language interactions with one another that are incomprehensible to adults. They are commonly described as babbling nonsensically to one another and laughing all the while. 'Babbling nonsensically' is a harsh way to put it. The sounds that the babies utter may well have meaning for them within a code system that they

Table 25.1   The language repertoire of a baby at 10½ months*

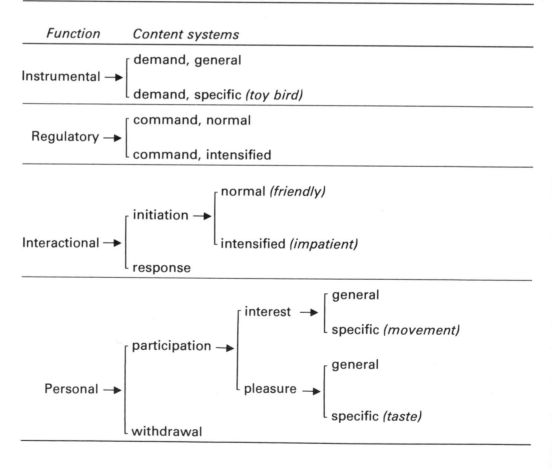

* The sounds cannot be accurately described except by using phonetic notation, shown in the Expression column. The entries under Approximate sound are very approximate indeed.

At 0:9, Nigel had two meanings, both expressed as [ø] on mid or mid-low falling tone; one interactional, 'let's be together', the other (usually with the wider interval) personal, 'look, it's moving'. He also had another three meanings expressed gesturally: two instrumental, 'I want that', grasping object firmly, and 'I don't want that', touching the object lightly, and one regulatory, 'do that again', touching person or relevant object firmly (e.g. 'making that jump in the air again'). The gestures disappeared during NL 1-2.

SOURCE: After Halliday, 1975.

Figure 25.3 Whereas a baby will reach for and grasp an object that is within reach, the gesture toward an object that is clearly out of range (*below*) looks more like pointing.

Expression (articulation)	Approximate sound	Meaning
nā - - -	nyah *(repeat)*	give me that
bø	bih *(as in bird)*	give me my bird
ə̄	nyih	do that *(again)*
m͡nŋ	mnying!	do that right now!
= ø; d́ø; d́ɔ	ih; dih; doh *(as in doll)*	nice to see you *(& shall we look at this together?)*
ən̩n̩n̩	ihng!ng!ng	nice to see you — at last!
ɛ ; ə	eh *(as in yes)*; ih	yes it's me
= ø	ih	that's interesting
d́ɔ; bø; ø	do *(as in dot)*; bih; ih	look it's moving (? a dog, birds)
a	ah	that's nice
ñ͡ŋ	nying	that tastes nice
ǵɤɪ - - -	*(gurgle)*	I'm sleepy

Table 25.2   The language repertoire of the same baby at 18 months*

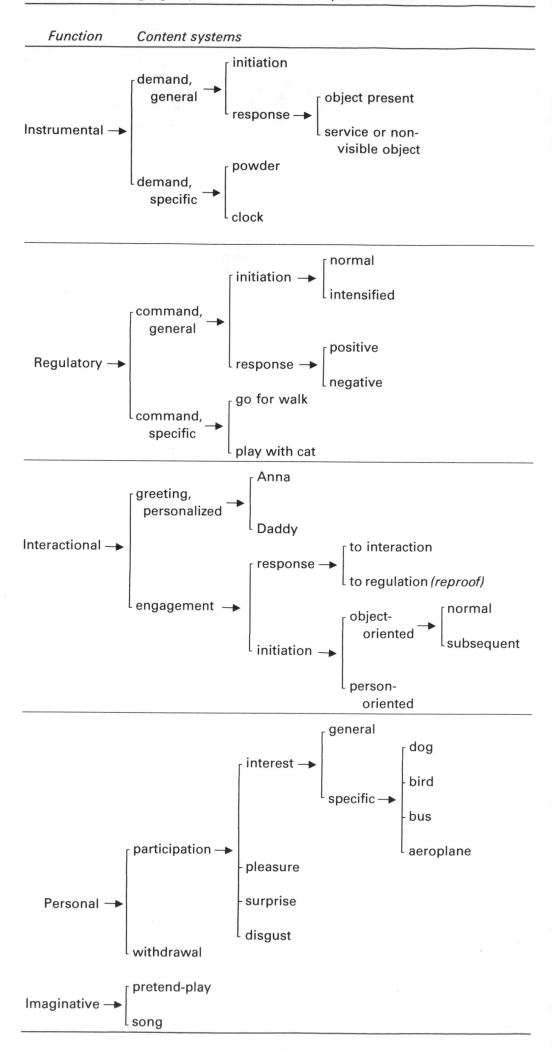

*The sounds cannot be accurately described except by using phonetic notation, shown in the Expression column. The entries under Approximate sound are very approximate indeed.
SOURCE: After Halliday, 1975.

Expression (articulation)	Approximate sound	Meaning
ʔnā - - -	gnyah (repeat)	give me that
yi - -	yee (repeat)	yes I want that
a:	ahhh	yes I want what you just offered
bʷǵa(-); buǵ(-)	biwigah (repeat); boog (repeat)	I want some powder
t́ka(-); t́kɔ(-)	tikah (repeat); tikoh (repeat)	I want (to go and get) the clock
a; ɜ; ɜ̄	ah; eh; nyeh	do that (again)
m̑nŋ	mnying!	do that right now!
ɜ̄ - - -	nyeh (repeat)	yes (let's) do that
āā ' - - -	nyahnyah —	no don't (let's) do that let's go for a walk
pʷi - - -; peʷ	pwee (repeat)	let me play with the cat
na; an; a	nah!; ahn-ah!	Anna!
da; dada ʔɛ:	dah!; dahdah! eh	Daddy! yes it's me; yes, I see
ø	ih	don't be cross with me
a::da	ahh-dah	look, a picture; you say what it is
'a::da	ahh-dahh	another picture; now say what that one is
=₁æ(dæ- -) dæ; ɛ(dɛ- -) dɛ	aahdaah; ehdeh	nice to see you (& shall we look at this?)
=₁æ(dæ- -) dæ da	aahdaah dah!	look, that's interesting a dog!
ba	bah!	birds!
ba	bah!	a bus!
œmœ ɛʸi:; æʸi:	ihhih! ehyee; ahyee	an aeroplane! that's nice
m̑nŋ	mnying!	that's funny (look where it's gone!)
bʷǵa(-); buǵə(-)	biwigah (repeat); boog (repeat)	a lot of talk!
=₂ǵ̣ʷˣ - - - =₂ʃ	(gurgle)	I'm sleepy let's pretend to go to sleep
bʷɛ - - -	bwiheh	tra-la-la

have developed. In an institutional environment there is less opportunity for language development to be reinforced and directed by adults, and therefore more opportunity for the babies to develop a private crib language to share with their neighbours. As well as this, there are a great number of reports of twins developing private languages which they do not share with their parents. Apparently the emergence of comprehensible sounds does depend on some shaping by co-operative adults.

The kind of change that goes on is illustrated in Table 25.2, which shows the range of vocalizations that Halliday's subject could produce at eighteen months. Note that the sounds are recognizable English now. Obviously a great advance has been made since the stage recorded in Table 25.1. This advance, however, has still not taken the baby into language proper. At this age the sounds are still situationally specific. Words which would be appropriate in many situations are still only used in the context in which they were learned. This baby, for example, used *more* only in the context of getting more cereal, although it would have been appropriate elsewhere. The commands or requests were tied to a specific stimulus situation.

Language proper begins when the 'words' in the vocabulary can be used in any situation. In a sense, this development is not limited to language. The child is using his responses in new situations throughout infancy. Possibly success in using established responses in new situations facilitates the generalization of utterances to all possible situations. This is something on which there are no data, something, indeed, on which it would be hard to gather data. The important point, however, is that all during infancy the baby is preparing in all ways to stop being an infant, to begin using language.

References
Condon, W. S. and Sander, L. (1974) 'Neonate movement is synchronized with adult speech: interactional participation and language acquisition', *Science,* 183, 99–101.
Eimas, P. D., Siqueland, E. R., Jusczyk, P. and Vigorito, J. (1971) 'Speech perception in infants', *Science,* 171, 303–6.
Halliday, M. A. K. (1975) *Learning how to mean: explorations in the development of language,* Arnold.
Lenneberg, E. H. (1964) 'Speech as a motor skill with special reference to non-aphasic disorders', *Child Development Monographs,* 29, 115–26.
Lenneberg, E. H. (1969) 'On explaining language', *Science,* 164, 635–43.
Trevarthen, C. (1975) 'Early attempts at speech' in Lewin, R. (ed.) *Child Alive,* Temple Smith.
Wolff, P. H. (1969) 'The natural history of crying and other vocalizations in early infancy' in Foss, B. M. (ed.) *Determinants of Infant Behaviour,* Vol. 4, Methuen.

Three processes in a child's acquisition of syntax.
A summary of an investigation by Roger Brown and Ursula Bellugi

Margaret Roberts

Roger Brown and Ursula Bellugi of Harvard University noted the observable sequence of language development which most children appear to follow. Some time in the second six months of life a first intelligible word is heard followed, a few months later, by the naming of things (and actions). Around eighteen months two-word utterances are constructed, such as, 'push car'. The sentence-constructing process continues to expand and reaches a high level towards thirty-six months or so when all the major varieties of English simple sentences are produced up to a length of ten/ eleven words.

Brown and Bellugi studied the development of English syntax (the sentence-constructing process) in children between eighteen months and thirty-six months including, from 1962, Adam, twenty-seven months, and Eve, eighteen months, the subjects of this paper. Three processes are identified and discussed:

1. imitation and reduction;
2. imitation and expansion;
3. induction of the latent structure.

The last of these three is described by Brown and Bellugi as by far the most complex and difficult to understand in terms of possible processes involved.

You will note that the study involved the mother in each case and that most of the speech to each child is hers.

Meaningful sounds related to human situation and responded to by parents are followed some time in the second six months of life by the first intelligible word. A few months later the naming of things and actions is developing. At about eighteen months to two years children are likely to begin constructing two-word utterances such as 'Bye-Bye Daddy', 'Doggie bite', 'all gone book'. By the age of thirty-six months some children are so advanced in the construction process as to produce all the major varieties of English simple sentences up to a length of 10 or 11 words.

Brown and Bellugi studied over several years the development of English syntax and the sentence-constructing process, in children between eighteen and thirty-six months of age.

This paper looks at a longitudinal study by Brown and Bellugi (1964) of a boy and girl referred to as Adam and Eve. The work began in October 1962 when Adam was twenty-seven months old and Eve eighteen months. These two children were selected from some thirty who were considered. Selection of these two was primarily because their speech was exceptionally intelligible and because they talked a lot. Both are children of highly educated parents and both were single children when the study began. Adam was nine months older than Eve but his speech was only a little more advanced than hers in October 1962. The best single index of the level of speech development is the average length of utterances and in October 1962, Adam's average was 1·84 morphemes and Eve's was 1·40 morphemes.

Method

Every second week each child was visited for at least two hours and a tape recording was made of everything said by the child *as well as everything said to the child*. The mother was always present and most of the speech to the child was hers. Both mother and child became very much accustomed to observers and followed normal routine.

A written transcription was made of the speech of mother and child (on the scene) with notes about important actions and objects of attention. Some experimental work was carried out with toys to test children's understanding, sometimes with amusing results, for example, 'Adam', we asked, 'which is right, two shoes or two shoe?' His answer on that occasion, produced with explosive enthusiasm, was 'Pop goes the weasel!'

Table 26.1 offers a sample section from an early transcribed record. The conversation was very much in the 'here and now'.

Table 26.1 A section from Adam's first record

Adam	Mother
See truck Mommy, see truck.	
	Did you see the truck?
No I see truck	
	No, you didn't see it? There goes one.
There go one	
	Yes, there goes one.
See a truck, see truck Mommy.	
Truck	
Put truck, Mommy	
	Put the truck, where?
Put truck window	
	I think that one's too large to go in the window.

In the course of the brief interchange of Table 26.1, Adam imitates his mother in saying, 'There go one' immediately after she says, 'There goes one'. The imitation is not perfect; Adam omits the inflection on the verb. His imitation is a reduction in that it omits something from the original. This kind of imitation with reduction is extremely common in the records of both children and is the first process to be discussed.

1. Imitation and reduction

The first thing to notice is that the imitators preserve the word order of the model sentence. The preservation of order suggests (to Brown and Bellugi) that the model sentence is processed by the child as a total construction rather than as a list of words.

Table 26.2 Some imitations produced by Adam and Eve

Model utterance	Child's imitation
Tank car	Tank car
Wait a minute	Wait a minute
Daddy's briefcase	Daddy briefcase
Fraser will be unhappy	Fraser unhappy
He's going out	He go out
That's an old time tram	Old time tram
It's not the same dog as Pepper	Dog Pepper

In English, the order of words in a sentence is an important grammatical signal. The imitation of the adult's word order by the child in his first sentences accounts in part for the ability of an adult to understand these sentences and so to feel that he is in communication with the child. Note that the imitations stay in the range of 2 to 4 morphemes. There is apparently a limitation on the length of utterance that the children are able to program or plan at this stage. The forms that are retained for the most part are nouns, verbs and adjectives, with some exceptions. Forms likely to be omitted are inflections, auxiliary verbs, articles, prepositions and conjunctions. These forms belong to syntactic classes that are small and closed – linguists sometimes call these 'functors'.

The child's speech at this stage may be described as a 'telegraphic' reduction – a telegraphic transformation of English generally communicates very well. Notice also that stress is important and in fact the heavier stresses fall for the most part on the words the child retains. It is possible that differential stress may be the cause of the child's differential retention. Telegraphic properties of these imitations appear also in the child's spontaneously produced utterances.

2. Imitation and expansion

One of the first things noticed in the early study of child speech was the frequency with which adults imitated children. Later it was noticed that the adult imitations were seldom exact reproductions; they were usually expansions.

Table 26.3 Expansions of child speech produced by mothers

Child	Mother
Baby highchair	Baby is in the highchair
Mommy eggnog	Mommy had her eggnog
Eve lunch	Eve is having her lunch
Mommy sandwich	Mommy'll have a sandwich
Sat wall	He sat on the wall
Throw Daddy	Throw it to Daddy
Pick glove	Pick the glove up

It should be noted that the words spoken by the mother preserve the order of the words in the child's sentence. From the mother's point of view an expansion is a kind of communication check; it says in effect: 'Is this what you mean?'

It is also important to note that the forms added to the child's utterance include the auxiliaries 'is' and 'will'; the prepositions, 'in', 'on', 'to' and 'up'; the verb forms, 'is', 'have', 'had', and 'having'; the articles, 'a' and 'the'; and the pronouns, 'her', 'he' and 'it'.

Notice that the decision on the correct expansion of the child's utterence is made in relation to the circumstance, and thus structure is related to meaning in the child's daily experience.

3. Induction of the latent structure

It is not easy to imagine an adult model for some of the children's utterances, for example, Adam's, 'No I see truck'. It seems more likely that the utterance was created by Adam as part of a continuing effort to discover the general rules for constructing English negatives. In Table 26.4 are listed some utterances produced by Adam or Eve for which it is difficult to imagine an adult model.

Table 26.4   Utterances not likely to be imitations

My Cromer suitcase
Two foot
A bags
A scissor
A this truck
You naughty are
Why it can't turn off?
Cowboy did fighting me
Put a gas in

It does not seem likely that these utterances are reductions of adult originals, it is more likely that they are mistakes which illustrate the child's search for the regularities of English syntax. When a child speaks correctly there is no way of telling whether he is simply repeating what he has heard or whether he is actually constructing, but when he says something like: 'I digged a hole', we can often be sure he is constructing. All children are able to understand and to construct sentences they have never heard but which are nevertheless well formed in terms of general rules that are implicit in the sentences the child has heard. Brown and Bellugi continued their study of the child's discovery of latent structure by examining the child's early use of noun phrases as independent utterances rather than as components of sentences, for example, 'That Adam', 'My Mommy', 'A hands', and the substitution of noun phrases by pronouns, for example, 'Ball go. Go get it', and pronouns produced together with nouns or noun phrases, for example, 'Mommy get it my ladder'. Brown and Bellugi see these utterances as further examples of the induction of latent structure in the sentence-construction process.

In describing the three processes involved in the child's acquisition of syntax, the induction of latent structure is seen to be by far the most complex and most difficult to understand.

The above material is taken from a Harvard Educational Review article by Roger Brown and Ursula Bellugi, reprinted in *New Directions in the Study of Language*, edited by Eric H. Lenneburg, published by MIT Press, 1966.

Discussion Guide N

Social interactions: words and people

You should allow at least 1¼ hours for this discussion. It would be helpful to divide into small sub-groups of 3 or 4 people in order to listen to individual cassette-recordings and discuss points arising from Activity 28.
Note: Active listening will require a considerable amount of concentration.
Bring:

1 Your cassette tape from Activity 28;
2 A cassette-recorder for the sub-group;
3 Your transcription of the cassette-recording;
4 Your observations of behaviour when mother was playing/talking with child *plus* basic data and comments.

Arrange to present your material in *age-order*, the youngest first. Give basic data including name, age, position in family first. Indicate briefly the observed situation, for example, toys available, whether other children were present and their ages. *Listen* carefully to the first five minutes of each tape, that is, Task 1 mother/child (5 mins × 3 = 15 mins). Give additional information from checklist.
Discuss major differences in terms of:

1 identifiable sounds used by child, if possible identifying the context from the checklist;
2 the use of two-word 'sentences';
3 mother's contribution, for example, does she:
   (a) repeat child's utterance;
   (b) expand child's two-word utterances, see Paper 26 (Brown and Bellugi's research);
4 child's response to mother's contribution.

Play back the next sections of tape(s) consecutively, that is, Tasks 2 and 3 in age-order. See Activity 28, to remind yourself that:
   in Task 2 the observer was using a passive role with the child;
   in Task 3 the observer was taking the initiative with the child.
   (time 5 mins × 6 = 30 mins.)
Discuss differences between the two sections (Tasks 2 and 3) in the same child and differences *between* the three children (transcripts will be helpful here). For example, marked differences in the number of verbal utterances used:
   (a) by the same child in the two sections 2 and 3;
   (b) between the three children, for example, the children may differ markedly in the number of two-word sentences used; some more complex utterances may be identified.
Check with Paper 26 (Brown and Bellugi's research).

Discussion Guide O

Role of the mother in early language development

You should allow at least 30 minutes for this discussion. Bring the cassette tape, recorder, transcriptions and observation records as for the previous discussion. Discuss the role of the mother or other care-giver in early language development. Refer to the Brown and Bellugi research findings in Paper 26.

Do you think that parents could be helped to give more assistance to their children in the early stages of language development? Suggest ways in which this might be tried.

What are some of the likely difficulties if other than very general guidance is given? Do you think that parents would tend to become self-conscious about talking to their children if precise suggestions were made to them? Can you think of ways around these difficulties?

Papers and discussions in Unit 3 of this module will take the matter further in the 0–2 age-range. From two years onwards this topic assumes increasing importance; (see Modules 5–8).

Unit Three

The Development of Imaginative Play — play with objects and 'pretend play'

- Read Paper 27 reviewing the period fifteen months to two years, and Paper 28 focussing on developments of imaginative play
- Complete Activity 30, Tasks 1 to 4, observing child at play with adult
- Work through Discussion P
- Read Paper 29 examining mother's contribution to child's play
- Engage in Discussion Q on the role of the mother in early play
- Bring Paper 29 with you to discussion

Reading	95 mins.
Activities	60 mins.
Discussion	75 mins.
Total	230 mins.
	= 3 hrs. 50 mins.

A review of aspects of development from fifteen months to two years
Margaret Roberts

We will consider some closely related characteristics of the child at this age under the following headings:

sensory-motor behaviour;

mental development: cognitive and linguistic activities;

emotional/social and attachment behaviour;

environmental influences.

Sensory-motor behaviour

The child's response to sensory experience through sight, hearing, touch, taste and smell is established from an early age. His mobility, how he gets around, whether crawling, walking or running, provides a measure of independence as far as his own movement in the home is concerned. He usually enjoys running, climbing and balancing. He will respond for a short time to a familiar adult's attempts to play ball with him, though when an eighteen-month-old 'throws' a ball, it generally goes over his head – behind him! His increased hand–eye co-ordination is demonstrated by reaching, grasping and manipulating objects, that is, bringing them together and relating them to one another. In addition to throwing objects away he will make efforts to retrieve them.

Mental development: cognitive and linguistic activities

There is increased evidence of the ability to reflect on experience; for example, he will search for objects no longer in view, he will look for people and things with expectation. He will imitate activities of familiar adults and may at times engage in imaginative, that is, 'pretend' play, representing one thing by another. He is beginning to project into the future and will respond to the adult's suggestion 'Let's do' so and so. He responds to his own name, may refer to himself by name. He is inventing his own names for things in his environment, for example, 'go-goes' for different kinds of vehicles. Two-word sentences, for example, 'Daddy gone', 'See lorry', indicate an important step forward in linguistic development. He understands very much more in terms of language within the home and normal surroundings than he is as yet able to express in words.

Emotional/social and attachment behaviour

A child of fifteen months to two years can express a range of positive and negative emotions, such as pleasure and annoyance, joy and anger, in response to pleasurable and unpleasurable, satisfying or frustrating situations. He is capable at times of expressing extreme distress or excitement when over-stimulated or tired. His sense of possession is developing towards two years of age in relation to his own toys. He is still very dependent on warm human relationships and not happy to be separated from known adults for any length of time. He may still show dependent behaviour towards his mother/father or another well-known person in a social group containing strangers, especially when under stress.

Environmental influences

It is most important to emphasize varying rates of development in the first two years of life and the wide range of developmental level within the norm at any particular age. Development and learning will be influenced by home background, stable/unstable family relationships, availability of other children to play with and members of the extended family to show an interest in the young child and his doings. The variety of play material and the child's awareness of the adult's interest in him and his activities are probably crucial factors in his mental development in the second year of life. The attitudes and behaviour of familiar adults will be among the most significant influences in his young life.

The unity of the child as expressed in his play life
Margaret Roberts

Having looked at certain aspects of behaviour separately through observation and in discussion we focus now on the unity of the child. We need to remind ourselves that the child, like the adult, is a unified human being and all aspects of his behaviour, development and learning are inter-related. This is not to say that all aspects of development take place at the same rate: clearly they do not do so. The perceptual, social and sensory-motor areas develop ahead of the linguistic in terms of actual behaviour. We tend to think that aspects that we can see developing as in walking behaviour between twelve and fifteen months are dominant at those times. In so doing there is a possibility that we may overlook important mental development, for example, the growth of the young child's thinking ability and imagination, which are also making considerable progress at this time.

In order to understand something of what is happening in the early stages of mental development it is helpful to consider briefly our own sensory, perceptual and imaginative experiences.

Sensation, perception and imagery
It may help to look at sensation, perception and imagery as a sequence starting with sensation, that is, the stimulation of our senses. Following sensory experience of any kind, seeing, hearing, smelling, tasting, touching or moving, the perceptual areas of the brain for those senses are stimulated and we become 'aware' of seeing, hearing, touching etc. These experiences are, through electrical and chemical changes in the brain cells, encoded and stored in the brain and we can 'see' and 'hear' mentally, that is, perceptually in mental images that relate to the objects in the outside world that originally stimulated our senses. Thus on some future occasion we may be able to visualize an object in our minds that is not actually present to our senses.

Mental imagery of various kinds is related to sensory experience through the central nervous system, for example:

Seeing	visual imagery
Hearing . . .	auditory imagery
Smell	olfactory imagery
Taste	gustatory imagery
Touch	tactile imagery
Movement . .	kinaesthetic imagery

This ability to image increases in complexity so that images become inter-related and we may experience visual and auditory imagery such as when we recall the experience of hearing and seeing an orchestra performing one of our favourite pieces of music. This capacity for imaginative thought, as it is called, enables us to hold events in mind, to memorize events, to relate to other past experiences and to plan future activities.

The above examples of imagery have been related to concrete experience, but early in life, between the first and second birthday, man develops the ability to use a more abstract form of imagery, that is the symbolism of words and later the most economical form of symbolism, that is, verbal thought.

We can often help ourselves to remember names of people, places and events by telling ourselves the information several times. People vary in the types of imagery they habitually employ; visual imagery appears to be particularly strong in childhood as demonstrated by children's spontaneous response to book illustrations, drawings and imaginative play. Adults vary from strong to weak visualizers and some claim to use mainly verbal imagery, that is, that they think 'in words' without visual imagery.

Symbolic representation and imaginative play
Imagery is a complex mental process that contributes to the development of imaginative thinking in different fields of experience, for example, in art, or science, or practical problem-solving. We are here concerned with the development of this mental activity as demonstrated by the young child in his day-to-day behaviour.

Between fifteen, eighteen and twenty-four months an important change in behaviour is seen emphasizing the unity of the child's physical and mental development. An important discovery is made by the child related to his earlier manipulation of objects and his developing imagery. He discovers that one object can be used to represent another; we say that he is 'pretending' or that he is playing imaginatively. Longer sequences of activity begin to appear in his play which is less repetitive and appears to be related to his thinking. It is noticeable that he is now happy to play on his own for longer stretches of time though he appreciates interaction with an adult who is sensitive to what he is trying to say and do.

Froebel, commenting on the importance of this stage in *The Education of Man* (1826), wrote: 'What man tries to represent or do he begins to understand.' At first the child's activities appear to represent what has impressed him from his experiences in his day-to-day life, aided perhaps by a toy, or a domestic tool. He will, for example, turn a small car into an ambulance by running it along the floor accompanied by a chant of 'Dee-dah, dee-dah, dee-dah' in imitation of an ambulance in a hurry. Later he appears to create his own ideas, combining experiences from the real world with his personal inventions. When his play seems to us beyond the realms of reality we call it fantasy play. This is not to detract from its value to the child, indeed fantasy play appears to exercise an important function at this stage. In extending the boundaries of the possible the child can explore 'as if' situations in imagination: the beginnings of hypothetical thinking.

Children's fantasy at times represents something that has made a strong impression on them, perhaps a frightening experience which may have a basis in reality, or an imaginary fear related to strong emotional feelings of anxiety or guilt. One theory, based on psycho-analytic treatment of disturbed children, suggests that fear of punishment for angry feelings is sometimes expressed by the child in the form of symbolic fantasy.

Fear, anger and aggression may be represented symbolically in the child's fantasy play, for example, in a game of 'burglars', or in aspects of doll play when aggression is directed towards the doll, such as the doll being punished for wetting herself. It is thought that this kind of play provides an outlet for pent-up emotions associated with guilt feelings related to past behaviour. The child is able to externalize his strong feelings which might otherwise be repressed from his conscious mind and experienced in the form of anxiety. The ability to express strong feelings in this way, without too much excitement and loss of control, appears to require the support of an understanding and calm adult. This is considered one of the values of nursery education at a later stage, which also provides a certain amount of time for 'free' play with real objects as well as toys as 'props', and the companionship of other children to share their world of make-believe. The role of the adult in extending the child's imaginative life is considered in later modules covering the years 2–5.

This unit will provide an opportunity for you to observe younger children at play, with certain objects we have come to think of as toys, in the company of their mother or other care-giver. We need to bear in mind that play is the child's 'life-work' at this early stage, being closely associated with his developing mental and physical skills. He works hard to develop his skill in manipulation and becomes deeply immersed in his imaginative play.

Martin Bax gives a helpful summary of the child's mental development at this stage:

> He is beginning to use ideas in a much more complicated way, to think out the relation between things without having to see or handle them. His skill in repeating sequences, in building up on what happens as a result of his actions,

in understanding the relationship between events, suggests that there may be important changes in the way his memory works, in his power of storing, recalling and comparing events over this period.

He goes on to link this development of symbolic processes with the acquisition of language. 'The beginning of a baby's use of words to express what he wants is very much tied up with these developments in the way he thinks – the ability to symbolize, to keep a stable image of something in his mind. From about fifteen months onwards (but the age is variable) the child starts adding to the four or five word "naming" vocabulary he had at one.'

An example from my own study of the beginning of imaginative play illustrates this point. Julian, aged twenty months, the middle of three brothers, all under five years, was fond of tipping objects out of their containers and then pushing them all back followed by another tip-out! He liked to play in this way with a home-made wooden dolls' house which had a flat roof. However, one day after tipping the miniature furniture out of the house, he selected certain pieces and proceeded to place them carefully one behind the other in a line on the floor. He then selected one of the small dolls and placed this on the top of the first piece of furniture which happened to be a table. He pushed the line of furniture along the floor for a short way making 'choo, choo' train noises followed by the words 'Tain, tain' in an excited voice. He then sat back holding himself tightly with both hands and beaming all over his face. As far as his mother and I could recall this was Julian's first attempt at imaginative play arising from his own spontaneous activity.

His mother later told me she had taken Julian on his own for a short train ride the day before from one station to the next and back again and that she had gone over the sequence of the journey in the form of a story at bed-time. Julian had joined in some of the actions and words such as, 'Shut-da-doors' though he was still speaking largely in jargon. Here again we can see the important part played by the mother. Although the mother was not present during this play episode it appears that her contribution in widening and highlighting the previous day's experience was contributory to Julian's recall and representation of his experience. The fact of my presence, a familiar and trusted adult, and my obvious interest was also an important aspect of this occasion.

Later, as the child extends his ability to represent his past experiences in imagination, he experiments with creating imaginary situations beyond the realms of reality; this, as stated earlier in this paper, we call fantasy play. The child of three or four years moves easily in his play from the reality level to fantasy and back to reality and in the one-to-one situation enjoys the familiar adult following him in his flights of fantasy. Winnicott (1971) sees the child's symbolic play, as he prefers to call it, as part of the child's realization of his own identity, an expression of 'I am, I am alive, I am myself'. It is not then surprising to find that he does not take kindly to direct interference in his fantasy ideas or attempts by the adult to redirect the theme or the sequence of his fantasy play. This is in contrast to his response to adult contributions when his play is directly representing happenings in the real world when the child may want the adult to play say, buses, with him. Then he usually wants reality rules to apply and resents it if the adult does not keep to the generally accepted rules for behaviour on buses.

Picture book behaviour

One of the most dramatic developments in the second year of life is the child's response to picture books, his looking and pointing and 'talking' about familiar pictures: 'doggy', 'car', 'bus' etc. A stream of jargon frequently accompanies a recognized picture and the child will often have a favourite book which he brings to the adult whom he knows well to 'read' to him. The close proximity of sitting on the adult's lap is, of course, part of the enjoyment. The sharing of this activity brings together the exercise of the imagination and the pleasure of human companionship. Very soon the young child between eighteen months and two years will be naming familiar objects and experiencing a sense of delight in his achievements.

Parental role

Research has shown that children from disturbed, socially deprived backgrounds where their early play has been of poor quality or non-existent, have little capacity for imaginative play at the pre-school stage, that is, at three to four years (Smilansky, 1968). It is therefore important to reflect at this point on the implications for young children of suffering the disadvantage of inadequate mothering due to the mental and/or physical ill-health of the mother, and also on the possible effect of a succession of mother-substitutes with different styles of response and understanding of the individual child's developing needs and/or lack of knowledge of the normal play needs of children in the second year of life.

Dunn and Wooding's study of 'Play in the home and its implications for learning' (Paper 29) looks at a small sample of twenty-four children from different social classes, aged between eighteen and twenty-four months, and their play with objects and early symbolic activity. The study is concerned with adult involvement with the children's play and distinguishes two levels of involvement: *joint attention* referring to the mother looking at what the child was playing with and commenting on; *joint play* referring to the mother actually manipulating the object with the child and taking part in the activity.

An important finding in this study related to the child's play and the interest of the mother. It was found that if joint attention of mother and child was focused on the object of the child's play, then the median length of the play bouts for each of the twenty-four children was significantly greater than the median length of play bouts when the mother was not paying attention.

Class differences

In this admittedly small sample it was found that the middle-class families provided more joint attention on the child's play with objects, that the middle-class mothers were more likely to join in play with their children and more time was spent in the middle-class families with representational material.

This picture suggests to the authors that class differences in parental conception of a guiding role and interest in teaching their children may be apparent by the age of eighteen months. These points will be further considered in your discussion groups after your observations of children at play in their own homes.

References
Bax, M. and Bernal, J. (1974) *Your Child's First Five Years*, Heinemann Health Books.
Smilansky, S. (1968) *The Effects of Sociodramatic Play on Disadvantaged Pre-school Children*, John Wiley & Son.
Winnicott, D. W. (1971) *Playing and Reality*, Tavistock Publications.

Play in the home and its implications for learning
Judy Dunn and Carol Wooding*

Introduction

In this paper we are concerned with two questions: 'How does interaction with the mother affect the patterning and quality of play in very young children?' and 'What are the implications of this involvement for learning?'

It has been suggested that it is in the context of intimate mother–child interaction that the young are given the opportunity to discover, to practise and to extend their skills (Bruner, 1974), and that the mother provides 'scaffolding' which enables the child to perform 'at the margins of his ability'. At present we have little systematic evidence on the extent to which (and the context within which) mothers provide scaffolding, or on the part children play in eliciting particular sorts of involvement.

Our information is particularly sparse and anecdotal for the second and third years of the child's life. Over this period, the ways in which the child's verbal environment and the responsiveness of the mother affect the early stages of language are beginning to be well-documented, but we know very little about the relation between other aspects of the development of symbolic thought and of the child's interaction with adults.

Most recent studies of play in children aged between one and two-and-a-half years have observed children either in group situations, in structured situations in which the children are presented with a series of toys or objects, or in playroom situations with a standard series of toys available. The increasing appearance of representational play, first with self, and later towards other objects, has been described (Lowe, 1975), and the increase in activity which involves bringing together objects according to common perceptual features has been studied (Fein and Apfel, 1975). Of course, these studies are not concerned with the rôle of adult interaction in the development of symbolic

thought. In one of the few studies on this issue of adult involvement, the Russian psychologist Fradkina asserts very positively that early symbolic play, with one object or name substituting for another, always originates from adult example or suggestion (quoted in El'konin, 1966). Some observations of 18-month-old and two-year-old children playing in their homes may help to illuminate these issues.

Authors' Observations

Twenty-four children aged between eighteen and twenty-four months have so far been observed. Thirteen children are from working-class homes (Registrar General III manual) and eleven from middle-class homes (Registrar General I and II). Observations were carried out by the two authors, only one of whom was present at each session. The observers arranged to sample, for each child, periods when the mother was doing housework and periods when she was relaxing. Apart from these two categories, no attempt was made to structure the observations. One hour of observation was made on each of at least two occasions.

The observations were made in the form of a running record, in a lined notebook with each line representing 10 seconds. A time marker was provided by an electronic bleeper. Categories of interaction between mother and child were precoded, and can be obtained from the authors. The details of the form of play and the object played with were written in narrative form. The verbal exchange between mother and child, and comments made by the child while playing, were recorded with a portable stereo tape-recorder.

Categories of Play

Two particular problems became apparent to us when we started observing children in their own homes. First, the categories of pretend or make-believe in these young children were

very difficult to use, since many of the 18-month-olds had very few words and classification necessarily involved subjective judgements about what the play meant to the child. If the child makes a 'train' of bricks, and moves them along the ground making 'choo-choo' noises, we might categorise this as pretend play. How should we categorise the play if he does not make the 'choo-choo' noise? We certainly cannot assume that he is imagining the bricks are a train. It is quite possible, for instance, that the whole sequence is a simple repetition of an adult's or an older child's play. In this study we have been very cautious about such incidents, and have only categorised as 'pretend' the less ambiguous play sequences. What we can examine, and what seems potentially of considerable importance, is the way the adult interprets and responds to these play activities. We looked particularly at the mother's response to, and interest in, behaviour that could be described as 'symbolic'.

Second, the usual play categories describing objects used by children under two years old in structured situations masked sequences of actions with objects that we felt were interesting. We observed a number of action sequences (such as the one following) and thought it would be interesting to group them.

Example 1: Kevin (18 months) in garden
Inspects small pool of water in drain cover – picks leaf of grass and drops it in water – picks dandelion head and drops it in water – picks up stone and drops it in water.

Piaget (1962) makes the distinction between two different kinds of knowledge: one that derives from logico-mathematical experience, and one that derives from experience with the physical world. He distinguishes between discoveries that are irrelevant to the properties of the objects – as in ordering and numbering objects – and discoveries where it is exactly 'the prop-

*Carol Wooding is now called Carol Kendrick.

erties of the objects themselves that are relevant – when the child begins to discover regularities in the physical world: water flows, sand also, but in a different manner; balls roll and can be made to bounce' (see Sinclair, 1970).

For the purpose of this preliminary analysis we have grouped together those sequences that might subjectively be described as making it possible for the child to discover the properties of the physical world. (The reasons why one cannot assume that any learning is going on in these sequences is discussed below.) In this first analysis we have also looked at two other classes of activity, and have examined their relationship to child/ mother interaction. Of course, many of the child's activities are not covered by these three classes, e.g. running and jumping, physical games played with others, verbal games, hide-and-seek games and household tasks. These activities were recorded during the observation, but are not discussed in this paper.

1. Symbolic Activity
A. Pretend activities. These include activities in which an inanimate object is treated as though it were animate, or is substituted for another object, and activities which resemble everyday activities but which occur in the absence of the necessary materials (e.g. drinking gestures with an empty cup). *B. Activities with representational material.* These include looking at pictures and books, naming and labelling from pictures, drawing involving naming or describing what is being drawn, and modelling involving naming or describing what is being modelled.

The sequences of pretend play tend to be very brief. The median bout length of play was four 10-second intervals, though there was a wide range, and bouts were considerably longer with the two-year-olds than with the younger children. (Developmental changes in play patterns are being examined in a follow-up study of the children seen at 18 months.) The total percentage of observation time that was spent in pretend play was low, with a median value of 3 per cent (range 0–10 per cent). The percentage of observation time spent with representational material ranged from 0–29 per cent, median 9 per cent.

2. Activity with Objects
In a recent developmental study, Inhelder and colleagues (1972) traced the progression of the child's actions with objects over the second year. Their classification of the child's activity distinguished three stages of activity with objects: in the first stage the child manipulates one object at a time – pushing, pulling, waving, etc.; in the next stage the child manipulates parts of objects, and also begins to place objects together – one object on top of, beside, into another, etc.; at a later stage the child plays with objects in a way which reflects the characteristics of the objects more specifically – he orders and organises objects together in a way that depends on their particular features. In this third stage, the child posts long, thin objects through holes, he systematically groups objects according to their shape, and he makes rows of objects which share particular features.

We categorised the children's activities with objects according to this three-stage scheme. In the analysis reported here, we have focused on the third stage of activity. This category includes activity where two or more objects are brought into relation with each other according to a common perceptual feature, e.g. bringing blocks together and arranging or aligning, and posting shapes through appropriate holes (Activity with Object Level III). The percentage of observation time spent in this category of activity ranged from 3–31 per cent, median 10 per cent.

3. Sequences of Actions with Objects
Sequences of different actions performed on the same object or material, accompanied by concentrated attention, such as Example 1 (above).

Mother's Involvement
We distinguished two levels of adult involvement with the child's play: *joint attention* referred to the mother looking at what the child was playing with, and commenting on it; *joint play* referred to the mother actually manipulating the object with the child and taking part in the activity.

Results
(a) Attention of the Mother and the Length of Activity Bouts
First, a general point concerning the child's play and the attention or interests of the mother. We found that if joint attention of mother and child was focused on the object of the child's play, then the median length of the play bouts for each of our 24 children was significantly greater than the median length of the play bouts when the mother was not paying attention.

This association could arise by mothers paying selective attention to those activities which in themselves tended to be continued for long time-bouts. However, when the different activities were examined separately, the association between the mother's

attention and length of activity bout was demonstrated for a number of different categories of activity: for pretend play; for activity with representational material; for activity with objects (Level III), and for practical household activities. The median length of activity bouts in each category of activities was longer when the mother paid attention at some point during the play bout, even if only for a few seconds, than when she paid no attention at all.

When we classified the bouts of activity according to length, we found that of the longest bouts (those exceeding 40 ten-second intervals in length), 86 per cent were bouts in which the mother had paid attention to the child's activity at some point. The only long bouts when the children played entirely alone were sequences of play with soil, sand, or water in the garden.

(b) Symbolic Activities
Figure 29.1 shows that the majority of pretend-play sequences were initiated by the child, but that comparatively few of these were *completed* by the child when playing on his own. In the majority of cases the child involved the mother by talking or demonstrating, or the sequence (though initiated by the child) took place while they were engaged in joint attention on the same object or material.

An equally high degree of maternal involvement was found with the incidents of play we have described as 'representational', *i.e.* those with books, drawing or discussion of pictures. Figure 29.1 shows that, in 63 per cent of the child-initiated bouts, the child involved the mother by taking the book or drawing and showing or commenting on it to her.

(c) Activity with Objects (Level III)
A very different pattern of involvement was found when we looked at the class of object play we have categorised as Activity with Objects Level III, according to the developmental account of Inhelder et al. (1972). The mother was involved in initiating 29 per cent of the bouts. In only four of the 82 bouts that the child initiated did he attempt to involve the mother (5 per cent of the child-initiated bouts). We distinguished between play with toy and non-toy objects, and it was noticeable that the mother initiated or joined in play of this kind only when it was concerned with toys.

(d) Sequences of Object Play
In the third class of play (sequences of actions with objects), none of the sequences was initiated by the mother (except in the sense that she was responsible for providing the object or

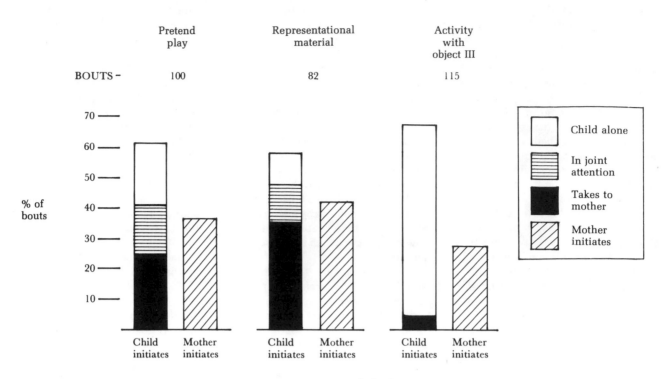

Figure 29.1. Initiation of play bouts.

material in two cases). In most of these bouts the mother did not intervene in any way. In five out of 46 sequences she made a 'pretend' suggestion, and in five others she prohibited the play. In the two cases where the child directly elicited the mother's attention the child was using the object in a 'pretend' way.

For these very young children, the first essays into symbolic play and representation seem very closely bound up with the mother. Not only is she active in initiating this play but the child, in the majority of instances, energetically seeks her comment and involvement. It is as if he looks for confirmation of his play with the new world of symbols. Catherine Garvey (1977) points out that much of what can be played with derives from socially-learned and socially-based rules for interpretation. Our observations suggest the mirror image to this – that in playing symbolically at this early stage the child actively involves the mother in a situation where it seems natural for an observer to judge that the child is learning how the physical world is categorised into classes of objects, and how items of behaviour are classified into appropriate and inappropriate actions. It is interesting to note in Thorburn's (1938) diary account, that between one-and-a-half years and two years the child, while happy to co-operate in games which an adult initiated, 'herself chose books to play with them'.

The contrast between the deliberate

way in which children turn to their mothers (as if for confirmation) in 'pretend' play or play with representational material and their independence when playing with objects in the 'sequences' was brought out in the two sequences mentioned above, where the child approached the mother when his play took a 'pretend' form.

Example 2: Kenny (18 months) alone in sitting room – mother washing in kitchen
Inspects bottle brush – waves it – pokes it through cardboard tube he has been playing with – pulls it in and out of cardboard tube – pulls it out and holds it out pointing it, runs to mother in next room pointing it still – points it towards her grunting 'uh uh' – she turns, looks at him holding it, says 'You got a gun, Kenny?' – K. looks at her, pointing and grunting 'uh uh' – turns and returns to other room.
On the few instances that a mother commented positively on what the child was doing in a sequence of object-manipulation, her comment was to suggest a 'pretend' element.

Example 3: Karen (23 months) in sitting room – mother sitting beside her with baby sibling
Inspects empty bottle in bowl of water – pushes it down – lets it bob up – holds it down – lets it bounce up – repeats sequence several times – raises bottle – examines water dripping off – scatters water on her knee – saying

'wet' – scatters water drops on water in bowl saying 'wet' – repeats pushing-down sequence – mother comments 'Are you washing up for me?'

It is extremely difficult to see whether one could in principle tell if these sequences are important for learning in any way – a point we will take up in discussion. What we would stress is that these sequences are 'private' for the child, in that he doesn't solicit adult interest, whether or not they are private experiments.

(e) Mother's Initiations
We have seen that the mothers initiated 42 per cent of the bouts of the child's play with representational objects, 39 per cent of the bouts of pretend play and 29 per cent of his Activity with Objects III. This does not of course tell us the comparative frequency of the mother's initiations of the different types of play. Figure 29.2 shows that 37 per cent of the mothers' initiations were in representational or pretend play. In column D we have listed the 'functional non-toy activities' that the mothers initiated. These were activities with household objects or tools where the objects were being used appropriately – usually cleaning with mops, dusting, polishing, cleaning shoes *etc.*, which the child was encouraged to do accompanying his mother round the house. This group of activities does not include those sequences where the mother or the child (it was usually the mother) turned the joint activity into a

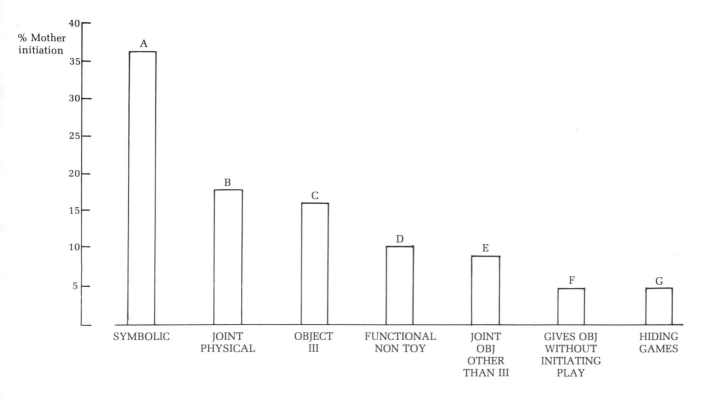

Figure 29.2. Relative frequency of mothers' initiations of different types of activity.

chasing, hiding, or physical game. Rather, the activities listed here have the connotations (at least for the mother) of the child learning and enjoying the activities of his mother's world.

One further point that must be emphasised about the mother's involvement with representational material is that it is overwhelmingly in *this situation* that we find explicit teaching on the mother's part. We have only just begun the analysis of the verbal interchange, and cannot present detailed data here, but it is striking that the tutorial functions described by Wood *et al.* (1976) are more evident here than in the other play situations we have looked at. An exception must be made for complex shape-matching toys such as elaborate 'posting' toys or workbenches. When the child is playing with these there is much direction, demonstration and direct help. Figure 29.3 gives the comparative frequency of the mother's suggestions – showing, acknowledging the child's comment or action, and extension of that comment – for 16 cases. When the mother and child are both looking at representational material, the mother's speech includes more extensions of the child's utterances, and more comments which elaborate on items that are the focus of the child's interest.

This feature of mother's speech, where her utterances are semantically related to the focus of the child's attention, has been shown to be related in an important way to rate of language acquisition (see Discussion below).

We have not shown the child's involvement here, but the general picture is that the child's active showing and dialogue between mother and child are most common with representational material.

(f) Child's Initiation of Interaction
By emphasising the mother's initiation and involvement with symbolic activity and Activity with Objects III, we should not give the impression that most of the child's activities were directed by the mother. Analysis of the start of each new verbal interaction, to describe the context in which mother and child come together, shows that it is equally likely to be child or mother that directly starts an interaction, and further, that the most common start to an interaction is where the child brings or shows an object to the mother (Table 29.1). Thirty-two per cent of the interactions in the cases so far analysed start with his attempt to draw attention to (and possibly her comment on) some physical object.

(g) Class Differences
With data analysed for so few subjects it is obviously foolish to attempt to make statements about class differences. However, since the differences between the middle-class and the working-class children are particularly large in the areas of mother involvement with symbolic activity, it seems worth presenting them for discussion. Table 29.2 shows that in the middle-class families there was more joint attention on the child's activity with objects, that middle-class mothers were more likely to join in play with their children, and that there were large differences in the amount of time the children spent with representational material. (Median time for middle-class children, 14 per cent; for working-class children, 0.7 per cent).

We also found a class difference in the involvement of the mother in the child's Activity with Objects III (Fig. 29.4). For the working-class children, 84 per cent of these bouts are initiated by the child, 16 per cent by the mother. For the middle-class children, 53 per cent are initiated by the mother, 47 per cent by the child. For the middle-class children then, much of the Level III Activity with Objects consists of playing with complicated toys (e.g. workbenches where screws of different shapes have to be matched with appropriate holes), which involves

Table 29.1 Initiation of verbal interaction sequences

Child initiates		Mother initiates	
Child initiates game	11	Mother initiates game	6
Child comments on or shows object to mother	158	Mother comments on or shows object to child	38
Child comments on future/past event, people absent	12	Mother comments on future/past event, people absent	5
Child comments on own action or event	27	Mother comments on child's action/suggestion	185
Child asks for help	37	Mother comments on own action	12

Table 29.2 Differences between working-class and middle-class mother–child pairs: percentage of observation time spent in joint activities and with representational material (Mann-Whitney U-test)

	Working-class N = 13	Middle-class N = 11	u	
% of observation spent in joint attention to objects (median)	12.0	20.0	25.0	p<.01
% of observation spent in joint play with objects (median)	0.1	6.5	4.0	p<.01
% of observation time with representational material (median)	0.7	14.0	14.0	p<.01

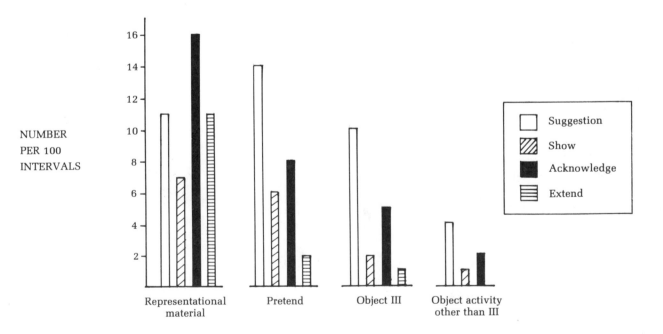

Figure 29.3. Frequency of mothers' positive comments in different types of activity (expressed per 100 intervals of each activity).

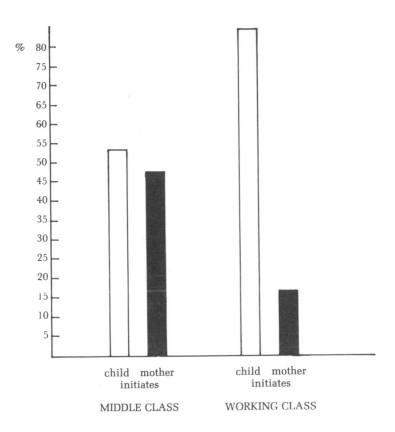

Figure 29.4. Percentage of bouts of Object Activity III initiated by mother and child: differences between social classes.

much direction and help from the mothers.

Discussion

There are considerable problems involved in any attempt to draw conclusions about what children may be learning from observations of their play. One approach is to examine the verbal interaction between mother and child in the contexts of the different activities. When the mother and child are looking at pictures or books together, we find that the mother's speech is characterised by features such as acknowledgement and extension of the child's utterances – features which studies of language development in children have emphasised as being particularly important (Cross, 1975). Evidence that supports and extends this point is provided in a recent study by Snow and her colleagues (1976): using a book-reading and free-play situation, it was found that the mother's speech was more complicated and elaborate in the book-reading situation than during free play. In another study, Bakker-Renes and Hoefnagel-Höhle (1974) compared six situations, of which three involved caretaking; the three others were playing, chatting after lunch, and reading a book. Again, it was found that mother's speech was most complex in the book-reading situation, as measured by length of

utterance and length of paraphrase.

It looks, then, as if joint attention to representational material provides a forum in which the verbal exchange between mother and child is particularly rich, and in which the child's span of attention is particularly long. And it is this situation, potentially valuable for the child's intellectual progress, which occurs much less frequently in the homes of the small groups of working-class children we looked at. Class differences in the way mothers expand and build on the 18-month-old child's interest in toys have also been demonstrated in another recent study (Lowe, 1975) using a more structured situation.

When we consider the greater time spent by the middle-class mothers in joint activity with representational material, and the differences in their involvement with guiding the children on complicated object activities, the general picture does suggest that the class differences in the parental conception of a guiding rôle, and the interest in teaching which has been reported for older children (e.g. Wootton's (1974) study of four-year-olds) may well be apparent by 18 months.

In conclusion, two points arise concerning the developmental significance of the activities and interaction we have been describing.

The first point concerns the question of context and early symbolic activity,

and two developmental issues. On the origins of symbolic play, the Russian claim that adult modelling is responsible for early symbolic activity has been mentioned; to test this one would have to follow individual children with meticulously close attention for the entire course of the early life (a procedure which not even Piaget can have found practicable). At the end of several of the observations we asked mothers about the incidents of symbolic play we had seen. In several cases they spontaneously described the symbolic play as originally demonstrated by adults. The question must remain open. Secondly, we have stressed that the loving mother–child relationship in nuclear families is the medium through which so much social learning (in the widest sense) is both taught and sought in play. It is thus important to attempt to judge the consequences of variations in the intensity and extent to which this opportunity for learning is exploited in different mother–child pairs. We may speculate on the consequences for M., who at 18 months spends 4 per cent of his time with his mother's attention on his activity, 28 per cent of whose interactions with his mother stem from her prohibiting his investigating and playing, whose mother's response to his presentation of objects is to ignore him or give the barest acknowledgement, whose mother rarely looks at books or pictures with him. What precisely are the developmental opportunities from which this experience excludes him?

If exchange with the mother is important for social learning at this early age, what are the implications of the differences in experience between a dependent first child, such as three of our sample who spent the whole day doing everything with their mothers (and by 24 months had even reached the stage of cooking stew and cakes) and a later born child whose interaction with his mother is much more fleeting and for whom it consists predominantly in the provision of food and comfort?

The final point is a warning to us on the issue of playing and learning, and the sorts of conclusions it is tempting to draw. When we examine these observations, there are two rather different sorts of thing we have described. First, there are actions by mothers that can be definitely described as *teaching* (in the terms of Wood *et al.*, 1976). Secondly, there is whatever the child is doing. This behaviour can be recorded, but whether or not it is an intentional act, and just what type of intentional act it is must remain a matter of construction. Whether or not a child is *learning* something is a question for which one can only have criteria *ex post facto*; and even if it is established that the child has learned something it is unclear whether what the child is *doing* is causally related to learning *ex post facto*. It is entirely possible that the child is learning when he is sitting there with a vacant expression. It is entirely possible that he is *not* learning when we see him performing a complex series of actions we have not observed him performing before. It is entirely possible that he is not learning when the mother is teaching, and that he is behaving in a way which he knows will placate her. However, it seems more sensible to assume that children learn the concepts of intentional action when teaching is organised in intentionalised action categories. Any assumptions we might make about an 18-month-old's 'private experiments' are much more dubious. The main difficulty in making progress in identifying such experiments and explaining their rôle in the development of human abilities is the difficulty of obtaining large enough samples of data to give us a reasonable chance to avoid building our explanatory findings into the descriptive categories which we use to record the data. Without this comprehensive sample of data we run the risk of being the theoretical victims of whatever 'transactions' we first happen to observe.

Acknowledgements
This work is supported by the Medical Research Council. We are grateful to the families in the sample for their generous help.

References
Bakker-Renes, H., Hoefnagel-Höhle, M. (1974) 'Situatie Verschillen in Taal Gebruik' ('Situation Differences in Language Use'), Master's thesis, Institute for General Linguistics, University of Amsterdam. (*Quoted by Snow, 1976.*)

Bruner, J. S. (1974) 'The nature and use of immaturity' in Connolly, K. and Bruner, J. S. (eds.) *The Growth of Competence*, Academic Press p.11.

Cross, T. (1975) 'Motherese: its association with rate of syntactic acquisition in young children', paper presented at the 3rd International Child Language Symposium, London, September, 1975.

El'konin, D. (1966) 'Symbolics and its functions in the play of children', *Soviet Education*, 8 (7), 35.

Fein, G. and Apfel, N. (1975) 'Patterns of play – time and place', paper presented at the Eastern Psychological Association Meeting, April, 1975.

Fradkina, F. I. (1946) *Psilhologii igri v rannem detsve (genetiches-kie kornie doshkol'noi igri)*, dissertation, Moscow.

Garvie, C. (1977) 'Play with language' in Tizard, B. and Harvey, D. (eds.) *Biology of Play*, Heinemann Medical Books.

Inhelder, B., Lezine, I., Sinclair, H. and Stambak, M. (1972) 'Les débuts de la fonction symbolique', *Archives de Psychologie*, 41, 187.

Lowe, M. (1975) 'Trends in the development of representational play in infants from one to three years; an observational study', *Journal of Child Psychology and Psychiatry*, 16, 33.

Piaget, J. (1962) *Play, Dreams and Imitation in Childhood*, Routledge & Kegan Paul; New York: Norton.

Sinclair, H. (1970) 'The transition from sensorimotor behaviour to symbolic activity', *Interchange*, 1, 119.

Snow, C. E. (1976) 'Mother's speech research: an overview' in Snow, E. and Ferguson, C. A. (eds.) *Talking to Children: Language Input and Acquisition*, Cambridge University Press.

Snow, C. E., Arlman-Rupp, A., Hassing, Y., Jose, J., Joosten, J. and Vorster, J. (1976) 'Mothers' speech in three social classes', *Journal of Psycholinguistic Research*, 5, 1.

Thorburn, M. (1938) *Child at Play*, Allen & Unwin.

Wood, D., Bruner, J. S. and Ross, G. (1976) 'The role of tutoring in problem-solving', *Journal of Child Psychology and Psychiatry*, 17, 89.

Wootton, A. J. (1974) 'Talk in the homes of young children', *Sociology*, 8, 277.

Discussion Guide P

Development of imaginative play

Allow at least 40 minutes for this discussion. The object for the group is the sharing and evaluating of information gained from your first-hand observations and play experiences with young children of fifteen months to two years during Activity 30. *Bring your observation records to the meeting.* Note that you will find it advantageous to sub-divide into small groups.

   Arrange to report individually according to the age of the children observed, starting with the youngest.

1 Read out the basic data first (to identify the child), and then a list of the toys available on this occasion.
2 Report examples of play under headings A to E of Activity 30, noting the mother's role in the play.
3 Report your own attempts to play with the child and his response to you.
4 Report any difficulties that you met with and how they were resolved.
5 Note similarities and major differences in the play records relating to:
   (a) age;
   (b) sex;
   (c) concentration on any particular type of play;
   (d) environmental factors, for example, space, furniture, frustrations etc.

Differences in environmental factors will provide a lead into the next topic for discussion.

Unit   3   Development of Imaginative Play – play with objects and
            'pretend play'

Discussion Guide Q

Role of the mother/care-giver in early development learning

Bring your observation records for Activity 30 to the meeting.
Allow at least 35 minutes for this discussion. *Read Paper 29 before this
discussion meeting.* The objective here is to discuss points raised in
Paper 29 relating to mother–child interaction and the role of the mother
in the young child's play life. Note particularly section (e) ('Mother's
initiations') in this paper and compare findings here with findings of
members of the group.

   Extend your discussion to the consideration of likely effects of social
disadvantages, including possible effects of inadequate mothering,
frequent change of care-giver, large family, over-crowding, lack of toys
and space to play.

   Consider the value of imaginative play in enabling the child to go
beyond the 'here and now'; to develop 'as if' situations and compare
them with reality; to think and plan in sequence and to reason.

   (a) Do you think the child gains from adult involvement in his early
       attempts to play imaginatively?
   (b) Does he need at least the expression of interest from familiar
       adults to reassure him that this is an acceptable form of behaviour?
       Would you go further than this?
   (c) What of the child who never receives any such form of
       encouragement?

Link with the work of language development in Units 1 and 2, and
consider whether interaction through play with the child could be a way
of involving parents in language development without making them
self-conscious about it. Check through your observation records to see if
you have any examples of language enhancing imaginative play or
imaginative play stimulating language. Is the adult's contribution needed
here? What developmental opportunities are likely to be missed if it is
not given, or is given without awareness of what is involved?

   As a child grows and develops his mental life becomes complex; his
ability to recall experience and to anticipate and plan develops along with
a wider range of language. Modules 5–8, dealing with the period two to
five years, will expand your knowledge and deepen your understanding
of the points raised here.

Module Five

Representation and Cognitive Development

The preceding modules of this seminar series, dealing with the development of infants from birth to two years, showed that their activities are for the most part of a sensory-motor kind, that is, they are confined to what is present to the senses. In order to plan activities with objects and events not present to the senses children must be able to recall and to anticipate, and this requires that they can represent in thought objects and events in their absence. Imagery is one way of representing reality, language is another.

The period from two to five years of age is marked by the growth of representational abilities. Two of these are symbolic play (make-believe play) and graphic representation (drawing and painting), both of which express imagery. When a child engages in make believe play he pretends something is other than it is in reality. He may pretend, for example, that a cardboard box is a truck. When he engages in this kind of play he imagines the object not present (the truck) and we can assume, therefore, that he can construct mental images of it. In his symbolic play a child may also imitate the actions of a person not present but whom he has seen engage in those actions in the past. For example, as he sits in the cardboard box he pretends to steer the truck and to change its gears. Thus we can assume that he can recall in imagery the actions of drivers he has seen. A child's first drawings are scribbles, a kind of sensory-motor exploration. Gradually the scribbles come to have meaning and the child will sometimes name the objects they represent, though they usually still appear indecipherable to adults. Yet later a child's drawings begin to resemble people and objects in however rudimentary a way and we are justified in assuming he can reconstruct through mental images the things he draws. Unit 1 in this module deals with aspects of symbolic play, while Unit 2 is concerned with the development of young children's drawings and paintings.

Unit 3 is concerned with the characteristics of thinking in early childhood. Bruner (Paper 33) describes cognitive development in terms of different modes of representation—enactive, iconic and symbolic representation. He shows how, in young children, the enactive and iconic modes predominate. It is important in reading Bruner's paper to be aware of the special ways in which he uses these terms. In everyday usage the word 'symbol' means something that stands for or denotes something else, in other words, any kind of representation. In Bruner's terminology representation through language is called 'symbolic' representation. He uses the term 'iconic representation' to refer to representation through imagery and 'enactive representation' to refer to representation through action. By contrast Piaget calls images 'symbols' and language 'signs'.

The remainder of Unit 3 deals with Piaget's account of thinking between the ages of two and five years. Paper 34 presents the main characteristics, while Paper 35 deals with one particular characteristic, egocentricity. In Paper 36 Donaldson describes some studies whose results challenge Piaget's claim that children under the age of seven years, on average, cannot take another person's point of view when it is different from their own, that is, that they think egocentrically. Donaldson's paper is important not only for these specific studies on egocentricity but also for the more general principle she puts forward that children's capabilities are greatest in contexts which, because they are familiar, make 'human sense' to them. This is a principle which has important educational implications discussed in Unit 4 (Paper 37).

Piaget's account of cognitive development is explanatory as well as descriptive. Whereas Unit 3 includes a description of some of the main characteristics of young children's thinking according to Piaget, Unit 4 deals with his explanation of how development proceeds. This aspect of his theory has some very important educational implications which are discussed in Paper 38.

Symbolic Play

- Read the introduction to Module 5 and then complete Activity 31
- Read Paper 30 and then compare your responses in Activity 31 with the arguments therein
- Read Paper 31
- Carry out Activity 32, which is designed to help you test your understanding of the difference between play and exploration explained in Papers 30 and 31
- Carry out Activity 33 which is designed to help you crystallize some ideas presented in Paper 31
- Carry out Activity 34 which should help you observe children's symbolic play and think about how best to provide for it
- Work through Discussion Guide R

Reading	35 mins.
Activities	175 mins.
Discussion	100 mins.
Total	310 mins.
	= 5 hrs. 10 mins.

Module Five   Paper 30

What is play?
Joan Tamburrini

There are two vital sets of questions about play confronting teachers of young children. The first concerns the importance of play in the curriculum: is it important and, if so, why? The second concerns the role of the teacher toward children's play: what kinds of facilities should she provide and should she intervene or participate in any way in children's play? The answers to the second set of questions depend to some extent on the answers to the first. We need to be clear about the importance of play to children's development if we are to make wise judgements about whether to facilitate it and how to enrich it. We cannot be clear about the importance of play to children's development, however, unless we are first of all clear about what play is and how it is different from other kinds of activity. Sometimes the word 'play' is applied rather indiscriminately to most of the activities in which young children engage in the nursery school, but if we do this we can neither understand the functions of play nor make effective decisions about how to cater for it.

Play is often described as a spontaneous activity. To say play is spontaneous, however, does not mean that an episode of play engaged in by one child cannot be initiated by another child or even by an adult, for clearly from common observation it often is. Almy (1966) distinguishes between spontaneous play and the kind of play evoked by materials which are so highly structured that they determine what the child does with them. What those who stress the spontaneity of play are drawing attention to is that play is unfettered, never obligatory. Coercion or even gentle persuasion will not lead a child to play unless he wants to. Perhaps a better word than spontaneity is voluntariness. Children freely engage in play.

Another characteristic of play emphasized by many psychologists and philosophers is that it is pleasurable. However, sometimes play is the way a child will externalize an emotional problem. In such cases it may seem strange to say play is pleasurable, for the emotional experience which a child expresses in his play may be a painful one. For example, a child may express in his domestic play his jealousy of a baby brother or sister and his fear that this new arrival has usurped his place in his parents' affections. Jealousy and fear are not pleasurable emotions. Freud, who described play as serving a pleasure principle, included relief from pain or tension as a kind of pleasure. When a child make-believes in play that he is the baby or that the new baby no longer exists, he com-

pensates for the reality and in doing so finds relief from his painful emotions. Thus we may say that play is nearly always pleasurable in the strictest sense of the word and always pleasurable if, like Freud, we think of relief from pain or tension as a kind of pleasure.

It would appear then that there is general agreement that these three qualities, spontaneity, voluntariness and pleasure, do for the most part describe play. Unfortunately they do not help us to differentiate play from other kinds of activities. People sometimes derive great pleasure from their work and engage in it voluntarily. Children often spontaneously begin to explore a phenomenon and appear to enjoy what they are doing, but, as Hutt's work discussed below indicates, play and exploration differ in certain important respects. It is important to determine in what way play is unlike other activities.

Dearden (1968) claims that play is different from other kinds of activities in that it is non-serious. At first glance this may seem a puzzling claim for three reasons. First, sometimes emotional concerns are expressed in play, particularly play of the compensatory kind discussed above, which are very serious to the child. Secondly, many psychologists and educationalists consider play to be of great importance to development. Bruner (1975) writes, 'Although we do not yet know how important play is for growing up we do know that it is a serious business'. Thirdly, children often become engrossed in their play: they would appear to be treating their play seriously.

However, by 'non-serious' Dearden does not mean unimportant or trivial. Nor does he mean that children do not become engrossed in their play. He is referring to an aspect of play which other philosophers and psychologists have drawn attention to in different ways and which concerns children's purposes. When he plays a child's purpose is not to find out about an aspect of external reality, not to learn something new, even though new learning may well be an incidental outcome of play. Play is 'for its own sake': it is not goal-directed. For example, if a child takes a cardboard cylinder and, pretending it is a feeding bottle, puts it to the mouth of the doll she is nursing, her purpose is not to learn more about the nature of cylinders or even about feeding babies. Some authorities would claim that through play of this kind a child does learn something about cylinders. This is no doubt true in many cases, but the point that is being stressed here is that finding out about cylinders is not the child's purpose. It is in this sense that Dearden seems to be claiming that play is 'non-serious': it is not 'for real'.

Piaget (1951) identifies the same characteristic of play when he calls it primarily an assimilatory activity. In order to understand what he means by this it is first necessary to give a brief explanation of three terms which are central to Piaget's theory. These are 'schema', 'assimilation' and 'accommodation'. A schema is a psychological organization of past experiences: it encompasses a pattern of activity with respect to certain kinds of objects or events and a set of ideas concerning a certain aspect of reality. Assimilation and accommodation are the central processes responsible for intellectual development. Assimilation occurs when an individual attempts to incorporate an aspect of reality into an existing schema, that is when he carries out an established pattern of activity without modification on an object or interprets something new in terms of what he already knows without modifying his ideas. In reality some modification is nearly always necessary. Objects frequently resist a particular kind of action on them, by being too heavy or an awkward shape, for example, and events can often not be understood unless one changes one's ideas. Accommodation is said to occur when a schema is modified in some way.

While most play must, therefore, involve an element of accommodation, it is, according to Piaget, primarily an assimilatory activity. In practice play a child repeats a pattern of activity (assimilates) with little modification (accommodation). His purpose in practice play is to repeat what he can already do for the pure pleasure of mastery. In symbolic or make-believe play a child makes aspects of the real world subserve his purposes. The cardboard cylinder that the small girl pretends is a feeding bottle in her doll play may well represent something quite different in another episode of her play. In her play the cylinder can mean anything she wants it to mean: she assimilates it to her purposes. Thus symbolic play is a different kind of activity from those in which a child's purposes are to find out about an aspect of reality such as the qualities of a cylinder. In the latter case she would need to accommodate to it, to adjust her ideas and actions to the nature of cardboard cylinders.

In exploration a child is concerned with finding out about objects and events in reality, whereas, as stated above, this is not a child's purpose when he plays. Corinne Hutt (1966) carried out a study which illustrates this distinction between play and exploration. The subjects were all nursery school children between the ages of three and five years. They were brought to a relatively familiar room containing a novel object, a box on four brass legs with a movable lever ending in a blue wooden ball, and some familiar toys. Each child had six sessions of 10 minutes in the room where his activities were observed and recorded. It was found that, in general, children approached the novel object first and explored it by looking, touching and manipulating the lever. When a child had thoroughly explored the novel object he then sometimes used it in symbolic play, for example by pretending it was a bridge or a seat. 'It was only when the child had apparently learned all there was to know about the object that it was incorporated in play activities, and any further learning was purely incidental.'

Garvey (1977) uses the expression 'non-literal' to refer to the non-seriousness of play. She draws attention to the fact that the same activity may be performed seriously or non-seriously, that is, as play.

> If we see someone running and another person running a short way behind him, we would probably see these events as related and say that the first person was being chased by the second or that he was fleeing from the second. We might use other behavioural clues to infer guilt or anger on the part of the runners, to decide perhaps that one was a thief, and thus construct a 'reasonable explanation' of their actions. This interpretation represents a *literal* orientation to the scene. (It might be changed to another literal interpretation if in the next second we saw a rhinoceros charge around the corner after the runners.) But what if we heard one of the runners laugh or noted that they were smiling? Then we would likely decide that we were not witnessing a 'real' pursuit, but that they were playing – or 'just' playing, as we usually put it. We would have attributed a *non-literal* orientation to the runners and constructed a non-literal interpretation of what we saw.

These differences between play and other kinds of activities to which Dearden, Piaget, Hutt and Garvey have drawn attention are important to a teacher, whose decisions about how to relate to a child in the context of his play should rest on a clear discrimination of these differences.

To say that play 'is for its own sake', that is not goal-directed like exploration, does not mean that it is unrelated to cognitive development. In the following paper evidence is discussed that play might be related to various aspects of cognitive development, particularly creativity.

References
Almy, M. (1966) 'Spontaneous play: an avenue for intellectual development', *Bulletin of the Institute of Child Study*, vol. 28, no. 2.
Bruner, J. (1975) 'The importance of play' in Lewin, R. (ed.) *Child Alive*, Temple Smith.
Dearden, R. (1968) *The Philosophy of Primary Education*, Routledge & Kegan Paul.
Garvey, C. (1977) *Play*, Fontana.
Hutt, C. (1966) 'Exploration and play in children' in Herron, R. E. and Sutton-Smith, B., *Child's Play*, Wiley: 1971.
Piaget, J. (1951) *Play, Dreams and Imitation in Childhood*, Routledge & Kegan Paul.

Teaching style in relation to play in the nursery school
Joan Tamburrini

There are a number of ways in which teachers can and do provide for play and relate to children in the context of their play. These ways can be categorized as four major styles which will be examined in this paper. As will be shown, each style involves different kinds of assumptions about and attitudes toward play. It will be argued that some of these assumptions are not supported by empirical evidence, and that some of the attitudes devalue play and implicitly fail to recognize some of the ways in which it is important to children's development.

1. Non-intervening style

The teacher who adopts this style frequently makes a rich provision of materials for children's play, but thereafter she adopts a comparatively bland and passive role, intervening in children's activities only to offer comfort when things go wrong, to provide more materials children might seem to need, and to resolve social conflict. The major characteristic of this style is that the teacher does not relate to the children in their play in any way that appears to be concerned with their intellectual development.

There are a number of assumptions that can lead a teacher to adopt this style. One may be the pseudo-Freudian assumption that the main function of play is as an outlet for emotional concerns and that it has little relationship to intellectual development. This notion is something of a distortion of psychoanalytic theory, but is, nevertheless, frequently reflected in nursery school practice. The assumption that play has little relationship to intellectual development is not valid in the light of experimental evidence. These experimental studies have been of three kinds. The first kind involves attempts to show a correlation between quality of children's play and the levels of their performance in other kinds of activities.

A study by Hutt and Bhavnani (1972) was of this kind. They investigated a sample of 48 children who were subjects of the earlier investigation by Hutt reported in Paper 30. The new study by Hutt and Bhavnani took place five years later when the children were aged between seven and ten years. It attempted to discover whether the children who in the first study played in many imaginative ways subsequently scored more highly on creativity tests (Wallach and Kogan) than the other children. These children did, in fact, achieve higher scores on the creativity tests especially when scored for originality. One must be careful, however, not to conclude that there is a cause–effect relationship between quality of play and subsequent performance on a creativity test. It may be simply that children who, for whatever reason, are most 'creative' reflect this both in the quality of their play and in their performance in creativity tests.

Firmer evidence comes from the second kind of experimental study. These are studies which have investigated the competencies of children after they have been exposed to adult tutoring aimed at increasing the quality of their symbolic play. Several of these studies have produced evidence that children tutored by adults in symbolic play activities have subsequently achieved higher scores on tests of creativity, for example, Feitelson and Ross (1973), and Rosen (1974). One study by Golomb and Cornelius (1977) even found that children exposed to such tutoring subsequently achieved higher levels on Piaget's test for conservation of quantity as compared with children tutored in constructional activities.

An experimental study carried out by Sylva (1977) was of a third kind. She set out to examine the relative contribution of play experience and adult demonstration on subsequent competence in a problem-solving task. The children were aged three to five years and the problem-solving task was to open a box placed out of reach. The solution to the task involved constructing a rigid tool from two sticks and a clamp near at hand. The children were divided into three groups. Prior to testing on the problem-solving task one group was allowed free play with a number of sticks and clamps, the second observed an adult first demonstrate one clamp tightened onto the middle of a stick and second demonstrate the construction of an elongated tool by joining together two sticks with a clamp, and the third group simply watched the adult tighten one clamp onto a stick. Sylva found that more children in the 'observe-principle' group solved the problem immediately, but more children in this group also opted out. Their approach seemed to be an 'all or nothing' one. By contrast children allowed to play reached the solution in a step-by-step fashion.

A pair of interrelated assumptions which may also lead a teacher to adopt a non-intervening style is that play is a natural and universal phenomenon and that if an adult attempts to intervene or participate in children's play she will inhibit it. Feitelson (1977) claims that it is only true to say that play is universal in the sense that among activities like mime, dance, games of chance and competitive activities, which play in its widest sense may be said to encompass, there is at least one found in every human society. However, she shows that the particular category of play called symbolic, make-believe or representational play is by no means found universally. Anthropological observations suggest it is almost non-existent in some communities and that in those communities adults either fail to encourage it or positively discourage it. Feitelson quotes El'konin's claim that symbolic play activity does not develop spontaneously but instead arises in interaction with adults who suggest it.

This is in direct conflict with the assumption that if adults participate or intervene in children's play they will inhibit it. While it is reasonable to assume that adults inhibit children's play if they intervene in a way that is clumsy and does not take its cues from the children, there is evidence to support El'konin's claim and to suggest that adult participation, providing that it is sensitive, can facilitate and enhance children's play. Paper 29, in the section on development from birth to two years, describes an investigation by Dunn and Wooding into the effect of mothers' involvement in the play of their eighteen-month to two-year-old children. The effects of the mothers' involvement were positive; the length of the play episodes was significantly greater than when the mother was not paying attention.

A number of studies have been carried out with older children into the effects of adult tutoring. Freyburg (1973) hypothesized that lower-class kindergarten children who receive training by an adult in imaginative play will play more imaginatively than a control group of children who do not receive such training. Her subjects were 80 five-year-old children evenly divided into experimental and control groups. The children in the experimental group were given eight twenty-minute training sessions in small groups of four children at a time. They were taken to a room equipped with a large table on which were spread a variety of fabrics, pipe-cleaners, clay, Playdoh, blocks, Tinkertoy sets and a wide variety of wooden shapes. During each of the eight sessions the investigator introduced a theme based on the children's interests and began to enact small plots in which pipe-cleaner figures were made to talk and to engage in make-believe roles. The children were encouraged to adopt a role using play equipment of their own choosing. The experimental group improved significantly in the imaginativeness of their play and in the degree of concentration shown in their play. These changes persisted two months after the training had ceased. Smilansky (1968) tried out the effects on Israeli children of adult play-tutoring, excursions and a combination of excursions and adult play-tutoring. Excursions had very little effect on the quality of subsequent symbolic play. Adult play-tutoring had some effect, but the most effective programme was the combination of excursions and play-tutoring.

By contrast Tizard (1977) reports that in nursery schools where the adults adopted passive roles the children's play was frequently of short duration, poorly elaborated and involved a narrow sampling of the available materials.

2. Pre-structuring style

This is a style in which, either by direction and/or by providing highly structured materials which virtually dictate to a child what he can do, children's play is to a great extent prescribed by the adult. Examples of this style are to be found in some Montessori nursery schools more common in the United States than in Great Britain. In these schools Montessori's materials are provided and the children are allowed to use them only in prescribed ways. A child is not allowed, for example, to use blocks intended for seriation to build a construction of his own invention. If the prescription is too firm it is probably inappropriate to call the children's ensuing activities 'play'.

This is a style which devalues children's symbolic play. We praise a child's play as imaginative when he is inventive, thinking up different themes and using materials in a variety of ways, as in the training for imaginative play carried out by Freyburg in her study discussed above. Children cannot easily be inventive if adults or materials prescribe what they can do. Pulaski (1973) has investigated the relationship between degree of structure of play materials and the imaginativeness of children's play. Five categories of play material were used: paints, clay, construction materials, dolls and dressing-up clothes. Each category included highly structured materials matched with equivalent materials which were minimally structured. For example, the minimally structured materials in the dolls' category were two rag dolls in simple gingham costumes representing male and female and the highly structured materials were two 'Barbie' dolls, one dressed as a bride, and a 'Ken' doll in a dark suit.* A plastic case held assorted clothes and accessories for both male and female dolls. There were also a G.I. doll in army uniform and a G.I. Joe diver doll in an underwater suit and helmet. Pulaski's hypothesis that the minimally structured materials help to produce greater imaginativeness in children's play than the highly structured ones was confirmed. When they played with the minimally structured materials the children produced a far greater variety of themes than they did with the highly structured materials.

Another drawback of some highly structured materials is that they tend to be matched to children at a specific level of development and not to be used spontaneously by children at other levels. Olson (1970) devised a highly structured educational toy to teach children the concept of diagonality. He found that only children who had mastered the diagonal tended to use the material, repeating what they had learned in their play. Most of the younger children who had not yet acquired the concept chose not to play with the toy at all.

*Barbie and Ken dolls are very realistic.

3. Redirecting style

Teachers who adopt this style, like the teachers who adopt the non-intervening style, often provide a diversity of materials and the children are allowed to generate spontaneous play activities. Unlike the non-intervening teachers, however, they are highly active in the context of the children's play. The major characteristic of the redirecting style is that how the teacher intervenes is based on her own preconceptions rather than on any prior assessment of what a child is paying attention to in his play. A teacher in this category may, for example, intervene in an episode of play with blocks by asking the children to measure the height of the structure they have built, when, in fact, they may well not be concerned with the height of the structure.

The redirecting style frequently includes the channelling of play activities by the teacher into other kinds of activities. These may include exploration and requiring the children to record the outcome of their activities in some way.

Like the pre-structuring style the redirecting style implicitly devalues children's spontaneous play and fails to recognize its importance in development, particularly in intellectual development.

4. Extending style

This style also involves the provision of a diversity of materials and spontaneous play with them is encouraged. The teacher adopting this style also participates with the children in their play in ways that are concerned with their intellectual development. She does so, however, only after first ascertaining the nature of the children's themes in their play and her strategies are concerned with helping them elaborate these themes. She may do this in a number of ways, for example, by judicious questioning, by suggestion or by providing more materials.

Of these four teaching styles it is clearly the extending style which would seem to reflect the greatest valuing of play in terms of its relationship to intellectual development. There is a good case for arguing, therefore, that the extending style should be the predominant one in a teacher's repertoire. This is not to suggest, however, that it is a style which should invariably be adopted. There may be occasions when a child's play reflects a deep emotional concern into which it might be undesirable to intrude at that particular time. In such instances a non-intervening strategy would seem to be appropriate. There are occasions too when children are engaged in group make-believe play in which they are being highly inventive and the themes of which show considerable elaboration. On these occasions it could be at best superfluous and at worst inhibiting for a teacher to intervene.

It could be argued that there are some situations when even the redirecting style should be adopted. Tizard (1977) reports examples of play which was 'repetitive and of a rather low level'. One of her examples is of a child running round saying 'I'm a Dalek'.* It is hardly surprising that play with this theme is of a low level, for in the television programme in which they appear Daleks' actions are repetitive. There is a good case for arguing that it would be less educationally profitable to try to get a child to elaborate a Dalek theme than to attempt to redirect his play.

Equally if not more important than the styles themselves are the attitudes and assumptions from which they spring. It has been shown that some of these assumptions are, in the light of empirical evidence, misconceptions. Any categorization in terms of teaching styles of what teachers do is bound to overlook some subtle differences in the kinds of provision they make and in the kinds of actions they take. But teachers' attitudes and assumptions are inevitably reflected in their pedagogical practices and different attitudes and assumptions lead to different practices.

These practices will, in turn, be reflected in the children's activities. The kinds of activity children are likely to engage in with prestructured materials are likely to be very different from those they would have pursued with less structured materials, as Pulaski's investigation revealed. Tizard reports a study where even the removal of table toys led to an increase in the amount of social play. Possibly the most dangerous misconception is the idea that a curriculum can be neutral, that we can so arrange matters in schools that children will develop spontaneously in directions natural to them as individuals. A curriculum can never be neutral. It is constructed by people with ideas about what is desirable and undesirable in the educational process and these ideas are reflected both wittingly and unwittingly in the curriculum and thence in what the children do.

References

Feitelson, D. (1977) 'Cross cultural studies of representational play' in Tizard, B. and Harvey, D. (eds.) *The Biology of Play*, Heinemann.
Feitelson, D. and Ross, G. S. (1973) 'The neglected factor – play', *Human Development*, 16, 202–24.
Freyburg, J. T. (1973) 'Increasing the imaginative play of urban disadvantaged kindergarten children through systematic training', in Singer, J. L. *The Child's World of Make-believe*, Academic Press.
Golomb, C. and Cornelius, C. B. (1977) 'Symbolic play and its cognitive significance', *Dev. Psychol.*, 13, 246–52.
Hutt, C. and Bhavnani, R. (1972) 'Predictions from play', *Nature*, no. 237.
Olson, D. R. (1970) *Cognitive Development: the Child's Acquisition of Diagonality*, Academic Press.
Pulaski, M. A. (1973) 'Toys and imaginative play' in Singer, J. L. (op. cit.).
Rosen, C. (1974) 'The effects of socio-dramatic play on problem-solving behaviour among culturally disadvantaged pre-school children', *Child Development*, 45, 920–7.
Smilansky, S. (1968) *The Effects of Sociodramatic Play on Disadvantaged Pre-school Children*, Wiley.
Sylva, K. (1977) 'Play and learning', in Tizard, B. and Harvey, D. (eds.) (op. cit.).
Tizard, B. (1977) 'Play: the child's way of learning?' in Tizard, B. and Harvey, D. (eds.) (op. cit.).

*A 'Dalek' is a robot appearing in a science-fiction television programme.

Discussion Guide R

1   Examine as a group your appraisals of the examples given by Manning and Sharp (Activity 32). Look for common agreement on which examples were of play and which of exploration. Try to resolve any disagreements. This should entail giving your reasons for categorizing a description as play or as exploration. Manning and Sharp call some of their examples of activities with sand and water 'exploratory play'. Do you think this term is helpful or not? What are your reasons?

2   Briefly examine the factors influencing play favourably and unfavourably (Activity 33). What educational implications would you suggest follow from your findings?

3   Critically appraise as a group your observations of children's play made in Activity 34 and your suggestions regarding how you could have related to the children in these episodes. Note points of agreement and disagreement. Make sure you give reasons for your judgements and, where possible, relate these to the paper presented in this unit.

You should allow about 20 minutes for each of topics 1 and 2. You will need at least 1 hour for topic 3.

Young Children's Drawings and Paintings

- Read Paper 32, which describes the major changes in young children's graphic representation and sets out various attempts to explain them
- Carry out Activity 35. This requires you to give children a task which is taken from Piaget's work. It will give you first-hand experience of this kind of experimentation and of the kind of data discussed in Paper 32 that Piaget uses to support his claims
- Carry out Activity 36. This, like the preceding activity, will give you experience of administering an experimental task, taken (this time) from Goodnow's work and again discussed in Paper 32
- In both these activities you should make sure that you have established rapport with the children before testing them. It may be possible to carry out both activities on the same visit, but you should not do this at the expense of tiring or coercing the children. Arrange a second visit if necessary
- Work through Discussion Guide S

Reading	40 mins.
Activities	240 mins.
Discussion	60 mins.
Total	340 mins.
	= 5 hrs. 40 mins.

Why young children paint and draw as they do
Joan Tamburrini

Psychologists have appraised the development of young children's drawings and paintings in three ways: first, they have described what children do at various ages and have noted the changes; second, they have tried to discover children's intentions and how these differ at different stages; and third, they have tried to interpret what children do in terms of psychological processes. There is a fair degree of agreement in the first and second cases. It is with respect to the interpretation of young children's drawings in terms of psychological processes that one finds differences.

Very young children, even before two years of age, begin to scribble. It is easy to conclude from a superficial inspection of these scribbles that they are all random and meaningless, but a closer examination of the scribbling of numbers of children over an age range suggests that order and meaning of some sort emerges out of randomness and that there are changes in what and how children scribble which follow a developmental sequence.

At about four years of age, although in drawing as in other activities there is a range of individual differences, children's drawings begin to look less like scribbles and become identifiable to the observer as expressing aspects of external reality. This is not to say that these early representations are naturalistic. On the contrary, children draw human figures without trunks, with hair unattached to the head, possibly with two limbs, usually the arms, missing, and perhaps with the nose placed above the eyes. Gradually, however, these characteristics disappear and children's drawings begin to resemble a little more what they represent. This process of change is a gradual one and, of course, much more detailed.

A number of psychologists and artists have described young children's scribbles, pattern making and early representations of the human figure and of objects. Their accounts differ mainly in terms of emphasis. Jameson (1968) emphasizes the preponderance of the oval. This shape emerges from early random scribbles and is then repeated by children, first in more intentional scribbles, and then as the basis for representations of many kinds, of birds, cats, houses, for example, but above all of human beings. Kellogg (1969) gives particular emphasis to the emergence of the 'mandala' and 'radials'. The mandala is a circular or ovoid shape overlaid by intersecting lines while the radial is a circular or ovoid shape from the circumference of which lines radiate. Kellogg says that these shapes predominate after the early scribbling stage and first involve combines of shapes which children have explored separately at an earlier stage. The mandala and radials are combines of circles and lines. At first the mandala and radial stand by themselves, the children simply repeating them with some variation. Subsequently these shapes become the bases for representations of people and things: the mandala may become part of a human figure while radials become spiders, suns, flowers and human hands. Eng (1931) emphasizes the development of scribbles from wavy scribbling to circular scribbling to variegated scribbling. The latter includes zig-zag lines, straight lines and cross-over lines. Kellogg's account is based on the study of some 100 000 children's drawings, whereas Eng's study is of one child.

These accounts of children's drawing are descriptive. A second way of appraising young children's drawings and paintings has been in terms of their intentions. There is fairly common agreement concerning the more general characteristics of children's intentions as they develop from the earliest scribblings. The first scribbles are really a form of sensory-motor exploration. Gradually they are given meaning by the child, but, at first, the same basic scribble is given several meanings. Steveni (1968) gives an example of the same basic scribble representing situations ranging from a motor car crash to 'a snake biting Mummy'. At the next stage which normally emerges between three and four years of age children give specific meanings to specific scribbles. They are still not clearly recognizable to the observer as representations of aspects of external reality but become more so when a child interprets for an adult what he has drawn or painted. At this stage children often begin to make marks on paper without having a clear intention of what they will represent, but what has begun as sensory-motor exploration changes in mid-stream when what a child has drawn so far suggests to him an object or theme and this then directs the remainder of his drawing. If at this stage a child is asked by an adult what he is drawing, he may well reply, 'I don't know because I haven't finished yet'. At the next stage children decide what they are going to draw before they begin, and at this stage they are able to tell an adult what they intend.

The major differences among the various commentators on children's drawings and paintings are a matter of explanation of the psychological states and processes which give rise to developmental differences. These explanations are of three kinds. First, there are interpretations based on the intrinsic properties of forms and the way in which children perceive these. The major proponents of this type of interpretation are Arnheim (1954) and Kellogg (op. cit.). Second, there is the explanation of children's drawings in terms of the development of their concepts of space by Piaget and Inhelder (1963). Third, children's drawings have been explained in terms of the strategies they adopt in planning and ordering them (for example, Freeman, 1977, Goodnow, 1977). Arnheim claims that young children's drawings are not attempts to copy specific objects in the real world, but are generalized representations and therefore contain only some of the properties of the original. It is for this reason, for example, that the drawings of hands on the human figure by young children seldom have the correct number of fingers: children are less concerned with a hand having five fingers than they are with the fact that it is a spreading form. Arnheim considers that the aspects that children select are determined in part by the form of the original. What the child selects is the essence of the original and what he omits is less essential. In the case of the human figure, for example, Arnheim considers that its essence is its verticality while its horizontal aspects are less essential and this accounts for the fact that young children's drawings of the human figure are more likely to include legs but omit arms than vice versa.

Kellogg suggests that there are two major factors that determine what children draw and paint. The first is a concern for order and balance. Children discover and repeat forms which are intrinsically 'good', that is which have order and balance. This accounts, she claims, for the prevalence of the mandala and radial. They are forms which are pleasing because of the balance in them. Our perceptual apparatus, she proposes, is inherently attuned to perceive and appreciate such forms. This explanation does not account for the changes in children's drawings and paintings. The second major factor in Kellogg's explanation is an attempt to do so. She suggests that at any one stage children's drawings include elements characteristic of an earlier stage. An example is when a radial which has previously stood on its own as a spider or the sun is used to represent human hands.

Unfortunately there have been no experimental investigations known to me to test the validity of Arnheim's and Kellogg's interpretations. By contrast both the explanation of Piaget and Inhelder of some of the features of children's drawings and the work reported by Goodnow on children's strategies are supported by experimental evidence. This is not to say that their interpretations are entirely correct and that Kellogg's and Arnheim's are not. These various explanations of why children draw as they do are not, for the most part, contradictory. To some extent they complement each other.

Between three and four years of age, on average, children's drawings and paintings begin to resemble what they are intended to represent. Thereafter they begin to display changes sufficiently marked and universal to be thought of as stages. Piaget and Inhelder use Luquet's terminology to categorize these changes in terms of three principal stages (1) synthetic incapacity, (2) intellectual realism and (3) visual realism.

Drawings characterized by synthetic incapacity begin to emerge on the average at between three and four years of age. The predominant characteristic of this stage is that some elements of a drawing are not arranged as they are in reality but in more bizarre and idiosyncratic ways. It is this apparent inability of the child to synthesize the elements in his drawings which led Luquet to call the stage one of synthetic incapacity. Examples of synthetic incapacity are particularly evident in children's early drawings of the human figure. Children commonly draw arms and legs attached to the head rather than the trunk and frequently there is no trunk. The facial features may be arranged in bizarre ways, for example with the mouth above the nose rather than below it. An inability to order and arrange elements as they are in reality is also found in young children's drawings of objects like houses and vehicles. Luquet gives the example of a child's drawing of a house in which the roof projects into the main structure instead of above it.

The next stage, that of intellectual realism, begins to appear at five to six years of age. Children's drawings now show a pictorial synthesis but the arrangement of elements still appears somewhat strange to adult eyes. These arrangements now reflect not the child's inability to synthesize but his attempt to draw everything that he knows is there. Thus he will draw a motor car in profile but with all four wheels visible. Similarly people in profile are drawn with two eyes, and a rider on horseback is drawn with both legs to be seen on one side of the horse.

Transparencies are a second characteristic of intellectual realism. For example, children draw houses in which the occupants are seen as though the walls are transparent, vehicles in which the entire figures of the driver and his passengers are visible, and human figures whose clothes are transparent. Luquet gives examples of children's 'X-ray' drawings of food in the stomach, a duck in its egg and potatoes in the ground.

A third characteristic of intellectual realism is expansion. For example, a house with both its sides as well as its front elevation may be drawn, looking in fact like a three-dimensional cut-out of a house expanded two-dimensionally.

It is not until eight or nine years of age on the average that children reach the stage of 'visual realism'. At this stage children's drawings are clearly attempts to take perspective, distance and proportions into account.

Luquet explains the differences among these three stages in terms of children's manual dexterity and their spans of attention. The characteristics of drawings at the stage of synthetic incapacity reflect, he claims, both clumsiness and limited powers of attention. This is not an entirely satisfactory explanation. While limitations of attention and manual control might account for some of the differences between earlier and later drawings they cannot adequately explain why certain differences are so universal.

Piaget and Inhelder explain the differences among the three stages in terms of the development of children's spatial concepts. Their investigations show, they claim, that young children first discriminate topological properties. It is not until they are seven or more that they discriminate Euclidean and projective relationships. Topological properties include proximity, order, enclosure and continuity. Euclidean properties include angularity, parallelism and distance. Projective relationships involve perspective. A square and a triangle differ in terms of their Euclidean properties but both possess the same topological property of being closed figures. One way of being clear about the difference is to imagine a rubber sheet on which are drawn a square enclosing a circle and next to them an equilateral triangle, and then to imagine the rubber sheet being stretched in a vertical direction. The figures would then become distorted: the circle would become an ellipse, the equilateral triangle would become an isosceles triangle and the square would become a rectangle whose top and bottom sides were shorter than the remaining two sides. In other words some of the Euclidean properties of the figures would be changed. The topological properties of the figures, however, would remain the same: the new rectangle would enclose the ellipse just as the square had enclosed the circle, and proximity would still be a feature of these and the triangle.

The investigations carried out by Piaget and Inhelder into the development of children's spatial concepts are too numerous to cover in their entirety in this paper. The following is one example particularly relevant to development in early childhood. Children between the ages of two and seven were asked to copy a number of shapes. These included, for example: (1) a large irregular shape with a small circle outside but close to it; (2) the same irregular shape with a small circle inside it and close to its boundary; (3) the same irregular shape with the small circle astride the boundary; (4) a large circle; (5) a square; (6) an equilateral triangle; (7) two circles 1 centimetre apart; (8) two intersecting circles; (9) an equilateral triangle containing a circle tangential to the three sides; (10) a vertical/horizontal cross; (11) an oblique cross.

Until the age of three, or thereabouts, the children produce scribbles showing little variation whatever the model. This is followed by Stage 1 which lasts until about 4 years of age. At this stage the scribbles vary according to whether the model is an open or closed shape, for example a circle (closed) or a cross (open). However, circles are not distinguished from squares and triangles and all three tend to be drawn as irregular but closed shapes. The child at this stage also represents the enclosed circles as enclosed shapes and his drawings attempt to reproduce proximity and overlapping. Thus the topological features of openness, closedness, enclosure, proximity and overlapping are represented. Towards the end of this stage some attention to Euclidean properties begins to emerge. Curved shapes begin to be distinguished from straight-sided ones, though the latter, for example the square and the triangle, are not distinguished from each other but are given straight sides without regard for how many.

Stage 2 starts at about the age of four and is marked by a progressive differentiation of Euclidean shapes. The angles and even the dimensions of shapes are taken into account. The square is distinguished from the triangle as is the circle from the ellipse. The two crosses are distinguished marking the discovery of oblique lines. The child at this stage is unable, however, to represent correctly the points of contact of circumscribed figures.

Stage 3 begins at about six years of age. All the problems are now overcome and the child can reproduce correctly a composite figure such as a circle emerging from a triangle at three places.

Piaget and Inhelder claim that this development from an understanding of topological features to an increasing understanding of Euclidean ones is reflected in children's spontaneous drawings. Thus if we examine children's drawings at the stage of synthetic incapacity we find that Euclidean relationships are ignored and that topological properties are beginning to be represented only when the simplest shapes are involved. The property of enclosure is clearly indicated in the case of simple shapes but errors arise with more complex shapes, and it is for this reason, they suggest, that we find eyes outside the head in a drawing of the human figure and a roof of a house projecting into it. Elements of continuity and discontinuity are evident in broad outline, but in a drawing of a human figure, for example, parts are juxtaposed instead of being continuously linked together. The relationship of order is in a primitive state so that one sometimes finds a reversal of left to right and upper to lower orders as when a child draws a tail on the side of a dog's head or the nose above the eyes in a human face.

At the stage of intellectual realism topological relationships are represented correctly. Proximities are correct so that limbs are attached to the trunk in drawings of the human figure. The relationships of order and enclosure are clear. In fact it is because the child adheres so strongly to these topological properties that, Piaget and Inhelder claim, one finds at this stage characteristics like expansion and transparencies. Expansions reflect a concern with order and transparencies reflect the importance the child gives to enclosure.

The stage of intellectual realism also sees the beginning of attention to Euclidean relationships: straight lines, angles, circles, squares and other geometric figures make their appearance in children's drawings but as separate elements. They are not integrated into a whole in complex drawings. Thus drawings of a head in profile but with two eyes visible are typical of this stage but are at variance with Euclidean relationships.

Projective relationships are also beginning to be understood, but children cannot yet represent them in a coherent way. Thus, we find that different elements in their drawings will be represented from different points of view which are uncoordinated. For example, trees may be drawn bordering each side of a path as though they are lying down and facing in opposite directions, or a road with its crossings and centre line may be drawn in such a way that it resembles an aerial view while on it are vehicles drawn in profile.

It is not until the age of eight or nine years on the average that intellectual realism gives way to visual realism, when children's drawings resemble more accurately things as they look. These more naturalistic drawings reflect an ability to represent Euclidean and projective relationships, so that distance, proportion and perspective are all taken into account.

The stage of intellectual realism is sometimes described as one in which children draw what they know rather than what they see, in contrast to the stage of visual realism when their drawings resemble what they see. This is not an entirely satisfactory description of intellectual realism. It seems a more plausible account of some aspects of young children's drawings than of others. When children draw X-ray houses and people or a vehicle in profile with all four wheels showing they seem to be drawing what they know to be there. But what are we to make of 'tadpole' drawings of the human figure in which there is apparently no trunk? It would be bizarre to suggest children see human beings without trunks and equally strange to claim that they do not know that human beings possess trunks. A more plausible explanation of these tadpole figures has been given in terms of the way children plan their drawings.

Freeman (1977) explains the omission of a trunk in children's 'tadpole' figure drawings in terms of a psychological phenomenon known as 'end-anchoring'. This is the term given to our tendency to focus more attention on the beginning and end of a sequence than on the middle elements. Young children, he found, drew in order head and legs and by 'end-anchoring' on them generate the 'tadpole' figure.

Goodnow (1977) also investigated sequence in children's organization of the elements in their drawings. She observed 'tadpole' figure drawings by 79 Australian pre-school children. Of these 68 children started with the circle, and 50 of these used the sequence circle, some face details and then legs. At this point 21 of the 50 children stopped, thus omitting arms, while most of the children who did draw arms did so last of all. At first glance Goodnow's results might seem to refute Freeman's hypothesis of 'end-anchoring'. If children draw arms last of all, the notion of 'end-anchoring' would seem to suggest that they should focus most attention on the head and arms and, thus, omit the legs rather than the arms. However, the matter is not that simple. Goodnow's investigations lead her to suggest that young children plan their drawings in chunks which include a core and accessories. The elements on the vertical axis (head, trunk and legs) comprise the core, and other elements including arms are accessories. Thus, when children draw the legs of a tadpole figure they do have a sense of having reached the end, the end that is of a chunk. Freeman's notion of 'end-anchoring' and Goodnow's hypothesis that young children organize sequences in chunks together explain the omissions of both the trunk and arms in their drawings.

Goodnow's notion that young children order their drawings in terms of sequences which include a core and accessories led her to investigate the phenomenon of X-ray drawings, or 'transparencies' as they are sometimes called. Children were asked for drawings such as 'a lady with a long skirt' or 'a man wearing a coat' which might provoke transparencies. This request did in fact produce a number of transparencies. The body was drawn first and the clothes represented in one of three ways: children superimposed the clothes without erasing the body; they drew an outline representing the clothes outside the outline of the body; or they scribbled over the body to represent the clothes. For a drawing to avoid transparency it needs to be planned as a whole in advance, not in piecemeal fashion in separate chunks.

There remains to be examined a claim by Arnheim (1954) that, although 'tadpole' drawings appear to be representations of the human figure without a trunk, in fact the circle is a combined head and trunk. Freeman explored this question by giving children drawings of a figure consisting of two circles to represent head and trunk and two stick 'legs', and asking them to put arms on the figure. Sometimes children appended the arms to the top circle (the head) and sometimes to the other circle (the trunk). The main factor determining which they chose seemed to be relative proportion. They tended to append the arms to whichever was the largest circle. Goodnow also explored the problem by giving children a 'tadpole' figure drawing and asking them to give the figure a 'belly-button'. In this case the placing seemed to depend on the relative sizes of the circle and stick 'legs'. If the circle was large they were likely to include the 'belly-button' in it, whereas if it was small and the legs were long they tended to place the 'belly-button' below the circle and between the legs. These experiments neither support nor refute Arnheim's claim. It is possible that children intend the single circle of a 'tadpole' figure to depict, as Arnheim suggests, a combined head and trunk, or that they intend the sticks to represent combined legs and trunk. It is also possible that children do not intend to represent a trunk and only pay attention to it when presented with the kinds of problems that Freeman and Goodnow generated in their investigations. Since we do not yet really know which of these explanations are valid and what young children's intentions are, it is important to heed Goodnow's advice not to say to them, 'You've left out its body'.

Goodnow has examined other aspects of the organization of elements in young children's drawings in addition to sequence. One of these is concerned with their strategies in relation to separations and boundaries. She hypothesized that young children tend to avoid overlapping spaces. She considers that this accounts for the fact that they seldom draw both hair and arms on a head: the arms and hair compete for the same space and one of these features is, therefore, omitted. Goodnow tested her hypothesis by devising situations which precipitated a problem of competing spaces. For example, she gave children a drawing of a simple circle and sticks figure (Figure

Figure 32.1

32.1) and then asked them to put in both arms and hair. Her hypothesis seemed to be supported by some of the results. Some of the children solved the problem by attaching the arms to the vertical stick legs, while other children kept the hair to the top of the head thus leaving room for the arms to emerge from the head. Solutions where the arms crossed the hair were rare.

In another study Goodnow and her colleague, Roslyn Dawes, gave children a drawing of a train which was a single carriage with two large wheels (Figure 32.2). The

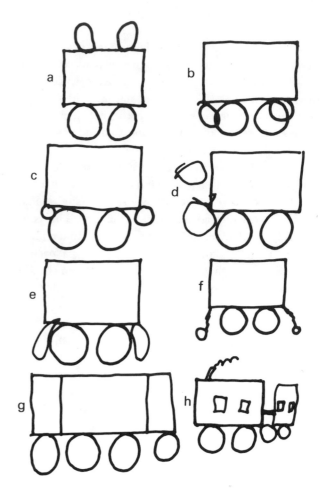

How do you add two more wheels to a train, where two wheels have pre-empted much of the lower space?

Figure 32.3

Figure 32.2

children were told, 'the child who drew this wanted to put in two more wheels, but didn't know how to do it. Could you finish the drawing?' If Goodnow's hypothesis that young children avoid overlapping is valid, this task presents a problem, for it is impossible to draw two wheels of the same size which do not extend beyond the carriage without overlapping them. Figure 32.3 is reproduced from Goodnow (1977) and shows some of the solutions children produced. A solution like (b) which involves overlapping was rare.

Piaget and Inhelder on the one hand and Freeman and Goodnow on the other interpret some of the same characteristics of young children's drawings but in different ways. In most cases these interpretations complement rather than contradict each other. For example, it may be that at a certain stage children adopt a strategy which avoids overlapping spaces because they are primarily concerned with the topological relationships of proximity and order and these conflict with overlapping. However, Goodnow's work does draw attention to and explain more details of young children's drawings than Piaget's and

Inhelder's does. It can also sharpen teachers' observations of children's drawings and paintings by drawing attention to the strategies they adopt.

The accounts of children's drawings discussed above are based on universal characteristics of young children's drawings, and these are explained in terms of psychological states and processes in development. It would be wrong, however, to conclude that other psychological processes and environmental conditions do not play a part and contribute both to individual differences among children and to differences in what one child may produce during a quite short period. There are three factors in particular which should be taken into account.

One important factor is a child's affective states and concerns. Piaget's and Inhelder's account and the work of Freeman and of Goodnow explain developmental differences in children's drawings in terms of aspects of their cognitive development. Affective factors such as what a child is interested in and the feelings and emotions he has about particular objects and events may also be reflected in his drawings and paintings. These interests, feelings and emotions influence what he chooses to represent and the intensity of his attention and effort. A five-year-old child produced a succession of drawings of houses, each of

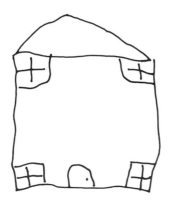

Figure 32.4

Teacher: 'Where's the door on your house?'
Girl: 'Hasn't got one.'
Teacher: 'How do you get in?'

Teacher: 'Poor daddy! He hasn't got any arms.'

In sum, what teachers conceive to be desirable ways of representing reality in pictures is defined by them in what they provide for children and in what they say to them. In this way children gradually learn to share their teachers' conceptions and to produce what is expected of them.

which had four windows placed straight on to the sides of the house as in Figure 32.4. This is a common stereotype of a house found in young children's drawings. Shortly after producing these the child was taken for the first time to visit an uncle's house which had slatted shutters on its five windows. The next day he drew a more detailed house with five shuttered windows which were now separated from the walls. His interest in his uncle's house had led to a drawing which is generally assumed to reflect a higher developmental level than the stereotype of Figure 32.4. As Kellogg and Goodnow emphasize we should be wary of jumping to conclusions about a child's developmental level on the basis of a single drawing.

Another important factor influencing the content of children's drawings and paintings is the experience they have had with the materials. A child given paints and paintbrush for the first time will often produce pictures which seem to be at an earlier developmental level than his previous products using a more familiar medium.

Finally, what and how children draw and paint is also influenced by what adults directly or indirectly suggest is desirable. In the previous unit, in Paper 31, it was claimed that it is impossible to produce a neutral curriculum, that teachers' attitudes toward and assumptions about play are inevitably reflected in what they provide and in how they relate to children in the context of their play. This is equally true of other areas of activity including drawing and painting. King (1978) describes how, in infant classrooms, teachers subtly influenced what the children produced. This influence was exercised in part by the material provided.

> The representations of houses, trees, flowers and people were versions of cultural images of these things. Although not directly presented to children by the teachers, these were displayed in the classroom, other than in other children's paintings and drawings. Lollypop (sic) trees and houses based on a rectangle and triangle were found on lotto cards, teacher-prepared and commercial word and number cards, mathematics work books and in some story books.

Teachers also influenced children more directly through their comments on children's paintings and drawings:

References
Arnheim, R. (1954) *Art and Visual Perception*, Berkeley: University of California Press.
Eng, H. (1931) *The Psychology of Children's Drawings*, Routledge & Kegan Paul.
Freeman, N. (1977) 'How young children try to plan drawings' in Butterworth, G. (ed.), *The Child's Representation of the World*, New York: Plenum Press.
Goodnow, J. (1977) *Children's Drawing*, Fontana.
Jameson, K. (1968) *Preschool and Infant Art*, Studio Vista.
Kellogg, R. (1969) *Analysing Children's Art*, California: National Press, Palo Alto.
King, R. (1978) 'Multiple realities and their reproduction in infants' classrooms', *Curriculum Studies*, 10 (2), 159–67.
Piaget, J. and Inhelder, B. (1963) *The Child's Conception of Space*, Routledge & Kegan Paul.
Steveni, M. (1968) *Art and Education*, Batsford.

Discussion Guide S

1 Compare as a group your findings in Activity 35 as follows:
   (a) Were there, on the whole, differences between the four-year-old and five-year-old children's responses to this task? If so, did they support Piaget's and Inhelder's claim that understanding of topological properties precedes that of Euclidean ones?
   (b) What was the extent of individual differences, if any?

2 Compare as a group your findings in Activity 36 as follows:
   (a) Do the results, on the whole, support Goodnow's hypothesis that young children avoid overlapping?
   (b) If there were any exceptions to this did they occur mainly among five-year-old rather than four-year-old children?
   (c) Discuss any other interesting aspects of the way in which the children completed the drawings, noting any examples which fitted with what you read in Paper 32.

3 (a) In what ways, if any, should teachers attempt to influence children's drawings and paintings?
   (b) In what ways, if any, should teachers try to avoid influencing children's drawings and paintings?
      Give your reasons.

Unit Three

Young Children's Thinking

- Read Papers 33, 34 and 35
- Engage in Activity 37 which is designed to provide you with more experience in giving young children a Piagetian task while, at the same time, giving you data to help your understanding of what is meant by saying young children are egocentric, a characteristic discussed in Paper 35
- Read Paper 36 which is also concerned with the concept of egocentricity
- Carry out Activity 38 involving experiment on egocentricity discussed in Paper 36
- Compare your results in Activities 37 and 38; note the differences. These will form part of the discussion for which Discussion Guide T should be used

Reading	65 mins.
Activities	150 mins.
Discussion	60 mins.
Total	275 mins.
	= 4 hrs. 35 mins.

Representation and cognitive development
J. S. Bruner

A useful concept for conceiving of the growth of intellect is the idea of representation. There is no need here for a long discussion of representation; only a few of the features of the concept need concern us. In effect, representation or a system of representation is a set of rules in terms of which one conserves one's encounters with events. A representation of the world or of some segment of one's experience has several interesting features. For one thing, it is in some medium. We may represent some events by the actions they require, by some form of picture, or in words or other symbols. There are many subvarieties within each of these three media — the enactive, the iconic, or the symbolic. A representation of an event is selective. In constructing a model of something, we do not include everything about it. The principle of selectivity is usually determined by the ends to which a representation is put — what we are going to do with what has been retained in this ordered way. Representations, by virtue of their summary nature, are rulebound in the sense that each representation is not an arbitrary or random sampling of what it stands for. That is to say, a representation of a spatially extended event uses a spatial notation that is common to a larger set of extended events. Much of spontaneous learning consists of inducing more general rules for more economical or more effective ways of representing similar events. And much of this learning consists of a kind of translation of one representational system into another, as when we become capable not only of following a given path habitually, but of representing it by an image in our mind's eye.

There are three kinds of representational systems that are operative during the growth of human intellect and whose interaction is central to growth. All of them are amenable to specification in fairly precise terms, all can be shown to be affected and shaped by linkage with tool or instru-mental systems, all of them are within important limits affected by cultural conditioning and by man's evolution. They are, as already indicated, enactive representation, iconic representation, and symbolic representation — knowing something through doing it, through a picture or image of it, and through some such symbolic means as language. With respect to a particular knot, we learn the act of tying it; when we know the knot, we know it by some habitual act we have mastered and can repeat. The habit by which the knot is organized is serially organized, governed by some schema that holds its successive segments together, and is in some important sense related to other habitual acts that facilitate or interfere with its learning and execution. What is crucial is that the representation is expressed in the medium of action with many features constrained by the nature of action, for example, its sequential and irreversible nature.

An image of a knot carried in your mind or on a page is not the same thing as the knot being tied, although the image can provide a schema around which action can be sequentially organized. An image is a selective, simultaneous, and often highly stylized analogue of an event experienced. Yet it is not arbitrary in its manner of referring to events as is a word. You can recognize an image of something, once having seen the something in question. You cannot recognize the appropriate word by knowing only the event is signifies. Linguistic signification is, in the main, arbitrary and depends upon the mastery of a symbolic code. A linguistic description, therefore, involves knowing not only the referents of words, but the rules for forming and transforming utterances. These rules, like the rules of image formation and habitual action, are distinctive to the medium of language.

Growth involves not a series of stages, but rather a successive mastering of three forms of representation along with their partial translation each into the others. The child in the early months of life literally defines events by the actions they evoke. Piaget's brilliant descriptions of the six- and seven-month-old child are readily replicated. The child has great difficulty at this age separating a percept and an act. To restore an object lost from view, he will perform an act appropriate to it. In time, perception becomes autonomous or relatively autonomous from action, and the child now has two semi-independent systems for representing things and a task of translation to master — to bring action and appearance into some correspondence.*

Symbolic representation is clearly the most mysterious of the three. Present evidence suggests that much of human syntax — rules of stunning power — is learned in the two or three years between the ages of two and four or five. There must be a huge innate component in this learning, in this unlocking of a syntactic component. It is not only mastered very swiftly and effortlessly, but first acquired in certain universal forms not to be found in the diverse adult speech communities into which children enter, so that pure imitation is hardly the relevant answer. Nor does syntactic competence bear much relation to the child's capacities on the semantic level. The child can say it correctly long before he can use his words and sentences in a fashion realistically appropriate to the situation. Only slowly does he learn to relate the language he speaks to his thoughts about things, to order his representation of the world by the syntactical logic

---

*See Bruner *et al.* (1966) for a fuller account of the process whereby a world of imagery comes first to be abstracted from action and then comes to be coordinated with it in a fashion that permits higher-order integration of sensorimotor behavior.

inherent in his speech. As he makes progress in that direction, again there is the task of translating from one mode of representation to another, of resolving the conflicts and contradictions that characterize the difference between how one does it, how it looks, and how one says it.

How does the idea of representation measure up to our four criteria? The formal properties of a representational system are, I believe, amenable to close and precise description, notably the languages in terms of which symbolic and iconic representations are effected. The description of action patterns remains obscure, though concepts of backput (Drever, 1962), the *TOTE* unit (Miller, Galanter, and Pribram, 1960), and reafference (Held, 1965) help to clear up our understanding of action patterns as modes of representing events. It is also plain that the notion of representation does not, so to speak, stop at the human skin. The technologies that a culture provides through language, myths and explanations, metrical and reckoning systems, tools, and its disciplines of knowledge, all reinforce, amplify, and enrich human representational capacities. With respect to a biological and evolutionary perspective, let me only comment that modern ethnological conceptions are centrally concerned with representation in such mechanisms as releasers and imprinting, much of it deriving from the originating idea of the *Umwelt* first proposed by von Uexküll. Finally, if education is not concerned with instilling skill and zest for representing one's experience and knowledge in some balance between rich particularity and economical generality, then I am not sure what else it is about.

Experiments

An experiment by Olson was carried out with the aid of a simple piece of apparatus: a rectangular board of five columns and five rows of small light bulbs. Each bulb, upon being pressed by the child, either lights up in brilliant scarlet red or remains unlit, depending upon whether the bulb is part of a pattern or not. The child's task is to discover, by pressing as few bulbs as possible, which one of several patterns presented to him are hidden in the bulb board. Only one bulb can be pressed at a time. Figure 33.1 shows the board with two alternative patterns. The child must press to determine which of the two is on the board.

Children are introduced to the task by being shown the correspondence between a single model and the board and then tested for their comprehension of the task. Different pat-

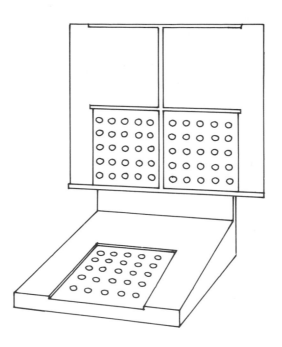

Figure 33.1. Apparatus used in the Olson experiment

terns, varying in difficulty and in number of alternatives, are presented to the child, his task always being the same: to press the bulbs that will tell him which alternative pattern lights up on the board. For ease and brevity, we consider now the pair of alternatives on the board in Figure 33.1: a T and a top horizontal bar.

The best way to describe the general course of development in the handling of this task is in terms of the strategies characteristic of the three-year-old, the five-year-old, and the eight-year-old. Their performance characterizes major turning points in development. The three-year-old is, in effect, searching the board for bulbs that will light up — his conception of positive instances. His search is not random. Likely he will start at an edge and, having pressed a bulb, the chances are that he will press one of its immediate neighbors. To put it figuratively in the interest of brevity, he is hoping that a perceptual pattern will spring from the board and often he must be restrained from pressing more than a single bulb at a time. His actions, he hopes, will produce the figure that can then be recognized as corresponding to one of the two before him. Needless to say, three-year-olds rarely succeed.

By age five, it is quite different. Now the child is quite capable of carrying an image representation to the task. But the procedure is striking in one

special feature. No matter how many alternatives are presented, the five-year-old will try out one at a time, testing it and eliminating or accepting it, the latter often on insufficent evidence. Each test of an alternative model is of that model and does not use priorly encountered information. In the task of discriminating the T from the top horizontal line, a five-year-old, for example, will check the five bulbs across the top and announce it is the horizontal bar. If you then urge him on to check whether it might possibly be the T, he will check the vertical as well. But if these should prove not to light, it is almost certain that the child will simply go back to checking the horizontal one again. Confirmation seems to involve direct test of a hypothesis presently in force about a particular image, or perhaps it is better to say direct test of an image.

What is striking about the eight-year-old is that he seems to be able to deal with information properly defined rather than simply in terms of single images. He can deal simultaneously with the patterns before him by dealing with their inclusion, exclusion, and overlap, in order to isolate distinctive features. The older child characteristically takes much longer to decide which bulb to press, though by age nine the choice time begins to speed up again as the child becomes master of the task of using symbolic operations as a basis for dealing simultaneously with many alternative images.

What are we to make of this shift from an active search strategy, to a pattern-matching strategy, and finally to an information-selection strategy? What does this tell us of the growth of representation? The initial search strategy shows a strong carry-over of an early interdependence of action and percept, as if the child were trying to create a response-produced stimulus, to get it all out there by his acts so that it may be discriminated. By the fifth year, the child's choice of bulbs to be pressed is controlled by the patterns before him — but one pattern at a time — and he is not able to embed the alternatives into the hierarchical structure that is the essence of symbolic representation. Only when the apparatus of symbolism can be applied to the task can the set of alternative images be fused into what can be described as an information space, characterized by distinctive features.

References
Bruner, J. S., Oliver, R. R., Greenfield, P.M. et al. (1966) Studies in Cognitive Growth, New York: Wiley.
Drever, J. (1962) 'Perception and action', Bulletin of the British Psychological Society, no. 45, 1.
Held, R. (1965) 'Plasticity in sensory-motor systems', Scientific American, 213 (5), 84–94.
Miller, G. A., Galanter, E. and Pribram, K. H. (1960) Plans and the Structure of Behaviour, New York: Holt.

Preoperational thought
D. W. McNally

When a teacher uses the word concept in the sense of referring to concept formation, he usually means that the child has abstracted a generalised notion from a series of particular examples. For example, the concept of a tree would be formed from experience with various types of trees such as pines, gums, willows and even dead trees. The important point here is the *generality* of the idea he has formed concerning a tree. A teacher intent upon developing the notion of area in children of about twelve years of age could proceed by using either *deduction* or *induction* or most likely both. Deduction refers to reaching conclusions about a specific case from an understanding of a general rule or principle. Thus, given the area of a rectangle as 'length by width', the child applies this to the problem of finding the area of a rectangle four inches by three inches because he can see that this specific case fits the general principle. Induction refers to the development of a general rule or principle from a series of specific instances. The child arrives at the concept of the area of rectangles from experience with calculating the area of specific rectangles.

But a child of two or three cannot reason either inductively or deductively but instead reasons *transductively*. In transductive reasoning the child goes from particular to particular without any apparent logical connection, as when Piaget reports that on an afternoon when Lucienne did not take a nap she said: 'I haven't had my nap so it isn't afternoon'. Similar reasoning can be seen in the young boy who wanted a lolly from the corner grocer shop after it had closed for the day. He stoutly maintained the shop was not closed but his mother insisted firmly that it was. A few minutes later the child rushed into the house and said, 'The grocer's shop is open because the grocer just walked past our house'. There is of course a certain logic in the thinking of Lucienne and the boy wanting to go to the grocer, but it is not a logical connection in the usual meaning of that term and is far different from the logic that can be applied by a twelve-year-old. At this preconceptual stage thinking is related to the wishes of the child as can be seen in the above example of the boy wishing to go to the grocer's shop. The child's desires distort his thinking and in a sense the child's reasoning is aimed at achieving a personal goal.

Transductive reasoning prevents the child from forming true concepts because he cannot cope with general classes. He is unable to distinguish between 'all' and 'some'. Piaget (1950, 127) gives an example of this when he notes that a young child did not know whether the slugs encountered in the course of a walk constituted a single slug which kept on appearing or a class of distinct individual slugs. Preconcepts are schemas which remain midway between the generality of the concept and the individuality of the elements composing them without arriving either at one or the other. They are as yet not true logical concepts.

To illustrate this inability to form concepts, consider the following example which comes from the author's research with children. Several three-year-old children were shown some of the attribute blocks which are part of the structured material of the 'Triad Mathematics Laboratory' for Kindergarten. They were asked to hand the experimenter some blocks that were alike. One child handed the experimenter in order a blue circle, a blue triangle, and a red triangle. The child had linked a blue circle to a blue triangle (by colour) and then the blue triangle to the red triangle by shape. A five-year-old presented with the same problem handed the experimenter a red and a yellow triangle. When asked for some more that were alike he handed the experimenter another red and another yellow triangle. When the experimenter put these four triangles on the floor and asked the child to point to some more that were alike he was shown a red and yellow triangle again. Another child of six handed the experimenter all the blue triangles that were in the pile. In the case of the three-year-old child no true concept was formed. With respect to the five- and six-year-old children, both were able to abstract to generality although one had abstracted at a higher level than the other.

The Intuitive (Perceptual) and the Concrete Operational Stages

The intuitive stage extends and develops the progress in thought made in the preconceptual period. In this sense it can be regarded as an elaboration of the preconceptual period and in fact it has already been stated that it is common for writers to discuss these two sub-periods under the one heading of preoperational, and to make no distinction at all. This is a matter of preference, but it is true that the distinction between preconceptual and intuitive is by no means as clear nor as dramatic as the distinction between the intuitive and concrete periods. Discussion proceeds, therefore, by first noting some general points about thought in the intuitive period and continues by contrasting the thought of the intuitive child with that of the child who has reached the level of concrete operations. It is impossible to discuss the intuitive stage adequately without reference to the concrete stage.

The Intuitive (Perceptual) Stage (4 to 7 years)

It is clear that at this stage the child has made considerable progress. His thought has developed to the stage where he can give reasons for his actions and for his beliefs. He is able to classify at a 'higher' level, e.g., sort coloured shapes either by colour or by shape, but not initially by colour and shape. Language too progresses rapidly and assists internalisation of behaviour through representation

Figure 34.1

which acts to speed up the rate at which experience takes place. Yet thought at this stage is restricted in quality and effectiveness by two things. It is dominated by immediate perceptions, by the dominant aspect of what is attended to, and by the fact that he is unable to keep in mind more than one relation at a time. These limitations have important consequences and clear implications for those who deal with pre-school and infant school children.

Teachers and parents of children in this stage frequently note that the child seems to contradict himself without any real concern for the facts. This is certainly true from the point of view of the parent for if the successive views of the child are compared by adults they quite often do contradict. This is not so from the point of view of the child because, unable to keep in mind more than one thing at a time, he forgets what went before. Consider the following example. A six-year-old child went recently to the Agricultural Show and on his return drew a picture of what he had seen. In the centre was a large pavilion on each side of which he had drawn a sign covered with wriggly lines to indicate printing (see Fig. 34.1). Asked to describe the picture the child said that the left hand sign said, 'Go in Here' and the right hand sign said, 'No Dogs Allowed'. The child

switched attention immediately to the left hand sign again and said, 'That says vegetables but not plants and grass' and pointing to the right hand sign said 'That says Chips and Drinks'. Ten minutes later the teacher said, 'I have forgotten what your signs said, could you tell me what they said again?' The child replied, 'That one [left hand sign] says "In" and that one [right hand sign] says "Out"'. The child here made no effort to stick to his original opinion and was quite unconcerned about the whole matter. To him there was no contradiction.

The same drawing provided a further illustration of thought in this period when the child was asked to say how he travelled to the show, what he did and saw and how he came home. His reply was 'I got a mask at the Royal Easter Show. When I went there I saw Mary. My brothers brought me home a present when they went to the show. I went on the Ghost Train at the show.'

The task given to this young child would, of course, tax the ability of much older children but nevertheless there is in this reply clear evidence of a lack of direction in thinking — successive, unrelated, in the sense of unordered, explanations. In response

to the question of 'What makes a car go?' the same child, on the same day, replied, 'The wheels. The motor. The petrol. By the steering wheel.' Here the child has put together a set of explanations, which although related to the movement of a car do not constitute an ordered explanation. The ideas are merely put side by side as they were when describing his visit to the show. In his earlier works Piaget used the terms 'juxtaposition' to describe this phenomenon which in effect involves an inability to see any relation among the parts which constitute a whole (Piaget, 1928).

Paradoxically, young children also engage in a type of reasoning in which they tend to connect a series of separate ideas into a confused whole and assign to quite different things a similarity which to the adult is illogical. To this type of reasoning Piaget gives the name *syncretic*. The child reasoning this way perceives the whole but does not see the differences within this whole.*

On the surface it would seem that juxtaposition where the child ignores the whole in favour of the parts and syncretism where the child can ignore the parts in favour of the whole are

*It should be noted that these findings with respect to young children's thinking belong to Piaget's earlier period where he was more concerned with analysis of verbal responses (op. cit., 1928).

irreconcilable. Analysis shows, however, that both effects are instances of the child focusing on one aspect of the situation at the expense of the other. The child is unable to attend to differences among things and to their similarities at the same time. Each is a special instance of the child focusing upon only one aspect at a time.

It is this characteristic of focusing on one dimension, of attending to a dominant feature, which is characteristic of thought at the intuitive stage. In his later work which was more experimental, Piaget looked at this phenomenon in great detail and it is the results of this work in the form of the various stages of thinking which are perhaps best known. Certainly such results have had a considerable influence on education and teaching in the last twenty years. Discussion proceeds by looking at the key concepts of Piaget's later views on intuitive thinking. It does so by first of all describing two typical experiments that Piaget conducts to determine whether the child is still at the intuitive stage or has progressed to the concrete operational stage. This provides a reference point for a discussion of the properties of thought characterised by these two periods.

A typical experiment of this kind is to present to a young child, say a six-year-old, two equivalent balls of plasticine. When the child agrees that the balls of plasticine are equivalent, one of them is distorted by being rolled into a sausage whose length is approximately three times the width. The child is then asked whether there is more, less or the same amount of plasticine in the sausage as in the ball. A child at the intuitive stage is likely to say something like, 'There is more plasticine in the sausage because it is longer', or 'There is less plasticine in the sausage because it is thinner'. The child who has reached the stage of concrete reasoning might say, 'There is still the same amount because you could roll the sausage up again and it would make a ball again', or, 'There is still the same amount because you didn't take any away'.

A similar experiment requires the experimenter to present the child with two beakers in which there are equal amounts of water. After the child agrees that they are equivalent, the contents of one beaker are poured into a tall thin glass and the child is asked whether there is more, less or the same amount of water in the tall glass as there was in the original beaker. The intuitive child says something like

'There is more because it is taller' or 'There is less because it is thinner'.

These two descriptions of experiments represent only part of each experiment. In the plasticine ball experiment the ball is typically deformed into a long snake, a ring, a cake, a flat pancake and frequently cut into many pieces. In the water experiment which is an experiment in the conservation of continuous quantity, the water is frequently poured into a number of smaller glasses. When the experiments are extended in this fashion it is usual to find three stages, not two as indicated above. The succession of stages is from intuitive, through a transition where a child may believe the sausage is the same as the ball but not believe the snake is the same, to conservation where equivalence is unhesitatingly asserted.

There are, of course, obvious similarities in these answers which give insights into the child's reasoning. First there is what Piaget refers to as *centration*. The child centres on one aspect of the situation. In the case of the plasticine ball test it is the shape of the sausage. The specific aspect he attends to is the length or width. He does not attend to both at the same time. In the case of the water in the long glass he attends to the shape again. He centres on the glass's height or thinness but is unable to take into account the reciprocal influence of both. In Piaget's terms he is unable to *decentre* his attention so that it becomes clear that height compensates for width and the amount of water remains the same. The child bases his judgments on what seems to be, on intuition.

It also becomes clear from these illustrations that the intuitive child focuses on successive states. He attends to the plasticine ball in the first instance and then to the subsequent shape. What he fails to take into consideration and what will be a feature of his thinking in the concrete period is the *transformation* between the state of plasticine ball to the state of plasticine sausage. The intuitive child cannot assimilate this because he does not attend to it. His attention is restricted to the particular perceptual event. First it is the plasticine ball that claims his attention, which then shifts directly to the final state, plasticine sausage.

What is required before the child can compensate for the changes described above is the development of a *logical structure* which can be applied to such situations. This is the subject of the next section on concrete reasoning but it is important to mention here that a very important aspect, indeed the key aspect of the development of that logical structure, is the development of *reversibility*. This refers to the ability to mentally return to the starting point of an event, and see, e.g., that the plasticine sausage could be rolled up again into a ball or that the water could be poured from the tall glass back into the beaker and leave the situation unchanged. The intuitive child cannot do this. He cannot shuffle mentally back and forth between the two states. It is this ability above all others which marks the concrete thinker off from the intuitive thinker because it enables him to *conserve*. He is able, by force of his ability to apply a logical structure, to compensate for the biasing distortions of perception.

References
Piaget, J. (1928) *Judgment and Reasoning in the Child*, Routledge & Kegan Paul.
Piaget, J. (1950) *The Psychology of Intelligence*, Routledge & Kegan Paul.

Egocentricity in pre-operational thought
Joan Tamburrini

The development of representational abilities in early childhood enables children to interact with their world in more complex ways than they could before the age of eighteen months to two years, on the average, when their interaction was of a sensory-motor kind and confined to what was present to their senses. In sum, the growing competencies of children between the ages of two and five years are highlighted when they are contrasted with earlier ways of functioning. In the same way some characteristics of intellectual functioning from two to five years can only be fully understood by contrast with the competencies that children acquire after the age of five. It is in this respect that Piaget's expression 'pre-operational' for the kind of thinking characteristic of early childhood is significant.

Operational thought begins to emerge between five and seven years of age, the time of onset varying among children and according to the complexity of particular concepts. In fact operational thought continues to develop in middle childhood and with respect to some rather complex concepts children do not think operationally until nine or ten years of age, on the average.

Operational thought is thought based on an understanding of certain relationships. An example may make this clear. Take the addition of numerical quantities, say 5 and 4. It does not matter whether one adds 5 to 4 or 4 to 5. The answer will still be 9. Moreover, if 5 and 4 or 4 and 5 are equal to 9, then it follows that, if 5 is subtracted from 9, 4 will remain, or, if 4 is subtracted from 9, 5 will remain. These are numerical relationships which a child must grasp if he is to add numerical quantities with understanding. It is possible to teach children tricks, for example to put out 5 objects and 4 objects and to count them, but getting the correct answer in this way does not mean the child understands the relationships set out above. Piaget believes that this kind of relational thinking involves mental actions and is the result of overt actions which have become internalized, and it is for this reason that he calls it 'operational'. The numerical relationships just discussed involve the actions of adding and taking away but these are performed internally, in thought, rather than in overt action.

Children's thinking before they are capable of these 'operations' is called, therefore, 'pre-operational'. Piaget divides the pre-operational period into the *preconceptual* and *intuitive* sub-stages. The preconceptual sub-stage precedes the intuitive sub-stage which emerges, on the average, at four years of age. Paper 34 by McNally describes the characteristics of these sub-stages.

As McNally states, one of the main characteristics of pre-operational thought is that the child, instead of grasping all the relationships in a situation, focuses or, to use Piaget's term, 'centres' on a particular aspect of it. One kind of situation in which this happens is that which involves a contrast between a child's own and another person's point of view. In these cases young children, according to Piaget, centre on their own points of view rather than the other person's, and this he calls 'egocentricity'.

It is important not to confuse egocentricity with selfishness. It is not a morally reprehensible state, but simply one which reflects the stage of a child's intellectual functioning. Nor should one assume that because young children are egocentric they cannot show empathy for other people. Recently on a visit to a nursery school I was approached by two children, a three-year-old and a four-year-old, hand in hand and both in tears. Some questioning elicited from the older child that his companion, a new entrant, was crying for his mother. The four-year-old's tears were in sympathy for his plight. Anyone familiar with young children will have observed similar examples of empathy. Young children are able to show empathy in this way because they have had similar experiences and can therefore identify the feelings associated with such experiences in others. It is a different matter when another person's point of view conflicts with or is different from their own.

One way of understanding the difference between situations in which a child can show empathy and ones in which he is egocentric is in terms of Piaget's concepts of assimilation and accommodation discussed in Paper 30. Children can show empathy when another person's situation can be assimilated to their own experiences; they are egocentric when another person's point of view requires an accommodation of which they are not yet intellectually capable.

One of the best known of Piaget's tests for egocentricity requires children to identify the perspective of a three-dimensional model as it will appear to a person in a different position from their own. The child is shown a three-dimensional model of three mountains whose differences are clearly identifiable (for example, by having different things on top of them). A doll is placed facing the model at different points. The child is given a set of photographs of the mountains from different points of view and is asked to select the photograph which represents what the doll can see from a particular position. Before the age of seven, on the average, children are unable to do this correctly. Instead they tend to select the photograph which represents their own points of view. Other tests for egocentricity taken from Piaget's work are given in Activity 7.

There have been some recent criticisms of Piaget's claims regarding the young child's egocentricity. Hughes (1978) gave a test for egocentricity similar to Piaget's described above but substituting three coloured dolls (red, blue and yellow) for the mountains. His sample consisted of 40 pre-school children aged four years to four years ten months. A child sitting at the table would see the full face of the doll nearest him and the profiles of the other two dolls. The experimenter also sat at the table oriented at 120° to the child, so that he similarly saw the full face of the doll nearest him and the profiles of the other two dolls. There were three pictures, one representing the child's view, one the experimenter's view and one showed a third view. The children were divided into two groups, A and B. Group B received preliminary questions before they were tested. These questions were designed to help them focus on relevant attributes before testing. Thus they were asked with no pictures present and for each position of the base, 'which face do you see?' and 'which face do I [the experimenter] see?' Three preliminary questions about the pictures ('which doll's face do you see in the picture?') were asked for each picture without the model present. Group A was the control group who received no preliminary questions before testing. The results indicated that these preliminary questions helped the children considerably. Thirteen out of the twenty children in group B succeeded in selecting the correct picture in the test compared with only one child in group A.

Another experiment for egocentricity, the results of which conflict with those of Piaget, is reported in Donaldson's paper (Paper 36). It is important to note that neither Hughes nor Donaldson claim that Piaget's results in his tests are invalid. Numerous investigators have repeated Piaget's test and, on the whole, have obtained similar results. What Donaldson is claiming is that young children's capabilities are greater than Piaget's results would lead us to expect, but these capabilities occur in contexts which are more meaningful to them than those of some of Piaget's tests.

The implications of Donaldson's thesis for education are of considerable importance and will form part of the discussion in Unit 4.

Piaget has stressed the importance for intellectual development of the child's experiences of manipulating objects, but has underemphasised the role of social experience. Light (1979) explored the egocentricity of a group of 60 four-year-old children and the connections between their abilities in identifying another person's point of view, which he called 'role-taking' and the quality of their social experiences. Some of the children, although only four years old, were very successful in the role-taking tasks he gave them, and he found that this ability seemed to be associated with several aspects of social experience among which was the tendency of their mothers to treat them as individual personalities rather than in terms of stereotypes of how four-year-old boys or girls ought to behave. If, as Light's study suggests, the quality of a child's social experience with his mother or other care-giver influences the development of his ability to identify another person's point of view, it would seem reasonable to suppose that the way in which teachers or other significant adults interact with young children can be potent in this respect.

Reference
Hughes, M. (1978) 'Selecting pictures of another person's view', *Brit. J. Ed. Psychol.*, 48(2), 210–19.
Light, P. (1979) *The Development of Social Sensitivity*, Cambridge University Press.

The ability to 'decentre'
Margaret Donaldson

In recent years Piaget has collected most of his data by devising tasks for children to do and then observing their behaviour when they deal with the task, questioning them about it, noting what they say. One of the best known of these tasks is concerned with the ability to take account of someone else's point of view in the literal sense — that is, to recognize what someone else will see who is looking at the same thing as oneself but from the other side.

For this task, a three-dimensional object or set of objects is needed. Piaget uses a model of three mountains. (See *The Child's Conception of Space* by Piaget and Inhelder.) The mountains are distinguished from one another by colour and by such features as snow on one, a house on top of another, a red cross at the summit of the third.

The child sits at one side of the table on which this model is placed. The experimenter then produces a little doll and puts the doll at some other position round the table. The problem for the child is: what does the doll see?

It would clearly be hard for the child to give a verbal description ('He sees a house on top of the mountain on his right . . .' etc.) for that description would have to be of considerable complexity. So in one version of the task the child is given a set of ten pictures of the model taken from different angles, and he is asked to choose the one which shows what the doll sees. In another version he is given three cardboard 'mountains' and he is asked to arrange them so that they represent what would be seen in a snapshot taken from the doll's position. Children up to the age of around eight, or even nine, cannot as a rule do this successfully; and there is a powerful tendency among children below the age of six or seven to choose the picture — or build the model — which represents their own point of view — exactly what they themselves see.

Piaget takes this to indicate that they are unable to 'de-centre' in imagination. He points out that in one sense they know perfectly well that the appearance of a thing changes when you walk round it. And yet he maintains that they are bound by what he calls 'the egocentric illusion' as soon as they are called upon to form a mental representation of some view which they have not actually seen. They 'really imagine that the doll's perspective is the same as their own'. They all think the doll sees the mountains only as they look from the child's position. What the child lacks is held to be the ability to see his own momentary viewpoint as one of a set of possible viewpoints, and to co-ordinate these possibilities into a single coherent system, so that he understands the ways in which the different perspectives relate to one another.

We are urged by Piaget to believe that the child's behaviour in this situation gives us a deep insight into the nature of his world. This world is held to be one that is composed largely of 'false absolutes'. That is to say, the child does not appreciate that what he sees is relative to his own position; he takes it to represent absolute truth or reality — *the world as it really is.* Notice that this implies a world marked by extreme discontinuity. Any change in position means abrupt change in the world and a sharp break with the past. And indeed Piaget believes that this is how it is for the young child: that he lives in the state of the moment, not bothering himself with how things were just previously, with the relation of one state to those which come before or after it. His world is like a film run slowly, as Piaget says elsewhere.

This is by no means to say that Piaget thinks the child has no memory of the earlier 'stills'. The issue for Piaget is how the momentary states are linked, or fail to be linked, in the child's mind.

The issue is how well the child can deal conceptually with the transitions between them.

All this has far-reaching implications for the child's ability to think and reason, and we shall come back to these implications later. But first let us consider how children perform on a task which is in some ways very like the 'mountains' task and in other extremely important ways very different.

This task was devised by Martin Hughes. In its simplest form, it makes use of two 'walls' intersecting to form a cross, and two small dolls, representing respectively a policeman and a little boy. Seen from above, the lay-out (before the boy doll is put in position) is like this:

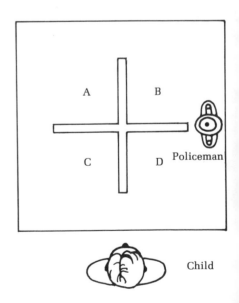

Figure 36.1

In the studies which Hughes conducted the policeman was placed initially as in the diagram so that he could see the areas marked B and D, while the areas A and C were hidden from him by the wall.

The child was then introduced to the task very carefully, in ways that were designed to give him every chance of understanding the situation fully and grasping what was being asked of him. First, Hughes put the boy doll in section A and asked if the policeman could see the boy there. The question was repeated for sections B, C and D in turn. Next the policeman was placed on the opposite side, facing the wall that divides A from C, and the child was asked to 'hide the doll so that the policeman can't see him'. If the child made any mistakes at these preliminary stages, his error was pointed out to him, and the question was repeated until the correct answer was given. But very few mistakes were made.

Then the test proper began. And now the task was made more complex. Another policeman was produced and the two were positioned thus:

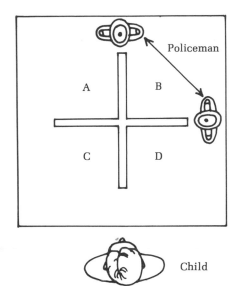

Figure 36.2

The child was told to hide the boy from both policemen, a result which could only be achieved by the consideration and co-ordination of two different points of view. This was repeated three times, so that each time a different section was left as the only hiding place.

The results were dramatic. When thirty children between the ages of three-and-a-half and five years were given this task, 90 per cent of their responses were correct. And even the ten youngest children, whose average age was only three years nine months, achieved a success rate of 88 per cent.

Hughes then went on to further trials, using more complex arrangements of walls, with as many as five or six sections, and introducing a third policeman. The three-year-olds had more trouble with this, but they still got over 60 per cent of the trials correct. The four-year-olds could still succeed at the 90-per-cent level.

It seems to be impossible to reconcile these findings with Piaget's claim that children under the age of seven are very bad at appreciating the point of view of some other person in the literal sense of being unable to figure out what that other person can see. However, though Hughes' findings cannot be reconciled with Piaget's *claim*, some way must be found of reconciling them with Piaget's *findings* — for these are not suspect. Research by other investigators has fully confirmed that, if children are given the Piaget 'mountains' task, they do indeed have extreme difficulty with it — but not, it now seems, for the reason Piaget suggests. For what reason, then?

One must obviously consider the differences between the two tasks — and these are many. One difference which Hughes noted is that the 'policemen' task, while it certainly involves the co-ordination of points of view, merely requires the child to figure out whether an object will be visible and does not require him to deal with left–right reversals and so on. That is, he must decide *what* can be seen but not exactly *how* it will appear. Now it is perfectly clear that the calculation of how something will look from a given position when the scene is fairly complex will give pause to many an adult. But this hardly seems to explain why young children, in tackling the 'mountains' task, so frequently choose their own point of view instead of a different, though wrong, one. When this fact is considered along with Hughes' findings, it is difficult to avoid the conclusion that the children who make 'egocentric' responses to the 'mountains' problem do not fully understand what they are supposed to do.*

By contrast it is quite evident that, in the 'policemen' problem, a situation has been found which *makes sense* to the child. Hughes was very careful about introducing the tasks in ways that would help the children to understand the nature of the problem, but in

fact his precautions were largely unnecessary: the children seemed to grasp the situation at once. We have then to ask why this was so easy for them.

Notice that we cannot appeal to direct actual experience: few, if any, of these children had ever tried to hide from a policeman. But we *can* appeal to the generalization of experience: they know what it is to try to hide. Also they know what it is to be naughty and to want to evade the consequences. So they can easily conceive that a boy might want to hide from a policeman if he had been a bad boy; for in this case it would be the job of the policeman to catch him and the consequences of being caught would be undesirable.

The point is that the *motives* and *intentions* of the characters are entirely comprehensible, even to a child of three. The task requires the child to act in ways which are in line with certain very basic human purposes and interactions (escape and pursuit) — it makes *human sense*. Thus it is not at all hard to convey to the child what he is supposed to do: he apprehends it instantly. It then turns out that neither is it hard for him to do it. In other words, in this context he shows none of the difficulty in 'decentring' which Piaget ascribes to him.

In respect of being humanly comprehensible, the 'mountains' task is at the opposite extreme. Within this task itself, there is no play of interpersonal motives of such a kind as to make it instantly intelligible. (There is the question of the experimenter's motives in asking the child to do it and of the child's motives in responding, but that is quite another matter.)

Thus the 'mountains' task is *abstract* in a psychologically very important sense: in the sense that it is abstracted from all basic human purposes and feelings and endeavours. It is totally cold-blooded. In the veins of three-year-olds, the blood still runs warm.

This is in no way meant to suggest that the ability to deal, in cold blood, with problems of an abstract and formal nature is unimportant. It is immensely important. Much that is distinctively human and highly to be valued depends upon it. And young children are bad at it.

The more highly one values this activity the more important it then becomes to try to understand the true nature of the difficulty to which it

*In another study, Hughes used a simplified version of the mountains task and found that it was possible, by taking great care over the way in which the problem was introduced, to get a high proportion of correct responses from pre-school children. So this lends further support to the view that Piaget's subjects did not understand.

gives rise. For the better we understand this, the more readily we should be able to help children to overcome it.

One obstacle that stands in the way of better understanding is that those who study such topics are, for the most part, accustomed to abstract and formal modes of thought to the point where they find it hard to appreciate that degrees of abstractness which present no kind of difficulty to them may render a task senseless and bewildering to a child. In other words, the research worker, like Laurie Lee's teacher, may often fail to decentre.

It may seem now that we have reached the curious position of claiming (a) that children are not egocentric, and (b) that sophisticated adults are. Not so, however. What is being claimed is that we are all egocentric through the whole of our lives in some situations and very well able to decentre in others. Piaget would not disagree with the claim that egocentrism is never wholly overcome. The dispute with him is only about the extent — and the developmental significance — of egocentrism in early childhood. I want to argue that the difference between child and adult in this respect is less than he supposes; and then to argue further that the critical differences lie elsewhere.

In the course of trying to reconcile Hughes' findings with Piaget's I suggested that Hughes' task is easy for the child to grasp because it makes human sense. It rests on an understanding of the interaction of two conplementary intentions of a very basic kind: the intention to escape and the intention to pursue and capture. Now it is worth observing that the appreciation of such a complementary pair of intentions, however simple and elementary, calls already for an ability to decentre that is not concerned with the literal understanding of another point of view: not with what another person *sees* from a given standpoint, but with what he is feeling or planning to do. Hughes' task, though designed primarily to test the former, also rests upon the latter. And what I have been suggesting is that the latter is a very fundamental human skill.

Reference
Hughes, M. (1978) 'Selecting pictures of another person's view', *Brit. J. Ed. Psychol.*, 48(2), 210–19.
Light, P. (1979) *The Development of Social Sensitivity*, Cambridge University Press.

Discussion Guide T

1 Compare as a group your results in Activity 37. What proportion of four-year-old children gave an egocentric response? What proportion of five-year-old children did so?

2 Compare as a group your results for Activity 38. What proportion of three-and-a-half, four to four-and-a-half, and five-year-old children gave non-egocentric responses? What can you deduce from this information?

3 Compare the results of Activities 37 and 38. Did they confirm Donaldson's findings?

4 Donaldson's claim is that young children's capabilities are greater in contexts which are meaningful to them because they have intentions and can recognize adult intentions. What do you consider to be the main implications of this for teachers of young children?

5 Nevertheless, young children do think pre-operationally in many situations as Piaget's tests show. What do you consider to be the main implications of this for teachers of young children?

Unit Four

Learning, Teaching and Cognitive Development

- Read Papers 37 and 38
- Carry out Activity 39 which is designed to help you think about the implications in terms of provision of materials in early childhood of these papers
- Work through Discussion Guide U

Reading	35 mins.
Activities	60 mins.
Discussion	60 mins.
Total	155 mins.
	= 2 hrs. 35 mins.

Performance and competence
Joan Tamburrini

It is a truism to say that effective education requires that account is taken of what the learner already knows and understands. It has sometimes been claimed that Piaget's account of the stages of development is of limited value to teachers because it frequently yields information concerning what children cannot do or understand, and this leaves teachers feeling helpless and powerless. This claim is valid only if Piaget's findings are interpreted in this limited way.

Such a view is limited in two ways, the first related to the problem of the relationship between performance and competence, and the second concerned with the problem of how cognitive development occurs.

The problem of the relationship between performance and competence may be put in the form of the following two questions:

(a) to what extent should we assume that a child's correct performance in one specific task indicates a generalized competence such that he can perform equally well in other contexts involving the same kind of thinking or concept?

(b) to what extent should we assume that a child's inadequate or incorrect performance on a task indicates an overall incompetence which would prevent him performing competently in another context involving the same kind of thinking or concept?

Donaldson's work has produced interesting insights with regard to the second question. It suggests that we should not assume that a child who cannot perform competently on one of Piaget's tests cannot 'decentre' or 'conserve' in another context which makes more 'human sense' to him. However, this finding does not invalidate Piaget's tests, for we have to explain the fact that children do reach a stage of development where they perform adequately not only in 'meaningful' contexts like those in the investigations reported by Donaldson, but also in orthodox Piagetian tests. It is legitimate to assume that when a child can conserve or decentre in a Piagetian test he has a more generalized competence than he had when he could 'decentre' or 'conserve' only in specific contexts like those of the tasks discussed by Donaldson. Such a generalized competence is of immense educational importance. Donaldson herself acknowledges this implicitly in a distinction she draws between 'embedded' and 'disembedded' thought. 'Embedded' thought operates within the supportive context of what our everyday experience makes meaningful, whereas 'disembedded' modes of thought move beyond the bounds of the specific contexts of everyday experience. One of the major tasks of education is to help children to develop 'disembedded' thinking.

This task leads inevitably to the second problem referred to earlier, the problem of how children develop the kinds of concepts investigated by Piaget at the level of competence to perform successfully on his tests, and of how teachers can facilitate this process. Paper 38 deals with this problem.

Piaget on memory: the case for constructivism and its educational implications*

Joan Tamburrini

Introduction

Teachers' assumptions about the nature of psychological processes are inevitably reflected in their classroom practices. It is obvious, for example, that a teacher who conceives of intelligence as predetermined and, therefore, fixed will organize his pupils and his curriculum differently from one who believes intelligence is largely environmentally determined and, therefore, plastic. Perhaps rather less obvious are differences in curriculum content and in teaching style that spring from empiricism and constructivism, two contrasting conceptions of how knowledge is acquired.

Empiricism versus constructivism

Empiricist conceptions of knowledge take different forms in modern psychology, some more refined than others, but Piaget claims that common to them all are two characteristics. Firstly the acquisition of knowledge is conceived of as a process which involves copying reality.

> If we look for common factors in these diverse approaches (of empiricism) we find a central idea: the function of cognitive mechanisms is to submit to reality, copying its features as closely as possible, so that they may produce a reproduction which differs as little as possible from external reality. This idea of empiricism implies that reality can be reduced to its observable features and that knowledge must limit itself to transcribing these features. (Piaget and Inhelder, 1976)

Secondly, empiricists implicitly attribute passivity to the knower, for to envisage that knowledge copies reality is essentially to conceive of it as a unidirectional process in which reality impinges with data on a mind that passively receives and records them.

Piaget rejects the empiricist view of knowledge and claims that it is the result of a process of construction. What the knower understands of external reality is, according to Piaget, never a copy of data received, but is modulated and transformed in terms of what he already knows and understands, or in Piaget's terminology in terms of his schemes.

Piaget and Inhelder's experiments on memory

The most convincing empirical support for Piaget's constructivist account of knowledge comes from his investigations of memory. In order to understand these investigations it is first necessary to understand his distinction between figurative and operative knowing. Figurative knowledge has to do with static aspects of reality, with observable characteristics and configurations. Operative knowledge has to do with relationships within things and between things, with relationships that are non-observable. Much of the knowledge we expect children to acquire in school has both figurative and operative aspects. The geography and science curricula, for example, involve properties of the physical world which are observable but organized through concepts of time, space, number and causality which are not directly observable. It is Piaget's contention that not even these figurative aspects are acquired as a result of a copying process, since an understanding of them also requires that the knower has structured the relevant underlying operative knowledge.

In one of their experiments on memory Piaget and Inhelder (1973) showed children between the ages of five and seven years the configuration in Figure 38.1. After one hour and again after one week the children were asked to draw from memory what they had seen. Only the youngest children had any difficulty with this task. Most of the other children were able to produce a fairly accurate drawing of what they had seen. This is a configuration, however, for which figurative knowing is adequate. By contrast children produce interesting deformations when they are asked to reproduce from memory the configuration in Figure 38.2. The main difference between the two configurations is that the lines in Figure 38.1 are continuous whereas Figure 38.2 is made up of discrete elements (matchsticks). The latter configuration, therefore, involves numerical and spatial correspondences. Piaget and Inhelder presented the latter configuration as a memory task to children between the ages of five and eight

*This paper was first published in *The New Era*, 50(3), May/June 1978.

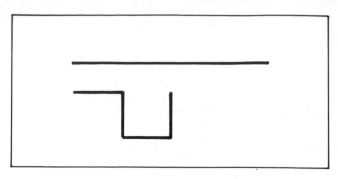

Figure 38.1

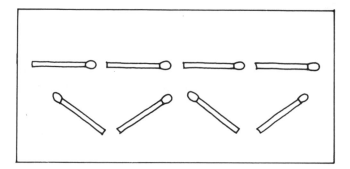

Figure 38.2

eliminate the conflict between numerical conservation and the coincidence of the spatial boundaries rather than by a tendency to copy the model'. In other words, although the array of matchsticks is a static model, what children reproduce corresponds not to the perceptible or figurative aspects of the model but to their understanding of its numerical and spatial aspects.

An even more remarkable result was obtained when children's memory was investigated in the same way with respect to a configuration of ten sticks ranging from 9 to 15cm in length arranged in a series from the shortest to the longest. The children, aged 3 to 8 years, were told to look carefully at the sticks so that they could remember them later. After a week and again after six months the children were asked to draw from memory what they had seen. As in the experiments already described there was no new presentation of the model. After they had completed their memory drawings the children were given sticks to make a series so that their levels of conceptual development with respect to seriation could be ascertained and so that the relationship between their conceptual levels and their memory drawings could be examined. The children's memory drawings showed varying levels of organization, examples of which are shown in Figure 38.4. The youngest children, mostly 3 to 4 years of age, drew a number of sticks of more or less equal length (1). Children of 4 to 5 years of age drew one of the configurations shown as 2a, b and c. From about 5 years of age children generally drew a correct seriation but with only a few elements and often with the bases not aligned horizontally (2d). On the whole the oldest children drew correct seriated configurations (3).

years requiring them to draw it from memory one hour and again six months after its presentation. There are inevitably some children within this age range for whom this configuration presents a kind of conceptual conflict. It is known that children achieve understanding of conservation of number before they aquire the concept of conservation of length. Children at this stage, therefore, will conceive the two rows of matchsticks to be equal with respect to number but unequal with respect to length, for they conceive that equality of length requires that the ends are coterminous. Thus, because 'they assimilate the (configuration) . . . to two schemata at one (one numerical and the other spatial) these children find themselves in a systematic quandary,' The reproductions of children between the ages of five to six years bear witness to the quandary, for instead of drawing a faithful copy of the configuration, as on the whole the older children do, they produce an illusory solution of the conflict by making the ends of the two rows coterminous as in both type II and type III solutions shown in Figure 38.3. The results indicate that 'memory retention is dominated by a tendency to

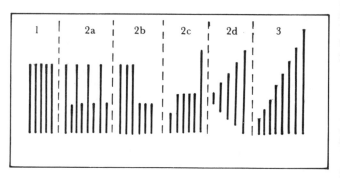

Figure 38.4

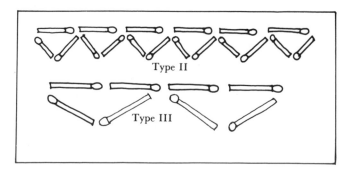

Type II

Type III

Figure 38.3

Seriation schemes and the memory code

The drawings proved to be similar to what the children did when asked to make a series with sticks. This alone would suggest some support for the hypotheses that memory is reconstructive rather than reproductive and that what a child reconstructs in memory is related to his schemes. But the results of requiring the children to reproduce the model from memory a second time after a lapse of six months support these hypotheses in an even more remarkable way. The reproductions of 74% of the children showed progress compared with their earlier drawings made one week after the presentation of the model. This progress always involved a move to the next sub-stage. Piaget and Inhelder suggest that over the six-month interval the children's schemes with respect to seriation have evolved through their experiences and actions to higher levels. The seriation schemes provide the code for memorizing and during the six-month period the modified scheme is used as a new code for the next memory evocation. Thus the memory code undergoes constant changes matching and determined by the corresponding schemes.

> Such a restructuring of the code takes place in close dependence on the schemes of intelligence. The clearest indication of this is the observation of different types of memory organisation in accordance with the age level of a child so that a longer interval of retention without any new presentation, far from causing a deterioration of memory, may actually improve it. In fact, such progress is due to and makes evident the general progress of intelligence during the interval concerned. (Inhelder, 1969)

Altemeyer's memory improvement experiments

There have been several attempts reported by Modgil and Modgil (1976) to replicate Piaget's findings on memory particularly in relation to the seriation task just described. Many of these studies have substantiated the long-term memory 'improvement' reported by Piaget. However, some of these investigators have interpreted the results differently from Piaget. Altemeyer *et al.* (1969), for example, have argued that there is a developmental tendency to seriate any drawing which involves an array which could be seriated and that this does not necessarily involve a recall of the original stimulus. In an investigation designed to test this hypothesis Altemeyer *et al.* presented a serial configuration of ten rods of different lengths similar to that used by Piaget and Inhelder to sixty-five children aged five to six years. A comparison between the children's drawings one week and six months after the presentation showed that 43% of the children's second reproductions were more serially ordered than their first ones, thus supporting Piaget's findings by showing an 'improvement'. A control group of twenty-nine children were given a slightly different task. They were presented with a scrambled series as in Figure 38.5. The second reproductions of 41% of these children were more serially ordered than their first ones and less like the scrambled series of the model. Thus their second reproductions were not an improvement in the sense of being closer to an accurate reproduction of the original display. While these results could be said to support Altemeyer's hypothesis, one could also interpret them as reflecting a rationalisation of the original configuration resulting from a development of conceptual understanding. It is as though the child has conceptualized the array as 'capable of being seriated'. His reproduction is more conceptually than figuratively accurate. The results of Altemeyer's investigation support rather than refute Piaget's contention that memory is not the copying process which a naive empiricism supposes.

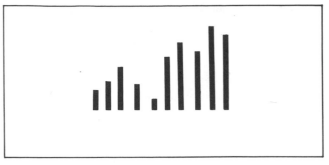

Figure 38.5

The acquisition of operative knowledge: Piaget's concept of action

Piaget maintains that the acquisition of operative knowledge is not a result of reproducing reality but is constructed by the knower through action. The concept of 'action' in Piaget's theory is complex and has three major connotations. Firstly, Piaget suggests that the logicomathematical operations whose development he has investigated are acquired as a result of abstracting from the results of one's actions on objects as distinct from abstracting from the perceived properties of objects, as is the case with concepts belonging to physics. Thus, for example, the concept of conservation of numerical quantity is achieved, Piaget maintains, through carrying out sorting and arranging activities with objects from which it is gradually abstracted that a numerical quantity is not changed by the configurational transformation.

Secondly, Piaget's notion of action involves an interactionist conception in contrast to the empiricist conception of the knower as passive.

> The object is known only so far as the subject achieves action on it, and this action is incompatible with the passive character which empiricism, at various degrees, attributes to knowledge. (Piaget, 1974)

Thirdly, Piaget's notion of action is not synonymous with physical activity. Cognitive development requires both physical manipulation and reflection upon action.

Empiricism and didactic teaching

An empiricist conception of the acquisition of knowledge is often the basis of didactic teaching. For if knowledge is thought to be acquired as a copying process then visual demonstrations and verbal presentations by the teacher of the facts and concepts the pupils are required to learn would seem to be the most effective way of teaching them. Of course, one must be careful not to over-simplify. No teacher supposes that a particular visual demonstration or verbal presentation will be equally effective with all pupils. Only a modicum of teaching experience makes it evident that some pupils do not have an adequate conceptual grasp to acquire certain representations with understanding. Faced with this fact of school life teachers then sometimes argue that pupils can catch up. In order to avoid setting up the complex individualized and diversified curricula that would be required to cater for differing levels of conceptual understanding, some material, such as mathematical rules and formulae and scientific laws, so the argument runs, must be presented to pupils before they have the necessary conceptual underpinning. But, it is claimed, at some point in the future those pupils will acquire the concepts and will then make sense of the material presented earlier. This argument only has force if memory is conceived of as a reservoir of 'traces' which accurately copy aspects of external reality. The problem is then only one of retrieval from this 'reservoir'.

This, of course, is an empiricist conception and quite different from the notion of a memory code continually restructured by evolving schemes and leading to the sort of 'improvement' found by Piaget and Inhelder in relation to the seriation task described above. Seriation is a concept which can show considerable evolution in children over a comparatively short period. With respect to other concepts whose evolution is slower Piaget and Inhelder found deterioration rather than improvement after a six months interval. This was the case, for example, in experiments designed to test children's memory for events the understanding of which involved an appreciation of causal relationships. The force of the memory for seriation experiment is that it provides strong support for the contention that memory is constructivist rather than a replicative process. It would be inappropriate to generalise more specifically from this experiment that 'improvement' in the memory code can always be expected.

A traditional didactic teaching approach often involves a strong emphasis on memorising compared with other cognitive activities such as questioning, problem-solving, inventing, checking and verifying. If it is supposed that knowledge is acquired as a replication of reality it is reasonable to give memorising a central place.

The traditional didactic teaching model is also characterized by ways of organizing the curriculum and the pupils that differ from those characterizing more informal models. Pupils tend to be organized in more homogeneous groups for teaching purposes than in the latter, for, if the acquisition of knowledge is thought to be a copying process, less attention needs to be paid to individual differences than would be the case for a curriculum based on the constructivist supposition that any specific curriculum content will be differently construed by each pupil. It would be unfair, however, to suggest that traditional didactic teaching pays no attention to individual differences. In some curriculum areas, in mathematics for example, the content is organized sequentially and the pupils are allowed to proceed through the sequence at different rates, some requiring more time and practice than others. Thus this is an acknowledgement of individual differences in terms of pace, that is in quantitative terms.

Informal teaching practices

By contrast more informal teaching practices usually involve heterogeneous grouping of pupils and more diversified curricula. At any one time pupils within a class may be involved with content in different curriculum areas, with different concepts and with different problems according to their interests and concerns as well as their levels of development. Thus individual differences are catered for in qualitative terms, not merely in the quantitative terms of a difference in pace.

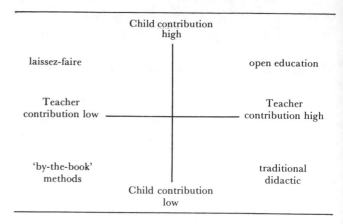

Figure 38.6

It would be wrong to think that an empiricist conception of knowledge is reflected only in traditional didactic teaching. It may well be the basis of certain 'progressive' or 'informal' practices. Figure 38.6 is an adaptation of a model proposed by Bussis, Chittenden and Amarel (1976) to characterize four teaching styles in early childhood education. Both of the upper quadrants represent teaching styles usually called 'informal', 'progressive' or 'child-centred'. Both of them are in a sense 'child-centred' but they differ in their view of the child and how he learns. The upper left-hand quadrant characterizes classrooms where the teacher plays a non-directive role. The children are likely to have a great deal of freedom of choice of activity. The teacher may well exercise careful forethought regarding the materials she provides for children's learning experiences, but beyond that she intervenes little in their activities. When she does intervene it is more likely to be in order to resolve a social conflict or an emotional problem than to extend a pupil intellectually. Thus there is a high contribution by the children and a low contribution by the teacher in terms of decisions regarding the content and process of learning.

The teaching style characterized by the upper right-hand quadrant is also one in which the children have a great deal of freedom of choice of activity, but, by contrast with the laissez-faire style, the teacher adopts an active role and intervenes in the context of the children's activities to promote learning and development. She takes her cue from the children by constantly diagnosing what they have understood or not understood, what problems they have generated and what ideas they have for the solution of these problems. These diagnoses in turn determine the ways in which she seeks to extend the activities, thinking and understanding of her pupils. Thus it is a teaching style in which both teacher and children make a high contribution to decisions regarding the content and process of learning.

There are a number of possible values and assumptions which could lead to a laissez-faire teaching style in early childhood education, but one of these may well be an empiricist conception of knowledge. Concepts are thought to be somehow embedded in the materials provided and it is assumed that if the children engage in activities with these materials they will automatically acquire those concepts. Thus careful thought is given to materials in terms of the concepts they exemplify, but intervention by the teacher is assumed to be superfluous if the embedded concepts are automatically transmitted to the pupils. This is essentially an empiricist conception of the knowledge process. Although this teaching style engages the children in activity it implies a view of their minds as passive. More activity, as has been stressed earlier, should not be confused with Piaget's much more refined concept of 'action'.

> The . . . confusion consists of believing that an activity with concrete objects is no more than a figurative process, in other words nothing but a way of producing a sort of precise copy, in perceptions or mental images, of the objects in question. (Piaget, 1971)

Conclusion: a constructivist teaching style

A teaching style based on Piaget's constructivist account of knowledge requires a high contribution from the teacher as well as the pupils. This high teacher contribution should involve educational dialogues with pupils which fulfil a number of inter-relating functions. Of these the following three are of major importance:

(a) observing and questioning pupils in such a way as to elicit diagnostic information,

(b) enabling pupils to reflect on their activities and on the conclusions they have drawn therefrom, and

(c) extending pupils' thinking in various ways.

The latter may often include visual demonstrations and verbal presentations by a teacher. But these would be based not on an empiricist assumption that a pupil would acquire the knowledge intended in a copying fashion, but instead would be designed to help a pupil crystallize and systematize the knowledge he has constructed.

References

Altemeyer, R., Fulton, D. and Berney, K. (1969) 'Long-term memory improvement: confirmation of a finding by Piaget', *Child Development*, 40, 845–57.

Bussis, A. M., Chittenden, E. A. and Amarel, M. (1976) *Beyond Surface Curriculum*, Boulder Colorado: Westview Press.

Inhelder, B. (1969) 'Memory and intelligence in the child' in Inhelder, B. and Chipman, H. H. (eds.) *Piaget and his School*, New York: Springer Verlag (1976).

Modgil, S. and Modgil, C. (1976) *Piagetian Research*, Vol. 2, NFER Publishing Co.

Piaget, J. (1971) *Science of Education and the Psychology of the Child*, Longman.

Piaget, J. (1974) *The Child and Reality*, Frederick Muller.

Piaget, J. and Inhelder, B. (1973) *Memory and Intelligence*, Routledge & Kegan Paul.

Piaget, J. and Inhelder, B. (1976) 'The gaps in empiricism' in Inhelder, B. and Chipman, H. H. (op. cit.).

Discussion Guide U

Compare your suggestions in Activity 39. What seem to be the concepts most frequently given by you as a group? Are there any concepts which were suggested only infrequently or not at all? If there are, try to think of equipment which might facilitate them.

Module Six

Language Development

In Module 5 the importance of the development of representational abilities to the development of cognition was discussed. Units 1 and 2 in that module dealt with symbolic play and graphic representation respectively. These are non-verbal modes of representation. Language is, as you will have read in Paper 33 by Bruner, an extremely important mode of representation. Its importance is acknowledged by devoting a whole module to it.

The first paper in the module, Paper 39, is introductory, its purpose being to explain some of the technical terms found in the literature on language acquisition.

In Paper 40 Wilkinson describes the stages in the child's acquisition of language between the ages of eighteen months/two years and five years. It is, of course, important that anyone whose work is with the education or care of young children has some knowledge of these stages. It is equally important, however, to be acquainted with the ways in which psychologists and psycholinguists have tried to explain how language is acquired, for the particular conception one has of this process will determine, in part, how one talks to a young child. Many adults believe that children acquire language purely by imitation. Paper 41 presents some of the evidence that suggests this to be a grossly over-simplified view, and Paper 42 discusses the main theories of how language is acquired. To say that language is not acquired purely by imitation is not to say that the adult does not have an extremely important role to play. Paper 43 is concerned with some of the ways in which adults can promote and facilitate the development of language in young children.

Among the major theories of language acquisition discussed by Donaldson is the 'cognition hypothesis' (for example, Bruner, 1975; Macnamara, 1972) which proposes that in early language learning a child first makes sense of objects and events at a non-linguistic level and that this understanding then determines the sense he makes of the linguistic input; effective language learning takes place when the adult tells the child what he already knows or sees.

On the other hand, there is no doubt that in various ways language can facilitate the development of children's understanding of their worlds. There is a close interdependence between language and the development of thinking. This interdependence was discussed with regard to children younger than two years old in Unit 1 Module 4. It was shown that how the baby makes sense of the world around him depends not only on his activities with objects but also on the way in which his mother or care-giver interacts with him providing verbal and non-verbal cues. In Paper 45 Francis gives examples of research into how mothers of children of two to five years interact verbally with them to facilitate their learning.

There is not just one relationship between language and thinking. As Francis's paper indicates language facilitates the development of thinking in at least three ways. It enables us to code experiences which in turn aids storage and retrieval. It helps focus attention on specific and relevant aspects of objects and events. It aids the expression of already acquired ideas and thus their communication. It is important to note, however, that saying that language facilitates thinking in these ways is not the same as saying that language determines thought. On the contrary, the 'cognition hypothesis' theory of language acquisition proposes the reverse, that what is already understood determines the language acquired.

Nevertheless, the notion that language determines thought has had a powerful influence. It is a view embedded in Whorf's (1956)* theory of linguistic relativity. Whorf's theory proposes that the language of a culture produces particular ways of perceiving and interpreting the world. Sometimes Whorf states explicitly that language determines thought. Sometimes he writes that language influences the way a person perceives objects and events. The former notion is known as the 'strong' version, the latter as the 'weak' version, of the Whorfian hypothesis.

The 'weak' version is unobjectionable providing it is interpreted only as meaning that a person *tends* to perceive the world in ways that are influenced by his language, and not that he *cannot* perceive the world in other ways. By contrast, the 'strong' version of Whorf's hypothesis has been strongly challenged, not only by the proponents of the 'cognition hypothesis' account of language acquisition, but also, as Francis discusses in her paper, by Piaget and his co-workers.

Whorf's hypothesis has been most directly tested in the work on social class language differences, and Bernstein's work has been particularly influential. This, together with contrary positions and evidence, is discussed in Paper 46 by Keats and Keats.

*This theory is sometimes known as the Whorf–Sapir hypothesis. Sapir had put forward a linguistic relativity hypothesis some thirty years previously, but his statements were elaborated by Whorf.

References
Bruner, J. S. (1975) 'The ontogenesis of speech acts', *Journal of Child Language*, 2, 1–19.
Macnamara, J. (1972) 'Cognitive basis of language learning in infants', *Psychol. Review*, 79, 1–13.
Whorf, B. L. (1956) *Language, Thought and Reality*, Cambridge, Mass.: MIT Press.

Unit One

The Child's Acquisition of Language and the Role of the Adult

- Read the introduction to the module and then read Papers 12 and 13 again. Read Paper 39; this explains some of the technical terms which appear in subsequent papers in the module
- Complete Activity 40 which is designed to test your understanding of these terms
- Read Papers 40 and 41
- Complete Activity 41; this again requires you to work with young children. Make sure you give yourself enough time to establish rapport with the children before giving them the tasks
- Read Paper 42
- Carry out Activity 42. This task is designed to give you data on a developmental sequence in children's understanding of prepositions; the significance of this sequence is discussed in Paper 43, which you should then read. (Do not read it before you have completed the activity.)
- Complete Activity 43
- Read Paper 44. After reading this paper the most desirable of the alternative adult responses given in Activity 43 should be clear. It is important, however, that you do not read this paper until you have completed the activity. Having read the paper you should then check your judgements in Activity 43 with what is discussed in the paper
- Complete Activity 44 which again involves making judgements about adults' verbal responses to children. This time your prior reading of Paper 44 should help you in your judgements
- Discussion Guide V should help you compare your judgements with those of your fellow students

Reading	85 mins.
Activities	225 mins.
Discussion	90 mins.
Total	400 mins.
	= 6 hrs. 35 mins.

An introduction:
some terms explained
Joan Tamburrini

In Unit 2 Module 4 the early stages in the child's acquisition of language were discussed. It was shown that until eighteen months to two years of age the baby's speech consists mostly of single-word utterances. These single words often have quite complex meanings. For example, if a baby says 'shoes' he may mean 'put my shoes on', 'my shoe has come off', 'where are my shoes?', 'there are my shoes' and so on. The word 'holophrase' has been given to these phrases or sentence meanings carried by a single word.

Complex in meaning though these single-world utterances are, one cannot yet speak of the child's language as having a 'grammar'. A grammar exists when the child puts together two or more words which include a noun phrase and a verb phrase. For example, if a child says 'Daddy wash', there is a noun phrase, 'Daddy', and a verb phrase, 'wash'. It has a grammar even though words are missing and the meaning is, therefore, ambiguous unless we are there with the child and can guess from what is happening that he means 'Daddy wash me' rather than 'Daddy is washing himself'. To say a child's early language has a grammar does not mean that it is grammatical in the sense that it exhibits 'correctness' as laid down in traditional textbooks on grammar. The word 'grammar' is used by linguists to describe young children's speech rather than to prescribe how they ought to speak.

The study of child grammar in the pre-school years has been of great importance not only because it is a way of describing the changes in children's language in those years but also because it gives us some insights into how children acquire language. This unit is devoted to both aspects.

In order to understand fully the papers in this unit it is necessary to understand the categories linguists use in analysing children's language. They distinguish three aspects of language—phonology, grammar and semantics. *Phonology* is concerned with the sounds of a given language, *grammar* with the form of its words and the way words are combined in *sentences*, and *semantics* with the meanings of words and their combinations.

Phonology is concerned with the features of sounds which are the basic units of a language. The basic speech sounds are called *phonemes*. The words 'pat' and 'bat' differ in their initial phonemes 'p' and 'b'. The words 'this' and 'thing' differ, of course, in their final phonemes 's' and 'ng', but they also differ in their initial phonemes, for 'th', though

written in the same way, is sounded differently in the two words. By contrast 'meat' and 'meet' are composed of the same phonemes even though they are spelt differently.

Phonemes are distinguished from *morphemes*. A morpheme is the smallest meaningful unit of speech. A morpheme may be a word, for example, 'dog', or a part of a word such as 'ed' in the past tense of verbs. It may even be a single letter such as 's' in the plural and possessive forms of nouns. Thus the word 'unflinchingly' consists of four morphemes, 'un', 'flinch', 'ing' and 'ly'. Morphemes may be *free*, that is they can stand alone. In the above examples 'dog' and 'flinch' are free morphemes. Those that cannot stand alone but must be combined with other morphemes are called *bound*. In the above examples 'un', 'ing', and 'ly' are bound morphemes.

The same distinction is that between *roots* and *affixes*. The morphemes 'dog' and 'flinch' are roots, whereas 'un', 'ing' and 'ly' are affixes. Affixes consist of *prefixes* and *suffixes*. As the terms suggest prefixes precede root morphemes, suffixes follow them. Thus in the above examples 'un' is a prefix while 'ing' and 'ly' are suffixes.

Some suffixes are called *inflexions*. These are suffixes which cannot be followed by any other phoneme. An example is the plural and possessive 's' on nouns.

Grammar is concerned with morphology and syntax. Whereas *morphology* deals with the internal structure of words, that is with how morphemes are combined, *syntax* is concerned with the rules governing the combination of words in sentences. Take the following sentences:

Indian Braves could bear pain unflinchingly.

How could Indian Braves bear pain unflinchingly?

Morphological aspects of both sentences include the combining of the morphemes 'Brave' and 's' to give 'Braves' and of 'un', 'flinch', 'ing' and 'ly' to give 'unflinchingly'. If we analyse the two sentences syntactically we notice that the auxiliary verb 'could' changes position. In the first sentence 'could' follows the subject 'Indian Braves', whereas in the second sentence it precedes it. These structures follow the rules for both kinds of sentence, a statement and a question. These are syntactic rules, that is, rules for combining words in sentences. There are, of course a great number of other syntactic rules.

Semantics is concerned with the meaning of words and is not, strictly speaking, an aspect of grammar. This does not mean, however, that linguists do not sometimes have to take meaning or semantic aspects into account when analysing a sentence grammatically. This is particularly important where there is ambiguity as in the following sentence given by Chomsky and quoted frequently in textbooks on linguistics:

Visiting relatives can be a nuisance.

This sentence may mean either that relatives who visit one can be a nuisance or that paying visits to relatives can be a nuisance. In the first case 'relatives' is the subject of the sentence and the word 'visiting' is adjectival, whereas in the second case 'relatives' is the object and 'visiting' is verbal. Linguists have been interested in ambiguous sentences because they illustrate a distinction made by Chomsky between the deep and surface structures of sentences. The *deep structure* is the underlying form of a sentence which represents the basic meaning or semantic relationships. The *surface structure* is the perceptible form of a sentence which represents the grammatical relationships. The above sentence is ambiguous because two sentences with different deep structures have the same surface structure. If relatives are the subject of the sentence the deep structure is different from what it would be if relatives are the object. Conversely, different surface structures may be derived from the same deep structure. For example the sentences 'Mary chased John' and 'John was chased by Mary' have the same deep structure though their surface structures are different. The process by which surface structures are derived from deep structures involves *transformations*. In the example just given 'Mary chased John' is the active transformation, 'John was chased by Mary' is the passive transformation.

As will be seen in some of the following papers it is very important to take meaning or semantic aspects into account as well as grammar in examining the language of young children.

The development of language
A. Wilkinson

Stages in language development 1–5

During the first five years when a child is learning language we may reasonably speak about definite stages in his language development, as long as we are content to confine ourselves to the grammar he uses, because that is reasonably easy to study. There are, however, no definite stages by which his vocabulary increases. We can certainly say that the vocabulary of a child at 5 years will be greater than it was at 18 months. It is, however, increasingly difficult as the child gets older to know the extent of his vocabulary: he may know many words he does not use, or we do not hear him use. As far as semantic development is concerned, it is often very difficult to be sure what he means by what he says; though we hope he talks more interestingly — 'talks more sense' — at 5 than at 1½.

Acquisition of grammar

There are three aspects of grammar to be acquired — the phrase structure rules, the transformational rules, and the rules of accidence.

Holophrases

Children begin with single words. These need not be words in our sense. A child can get a long way with a single sound combination like 'uhuh' to mean a variety of things. Sometimes they are more than single words to an adult, but the child learns them as one: 'what's that' is one example of what is known as a 'giant word'. These single word equivalents are called *holophrases*.

They are used in a variety of ways: linked with action ('down' meaning 'I want to get down'); as a name ('dindin'); to express emotion, such as approval or disapproval ('uhuh'). It is interesting to note that the child's use of a holophrase may indicate a greater grammatical knowledge than is immediately evident. Thus, when he uses 'door' to mean 'open door', he is using a noun to mean verb plus noun in our terms.

Phrase structures

(a) Pivot and open classes The next stage seems to be when the child uses words in combinations, and can change the combination. Thus we can only regard 'what's that' as a holophrase until we know the child can use 'what's this', 'what's book', etc. It seems that children have a small number of words (pivot class) that are frequently employed, which they use along with a larger number of others (open class) that are less frequently employed. Thus, 'allgone' or 'see' or 'my' could be pivot words used alongside 'milk', 'shoe', 'hand', 'sock', 'apple', and so on. Pivot words seldom occur in combination with each other, but open words may do so ('horsey, cow').

This notion is useful in indicating how children do combine words; but it may also be doing them an injustice to run all such combinations together as a pivot/open class. It seems that in effect they may be using a form of adult grammar. A child saying 'allgone milk' is using adult terms *verb and noun*, whereas in 'my sock' he is using possessive pronoun and noun.

(b) Further phrase structures Further combinations that occur are more in accordance with adult grammar, often in stripped down or telegraphic form. Thus Susan, aged 2½, is looking at a picture book with her mother:

Mother Shall we find a picture of your dolly?
Susan yes/there dolly/there dolly (*book falls*) oh dear/dolly gone/get dolly mummy/get dolly/I get dolly

We find here two complete sentences syntactically speaking ('get dolly mummy', 'I get dolly'), though the definite article is not yet used. The verb 'to be' is also missing ('there dolly').

Early transformations

Emerging rather later than the first phrase structure are some trans-formations, such as questions with a word like 'where' or 'what' (known as '*wh*-transformations'), in a sentence like 'Where mummy gone?' Auxiliary verbs are not used (for example, 'Where *has* mummy gone?'). The child will also use a negative transformation using 'no' or 'not', for example, 'No mummy go' (with the negative probably used in front of the sentence).

Here is part of a dialogue between Guy, who is nearly 3, and his mother. They are playing with his toys, principally a 'wheel van' and model animals. The van is loaded and is supposed to be going to school.

Mother Where's the school bus? Is this the school bus in the car park?
Guy No the wheel van, wheel van.
Mother That can't be a school bus.
Guy No a the wheel van. Where school bus mummy? Where school bus? Where school bus? . . .
Mother Which way is it to school? Which way is the bus going?
Guy That my wheel van. Open it. Daddy do that. Daddy do that.
Mother Daddy's opened the doors.
Guy Here school mummy. Here school.
Mother Good, you'd better stop there then.
Guy Pig get out/pig/pig get out.
Mother Let him get out.
Guy Yes, wheel van. Going brm. Doing writing.
Mother He's doing writing at school. He's a very clever pig.
Guy Sit down. Sit down. Sit going down. School bus in here. This one. This one wheel van going this. This one going school. This one. This one going school. This horsey going school. In school, this horsey.
Mother Can he get in?
Guy Yes.
Mother Yes, just about.
Guy Going school, your school, going school. Get out, get out

lamb. Err . . . get out. Doing writing, writing.

Mother Do they do anything else at school?

Guy Yes. Sums. Sums. Going school Zoe, going school, going school. That one going wheel van, in wheel van. No. Brm. Legs in it. Going school. Going school. That little, little big lamb going school. That big lamb. Go school Zoe, go school. No touch it. Doing writing. Go away. Go away. No touch it. Here school. Here school. Yes. Brm here — that — that school. No touch it. Go away. Go away. Play daddy. What's that for? What's that for?

Mother What's it for?

Guy Look out. Look out.

Mother Yes, that's the lookout, that's the windscreen.

Guy Yes.

Mother What are you going to use it for?

Guy To look out. Drive, driving. Me driving.

It is clear that Guy's understanding is considerable: he may not know the word 'windscreen', but he knows the concept and its function. As far as his grammar is concerned, to judge from this sample he can use *wh*-transformations ('Where school bus?' 'What's that for?'), and negative transformations by inserting 'no' ('No touch it'), neither of which, of course, are accurate in terms of adult grammar. He uses some verbs ('touch') but not auxiliaries ('This one going school', not 'is going'), and the verb 'to be' is omitted ('Here school'). He is moving to the stage of being able to use some prepositions ('Legs in it'), but is not secure in this ('going school'). He can use the definite article ('the wheel van').

At this stage, at least in this passage, there is no evidence that he can use rules of accidence (for example, tense, number, possession).

Further transformations and accidence

Between the ages of 3 and 4 many children acquire auxiliary verbs which enable them to carry out interrogative transformations (for example, 'you think' becomes 'do you think?'). Sentences become less telegraphic in form as words such as definite and indefinite articles and prepositions are used. Features of accidence (for example, agreement of singulars, tense other than the present) appear. Sentences may become more complex.

The following is a transcription of part of a conversation with Francesca, aged 3, about her tortoise. Pet tortoises are a pretty torpid lot, but Francesca's is a toy powered by the dynamos of her imagination, so there is very little it can't do.

yes he does/he eats/and he eats a apple/he eats lots of things/to eat/in the winter/eats leaves cabbages vedables and apples and nanas and grapes and he eats/hollies/they won't prick/his teeth/won't prick it teeth/and and/and he eats flowers and roses/and petals/no he doesn't eat the stalks up/no he don't make his teeth/he don't pick the flower up off/the stalk/he doesn't/no he only eats petals/and they fall off the flower/ and he like them/and he/and he picks them up to eat . . . that's what he wants to eat . . . cat enters hallo/hallo/going to go in your room/I don't know where he's going to go/do you think he's going to go on your bed.

At this stage later and earlier forms of accidence exist side by side ('he eats', 'he picks them up', 'they fall off', as against 'he like them'). There are assured negatives ('he doesn't eat the stalk up'), and interrogatives ('do you think he's going to go on your bed'). The most advanced feature is what is now known as 'embedding', where a sentence (or subordinate clause) is included in another ('I don't know' and 'he's going to go where' as 'I don't know where he's going to go').

There are no signs in the passage that Francesca can yet handle tense by means of inflections, but she can certainly handle a future meaning in 'going to go'. Could she also have said 'will go'? There is insufficient evidence on this. Certainly Amanda, who is just 4, in this next transcript has no difficulty with past inflections.

Once upon a time mousie lived/and he couldn't have a hole because/he was so fat/and he didn't have a time to spare because he was so happy/and I didn't know what to do/so he had an idea/I've giving him a new home so I did/that was in my mummy and daddy's room/ there was a little mouse hole.

was there?

and they/there really is.

Command of inflections is apparent, as well as the ability to use complex embedded constructions ('I didn't know what to do'). The unacceptable forms ('I've giving') are doubtless slips.

Almost complete command

By Francesca's age (just over 3), and certainly by Amanda's age (4), many children have got a considerable command of English grammar — the phrase structure, the transformational rules, and the rules of accidence. They may be said to 'know' English grammar.

There are, however, some syntactic rules which children do not seem to master until they are older. Carol Chomsky, the wife of Noam Chomsky, has investigated these in *The Acquisition of Syntax in Children from 5 to 16* (MIT Press, 1969). Take, for instance, a sentence like 'John is eager to see'. Children will easily understand that it is John who wants to do the seeing. But if we take 'John is easy to see', they will not readily grasp that it is John who will be seen. They need to realize that the subject of the second sentence is 'to see John'. (Every adult realizes this, even though he might not be able to formulate it in this way.) Thus children were shown a blindfold doll and asked 'Is this doll easy or hard to see?' A child who answered 'hard to see' would be asked to make it easy to see: the typical response of the younger children would be to remove the blindfold.

Again, children may be confused about who does the shovelling in a sentence like 'John promised Bill to shovel the driveway'. The younger children think that Bill shovels, on an analogy with, say, 'John told Bill to shovel the driveway', where it would be Bill. Similarly, distinctions between 'ask' and 'tell' present problems. In all these cases the 5-year-olds predominantly got the wrong answers, but improved as they grew older so that by the age of 10 nearly all of them understood the constructions.

It should be added that, as far as accidence is concerned, many regional and class dialects have forms of their own, different from the standard forms. Forms such as 'I done it', 'us be going', 'we'm going', 'I told he' are commonly used in such cases. Such forms almost never result in any confusion in understanding, though they are often stigmatized as 'bad grammar'. 'Us isn't doing nothing' breaks three rules of accidence (but none of syntax) and the meaning is never in doubt except to the pedant who wishes to score a debating point.

Summary

It is possible to trace the stages in the acquisition of grammar from holophrases (single 'words') to combinations of words, first organized according to the child's own syntax, and then increasingly along the lines of adult grammar. In the later stages variation on simple patterns ('transformations'), and alterations to individual elements for particular purposes, accidence, are learned. By the time they enter school, children normally have a considerable (though not complete) mastery of grammatical rules.

The significance of errors and omissions

Joan Tamburrini

A few years ago a television interviewer stood in a busy city street and asked several passing adults how they thought children learned language. Without exception they answered that children learned language simply by imitating the adults they heard. The studies of professional psycholinguists suggest that this common-sense view is an oversimplification. Of course, there must be an element of imitation in children's language acquisition. If a child does not hear speech he will not learn to speak. But imitation is just one of a number of factors involved in language acquisition. Language is acquired by a process much more complex and interesting than simple imitation.

The study of young children's linguistic errors furnishes evidence against the view that children learn language simply by imitation. Children commonly produce grammatical errors which result from the overgeneralization of a rule. The child cannot state the rule, of course, but, nevertheless, he uses it systematically and to the point of overgeneralizing it to apply to exceptions of the rule. This is found with certain inflexions. For example, children learn to add the inflexion 'ed' for the past tense of verbs and then use it for verbs whose past tense is not of that form, as in the case of the child who said, 'We went for a picnic and a wasp bited me'. The same overgeneralization is commonly found with the inflexion 's' for plural nouns. It has even been found that some children produce a correct form and then later learn a rule which they overgeneralize and wrongly apply. Francis (1975) reports that her son Jonathan first said 'chessmen' and 'children' and later, overgeneralizing the rule of adding 's' to make a noun plural, said 'chessmens' and 'childrens'. Two months later he again used the correct form.

The development of grammatical rules in young children has been investigated by Berko (1958). She devised a test in which the child was required to apply rules such as those for the plural noun, the past tense and the comparatives and superlatives of adjectives, to nonsense words. For example, one of the nonsense words 'wug' was invented for the name of a strange animal. The experimenter would show the child a picture of one of these strange animals and say, 'This is a wug'. Then another picture of two of the creatures would be shown as the experimenter said with a questioning intonation, 'Here are two . . .?' At three years of age most children can supply the correct form 'wugs'. They had successfully learned the rule and could apply it to a word they had never heard before.

The errors children produce through overgeneralization of a rule cannot have been learned by imitation for the child has never heard adults say, 'feets', 'bited', 'him's stomach' or 'why I can't have some?', just as he has never before heard the word 'wugs'. When children produce word forms or combinations they have never heard they may be said to be using language creatively. Children also use language creatively by inventing words or word combinations to convey meanings when they do not know the correct word or words. A five-year-old boy of my acquaintance had seen children roller-skating in the park and wanted some skates. He did not know the name to give them and asked his parents for some 'shoe-bicycles' for his birthday. The Russian poet Chukovsky (1966) gives the amusing example of the small girl who, when found admiring herself in the mirror, was asked what she was doing and answered, 'I pretty-mire [for admire] myself'.

Bellugi (1971) carried out a study which suggests that children may sometimes be unable to imitate grammatical structures that they do not already produce spontaneously. Bellugi had observed the language development of a boy, Adam, and found that when he was about three years and three months old he used the correct sequence of auxiliary verb–pronoun/noun for yes–no questions. Thus he would say correctly:

> '*Can I* have a piece of paper?'
> '*Will you* help me?'
> '*Does the kitty* stand up?'

But he did not use the correct sequence in 'wh' questions. Thus he would say:

> 'What *I did* yesterday?'
> 'Which way *they should* go?'
> 'Why *we can't* find the right one?'

Bellugi tested Adam by playing a game in which he was told, 'You say what I say'. Adam was unable to imitate correctly the structure for 'wh' questions:

> Adult: Adam, say what I say: 'Where *can he* put them?'
> Adam: 'Where *he can* put them?'

These findings are further illuminated by studies of

children's spontaneous imitations of adult language. These show that children imitate selectively, and that what determines the selection is understanding. In other words they tend to imitate either those grammatical structures that are already appearing in their own speech or those which they are on the verge of acquiring.

It has been shown that we can begin to understand something about the ways in which children learn language by examining their errors. Equally informative are the omissions in their speech. Young children's sentences are often condensed and incomplete. They are what Brown and Fraser (1963) call 'telegraphic'. Hazel Francis (1975) gives a number of examples from Jonathan's speech some of which follow:

> 'Daddy gone work', instead of 'Daddy (has) gone (to) work'.
> 'My lorry', instead of '(That is) my lorry'.
> 'I going on a horsie', instead of 'I (am) going on a horsie'.
> 'Bus stopped', instead of '(The) bus (has) stopped'.

This kind of speech is aptly called telegraphic. Just as we usually understand without difficulty the meaning of a telegram in spite of the omission of some words, so Jonathan's telegraphic statements were usually intelligible to the adults who heard them. Where there was some ambiguity the context usually made it clear whether the child meant, 'That is my lorry', 'Give me my lorry' or 'Where is my lorry?'

Most children will have heard adults use the words such as 'to' and 'the' and word combinations such as 'has gone' and 'I am' much more frequently than they have heard words such as 'lorry' and 'horsie'. If children learned language by simple imitation it would be reasonable to suppose that they would learn with most ease the words they heard most frequently. An examination of omissions in children's telegraphic utterances suggests that this is not the case and that one of the main factors determining the language a child produces is meaning.

Further support comes from a study by Brown (1973) in which he compared the frequency with which the parents of three young children, Adam, Eve and Sarah, used certain words or word forms with the order of the children's acquisition of those words. Brown found that once a child had learned a new word or word form it appeared regularly in a number of phrases regardless of the frequency with which the parent had used it. For example the word 'in' is absent from Eve's speech in samples 1–6, whereas it is always present when required in samples 7–12. Brown concludes that 'there is no clear evidence at all that parental frequencies influence the order of development of the forms we have studied'.

In sum, children are not passive imitators of the language they hear. They actively select from adult models in relation to the rules they have already acquired and to the meanings significant to them. Thus they do not learn language in a piecemeal way but rather in an orderly, systematic fashion. It is the behaviourist theory which views children as somewhat passive imitators of the language they hear. Two alternative theories of how children acquire language are Chomsky's theory and a more recent one sometimes known as the 'cognition hypothesis'. The following paper by Donaldson examines these two theories.

References
Bellugi, U. (1971) 'Simplification in children's language' in Huxley, R. and Ingram, E. (eds.) *Language Acquisition: Models and Methods*, New York: Academic Press.
Berko, J. (1958) 'The child's learning of English morphology', *Word*, 14, 150–77.
Brown, R. (1973) *A First Language*, Allen & Unwin.
Brown, R. and Fraser, C. (1963) 'The acquisition of syntax' in Cofer, C. W. and Musgrave, S. S. (eds.) *Verbal Behaviour and Learning*, New York: McGraw-Hill.
Chukovsky, K. (1966) *From Two to Five*, University of California Press.
Francis, H. (1975) *Language in Childhood*, Paul Elek.

Module Six   Paper 42

Learning language
Margaret Donaldson

It has become fashionable recently to talk, not of *learning* to speak, but of *acquiring* language. This is the result of a kind of revolution which took place in the 1960s and which was due to the work of the American linguist, Noam Chomsky.

As regards the growth of a child's knowledge of his language, Chomsky's central thesis was — and is — that we are innately equipped with knowledge about what human language is like — about the *kind* of system it is. He supposes us to be provided from birth with a special sensitivity to those features of the grammars of human language which are 'universal' — that is, not specific to any given tongue. Thus we are able quickly to recognize, or 'latch on' to, the ways in which these features manifest themselves in the particular human language with which we happen to be dealing — Chinese or Finnish or Hebrew or whatever, as the case may be.

Notice, first of all, that in this account the stress is on *grammar*. The emphasis is on how the child comes by his knowledge of the structure of the language, of the rules which control the ways in which words may be combined with other words to form acceptable utterances.

This was a topic which had previously received very little attention from students of child language, and Chomsky's work generated a sudden rush of interest in the problem — an interest so great that, for a while, almost every other aspect of language learning was ignored. The research to which this interest gave rise seemed at first to confirm the claim that children had mastered the grammar of their language at a very early age. And this mastery appeared to involve the child in really formulating the rules for himself. Much was made of the fact that children's errors were sometimes 'rule-revealing'. It was argued that a child who says 'I bringed it' must have formulated (in some sense, though presumably not consciously) the rule

that you make the past tense of a verb by adding -*ed* to the present tense. The error would then arise simply because he applied the rule too widely, not yet having come to know the exceptions. At any rate it was clear that he had not learned 'I bringed it' by direct imitation of adults, for this is not an error that they are at all likely to make.

What was specially exciting against this background was the finding that children will sometimes begin by saying 'I brought' correctly and then for a time abandon the correct form in favour of the erroneous one. This made it seem clear that the child's active building of his own grammar was a process which could over-ride other kinds of learning; and students of child language spent a great deal of time trying to specify the grammar which a child was using at any given stage in his development. They did this by collecting a 'corpus' of as many as possible of the things the child had said, and then trying to work out a set of rules by which just these utterances might have been generated.

Little attention was paid, at the height of this activity, to the question of what the child might mean by the things he was saying, and still less to the question of his ability to understand the words of others. It was widely accepted, however, that his understanding would be generally in advance of his ability to speak. 'Comprehension precedes production' was the dictum. This seemed like common sense and such research as had been done appeared on the whole to support it.

In order to understand how significant the work on child grammar appeared a decade ago, it is necessary to think of it in relation to the ideas that were then dominant concerning other aspects of the development of the mind. In particular, the work on child language has to be seen in relation to the work of Piaget, and to Piaget's claim that the child under the age of seven is in many ways extremely limited in his ability to think and

reason. We have already seen that the Piagetian pre-school child is not supposed to know what an object would look like from the other side. To give some further examples of his limitations, he is supposed to think that if you pour water from a jar into another jar of a different shape you change the amount of the water. Further, he is not supposed to realize that if a red stick is longer than a yellow stick, and if that yellow stick is longer than a blue stick, then the red stick must be longer than the blue stick; and so on.

By the mid-1960s, a flood of researches had been pouring out of Geneva for years, all of them tending to the same conclusion: the child under seven is very restricted intellectually. He has developed considerable skills on a practical level, mastering these rapidly during the first eighteen months of his life. But he is not much of a thinker.

During the 1960s this work by Piaget and his colleagues was at the peak of its influence. It was very widely known and very widely accepted.

Against this background the claims about the child as a grammarian were dramatic. How was one to explain that a child who, on the one hand, was baffled by many things which seemed utterly simple and obvious to an adult could, on the other hand, work out for himself the rules of such a highly complex system as a human language?

To this question Chomsky proposed an answer: the child must have a *highly specific* predisposition to understand this kind of system. He must be born with a 'language acquisition device'.*

The language acquisition device, or LAD as it was called, was pictured as a kind of box. Into this 'box' (which was presumably located somewhere in the central nervous system, though not literally as a box, of course) there went, via the child's ears, linguistic input — input that was often very scrappy, fragments of the discourse that the child was hearing around him. But the device was so well tuned to the key features of human language that from this inadequate input it could extract the rules of the grammar — so sensitive and well prepared that it could produce almost immediately the right hypotheses about what these rules might be.

It proved to be an extraordinarily compelling idea. Almost everyone in the affected disciplines succumbed at least for a time to its seductive power. One of its consequences was to set human beings very firmly apart from the other mammals, who evidently lacked such a device. It was of course no new idea that man is set apart by his language-learning skills. But this notion of the special human LAD provided a new kind of focus for the old apartheid.†

In 1965 Chomsky stated his position like this:

> It seems plain that language acquisition is based on the child's discovery of what from a formal point of view is *a deep and abstract theory* — a generative grammar of his language — many of the concepts and principles of which are *only remotely related to experience* by long and intricate chains of unconscious quasi-inferential steps. [My italics]

Before Chomsky, the closeness to experience of the language-learning process had been the main emphasis. This emphasis is now returning, but in a very different form.

In the 1930s, 1940s and 1950s there was a conception of how language was learned which in its broad outlines went almost unchallenged at that time. Many variant theories existed, but the basic notion was that a word acquired its meaning by occurring, *together with* the thing which it meant or *stood for*. Language was conceived as a vast network of associative links between separate elements: individual words and individual 'things'. Thus a child's language-learning history was the history of the formation and strengthening of these bonds. And sometimes the following sort of account was offered to explain how the process got begun.

While a mother is looking after her baby she normally makes human speech sounds. The child has a natural tendency to vocalize randomly himself. Some of his sounds will come close to those his mother makes and will thus be associated with the relief and satisfaction which her presence and her care bring to him. He will then tend more and more to make those sounds rather than others in his repertoire — and gradually he will discover that these sounds not only satisfy him, but produce desirable responses from his parents. Thus he will begin to *use* them.

There is no point now in discussing how, starting from one or other version of the 'associationist' position, psychologists tried to explain the full development of language in all its richness and flexibility. The attempts were sometimes ingenious. They achieved some partial successes that looked promising. In the end they all failed.

The Chomskyan revolution was a revolt against them; and Chomsky's attack on the significance of experience was the flag to which the rebels rallied. A child with a language acquisition device had need of experience indeed, but only to set going processes which were destined to depend upon it very little thereafter.

Now in the 1970s another revolt has begun. It is milder, and it lacks one powerfully dominant leader. But it is gathering strength.

In 1972 John Macnamara wrote a paper which stands Chomsky's argument about the language acquisition device upon its head. In place of the claim that children have an 'acquisiton device' whose content is highly specific to language, with the result that language acquisition shoots ahead of the other skills of the mind, Macnamara proposed that children are able to learn language precisely because they possess certain other skills — and specifically because they have a relatively well-developed capacity for making sense of certain types of situation involving direct and

immediate human interaction.

To understand how this might work, imagine, for instance, the following scene. An English woman is in the company of an Arab woman and her two children, a boy of seven and a little girl of thirteen months who is just beginning to walk but is afraid to take more than a few steps without help. The English woman speaks no Arabic, the Arab woman and her son speak no English.

The little girl walks to the English woman and back to her mother. Then she turns as if to start off in the direction of the English woman once again. But the latter now smiles, points to the boy and says: 'Walk to your brother this time.' At once the boy, *understanding the situation* though he understands not a word of the language, holds out his arms. The baby smiles, changes direction and walks to her brother. Like the older child she appears to have understood the situation perfectly.

These events occurred as I have described them. The thing to notice is that the words 'Walk to your brother this time' were such as to fit with complete appropriateness the patterns of interaction. All the participants understood the situation in the sense that they understood one another's intentions. The language was unnecessary but it was uttered — and its meaning was highly predictable in the human context of its occurrence. What the people meant was clear. What the words meant could in principle be derived from that.

It is evident that some kind of association is involved here — and is indeed essential to this account of what is going on. It is possible to figure out what the words mean because they occur *together with* certain non-linguistic events. But beyond this all likeness to the old associationist accounts disappears. The whole nature of the explanation is different, for it implies a totally different conception of the nature of the human mind.

The old idea was that the associations were built up in quite mechanical automatic ways. They were bonds between isolated elements. The person in whom these bonds developed was passive. Something happened to him, and an association between, say, a word and a thing was the result. The associations came first. Insofar as there was 'meaning' it was an outcome of the (conditioning) process by which the associations were established.

The newer account differs from this in the most fundamental way. The primary thing is now held to be the grasp of meaning — the ability to 'make sense' of things, and above all to

*I do not intend to imply that Chomsky himself was directly influenced by Piaget's work when he postulated the language acquisition device. But I think that, for many psychologists, Chomsky's claims were rendered more striking and interesting by being considered in the context of Piagetian findings. On the other hand, Piagetian theory conflicts in many ways with the Chomskyan position. It would take a whole book to do justice to the relations between the two.

†Yet in June 1966 two American psychologists, Allen and Beatrice Gardner, were already undertaking the apparently hopeless task of teaching American Sign Language to Washoe, a chimpanzee — a task which turned out not to be so hopeless after all.

make sense of what people do, which of course includes what people say. On this view, it is the child's ability to interpret situations which makes it possible for him, through active processes of hypothesis-testing and inference, to arrive at a knowledge of language.

Now there is an important condition which must be satisfied if this account is to hold: the child must be in a general way capable of inference. For it is no longer being claimed that when he learns language he is using skills highly specific to that task. On the contrary, language learning is now presented as being closely bound up with all the other learning that is going on.

Indeed for a long time the learning of language may be bound up with non-linguistic concerns more inextricably than has appeared in anything that has been said so far. It may turn out to be a very long journey from the primary understanding of what people mean by the words they speak and by their concomitant acts to the ultimate and separate understanding of what *words* mean. Perhaps the idea that words mean anything — in isolation — is a highly sophisticated adult notion, and a Western adult notion at that.

Heinz Werner tells the story of an explorer who was interested in the language of a North American Indian tribe and who asked a native speaker to translate into his language the sentence: 'The white man shot six bears today.' The Indian said it was impossible. The explorer was puzzled, and asked him to explain. 'How can I do that?' said the Indian. 'No white man could shoot six bears in one day.'

To Western adults, and especially to Western adult linguists, languages are formal systems. A formal system can be manipulated in a formal way. It is an easy but dangerous move from this to the conclusion that it is also learned in a formal way.

Chomsky's LAD is a formal data processor, in its way just as automatic and mechanical as processes of an associationist kind. In go the linguistic data, out comes a grammar. The living child does not seem to enter into the business very actively (not to say fully) in either case. What does the warm blood in the veins matter? It actually figures more in some associationist accounts than in the Chomskyan one.

Reference
Macnamara, J. (1972) 'Cognitive basis of language learning in infants', Psychol. Review, 79, 1–13.

Commentary on Activity 42
Joan Tamburrini

If the 'cognition hypothesis' account of language acquisition proposed in particular by Macnamara and discussed by Donaldson in the preceding paper is correct, one would expect to find that the child's acquisition of language proceeds apace with his acquisition of the concepts the language expresses. There is some evidence to suggest that this is the case. For example, the words 'in', 'on', 'beside', 'below', 'through' and 'along' all express spatial concepts. Some of these concepts we know, from the work of Piaget, children acquire before others. The words 'in' and 'on' express what are called topological relationships, the words 'under' and 'beside' refer to what are called Euclidean relationships, and the words 'along' and 'through' express yet more complex relationships involving movement through space. As you will have read in Paper 32 Piaget's work suggests that children acquire these spatial concepts in that order. If there is a close relationship between the development of language and the development of concepts, it could be predicted that children acquire an understanding of the words expressing spatial concepts in the same order as they acquire the concepts themselves. There is some evidence to suggest that this is indeed the case.

Brown (1973) studied the acquisition of prepositions in Adam, Eve and Sarah and found that 'in' and 'on' were the first to be acquired. Palmer (1970) investigated 240 New York children's understanding of words expressing spatial concepts. These included 'on top of', 'into', 'under', 'around', 'bottom', 'backward' and 'side'. She found that only 18 per cent of the children understood the word 'under' at two years of age. At age three years 70 per cent of them had done so. Words which were still difficult for the three-year-olds were 'bottom', 'backward' and 'side'.

The activity you have just completed is designed to examine this trend. However, one student's results may be influenced by individual differences among children in such a way that a three-year-old obtains more correct responses than a four-year-old, for example. Nevertheless, if you examine the results for a number of children by combining your results as a group you are likely to have found similar results to Palmer's. You are asked to discuss your findings in Discussion Guide V.

Further details and implications of a close connection between intellectual development and language, which Macnamara's position and findings like those of Palmer would suggest, are presented in the following unit.

References
Brown, R. (1973) *A First Language,* Allen & Unwin.
Palmer, F. H. (1970) 'Sociometric status and intellective performance among Negro pre-school boys', *Dev. Psychol.,* 3, 1–9.

Correction, expansion, extension and match
Joan Tamburrini

The A type response by the adult in each of the examples given in Activity 4 is clearly a correction of a child's grammatical error. In each case it begins with a negative to alert the child to something being wrong and the word which replaces the child's error is stressed. Common sense might suggest that such clear correction is the most effective way an adult can help a child to eliminate grammatical errors. It is doubtful, however, whether this common-sense judgement is a correct one. A number of investigators now suggest that perhaps expansion is more effective than correction.

In Paper 41 the study by Brown and his colleagues of the language development of three young children, Adam, Eve and Sarah, was introduced. Brown, Cazden and Bellugi (1969) examined the samples of the children's statements and their mothers' responses for instances of correction. They found no case where a mother corrected the child's grammatically 'incorrect' utterance. Wherever a correction was found it followed a mis-statement of fact rather than a grammatical error. Thus, for example, when Eve said, 'He a girl' and on another occasion when she said, 'Her curl my hair' her mother did not correct her. By contrast, when Sarah said, 'There's the animal farmhouse' she was corrected because the building she referred to was in fact a lighthouse. Similarly when Eve said, 'Watching the men – building hole', her mother corrected this mis-statement of fact, saying, 'Well they aren't building a hole, sweetie. They're building a building now. First they dug the hole and now they're building the building.' Brown, Cazden and Bellugi comment, 'It seems to be truth value rather than syntactic well-formedness that chiefly governs explicit verbal reinforcement by parents.'

In the first two examples in Activity 4 the child's error is based on using a rule (the past tense ends in 'ed'), to apply to cases which are exceptions to the rule. Paper 41 discussed the importance of the child's unconscious acquisition of rules in his language development, and how this leads to overgeneralizations of these rules. It was shown that a child cannot imitate correctly grammatical structures which he has not yet acquired. Several investigators have shown how impervious a child can be to a grammatical correction before he is ready to understand that there are exceptions to the rule that he has learnt and overgeneralized. Cazden (1972a) quotes the following examples:

Four-year-old child: 'My teacher holded the baby rabbits and we patted them.'
Adult: 'Did you say your teacher held the baby rabbits?'
Child: 'Yes.'
Adult: 'What did you say she did?'
Child: 'She holded the baby rabbits and we patted them.'
Adult: 'Did you say she held them tightly?'
Child: 'No, she holded them loosely.'
(from Gleason, 1967)

Child: 'Nobody don't like me.'
Adult: 'No, say "Nobody likes me".'
Child: 'Nobody don't like me.'
(eight repetitions of this dialogue)
Adult: 'No. Now listen carefully; say "Nobody likes me".'
Child: 'Oh! Nobody don't likes me.'
(from McNeill, 1966)

Cazden (1972b) suggests:

> Rule-governed errors ... seem to be open to shedding when the child is in some sense 'ready' to move on, no matter how well-practised they may be. This was true of overgeneralizations like 'goes' and 'mines' in the acquisition of inflexions ... The implication for education is that teachers may be interfering with the child's learning process by insisting on responses that superficially look or sound correct.

The B type responses by the adult in Activity 4 are examples of expansion. Whereas each of the correction responses begins with a negative to alert the child to error, the expansion responses begin with an affirmative that tacitly acknowledges the *sense* of the child's statement. There is incidental correction of the child's error but the emphasis is on the meaning he intends to express rather than on his mistake. Cazden (1972b) writes:

> The warm confirming quality of the expansion contrasts with the critical and impatient manner of the correction. The expansion in substance and tone focuses on how much the child has already achieved, while still pointing the direction for further growth; the correction stresses the gap still remaining between where the child is and where he is supposed to arrive.

Another category of adults' responses to children's statements and questions may involve extensions. Whereas expansion involves expanding the child's utterance into a form that is grammatically more correct or complete, extension concentrates on meaning. It may include a grammatical expansion but, in addition, it takes the idea expressed by the child and extends it in some way.

Extension is an extremely important quality of the way adults should respond to children.

Cazden (1972b) reports an experiment to examine the relative effects of expansion and extension on children's language development. The subjects of the experiment were 12 children in a private day-care centre aged between twenty-eight and thirty months. The children were divided into four trios in each of which they were matched on the basis of age, talkativeness and their language development. Within each trio the children were then randomly assigned to one of three groups: group 1 were to receive 40 minutes per day treatment involving expansion, group 2 were to be exposed to an equal number of sentences which involved extension and group 3 was the control group, that is, the children received no language treatment but were brought to the treatment room at intervals to keep them familiar with the materials and the staff. Thus, if a child in group 1 said, 'Dog bark' the adult would respond, 'Yes, the dog is barking' (expansion). If a child in group 2 said, 'Dog bark' the adult might respond, 'Yes, but he won't bite' or 'Perhaps he's mad at the kitty' (extension). The results of this experiment suggest that extension was slightly more helpful than expansion.

Cazden's investigation compares expansion and extension. It does not examine differences in quality of extension. Such differences exist and are likely to be important not only to language development but to intellectual development. If a child comments on some occurrence with a description of what he sees an adult might respond in a number of ways: she might extend the description, picking out further characteristics; she might ask the child to predict what will happen next; she might ask him for an explanation of what he has seen; or she might ask him to recall a similar past occurrence and to make comparisons. Each of these would be an extension but would involve different uses of language; the examples just given can be classified under Tough's (1976) headings. Tough's analysis can help adults be more aware of their own language to children as well as of the children's uses of language.

Both expansion and extension refer to adults' responses to children's utterances. Often, of course, adults initiate talk. In this case, too, positive and informative talk seems to facilitate children's language development more than negative and non-informative talk. Tizard et al. (1972) examined the conditions in residential nurseries that seemed to promote language development. They categorized the adults' talk in terms of informative talk, supervisory comments and control remarks. Informative talk included reading to a child, telling a child something about present, past or future activities, naming objects, asking for or giving an opinion, an explanation or a piece of information. Supervisory comments were 'a category of talk used by adults when they wish to respond to children but have no real communication to make'. They included remarks which simply repeated, confirmed or contradicted what a child had said, such as, 'Did you?', remarks which were ritual accompaniments to actions, such as 'Here you are' and 'Off we go' and ritual-type responses to a child's statement, for example, 'That's nice'

and 'Aren't you clever'. Control remarks could be positive (instructions to carry out an activity) or negative (instructions to stop an activity).

The children, aged two to five years, were tested using the Reynell Developmental Language Scales which cover children's ability both to understand (comprehension score) and to use (expression score) spoken language. Tizard et al. found a significant correlation between the frequency of informative staff talk and the children's comprehension score. They also found that time-passing remarks tended not to produce a response in children while informative remarks did.

Another quality that good adult talk to children possesses is that it is an appropriate match to a child's developmental level. It would be inappropriate for an adult to respond to a two-year-old child's telegraphic utterance with the same sophisticated vocabulary and complex syntactic structures that he might use when speaking to another adult. Snow (1972) carried out an investigation into the ways in which mothers talked to their two-year-old and ten-year-old children. Their speech to the two-year-old children was found to be simpler and more redundant than that to the ten-year-old children. They used fewer subordinate clauses. For example a mother might say to a two-year-old child: 'That's a lion. And the lion's name is Leo. Leo lives in a big house. Leo goes for a walk every morning. And he always takes his cane along.' Snow suggests, 'If there are fewer clauses in a sentence the child is faced with fewer subject–verb and subject–verb–object relationships to puzzle out, and related subjects and verbs are more likely to follow one another directly. Thus the child might discover the subject–verb–object rule for sentence production with greater ease than if he were faced with sentences composed of many interembedded clauses.' Another example of simplification found in the mother's speech to the two-year-old children was the use of fewer third-person pronouns. Mothers repeated the subjects and objects of their sentences rather than substituting pronouns for them. Thus the children in the early stages of forming rules in language did not have to deal with the difficulties of pronoun reference. This is especially important for children who are not yet sure which pronouns refer to which classes of nouns. Snow concludes, 'Simplified speech is admirably designed to aid children in learning language.'

Using simple grammatical structures is one way in which adults match their talk to young children. Another aspect of match is concerned more with meaning. Tough (1973) describes a mother who consistently failed to base her responses on her three-year-old son's meanings, as the following exchange illustrates:

Jimmie: 'Look, look what I've found.'
Mother: 'Just look at your hands – black bright aren't they?'
Jimmie: 'Look at this thing – this ladybird – look it's right little.'
Mother: 'Go and wash your hands now – just look at the colour of them.'

Matching one's response to a child's meaning is a more complex matter than might appear at first glance. What a child means is sometimes ambiguous and depends on his level of intellectual development. There is a well-known story, probably apocryphal, of the mother who replied to her young child's question, 'Where did Johnny come from,' with an account of the processes of conception and birth. What the child really wanted to know was the country of origin of his friend, Johnny. Nathan Isaacs (1930) has shown that young children's 'why' questions cover requests for a range of kinds of explanation, including questions about motives and purposes, about reasons for statements and rules, and about physical causes. These different kinds of 'why' questions to some extent follow a developmental sequence.

References

Brown, R., Cazden, C. B. and Bellugi, U. (1969) 'The child's grammar from 1 to 111' in Hill, J. P. (ed.) *Minnesota Symposium on Child Psychology*, University of Minnesota Press.

Cazden, C. B. (1972a) 'Suggestions from studies on early language acquisition' in Cazden, C. B. (ed.) *Language in Early Childhood Education*, Washington D.C.: National Association for the Education of Young Children.

Cazden, C. B. (1972b) *Child Language and Education*, Holt, Rinehart & Winston.

Gleason, J. B. (1967) 'Do children imitate?' *Proceedings of the International Conference on Oral Education of the Deaf*, vol. II, 1441–8.

Isaacs, N. (1930) 'Children's why questions' in Isaacs, S. *Intellectual Growth in Young Children*, Routledge.

McNeill, D. (1966) 'Developmental psycholinguistics' in Smith, F. and Miller, G. A. (eds.) *The Genesis of Language: A Psycholinguistic Approach*, Cambridge, Mass.: MIT Press, 15–84.

Snow, C. E. (1972) 'Mothers' speech to children learning language', *Child Development*, 43, 549–65.

Tizard, B., Cooperman, O., Joseph, A. and Tizard, J. (1972) 'Environmental effects on language development: a study of young children in long-stay residential nurseries', *Child Development*, 43, 337–58.

Tough, J., (1973) *Focus on Meaning*, Allen & Unwin.

Tough, J., (1976) *Listening to Children Talking*, Ward Lock.

Discussion Guide V

First you should make sure that you understand the terminology discussed in Paper 39. In order to do this compare as a group your answers in Activity 40.

The rest of your discussion should be concerned with the educational implications of some of the theoretical issues presented in this unit.

1 Compare the results you obtained as a group in Activity 42.
   (a) What differences were there among the children? To what extent did these differences reflect an age trend? To what extent were there individual differences among children of roughly the same age?
   (b) Did the children find the task easier with the model toys than they did with the stick, ring and tube?
       What educational implications would you derive from your findings?

2 What different kinds of practices might one expect from teachers according to whether they conceive language acquisition to be explained in terms of (i) imitation alone or (ii) the cognition hypothesis?

Unit Two

Language and the Development of Thinking

- Reread the introduction to the module. This introduces the Whorf-Sapir hypothesis which is at the centre of the controversy concerning the relationship between language and thought
- This controversy is elaborated in Paper 45 which you should read next
- Complete Activity 45 which is designed in part to test your understanding of Paper 45
- Read Paper 46 which introduces Bernstein's work on language and social class
- Carry out Activity 46 which should test your ability to categorize young children's language, where appropriate, in terms of Bernstein's description of restricted and elaborated codes
- You should then be able to pool your results from the above activities in Discussion Guide W

Reading	55 mins.
Activities	180 mins.
Discussion	120 mins.
Total	355 mins.
	= 5 hrs. 55 mins.

Talking for learning
Hazel Francis

In any new learning both verbal and non-verbal aspects of communication may be involved. They may come together, or some marginal advantage may lie with one or the other in any particular situation. They may aid the grasp of a problem or the advent of a new insight, but new learning may also require the extension of language skill.

Gregory (1973) studied the way mothers helped young children to learn to put shapes into a form-board:

> Very early on, the mother is involved in getting the child to play with the board. She makes the board 'rich', i.e. she makes it the focus of a large number of associated activities. She deliberately sets up events for the child in order to hold, maintain and guide his attention. Informal games evolve ... The mother does not set up activities separate from the child, but seizes on and utilises what the child is doing, and can do ... Later on in the learning sequence there is the act of getting the piece into a hole. Implicit in this activity is its termination, but the mother makes the act especially significant. There is a release in the tension of the situation as the piece goes in, often marked by saying 'Good' or clapping. For the child there must seem to be a gradual build up in tension which is released as the piece goes in.

Here we see how verbal, accompanying non-verbal, signals can be used to guide the learning as distinct from conveying what is to be learned. They can signpost beginnings and ends and fruitfully guide the tension of learning. Other observations made in the Nottingham research unit by colleagues of Newson show the strategies mothers adopt with children from 3 to 5 when helping them to solve jigsaw puzzles. Guiding speech is very evident, though each mother–child pair has its own particular communication style.

Another insight into mothers' instruction of children can be gleaned from a study by Hess and Shipman (1965) of mothers from different social backgrounds teaching their 4-year-old children three simple tasks — toy sort-ing, block sorting on a basis of two characteristics, and design copying. The teaching styles varied considerably, as the following examples of remarks introducing the toy sorting task show clearly:

First mother: All right, Susan, this board is the place where we put the little toys; first of all you're supposed to learn how to place them according to colour. Can you do that? The things that are all the same colour you put in one section; in the second section you put another group of colours, and in the third section you put the last group of colours. Can you do that? Or would you like to see me do it first?
Child: I want to do it.

Second mother: Now, I'll take them all off the board; now you put them all back on the board. What are these?
Child: A truck.
Mother: All right, just put them right here; put the other one right here; all right put the other one there.

Third mother: I've got some chairs and cars, do you want to play the game?
Child does not respond.
Mother: O.K. What's this?
Child: A wagon?
Mother: Hm?
Child: A wagon?
Mother: This is not a wagon. What's this?

The first mother made the task clear and gave specific verbal guidance about the basis of sorting. Although the expression *group of colours* seems ambiguous it posed no problem in that particular partnership. The mother looked for evidence of understanding, in this case non-verbal, and checked the child's feelings about doing the task before withholding further guidance and letting her try. The second mother began to demonstrate the basis of grouping, but without correcting the false cue she elicited verbally from the child, nor giving correct verbal guidance. The third mother gave no lead at all into the sorting, and reduced the verbal exchange to attempts to get the child to name the toys. Hess and Shipman found a marked tendency for middle-class mothers to behave like the first and for other mothers to be less helpful the lower their social class status. Not surprisingly, the middle-class children were better able to perform the tasks and to explain the basis of their sorting. One might ask how far the experimenters had been successful in instructing the mothers about their task, but this would take us into another problem — what different kinds of learning task mean to different parents and different social groups.

These studies of early learning show that before entering school it is possible for the child to have become familiar with many of the ways language can be used to facilitate learning — informing, expressing feelings, assisting, directing, confirming, testing, correcting and approving. In earlier discussion we have indicated something of the informing and expressing functions in maternal instruction, for while we were discussing language learning itself it was obvious that such learning went hand in hand with the growth of perceptual-motor, cognitive and social skills. Judgement as to what forms of speech are helpful and what are so much beyond the child as to be totally incomprehensible, misleading or discouraging is an art to be developed by the teacher. At its best it requires a good understanding, not only of the probable general features of a child's language skill, but also of the particular characteristics that derive from his personal experience.

In addition to observation of teaching attempts by mothers we can look to other sources for analyses of the ways language might be used to guide other forms of learning. Holding (1965) summarised and discussed some useful points arising out of research into training. Since this might include such skills as trouble-shooting, the analysis is not inappropriate for much of what is more usually termed education. If we consider that the nature of the learning to be achieved lies on a continuum of skill from the more specifically perceptual-motor, e.g. tracing and handwriting to the more cognitive, e.g. rule discovery and problem solving, we can see that any such learning requires a grasp of constituent parts and integration, planning, checking and smoothing of these in the total performance. How far symbolic representation is necessary or helpful in learning these skills is a matter that can be empirically explored. Holding took up three main issues in guidance — instructions, aid during learning and knowledge of how well each performance is carried out. In all three it is possible to inform the learner non-verbally, as with physical demonstration and guidance or by signals or diagrams or charts, but verbal information has been shown to carry certain advantages. Verbal instructions are more easily memorised than others, particularly for complex tasks, because they take advantage of the prior experience of the learner that gives them meaning. If they do not recall relevant 'know-how' then either some additional training is needed or a different form of instruction is called for. For similar reasons verbal guidance or hints during the task are often more readily taken up than non-verbal, and in tasks where transfer of training from some other skill is helpful the verbal definition of what is involved may help to focus attention on relevant features. Verbal guidance is not sufficient to develop skill however, for although it may shorten the learning time needed, practice in the performance is essential. A further run-through always benefits from knowledge of the result of the last, and verbal description of the outcome has the dual advantage of conveying a variety of information with more lasting effect. Moreover, if feedback is delayed a verbal report is more likely to be related meaningfully to what was done than is a tick or a cross! In spite of these advantages it can nevertheless be shown that there are possible drawbacks to verbal instruction; but these tend to rest in inappropriate use. Individual learners are not equally able to take it up — older persons, for example, sometimes finding it harder than the young in industrial skills. This may be because 'translation' into activity is required, a process whose speed will vary not only with personal attributes, but also with the complexity of the task. In addition, the instructions might fail to be as clear and as simple as possible and thus lead to confusion or slow understanding; or the learner might simply not have the prior experience to use the information in them.

While the powerful coding properties of language make verbal guidance so useful in the teacher's hands, they can also be used to advantage by the learner for self-direction. Knowing what is to be attempted can lead to verbal encoding whether it be in thought, subdued muttering or even overt talking to oneself. Luria (1959) explored the young child's capacity to direct his own activity verbally as part of a developmental account of more general response to instruction. Apparently the very young child, under 2 years, is unlikely to be able to respond to a verbal instruction that conflicts with his tendency to repeat a previous action or that requires a choice to be made between the object of the instruction and some other object that interferes with access to it. For example, if asked to give the speaker a toy brick that lies before him the child may well hand over another toy if it happens to lie nearer. His ability to follow an instruction when no such conflict exists seems therefore to be less stable than we are inclined to believe. After 2 years the response to verbal instruction to attend in some way to specific objects seems to be firm, but there is considerable difficulty in responding to more complex instructions such as When the bell rings, press the switch. This is not very surprising in view of what we know of the child's language abilities; nor, in view of the repetition tendency referred to above, is it surprising that at the level of more simple instruction, when the child is told what to do at the time of the signal, he at first finds the inhibiting instruction more difficult to observe. The speech signal functions as a command to act 'positively' whether it is positive or negative. But it is surprising that the child's own spoken command to himself, conditioned appropriately to the signals, functions reliably only as the fifth year is approached. It seems, on the basis of this kind of work, that it is debatable how far language promotes learning or guides action in the early years and how far the learning or action guides the acquisition of verbal skills. This is a considerable problem when we turn to the more cognitive rather than the more perceptual-motor skills.

Suggested answers to the question of the place of language in such learning have been both varied and disputed. If we suggest that verbal expression aids the coding of recognised categories of experience, thus aiding memory, recall and problem solving, it might be argued that stored and available memories can be readily used without resort to verbal symbols.

Kuenne (1946) attempted to throw light on this matter in an interesting set of experiments with children of about 2 to 3 years. For example they learned to find a sweet placed consistently beneath the larger of two squares of different sizes. They were then expected to find a sweet under one of another pair of squares, one of which was the same size as that under which the sweet had first been reliably found, while the other was larger. The question was whether the children would transfer their expectations to the same-sized square as before or to the one which stood in the same size relation to the other square of the pair. Since the size relationship was the criterion the sweet was to be found under the larger square. Those children who were observed to mutter such phrases as under big one or big one in their first learning found the second task much easier than did the others; but, when in a further experiment children were given prior training on a size relation task before trying to find the sweets under the squares, they performed just as well as the children who had shown that they could verbally encode the relation. Speech did therefore seem to aid thinking under the first conditions, but the second experiment suggested that while it could be useful it was not essential. We cannot know, though, how the children who did not speak were encoding their thinking and learning.

With more complex concepts Vygotsky (1962) was able to show how verbal labels acquired meaning. He used nonsense syllables to stand for the concepts which formed the rather difficult basis of sorting a set of coloured bricks of various shapes and sizes. Combinations of height and area of cross-section were the relevant attributes, and the bricks were labelled beneath with the chosen syllables. Children were shown the label on each brick after they had allocated it to a group, and if the grouping was incorrect the brick was reallocated until it was placed correctly. It was shown that whereas 5- or 6-year-olds could group the bricks according to single perceptual attributes such as red or round, the more complex basis of grouping was not grasped until the age of 9 or 10 years. Stones (1970) was able to show that the verbal label aided further sorting of different sets of objects possessing the same criterial attributes. Children who had sorted the Vygotsky bricks without the verbal labels were much less able to extend their skill to the different materials. These studies show that different kinds of thinking underlie children's use of different words, and that whatever has been encoded in the use of a particular word or set of words is potentially available as part of the ground for further learning.

The role of verbal self-guidance in adolescence was explored by Gagné and Smith (1962) in a review of studies of the use of language in problem solving. In their own work with adolescents they used a difficult problem — a game requiring a particular pattern of moves and with a specifiable minimum number of moves to the end. The pupils were allowed to practise simple, but similar, games; and they were fully informed about the materials of the game, its aim, and the minimum number of moves needed to achieve it. They were then divided into four equivalent groups, and each group was given a different additional instruction. One was to make a verbal statement of the reason for each move as it was made and to try to find a rule to tell some other person how to solve the problem. Another group was to make similar statements but not to find a rule. The third group was asked to find a rule, but was not required to explain the moves; while the fourth was not asked to do either. In general, both in terms of solving the problem and of formulating the rule, the groups that were required to explain their moves did better than the others; but the instruction to find a rule did not seem to have any appreciable effect by itself. Certain questions remained unanswered, however, for differences in the patterns of moves made by the pupils were not explored and the ways verbalisation helped were not clarified. Is it somehow easier to make a rule from repeated verbal statements than from repeated action patterns? And if so, at what ages would this apply?

So far we have thought about the use of language in guiding learning, but, because most human learning is the building and consolidation of skill or knowledge, we have necessarily touched upon the problem of the relationship between language and thinking. A long-standing controversy can be discerned between those who maintain that thinking largely depends on language and those who regard it as primary. To some extent the opposition of ideas diminishes when the ways in which proponents use their terms are examined, and this seems particularly true of the arguments of Vygotsky and Piaget, as can be seen in the latter's reply (1962) to Vygotsky's (1962) criticism of his earlier writing. Both had observed young children talking aloud while playing alone, but they attributed different importance to such monologue. Piaget saw it as

fading away and having no great significance in the development of logical thought, while Vygotsky described the development of verbal reasoning as dependent on the meeting in monologue of early thinking and of early speech learned in social exchange — such monologue developing into inner speech and so into verbal thought. It is surely incontrovertible that speech develops in forms of dialogue, but its grasp depends on the ability to symbolise; and while Vygotsky stressed the social aspect Piaget explored the latter, claiming that language development was based on and related to the symbolic representation of experience in both enacted and imagined forms. For Piaget, the greater importance of dialogue was not in providing a language model but in informing the child of the viewpoints of others when he had outgrown his infant egocentrism, of which monologue was but one feature. The adaptation to other points of view was an important step in the growth of logical thought. It is clear from Piaget's reply to Vygotsky that a distinction must be made between verbal thinking and logical thought, and that the difference between the writers was more a matter of emphasis than of opposition. The difference should not, however, be lightly dismissed, for a reliance on one account rather than the other has implications for education. The Russian viewpoint of language as a second signalling system suggests that verbal skill may be additional to cognitive rather than derived from it, and that it may therefore be used to advance the latter, while the Genevan viewpoint suggests that language is so intimately related to other symbolising activities that it can only marginally advance thinking. In considering the implications for teaching and learning we should bear in mind that the Genevan work clearly specifies the development of logical thought against particular models of mathematical groups and propositional logic. It is debatable whether this can be said to encompass all that is involved in processes of thinking, and it may be that such thought is involved in different ways and to different extents in various learning tasks. Thus, while experiments which tend to confirm the Genevan approach are to be taken seriously as suggesting limitation in the use of language to promote the development of logical thinking, they should not be read as indicating that it has little facilitating effect in all thinking tasks.

The most important point at which the limitations of language have been

shown is that of the transition from pre-operational to operational thought (to use Piaget's terminology) when the child is between 5 and 7 years of age. By 7 years children begin to assert that, in spite of appearances, certain operations do not alter some fundamental properties of matter and are reversible. Thus, pouring an amount of water from one container to another of different proportions, while altering the appearance, does not alter the amount, as will be evident if the water is poured back. Rolling a piece of plasticine into different shapes does not change the amount and the original shape can be reformed. Before they can confidently make such assertions children are said to be at the age of pre-operational thought, and are also described as non-conservers in contrast with the conservers who see the unchanging properties. The non-conservers compare the appearance of water poured from one jar into another of different proportions with that of the same amount in a container identical with the first, and tend to say that there is more or less rather than the same amount. But conservers judge them to be the same, commenting on the identity of the poured water, the possibility of pouring it back, or the compensatory features (e.g. taller but narrower) of the shape of the second container. Bruner (1966) has pointed to the complexity of the judgements, showing that a grasp of the unchanging identity of the water is one aspect, but that the recognition of equivalence of amount through ideas of reversibility and compensation is needed to counter the tendency for perceptual evidence to outweigh the knowledge of identity. Non-conservers may mention any aspect of these judgements, but they do not grasp the whole. One might consider the step from pre-operational to operational thought as a movement towards a higher level ability to combine judgements. Bruner comments: '. . . language obviously does not help him "put things together", nor is it adequate as a medium for communicating to an adult what the child experiences' (Bruner, 1966, p. 205). The term *the same amount* covers a complex of meanings which is not evident in any particular example of its use. For the child to use it therefore does not necessarily imply an understanding comparable to the adult's.

Sinclair-de-Zwart (1967) offered evidence that language training did not really help children not yet at the stage of operational thinking to express the relations involved in comparing objects on the basis of two criteria at once. Pencils in one group could be described as both longer and thinner than those in another group of shorter, fatter crayons. Children who gave independent evidence of attaining operational thought in conservation tasks tended to be able to express the relations between attributes of the pencils, but only those who were marginally conservers were able to improve their expression of comparisons after appropriate language training. For most non-conservers the training itself proved to be difficult, and the results showed no improvement. Furthermore, the language training did not help children to become conservers in a plasticine-rolling demonstration in which the relevant perceptual changes were the sort they had been trained to express. In a more recent account written with colleagues, Inhelder (1974) reported various attempts to facilitate the development of operational thought, including verbal training, but the latter was found to give only marginal help. Nevertheless it was concluded that language aided the expression of already acquired ideas; it tended to draw attention to specific features of tasks very usefully; and it could with some children give rise to limited correct solutions and with others just tip them over into operational thinking.

References
Bruner, J. S. (1966) 'On the conservation of liquids' in Bruner, J. S. et al. (eds.) *Studies in Cognitive Growth*, New York: Wiley.
Gagné, R. M. and Smith, E. C. (1962) 'A study of the effects of verbalisation on problem-solving', *Journal of Experimental Psychology*, 63, 12–18.
Gregory, S. (1973) 'Learning to discriminate – the learning of meanings', paper presented at the British Psychological Society Developmental Section Conference, September 1973.
Hess, R. D. and Shipman, V. C. (1965) 'Early experience and socialisation of cognitive modes in children', *Child Development*, 36, 869–86.
Holding, D. H. (1965) *Principles of Training*, Pergamon.
Inhelder, B., Sinclair, H. and Bovet, M. (1974) *Learning and the Development of Cognition*, Routledge & Kegan Paul.
Kuenne, M. R. (1946) 'Experimental investigation of the relation of language to transposition behaviour in young children', *Journal of Experimental Psychology*, 36, 471–90.
Luria, A. R. (1959) 'The directive function of speech in development and dissolution: Part 1' *Word*, 15, 341–52.
Piaget, J. (1962) *Comments on Vygotsky's Critical Remarks* concerning The Language and Thought of the Child and Judgment and Reasoning in the Child, Cambridge, Mass.: MIT Press.
Sinclair-de-Zwart, H. (1967) *Acquisition du Langage et Développement de la Pensée*, Paris: Dunod.
Stones, E. (1970) 'Verbal labelling and concept formation in primary school children', *Brit. J. Educ. Psychol.*, 40, 245–52.
Vygotsky, L. S. (1962) *Thought and Language*, Cambridge, Mass.: MIT Press.

Evidence significant in the language —thought relationship

D. M. Keats and J. A. Keats

Language deprivation of a social kind has been found in cases in which the language used by or available to some speakers is restricted in some way. Under certain social conditions the language mode commonly employed does not make use of the entire range of the language, but is limited in vocabulary and syntax to a relatively small segment of the total usages. Such conditions may include, for example, class or ethnic minority membership, and geographical or institutional isolation. To what extent is there evidence that socially-based limitations on linguistic development interfere with thinking processes or not?

One source of such evidence which has had considerable influence and excited some controversy is the work of Bernstein. Bernstein proposed that there was a relationship between the mode of linguistic expression and the mode of structuring ideas and feeling in the middle classes versus the lower classes. He saw these two groups as differing fundamentally. The middle classes possessed a cognitive and affective awareness of the importance between means and long-term ends; they were disciplined to orient their behaviour toward certain goals and values, and at the same time placed a premium on individual differentiation; they had an instrumental attitude to social relations and objects; they were sensitive to structure rather than content; and they discouraged direct expressions of feeling, particularly feelings of hostility. In the middle classes words were used as mediators between the expression of feeling and its approved social recognition. Thus a value was placed upon the verbalization of feeling. The attitudes of working classes and the semiskilled, on the other hand, were non-instrumental and more sensitive to content than structure. They expressed feelings directly and more often through action than through words (Bernstein, 1958).

Bernstein considered that these tendencies were universal to all societies where such class structures are to be found. The important determining factor was seen as being the nature of the words and the type of language-use, not so much in the size of vocabulary as in the way that a particular social emphasis might mediate the relation between thought and feeling. In terms of the Whorfian hypothesis he was following the weaker form of Hockett (1954), Fishman (1960), and Hymes (1964) rather than the purely lexical version.

The 'restricted' code, more typical of the lower classes, was said to be characterized as follows (Bernstein, 1959):

(1) Short, grammatically simple, often unfinished sentences, a poor syntactical construction with a verbal form stressing the active mood.
(2) Simple and repetitive use of conjunctions ('so', 'then', 'and').
(3) Frequent use of commands and questions.
(4) Rigid and limited use of adjectives and adverbs.
(5) Infrequent use of impersonal pronouns as subjects ('one', 'it').
(6) Statements formulated as implicit questions which set up a sympathetic circularity, e.g. 'Just fancy?', 'It's only natural, isn't it?', 'I wouldn't have believed it'.
(7) A statement of fact is often used as both a reason and a conclusion, or more accurately, the reason and conclusion are confounded to produce a categoric statement, e.g. 'Do as I tell you', 'Hold on tight', 'You're not going out', 'Lay off that'.
(8) Individual selection from a group of idiomatic phrases will frequently be found.
(9) Symbolism is of a low order of generality.
(10) The individual qualification is implicit in the sentence structure; therefore it is a language of implicit meaning. It is believed that this fact determines the form of the language.

In contrast, the 'elaborated code' of the middle classes is characterized by:

(1) Accurate grammatical order and syntax regulate what is said.
(2) Logical modifications and stress mediated through a grammatically complex sentence construction, especially through the use of arrangement of conjunctions and relative clauses.

(3) Frequent use of prepositions indicating logical relationships, and temporal and spatial contiguity.

(4) Frequent use of impersonal pronouns such as 'it', 'one'.

(5) A discriminate selection from a range of adjectives and adverbs.

(6) Individual qualification verbally mediated through the structure and relationships within and between sentences.

(7) Expressive symbolism which distributes affectual support rather than logical meaning to what is said.

(8) A language use which points to the possibilities inherent in a complex conceptual hierarchy for the organizing of experience.

These characteristics are relative to those of the restricted code. It would seem that Bernstein is suggesting a continuum rather than different dimensions and also that the restricted code as he describes it above is rarely found in a pure state. However, it is clear that he regards the restricted code as both less precise and less conducive to expressing affective states. Bernstein (1959, p. 318) suggests that learning is affected because a correlate of such a code is a

> ... low level of conceptualisation — an orientation to a low order of causality, a disinterest in processes, a preference to be aroused by and respond to that which is given rather than to the implications of a matrix of relationships, and thus, it is suggested, partly conditions the intensity and extent of curiosity, as well as the mode of establishing relationships.

Bernstein's evidence for these claims was mainly derived from studies carried out with 300 male adolescent apprentices of the lower class in London (aged from fifteen to eighteen years). The boys were tested using the Raven Progressive Matrices, 1938 (RPM 38), and the Mill Hill Vocabulary Test. Results of the first stage of this study showed that scores on the RPM 38 ranged from 71 to 80 IQ to 121 to 126. This group came from skilled and semiskilled backgrounds, randomly distributed geographically in inner and outer suburbs (295 had left school at the age of fifteen). It was predicted that the higher the score on Matrices the greater the difference between the Progressive Matrices and Mill Hill scores. Results supported the hypothesis (Bernstein, 1958). In the second stage of this study (Bernstein, 1960) two extreme social groups were used: sixty-one students, all of whom were employed as messenger boys and none of whom had had a grammar school education, and forty-five subjects matched for age and sex with the former, all pupils of major public schools with a cross-section of scholastic attainment and educational interests. Subjects were given the Raven Progressive Matrices 38 and Mill Hill Vocabulary tests as before and a similar result was obtained. The language scores of the working-class group tended to remain depressed in relation to their higher Progressive Matrices scores, but for the middle-class group there was relatively no difference between the levels of vocabulary and Progressive Matrices at each IQ level.

In regard to the relationship between the language and cognitive measures, Bernstein concluded from his results that the lower-class boys were disadvantaged on the language measure. However, while the results in the two groups clearly differ, there are some problems in accepting Bernstein's interpretation. It could be, for example, that the increasing discrepancy at the upper levels of the lower-class group illustrates not dependence of thinking upon language but independence, an interpretation at odds with the Whorfian aspects of Bernstein's basic predictions. Also, it might be argued that the choice of the Mill Hill Vocabulary Test was inappropriate for eliciting differences in language performance because this test can show only *recognition of vocabulary*, not use of either vocabulary or syntax. The presence or absence of formal language devices, as set out in Bernstein's description of the elaborated code, therefore would not be tapped. What Bernstein claims to be universal characteristics may well be culturally endemic and limited to special groups of disadvantaged speakers of English. Despite these problems, Bernstein's notions are provocative and testable, and since the original statement much research has taken up the question of how socially-based linguistic styles may affect thinking. The result is some qualified support for the hypothesis from studies in England (e.g. Lawton, 1968; Robinson, 1965; Robinson and Rackstraw, 1972, 1975) and some contrary evidence from Australia (Owens, 1976; Poole, 1972a, 1972b) and the United States (Labov, 1972).

Lawton found such differences in syntactic structures in written material. He argued that the restricted code was adequate for expressing and describing concrete things and events rather than ideas and reflections upon events. Although Robinson and Rackstraw (1972) found differences in speech patterns between working-class and middle-class children, they argued that social class can have no causal significance (Robinson and Rackstraw, 1975) and planned a programme of assistance to working-class mothers aimed at helping them to respond more effectively to their children's questioning.

Poole (1971, 1972a, 1972b, 1973) carried out a series of studies of the oral and written language used by university students in Australia. For the oral language Poole used structured interviews which were subjected to detailed linguistic analysis. She found that students from middle-class backgrounds used sentences of greater length and complexity, a wider variety of adjectival qualifiers and adverbial modifiers, more egocentric references, and fewer fragmented or repetitious sentences. However, lower-class students did not use a higher proportion of non-specific and sociocentric speech as was predicted from the Bernstein hypothesis (Poole, 1971).

The written language was examined using the Cloze method. In terms of lexical and structural predictability, the middle-class messages were more difficult to predict than the lower-class messages, which were more stereotyped and limited in lexicon, but overall support for the Bernstein position was limited. Poole suggests that some conformity tendencies in completing the Cloze items might have accounted at least in part for the findings. Unfortunately the relationship between linguistic performance and general academic performance was not tested, but it should be noted that as all subjects were university students they had already shown evidence of academic superiority.

The work of Owens (1976) has provided an extremely thorough and rigorous testing of the Bernstein theory in regard to syntactic aspects of written language. Owens used a sample of 240 boys and girls from Grade 5 (primary school) and Forms I, III and V (high school) in Sydney, Australia. The sample was balanced on grade, sex, and upper and lower socioeconomic status. Owens collected compositions on three topics all in the narrative descriptive mode, and gave a brief test of cognitive development designed to elicit intuitive, concrete or formal operational thinking, and some transitional categories, from the comprehension of short verbal passages. The test was devised originally by Peel (1966, 1967) but incorporated some local modifications by McNally (1968) and others. From this testing Owens obtained a group of 128 subjects from Forms III and V such that there were equal numbers of each sex, equal numbers of middle-class and lower-class socioeconomic status, and equal numbers of concrete and formal operational thinkers. IQ was treated as a covariate. Social class was assessed on the basis of parents' occupation and education. Four indices of syntactic development were devised: clause-to-sentence development; depth of subordination; subordinate clause type, i.e. use of adverbial, adjectival, and noun clause; and use of passive voice. These indices were based directly on work arising from the Bernstein theory. Clause-to-sentence development was defined operationally as the 'T-unit', the minimal terminal unit, namely one main clause with all its subordinate clauses. Depth of subordination was related directly to the work of Loban (1963) and Lawton (1963, 1964). The use of passive was also justified on the basis of Lawton's work. In accord with the Bernstein position it was predicted that the lower class would be inferior on all indices and on the cognitive task.

The analysis failed to support any of the eight major predictions. There were no social class differences on any of the indices of psychosyntactic development and there was no relationship between either social class or syntactic development and cognitive level. Nor were there any significant interaction effects between the major language and class variables. In the case of the analysis by cognitive level, some interactions between level, sex, clause length (T-unit), and use of passive verbs were obtained such that boys at the formal operational level were superior to girls on the syntactic measures. At least for these Australian adolescents on this task there can be no support for the Bernstein position. Two problems suggest themselves, however. One is that the use of school compositions as the sample of written English would be biased towards the use of the elaborated code. The bias would necessarily favour the lower SES since good writing style also sets limits to the number of subordinate clauses, sentence length, and use of passive. The other is that as the cognitive screening test was itself a verbal test it could be a possible source of confounding, in that children who did well on a verbal comprehension test would also do well in a written task. In Bernstein's original work the lower-class boys performed differently on the Mill Hill test from the RPM but the middle-class did not. On the other hand, the use of a verbal task would seem to have been an appropriate instrument to detect evidence of the cumulative developmental lag proposed by Robinson and Rackstraw (1975). Even had individual testing been carried out the problem of the verbal content of explanations would still have remained.

The work of Labov (1972) on negro speech in the United States also provides a contrary case. After examining the nature of the speech of socially disadvantaged and middle-class negroes, Labov concluded that they indeed suffered a language disadvantage. However, the disadvantage did not arise from any lack of richness or creativeness in the lower-class negro speech but rather from its being different from the standard American English, favoured by, if not necessarily always spoken by, their middle-class negro and white teachers. Labov would agree with Bernstein that such differences could lead to a breakdown in communication between a lower-class negro child and his teacher, hence poorer performance might be expected of such speakers.

Social class-based and ethnically-based deficiencies in language may be compared with those studies of peripheral language deficit in the deaf, described above. The language input and output are restricted in each case, but in different ways. Yet in both types of work there is at least some evidence that performance on tasks generally considered to reflect the presence of intellectual functioning need not necessarily be impaired. That impairment does occur may depend on many factors other than language. Indeed, the importance of Labov's findings lies in showing the compounding of the effects of social disadvantage which arise from an interaction between class and ethnicity with those of language disadvantage, or language difference, whichever way one may interpret the non-standard use of English by negro speakers.

References

Bernstein, B. (1958) 'Some sociological determinants of perception: an enquiry into sub-cultural differences', *British Journal of Sociology,* 9, 154–74.

Bernstein, B. (1959) 'Public language: some sociological implications of a linguistic form', *British Journal of Sociology,* 10, 311–26.

Bernstein, B. (1960) 'Language and social class', *British Journal of Sociology,* 11, 271–6.

Fishman, J. A. (1960) 'A systematization of the Whorfian hypothesis', *Behavioural Science,* 5, 323–39.

Hockett, G. F. (1954) 'Chinese versus English: an exploration of the Whorfian hypothesis' in Hoijer, H. (ed.), *Language and Culture,* Chicago: University of Chicago Press.

Hymes, D. H. (1964) *Language in Culture and Society: A Reader in Linguistics and Anthropology,* New York: Harper & Row.

Labov, W. (1972) *Language in the Lunar City,* Philadelphia: University of Pennsylvania Press.

Lawton, D. (1963) 'Social class differences in language development: a study of some samples of written work', *Language and Speech,* 6, 120–43.

Lawton, D. (1964) 'Social class differences in group discussions', *Language and Speech,* 7, 183–204.

Lawton, D. (1968) *Social Class, Language and Education,* Routledge & Kegan Paul.

Loban, W. D. (1963) *The Language of Elementary School Children,* Champaign, Ill.: National Council of Teachers of English.

McNally, D. W. (1968) 'The nature of sociometric choice process', unpublished Ph.D. thesis, University of Sydney.

Owens, L. (1976) 'Syntax in children's written composition, sociometric status and cognitive development', *Australian Journal of Education,* 20 (2), 202–22.

Peel, E. A. (1966) 'A study of the difference in the judgements of adolescent pupils', *Brit. J. Educ. Psychol.,* 36, 77–86.

Peel, E. A. (1967) *The Pupils' Thinking,* Olbourne.

Poole, M. E. (1971) 'Social class differences in code elaboration. A study of oral communication at the tertiary level', *Australian Journal of Education,* 15, 152–60.

Poole, M. E. (1972a) 'Social class and language predictability' *Brit. J. Educ. Psychol.,* 42, 127–36.

Poole, M. E. (1972b) 'Social class differences in code elaboration. A study of written communication at the tertiary level', *Australian and New Zealand Journal of Sociology,* 8, 46–55.

Poole, M. E. (1973) 'Social class differences in language predictability: written', *Australian Journal of Education,* 17, 300–13.

Robinson, W. P. (1965) 'The elaborated code in working class language', *Language and Speech,* 8, 243–52.

Robinson, W. P. and Rackstraw, S. J. (1972) *A Question of Answers* Vol. 1, Routledge & Kegan Paul.

Robinson, W. P. and Rackstraw, S. J. (1975) 'Questioning and answering of school children', Macquarie University, Joseph Rowntree Memorial Trust Fund, Sydney.

Discussion Guide W

Discuss your findings in Activity 46 as follows.

1 Examine the provision of materials in the various contexts within which you carried out your observations. Were there any marked differences in the quality of provision of materials?

2 Look for common agreement on:
   (a) whether there was any particular kind of situation in which the use of a restricted code was especially marked;
   (b) what particular differences emerged between the language of the younger and older children.

3 Do any strong educational implications emerge from your findings?

Module Seven

Social Development

In Unit 1, Module 3, Schaffer's work on social interaction between mothers and infants was discussed. Schaffer insists that social development is not a one-way process. It involves an interaction between adult and infant, and how a mother behaves not only influences the infant's behaviour but is also influenced by it. This is a conception of the child as an active participator rather than as a passive recipient in the process. If Schaffer's theory is valid – and there is a considerable body of empirical evidence to support it – it follows that a child's response to adult socializing behaviour will be selective, and an adequate account of socialization should do more than describe adult actions. It should also identify the nature of the processes which determine which of these actions are most effective, and when and why. Paper 47 by Schaffer discusses the process of identification which is central to socialization, and the part played by imitation and modelling in identification.

Identification, imitation and modelling are processes of a universal kind, but there are also variations in what parents see as desirable behaviour and in the kinds of strategies they adopt. Two of the most significant factors giving rise to these variations are the sex of the child and the cultural or social class group to which the parents belong.

From an early age boys and girls show differences in preferred activities, in social interaction and the quality of personal relationships. No doubt some of these differences are biological in origin, but they are also influenced by the kind of support or discouragement they receive from parents and other influential adults. Hutt (1975) in studies of over two hundred nursery school children found that different life-styles in boys and girls were beginning to emerge even at the age of three and four years.

> Boys were more active and energetic, more exploratory, more 'thing-orientated' and more effective with the inanimate. Girls were more affiliative and 'person-oriented', more easily inhibited by novelty or uncertainty; they tended to construe personal relationships and social situations in a more complex manner and differentiate more subtly along social and emotional dimensions. Boys we found were twice as aggressive as girls, both physically and verbally. But not only did they *display* more aggression, they also *elicited* it more frequently.

Hutt suggests that the more aggressive characteristics of the boys reflect the action of the male hormone. Nevertheless, societies differ in the extent to which they reinforce or discourage aggressive behaviour in boys and the extent to which they react differently in this respect to girls.

An investigation by Fagot (1978) found that even toddler children are treated differently according to their sex by parents. Girls received more negative reactions when they manipulated objects and were given more positive feedback when they asked for help or tried to help an adult with a task. By contrast, boys seemed to be allowed to explore objects, to learn about the physical world, with less chance of criticism than the girls, but were more likely to receive a negative response when they asked for help.

In Paper 48 Robinson discusses patterns of social class differences in child rearing. Robinson confines himself mainly to the role of language in the socialization process, and social class differences are examined in large part in terms of the work of Bernstein and his colleagues. Socialization involves more, of course, than its linguistic realizations, but language is a powerful and important aspect.

Bernstein's distinction between the restricted and elaborated codes has already been discussed in Paper 46 in the unit on language and the development of thinking. It will be remembered that two differences between the codes according to Bernstein are that the restricted code is particularistic whereas the elaborated code is universalistic, and the restricted code deals in implicit meanings in contrast to the elaborated code which makes meanings explicit. It is to be expected that the characteristics of an elaborated code are more favourable to cognitive development than those of a restricted code, for cognitive development is in part concerned with the increasing ability to deal with universals and with explicit meanings. However, Bernstein has strongly emphasized that his main concern has been to show how the codes 'are both realizations and regulators of the structure of social relationships' (Bernstein, 1971).

Unit 1 in this module is concerned with the ways in which adults influence the social development of children. It is also influenced by social interaction in the peer group which is the subject of Unit 2. Paper 49 is concerned with the development of social play among pre-school children. Paper 50 discusses the development of moral judgement in young children and the part played in this process by interaction with other children.

References
Bernstein, B. (1971) *Class, Codes and Control,* Vol. 1, Routledge & Kegan Paul.
Fagot, B. (1978) 'The influences of sex of child on parental reactions in toddler behaviour', *Child Development,* 49, 459–65.
Hutt, C. (1975) 'Sex differences: biology and behaviour' in Lewin, R. (ed.) *Child Alive,* Temple Smith.

The Child, the Adult and the Culture

- Read the introduction to the module and then read Paper 47

  Complete Activity 47 which is designed to help you crystallise your understanding of some important concepts in Paper 47
- Complete Activity 48. It is important that you keep the data acquired in this activity; it will be required again
- Complete Activity 49 which is designed to help you think about a teacher's responsibilities in relation to the social development of young children
- Read Paper 48

  Complete Activity 50 which is designed to help you gain some experience of differences in behaviour of young children according to sex
- Work through Discussion Guide X

Reading	75 mins.
Activities	210 mins.
Discussion	120 mins.
Total	405 mins.
	= 6 hrs. 45 mins.

Identification
H. R. Schaffer

Having formed a strong bond to certain selected individuals, the child will inevitably wish to conform to their standards of behaviour and avoid their disapproval of inappropriate conduct. He does so by becoming like them — by incorporating their standards and thus identifying with them.

The task of socialization is at first almost entirely in the hands of the child's family. This is the primary social group in which he is introduced to the mores of society and which helps him to acquire the basic skills necessary to cope with the environment. In so far as social learning is a function of social contagion, i.e. the extent to which the individual comes into contact with others, the family is likely to provide the most powerful formative influence on personality development, for in the early years, at the time of maximum susceptibility, the child will be in almost continuous contact with family members. On an overt level, their influence manifests itself in the child's tendency to imitate their ways of behaviour and consequently to become more and more like them in speech, dress, eating habits and other personal characteristics. Habits of imitation can, in fact, be learned if the child is suitably rewarded for doing so (Miller and Dollard, 1941). However, imitation is not merely conditioned by overtly given rewards and instructions but depends on the total parent–child relationship and the powerful, though often subtle, feelings which a child develops towards those on whom he is emotionally dependent. The whole process that leads the child to think, feel and act as though the characteristics of another person were his own is called identification. The person with whom the child identifies is known as the model, and identification may thus also be regarded as the wish to be the model. Two qualifications must, however, be added: in the first place, a child need not necessarily identify with the whole model but may do so with only certain of its parts or attributes, and in the second place this tendency can be a wholly unconscious process.

Most of the difficulties of studying identification arise from this latter point. Freud, to whom much of the credit must be given for drawing attention to this process, was mainly concerned with it as a defence mechanism, i.e. as a way of dealing with the anxiety which the child experiences as a result of the feelings of hostility that parental frustrations engender. Afraid of losing the parents' affection as a result of these hostile feelings, the child solves the conflict by repressing his aggression and instead adopts the safer course of himself, as it were, becoming the aggressor through incorporating the parents' characteristics. The Freudian theory thus views identification as being mainly based on the child's negative feelings towards his parents and in this way differs from the learning theory account, which proposes instead that the child's wish to be the parent arises from his past experiences of feelings of gratification and pleasure associated with the presence of the parent, as a result of which he adopts his characteristics in order, so to speak, to supply his own rewards.

Whichever view is the correct one, the process is clearly a very important one in making the child into an acceptable member of society. Most of the research dealing with it has investigated it in relation to two areas: sex-typing and the development of conscience.

From a very early age on boys and girls are expected to behave differently. Already at three and four years of age children have formed definite and sex-appropriate preferences when asked to choose from such toys as guns, dolls, kitchen utensils and soldiers (Hartup and Zook, 1960), and the strength of these sex-linked preferences tends to increase with age. To some extent learning the appropriate role is due to direct training procedures employed by the parents, but there is evidence suggesting that it is also a result of identification with the same-sex parent. The little boy is expected to be 'like daddy' and to engage in masculine activity like hammering in nails and kicking footballs, while the little girl is similarly encouraged to imitate her mother's interests in cooking, knitting, etc. Society thus guides the child towards the appropriate model and gives him or her the opportunity to form the relevant identification with it. This process involves, of course, not merely the imitation of certain interests and hobbies but also the incorporation of more basic personality characteristics. Aggression, for instance, is regarded as being a mainly masculine trait and therefore fostered in boys by contact with their father. In one investigation (Sears, 1951) pre-school boys whose fathers were away on military service were found to have developed less aggression than boys whose fathers were at home. No such difference was found between father-present and father-absent girls of the same age.

Many attempts have been made to ascertain those characteristics in a child's family environment which foster strong sex-identifications. There is general agreement that the quality of the relationship with the parent is the most decisive factor in this respect. In a study of five-year-old boys (Mussen and Distler, 1959) a test was administered to measure strength of masculine identification. The scores were then compared with the boys' perception of their fathers (as obtained from the endings which the children supplied to incomplete stories), and it was found that boys with high male identifications tended to see their fathers as warmer and more affectionate than boys with low male identifications. Similar evidence has come from another study (Payne and Mussen, 1956), this time on adolescent boys and using 'test similarity' as a criterion of father-identification: again the strength of identification and the perception of the father as warm, helpful and kind were related. The same finding also applies to girls, for those with high femininity scores on sex-role tests have been found to have warmer relationships with their mothers than girls with low scores. It is thus the rewarding, positive qualities of the parents that promote identification rather than their negative, fear-arousing characteristics.

Another parental quality which encourages the child to model himself on the parent can be described as the latter's 'power'. In the study of five-year-olds quoted above the boys with high male identifications described the father not only as warm but also as strong, powerful and competent: clearly all qualities which aroused the child's incentive to be like the father. Similarly, the parent's interest in the child and the amount of time spent with him promoted identification, suggesting that it is primarily those variables which describe the parents' salience in the child's experience that affect this process.

A child's parents will usually, of course, exercise the most decisive influence on the nature of his identifications. They are, however, by no means the only individuals who will serve as models, and indeed identifications may subsequently be formed with groups and institutions as well. In the case of sex-identification, a study by Koch (1956) shows the importance of family members other than parents. Girls who have older brothers, it was found, tend to be more 'tomboyish' than girls with older sisters, and likewise boys with older sisters have a somewhat higher proportion of feminine traits than boys with older brothers.

Whether sex-linked behaviour is, in fact, solely a function of social learning, as so many writers seem to assume, or whether constitutional factors do not also play a part, remains as yet an unsolved problem. Certainly anthropological material concerning the very different conceptions of sex-roles found in other societies indicates that behaviour regarded by us as 'natural' may turn out to be a product of socialization rather than inheritance. Yet in the area of sex-linked behaviour above all the assumption of the 'tabula rasa' child ought to be avoided until more data have been gathered to enable us to make more precise statements regarding aetiology than we can make at present.

The other main area in which the process of identification has been studied is the development of conscience. The learning of moral standards and prohibitions starts early in life in relation to such mundane things as feeding, elimination and aggression, and it is here rather than on the lofty plane of morality and ethics that the foundations of conscience are laid. At first 'right' and 'wrong' are, from the child's point of view, purely arbitrary notions that are imposed on him by external agents. Sooner or later, however, he learns that these agents will follow 'right' actions with praise and 'wrong' actions with punishment and withdrawal of love. In order to avoid the latter consequences he begins to incorporate the rules of behaviour expected of him, so that his conduct is no longer exclusively governed by sanctions employed by other people but becomes increasingly regulated by the feeling of guilt which he experiences after all transgressions. Thus, in the adequately socialized child, the tendency to model his behaviour after that of his parents results in the incorporation of adult moral standards and the capacity for self-punishment.

The progression from external to internal regulation of behaviour takes a long time and may, in some individuals, never be completed. Again, a satisfactory relationship with the parents appears to be an essential prerequisite for such a development, for children with a highly developed conscience have mostly been found to have warmer, more accepting parents than children of the same age with less well developed consciences. A further influence, however, has also been isolated, namely the actual technique which parents employ in order to impose conformity. In general, withdrawal of love has been found far more effective in producing a strong conscience than physical punishment, deprivation of privileges, or the giving of tangible rewards (Sears, Maccoby and Levin, 1957). However, this relationship only holds in those cases where the parents are also generally warm and affectionate towards the child, for otherwise, presumably, there would be less love to take away and the child would not be as affected by the threatened loss as a child who has a rather more affectionate relationship with his parents. Thus the children most advanced in conscience development appear to be those whose parents are relatively warm towards them but who make their love contingent on the child's willingness to conform to their demands.

Once again one must remember, however, that parents are not the only models a child encounters. Influences outside the home also play their part in shaping conscience: a conclusion borne out by an interesting finding on boys with criminal fathers (McCord and McCord, 1958). This investigation showed that such boys are less likely to become criminals themselves if accepted by their fathers than if rejected by them. Where the parent model is found by the child to be opposed to society's norms, parents' acceptance may actually operate against identification.

Just in what way identification is to be differentiated from imitation is still an open issue. Some writers distinguish between these terms on the basis of the degree of specificity of the behaviour pattern which is learned; others consider that identification presupposes the existence of an attachment to the model, whereas this is not a necessary precondition in the case of imitation; and still others believe that imitation is a process that requires the model's presence at the time, whereas identification refers to the performance of the model's behaviour in the latter's absence. However, one recent body of research stemming from the work of Bandura and Walters (1963) has proceeded from the assumption that the two terms refer in fact to the same set of behavioural phenomena and to the same learning process, and that no useful purpose is served by making any distinction between them. Both terms, according to these writers, apply to the manner in which patterns of social behaviour are acquired through a process that may most suitably be labelled as *observational learning*. Whereas previous theories had stressed the need for rewards to be made available if imitation is to occur, these investigators have shown that, through simple exposure to a model and the opportunity to observe him perform certain activities, children will acquire new responses that match those of the model and which can, moreover, be reproduced not only at the time but also be replicated at a later date. Thus, in a typical experiment (Bandura, Ross and Ross, 1963), nursery school children watched a model behaving aggressively in a play situation by showing, for instance a number of unusual hostile responses towards a large inflated rubber doll. When the children were subsequently allowed to play in the same situation it was found that they showed precisely matching responses and tended to behave far more aggressively than children who had not previously been exposed to a model. Moreover, there was no difference in the extent of imitation between children who had observed a real-life model and children who had observed a filmed model, suggesting not only that exposure to aggression can heighten and also shape the nature of children's aggressive reactions, but also that this influence can be exerted by means of pictorial as well as real-life stimulation.

From experiments such as these Bandura (1962) concludes that social behaviour is typically acquired by means of imitation, that this may take place merely on the basis of 'sensory contiguity' (i.e. the opportunity to observe and attend to the activities of others), and that such learning usually involves the imitation of large segments of behaviour or whole sequences of activities rather than proceeding through the slow, gradual acquisition of isolated responses, each of which must be differentially reinforced by a suitable programme of rewards and punishment. However, imitation is by no means conceived of as a purely passive process, as exposure of an individual to a set of stimuli is no guarantee that he will attend to and learn the relevant cues. It is, however, a virtue of this conceptual approach that it is possible, through a variety of laboratory experiments (cf. Bandura, 1965) to isolate the conditions under which imitating does occur and thus to specify both the environmental and the subject factors which make for optimal susceptibility to the influence of social models. In this way those adult–child similarities of behaviour, which have given rise to the concept of identification in psychodynamic theories, can be studied empirically and traced back to their developmental origins.

There can be little doubt that identification is an extremely complex process and that it is as yet little understood despite the growing amount of research into it. This is partly because of the rather crude techniques that have been used to investigate it: for instance, parental identifications have been measured by the relative amounts of handling of father-dolls and mother-dolls in structured doll-play situations, yet the validity of this technique remains unknown. Similarly in research on moral development the choice of criteria for conscience, such as the type of endings which a child supplies to uncompleted stories, is not based on any established association with actual behaviour. Nevertheless, this area does represent an earnest attempt to find out how society impinges on the growing child and the manner in which it shapes and canalizes his behaviour. At present our theories about identification may be rather more impressive than their empirical underpinnings, but at least they serve to draw attention to some of the more subtle forms of interaction between the child and his social environment and to the wide range of variables which may influence any one behavioural activity.

References
Bandura, A. (1962) 'Social learning through imitation' in Jones, M. R. (ed.) *Nebraska Symposium on Motivation*, Lincoln: University of Nebraska Press.
Bandura, A. (1965) 'Behavioural modification through modelling procedures' in Kradner, L. and Ullmann, L. P. (eds.) *Research in Behaviour Modification*, New York: Holt, Rinehart & Winston.
Bandura, A. and Walters, R. H. (1963) *Social Learning and Personality Development*, New York: Holt, Rinehart & Winston.
Bandura, A., Ross, D. and Ross, S.A. (1963) 'Imitation of film-mediated aggressive models', *J. Abnorm. Soc. Psychol.*, 66, 3–11.
Hartup, W. W. and Zook, E. A. (1960) 'Sex-role preferences in three and four-year-old children', *J. Consult. Psychol.*, 24, 420–6.
Koch, H. (1956) 'Attitudes of young children towards their peers as related to certain characteristics of their siblings', *Psychol. Monogr.*, 70, no. 19.
McCord, J. and McCord, W. (1958) 'The effect of parental role model in criminality', *J. Soc. Issues*, 14, 66–75.
Miller, N. E. and Dollard, J. (1941) *Social Learning and Imitation*, New Haven: Yale University Press.
Mussen, P. and Distler, L. (1959) 'Masculinity, identification and father–son relationships', *J. Abnorm. Soc. Psychol.*, 59, 350–6.
Payne, D. E. and Mussen, P. (1956) 'Parent–child relations and father identification among adolescent boys', *J. Abnorm. Soc. Psychol.*, 52, 358–62.
Sears, P. S. (1951) 'Doll play aggression in normal young children: influence of sex, age, sibling status, and father's absence', *Psychol. Monogr.*, 65, no. 323.
Sears, R. R., Maccoby, E. E. and Levin, H. (1957) *Patterns of Child Rearing*, New York: Harper & Row.

Social class, language and socialization
W. P. Robinson

Introduction

The agglomeration of social class differences in child-rearing beliefs, attitudes and practices enforce the use of some selective principle here, even though our interest is already confined to the development of verbal skills only. While we might properly be concerned about each of the four activities of speaking, listening, reading and writing at all levels of linguistic analysis and could cover development from birth to maturity, we shall not. If we assert that essentially what we wish to know here is whether or not we can establish a *prima facie* case for the existence of functional differences in the use of language, with the lower working class emphasizing direct control of behaviour and role definition, we can answer this most readily by making a mainly patriotic survey of the work of Bernstein and his colleagues.

We could start with the presumption of social class differences in interactions of mothers with their children along the theoretical lines suggested. It is their behaviour that we would expect most generally to be relevant to what young children acquire, purely on the basis of time spent together. The simplest principle of transmission would claim that the children's learning is a direct and simple function of what is made available for them to learn. The actual mechanisms might be specified in terms of Skinnerian and/or Piagetian concepts. What the children learn will guide their behaviour.

In the other direction, the mother's behaviour will be determined by a combination of her knowledge, beliefs, attitudes and relevant constraints in the total context: one would expect her 'ideal strategies' to be modified by such constraints, whether these be acute, e.g. very busy and tired, or chronic, e.g. seven children in the family. The attitudes of the mother herself have no direct relevance to the child's behaviour for they are at two stages removed from it. More distal

still, the mother's basic capacities and dispositions will be related back to social class. Why members of particular social classes should have the capacities and dispositions they do is a sociological and historical problem.

These different features of the problems are mentioned here because some odd thinking can result if the distinctions are not preserved between what used to be called immediate and final causes on the one hand and between social psychology and sociology on the other. Social class of mother does not cause children to answer questions in peculiar ways, mother's beliefs that children should answer interviewers' questions does not cause them to do so. As we have already mentioned, this type of mistake is not discouraged by the design of the many investigations that do directly relate mother's social class to child's behaviour in terms of the statistical analyses conducted. The intermediary links are often assumed rather than made explicit.

In what follows three levels are separated out: mothers' attitudes; mothers' actual and reported behaviour; children's behaviour. All of these are related back to social class. The inter-relationships of the three are not explored both because it is social class which is of direct relevance to the theoretical framework and because so few studies have tried to descend to social psychology for both sets of the variables believed to be related.

Mothers' attitudes towards language and language development

Henderson (1970) analysed data relevant to mothers' reported frequency of speaking for each of a listed variety of reasons. A set of items labelled 'social chit chat' did not differentiate between MC and LWC mothers, but LWC mothers claimed to speak more often than MC mothers for affective (e.g. to show my feelings to others) and role defining (e.g. to decide what is right and wrong) reasons, while the reverse

was true for what were labelled cognitive reasons (e.g. to exchange ideas). These preliminary results pose the problem of how far even self-report inventories might shed light on what people do with language.

More directly related to child-rearing, Bernstein and Henderson (1969) asked mothers how much more difficult it would be for a dumb mother to teach her child a number of things. Items were grouped into 'general cognitive', 'affective' and 'specific skills'. MC mothers saw greatest difficulties overall, but this was particularly pronounced in the general cognitive area. LWC mothers reported that the teaching of specific skills like learning to dress would be most affected and emphasized difficulties in this area more than MC mothers. (Work on complex sensori-motor skills in fact stresses the desirability of actual practice with knowledge of results for efficient learning of these.) MC mothers also expressed a readiness to talk with their children across a wider variety of situations and a greater willingness to answer difficult questions than LWC mothers (Bernstein and Brandis, 1970).

Mothers' beliefs about language development in children, how they think it comes about, and what relevance they consider their own behaviour has for this remain unknown. From more general evidence, it might well be expected that MC mothers believe that children have to be taught how to speak and that it is part of their role to encourage such development in a systematic way. As we shall see below they also use language as a means of communicating information of a referential nature. On the other hand, LWC mothers are probably more likely to adopt a passive view believing that children learn to speak 'naturally' or 'automatically'. This *laissez faire* policy is supplemented by beliefs in boundaries being maintained between school and home — teachers teach children school topics and the mother teaches the child role-appropriate behaviour. These possibilities have not been systematically examined.

Reported behaviour of mothers

Cook-Gumperz (1973) has analysed mothers' responses to questions about controlling their child's behaviour, namely, discipline problems. A distinction was made between 'imperative techniques', 'positional appeals' and 'personal appeals'. *Imperative* techniques included brief commands such as 'Shut up!' as well as non-verbal intervention like smacking and forcible removal from situations. Of the other two verbally based strategies, *positional appeals* comprised those reasons given for behaviour in which membership of a general status category was invoked, often age, sex, or family, e.g. 'Only little boys pull their sister's hair!' What are given here are prescriptions for behaviour appropriate to a given role, e.g. 'five-year-old boys'. By contrast, *personal appeals* invoke the consequences, affective and/or behavioural, for specified individuals such as self, mother, sister, e.g. 'Now you've broken that cup and I am very angry. You will not take advice. You have to learn the hard way, upsetting everybody'. These appeals tend to combine specificity and generality, specific acts being related to general consequences for specific people. There is also in the example an implicit higher level principle 'You should not make people angry.'

There were no social class differences in the incidence of positional appeals, but MC mothers used more personal appeals specifying consequences for the child than LWC mothers, while the exact reverse was true for imperative techniques. Comparable results have been obtained with slightly younger children in Nottingham (Newson and Newson, 1970) and with Negro children in Chicago (Hess and Shipman, 1965).

What do these results imply? In the first place LWC mothers are less likely to use language in discipline situations except in the form of direct commands. Their greater use of simple commands or non-verbal strategies leaves the child to work out for himself the connections between other events and the maternal intervention. On a classical conditioning paradigm, avoidance learning, mediated or not by anxiety, should associate contiguous events with the maternal behaviour, e.g. looking at the clock, day-dreaming about sweets, as well as spilt tea. Repeated trials with consistent reinforcement should render the learning more specific to 'offences', but the other associations

might well remain unextinguished. On cognitive developmental theory, the child should seek to accommodate such experiences and derive working rules to apply to them, but the representation of this knowledge at five is likely to be mainly enactive and ikonic, neither of which permit higher order abstraction. There is the further possibility that maternal interventions are not perceptibly rule-following with sufficient consistency for successful accommodation to be possible. Newson and Newson (1970) remark upon the relatively high incidence of threats used by WC mothers, often involving outside authority figures such as policemen. Since policemen seldom come in to carry out maternal threats Newson and Newson ask how far such tactics encourage both a fear and ultimately a contempt (at the impotency) of authorities.

Given that the child can learn the positional appeals, these do afford definitions of role-appropriate behaviour. Where the appeal is based on sex or age relation, such rules have potential durability, but where they are based on age they do not. A caricature might offer a picture of a child spending his sixth birthday checking which rules for five-year-olds continue to apply — and perhaps sadly finding that many still do. It may also be noted that positional appeals define only a small number of roles and that these are ascribed and hence inescapable.

Personal appeals have rather different possibilities as opportunities for learning. They are in fact used to make referential statements about the material and social environment. Emotional states are defined verbally, and actions leading to their occurrence specified; they are made specific to individuals, hence allowing that differences between persons may exist. But children may also acquire information about more general social matters: where one buys teacups to replace broken ones; that lemon juice removes tea stains from tablecloths. It has already been mentioned that such appeals often invoke rather general moral principles, like not hurting other people. Such principles give explanations for behaviour — whereas positional appeals only assert what is allowed or proper — and hence the child has the opportunity of applying them to new situations. He can pose problems in terms of who will be hurt. 'I give you a new commandment: love one another . . .' is used to transcend eight of the Ten Commandments. Cook also found that MC mothers were more likely to take the child's intention into account, and we may note in passing

that this is referring to an unobservable variable less easily inferred than emotional states.

To summarize briefly, LWC children are exposed either to conditions similar to those that a rat in a maze enjoys when learning to avoid electric shocks, or to prescriptions for role-appropriate behaviour. Language is used as a medium for the direct control of behaviour by commands or to define roles. MC children also receive such prescriptions, but in addition are given verbally expressed reasons for certain behaviours and information about the material and social environment in general. For the LWC child to contest the validity of a positional appeal or an imperative is to challenge the authority of the mother. A MC child can question the empirical basis of personal appeals without necessarily evoking such a confrontation.

Robinson and Rackstraw (1967) analysed answers that mothers said they would give to a variety of 'wh' questions supposedly posed by their five-year-old children. In this situation MC mothers were more likely to answer the questions, gave more factual information when they did, the information was more accurate and the types of explanations to 'why' questions differed. MC mothers were more likely than LWC mothers to mention causes, consequences, analogies, and class (not social for once) membership as reasons; LWC mothers were more likely than MC mothers to answer by re-organizing the question as a statement — 'Because they do', or by making an appeal simply to the regularity of the event — 'They always do'. These LWC replies make it tempting to argue that, as in the discipline situations, LWC mothers are more prone than MC mothers to control the child directly than to extend his general knowledge. Rackstraw (Robinson and Rackstraw, 1972, p. 244) argues for a grouping of certain types of reply to 'why' questions which she calls answers that 'focus on the proposition'. To use these a person need have no empirical knowledge relevant to the question, but only a small set of sentence frames, e.g. '. . . always . . .'. What are called appeals to essence, denials of a need for an explanation, and appeals to unspecified authority or tradition for moral and social questions are combined with repetitions of questions as statements and appeals to simple regularity to form the total set. In a subsequent analysis of similar data, Robinson (1973) found LWC mothers used 'focus on proposition' modes of reply more often than MC mothers. This study also found that MC mothers were more likely than LWC mothers to use more than one mode of explanation and more likely to point to similarities and differences in their answers.

What is made available for children to learn in this situation? The fact that LWC children are more likely to receive no answers or to receive only 'focus on proposition' modes to 'why' questions might be expected to discourage them from asking questions. Curiosity is neither satisfied nor encouraged. LWC children are receiving less information of a referential nature and what they do receive is less accurate. The relative absence of analogies, or specifications of similarities and differences, or appeals to categorization for 'why' questions reduces the chances of knowledge becoming organized — co-ordinate, super-ordinate and sub-ordinate groupings are less likely to develop. The relative shortage of appeals to cause and consequence reduces the extent to which knowledge acquired is ordered sequentially and meaningfully. Language is the medium by which these differences are made explicit.

A methodological critique

It might be argued that what mothers report does not relate in any systematic way to what they in fact do. Perhaps LWC mothers are nervous talking to interviewers, and this anxiety affects their verbal behaviour in interviews. If this were so we might expect to find a higher refusal rate among the working class, in what was after all a voluntary situation, and we might expect to detect some of the signs of anxiety metioned in chapter 4.* The first was not true. The second was not systematically investigated, but superficial impressions of the tape recordings do not support this idea. Alternatively, MC mothers may be operating under the influence of a 'social desirability' response set, the tendency to give some type of ideal rather than true answers (Edwards, 1957). Investigations into social desirability as a factor influencing replies normally exploit overtly obvious statements of opinion to which it is relatively easy to distort replies, whereas in this investigation no easy opportunities for distortion were available; mothers had to construct their replies from their own resources and had no foreknowledge of how their answers were likely to be scored. It is possible that the maternal replies provided would not in fact be employed with

*This reference refers to the original source, viz. W. P. Robinson, *Language and Social Behaviour*, Penguin.

their children; especially perhaps when domestic situations become fraught with many simultaneous demands, informative causal answers to 'Why are you so red in the face, Mummy?' may not have a high frequency of occurrence. On the other hand, when moods are good and pressing problems few, we might reasonably expect MC mothers to offer more. One way of looking at the problem would be to suggest that, while almost all mothers may well use non-verbal means of control and not reply to questions under some conditions, some mothers are less likely to start in this way under favourable conditions, conditions describable in terms of numbers, types and strength of pressures to do other things.

While these worries about the validity of maternal reports should be exposed and their force investigated, it is also possible to check what the children are like. If the children's behaviour relates to the maternal reports, and we can generate reasonable explanations for such associations, the likely validity of these reports is enhanced.

Behaviour of children

Robinson and Rackstraw (1972) interviewed fifty-six children whose mothers' answers had been collected two years earlier. These children answered some of the same questions as their mothers, but the number of questions was made up to thirty, covering the full range of common interrogative words as well as different content areas for 'why' questions. In reply to these, MC children gave more information, the information was more accurate and their answers were less likely to be irrelevant to the question asked. For 'when' and 'where' questions, distinctions of convenience were made between absolute (e.g. on 17 October 1941) and relative (e.g. when my sister got married: when the bell goes) answers. In contexts where absolute answers were more likely to be useful, MC children gave more of them. In answer to 'why' questions LWC children used more appeals to simple regularity (e.g. always) and unspecified authority (e.g. it's naughty), while MC children made more appeals to classification, cause and consequence, more to wants of individuals, and mentioned effects upon other people more often. Among appeals to consequence, LWC children were more likely to mention avoidance of punishment as a reason for not

doing things, the reality-based wisdom of this being complemented by Cook's data.

The parallels between the social class differences of both mothers and children have been developed in an extended re-analysis of these data in mother–child pairs within social class (Robinson, 1972). Although the sample size was small and there had been a two-year gap between the collection of mothers' and children's answers, in which children had been exposed to the influence of their schools, mother–child similarities could still be found — although some strange findings emerged as well. The simplest interpretation remains: that the learning opportunities offered by the mother are determinants of the verbal behaviours of the children.

Turner (1973) has also used the factorial sample of five-year-old children whose mothers were included in the Robinson and Rackstraw study (1972), as well as a sub-sample of the same children at seven, for an analysis of control directed speech. These children had to tell a story to a series of questions asked about a four picture cartoon strip in which some boys appear to kick a football through a window, and subsequently interact with a man and possibly with a woman as well. In summary, he found that LWC children were more likely to cite tellings off and use abrupt imperative commands and context-specific threats, while MC children were more likely to use positional appeals focused upon the affective state of the controller. MC children made more explicit reference to attributes of offenders and the effects on controllers; used intensifiers (e.g. very) to make more specific reference to states; and they offered fewer examples of implicit reference marked by exophoric pronouns.

As with the question-answering, so with the control situation: if we make allowance for the difference in level of cognitive development between mothers and their five-year-old children, the social class differences among the children echo their mothers.

Observed mother–child interaction in a teaching situation

Hess has conducted a series of investigations examining relationships between maternal attitudes and behaviour and children's cognitive development. Of immediate interest are those studies which show social class differences in maternal control procedures and in maternal teaching styles (Hess and Shipman, 1965). With

Negro mothers of four social groups equivalent to upper middle ($n = 40$), upper working ($n = 42$), lower working ($n = 40$), and a fatherless public assistance group ($n = 41$), they found control differences similar to those reported by Cook (1971). The categorizations of control were different in that non-verbal strategies and positional appeals were combined into an imperative–normative category, but personal appeals were divided into those with an affective basis and those with a cognitive–rational one. The results were like Cook's. Social class differences appeared on all three categories in the expected directions. These results are mentioned not so much to demonstrate cross-cultural similarities, but to suggest that Hess's subsequent results on maternal teaching styles and children's behaviour are likely to have been found with the London sample as well.

As a warm-up task a preliminary teaching problem was set to each mother with her four-year-old child as pupil. This was followed by a block-sorting problem requiring simultaneous categorization on two attributes (each two valued). The mother was given as long as she wanted to teach her child and was told to continue until she was satisfied with her child's performance on the task. The child was then tested both for the accuracy of his performance and for his ability to verbalize the basis of his sorting. The mother–child interaction was recorded. The higher social class children made more correct sortings and verbalized these more accurately, although no co-variance analysis appears to have been used to ascertain whether the more effective verbalizations were not simply a direct function of having more correct solutions to verbalize. In their teaching, MC mothers were more likely to seek to motivate the child, establish an appropriate set, give positive verbal reinforcement, give specific instructions and seek verbal responses from their children. They were less likely to give negative verbal reinforcement or seek non-verbal feedback, i.e. to get the child to move the blocks around.

The second task, Etch-A-Sketch, utilized a commercial toy which consists of a rectangular white screen with two control knobs that can be turned to produce black vertical and horizontal lines respectively. The toy was explained to the mother and it seems to have been established that she knew how to work it effectively. The child was brought into the situation and the instructions given: the mother was told she was to operate one knob, the child the other; she could say or do

anything except actually turn the child's knob (or his hand on the knob), and after three minutes practice, they were to copy five patterns. The interaction was observed, tape-recorded and accuracy scores computed. The three-minute practice session was rated for preciseness and specificity of instructions given; a sample of twenty-five instructions in the test session was scored for specificity of instructions; and a count was made of the number of designs to be copied shown to the child. A combination of these scores gave a multiple correlation of 0.64 with a measure of task performance. The class differences were considerable; the middle class performed better, but spent less time on the task. MC mothers gave more specific instructions and showed their children more of the designs and were rated more highly in the practice sessions. Some of the differences were extraordinary. The 'highest' level of instruction given by any working class mother was 'Turn your knob'. The mean number of designs shown to working class children by their mothers was only 1.2 out of the five possible.

Hess and Shipman summarize the position of the working class child in this situation:

> The lack of meaning in the communication system between mother and child is clearly exemplified in the behaviour of many of the mothers on this task. Consider the plight of the child whose mother is low on these three measures (see above): during the practice period, his mother demands that he turn his knob, but she fails to explain why or to relate it to the lines on the screen. During the task she doesn't show him the models and fails to give specific turning directions. For such children, the effects are these: (a) the child is not given a goal to make his individual responses meaningful (that is, he is not shown the model). (b) The mother is not specific in her directions: each new response is essentially a guess. (c) The sequence and pattern of response is not explained. The child has no way to tell ahead of time how to respond, and even after he does respond, he cannot predict the mother's reaction. He is hindered in learning anything from one response that will generalize to the next. (d) Nevertheless, his responses are being rewarded or punished, usually with maternal praise or disapproval, which provided belated feedback for a particular response if the mother is not giving specific directions. In either case, reward or punishment performs a motivating function.
>
> As a result of the interaction of these factors, the child is being made to produce responses that from his point of view are not related to any visible goal, are unrewarding in themselves, and do not bring cor-

rective feedback that will enable him to avoid punishment.

> Nevertheless, reinforcement continues, and punishments are usually more frequent and intense than rewards (1967, p. 79).

Discussion

The data on socialization procedures are generally much more informative about functions of language and social class than the earlier work focusing mainly directly upon grammar or lexis. A number of the studies mentioned are able to relate functions and their structural realizations, particularly that of Turner. This is presumably a direction that should lead to progress. A detailed list of functionally based modes of control can be defined in terms of linguistic structure and lexis. Hence the function of 'controlling behaviour of others' can be sub-divided into a variety of means and these can be cross-referenced to other functions. Abrupt commands are one form of control, but might involve some affective instrumental component. Positional and personal appeals involve role definition, the former in terms of crude status-based categories, the latter at a most general level of how human beings should behave. The personal appeals can also be linked to the affective instrumental and to the referential functions. The successful production of articulations of function and structure in limited contexts should help to lessen the force of Labov's stricture that Bernstein's theoretical framework has gaps between the two.

While the investigations reported throw a light on the mother–child interaction situation, especially at the social class level of analysis, there are at least two obvious next steps. One is the shift to a social psychological analysis within or independent of class and one or two studies have begun to explore this. The other is to examine teacher–child interaction in the schools. Unpublished data from Bernstein's team on this topic may well turn out to show a correspondence between teachers' and mothers' control strategies, teachers in solidly working class schools tending to use working class strategies, those in solidly middle class schools, a middle class pattern. Demonstrations of such differences would further substantiate Bernstein's thesis. If LWC children, already orientated towards the use of language for direct control and role definition, find their teachers biased in the same way, then what has been said about encouraging and discouraging development along Piagetian lines in the home may be continued into the educational system. At present we do not know whether or not this is the case.

If it is, then it would add further support to Bernstein's explanations of how the restricted code of language usage and its consequences for the development of intellectual maturity are transmitted from one generation to the next. It has been suggested that the family and peer group will act to confuse the child, while his own cognitive-motivational pre-dispositions and the school will facilitate his intellectual development. If it does emerge that the school joins parental and peers' pressures, then it is the child alone who is wishing to insist that the emperor is naked.

References
Bernstein, B. and Brandis, W. (1970) 'Social class differences in communication and control' in Brandis, W. and Henderson, D. *Social Class, Language and Communication*, Routledge & Kegan Paul.
Bernstein, B. and Henderson, D. (1969) 'Social class differences in the relevance of language to socialization', *Sociology*, 3, 1–20.
Cook-Gumperz, J. (1973) *Social Control and Socialization*, Routledge & Kegan Paul.
Cook, M. (1971) 'The incidence of filled pauses in relation to part of speech', *Language and Speech*, 14, 135–40.
Edwards, A. L. (1957) *The Social Desirability Variable in Personality Assessment and Research*, Holt, Rinehart & Winston.
Henderson, D. (1970) 'Contextual specificity, discretion and cognitive specialization: with special reference to language', *Sociology*, 4, 311–37.
Hess, R. D. and Shipman, V. C. (1965) 'Early experience and the socialization of cognitive modes in children', *Child Development*, 36, 860–86.
Hess, R. D. and Shipman, V. C. (1967) 'Cognitive elements in maternal behaviour' in Hill, J. P. (ed.) *Minnesota Symposium on Child Psychology*, vol. 1, University of Minnesota Press.
Newson, J. and Newson, E. (1970) *Four Years Old in an Urban Community*, Penguin.
Robinson, W. P. (1973) 'Where do children's answers come from?' in Bernstein, B. (ed.) *Class, Codes and Control*, Vol. 2, Routledge & Kegan Paul.
Robinson, W. P. and Rackstraw, S. J. (1967) 'Variations in mothers' answers to children's questions', *Sociology*, 1, 259–79.
Robinson, W. P. and Rackstraw, S. J. (1972) *A Question of Answers*, Routledge & Kegan Paul.
Turner, G. J. (1973) 'Social class and children's language of control at ages five and seven' in Bernstein, B. (ed.) *Class, Codes and Control*, Vol. 2, Routledge & Kegan Paul.

Discussion Guide X

1 In the light of your reading on identification and modelling in social learning discuss as a group what you think this entails for teachers in early childhood education in terms of:
(a) responsibilities;
(b) knowledge;
(c) skills.

2 Compare as a group your findings in Activity 48. What categories of behaviour predominated? What kinds of models predominated? What conclusions would you draw from your findings?

3 Compare as a group your suggestions in Activity 49. Look for common agreement on the kinds of strategies you have advocated and the reasons for them. If there are instances of disagreement among you, give your reasons and discuss them.

4 Discuss what you consider to be the teacher's responsibilities in the light of the cultural and subcultural child-rearing differences you have read about.

5 What were the major differences to emerge from your findings in Activity 50? What changes, if any, would you wish to make in nursery school provision in the light of these?

Peer-group Relationships

- Read Paper 49
- Complete Activity 51 which should help you observe children's play in terms of the characteristics discussed in Paper 49
- Read Paper 50
- Complete Activity 52 which is designed to help you test children's moral judgement as discussed in Paper 50
- Work through Discussion Guide Y

Reading	40 mins.
Activities	135 mins.
Discussion	120 mins.
Total	295 mins.
	= 5 hrs. 45 mins.

A longitudinal study of social participation in preschool children: solitary and parallel play re-examined

Peter K. Smith

Longitudinal observations were made over a 9-month period of the social participation of 48 preschool children. Group play increased and solitary play decreased during the period, while parallel play did not vary much in overall occurrence. Some 2-year-olds went through successive stages of predominantly solitary, then parallel, then group play, but many others did not. Some 3- and 4-year-olds alternated between periods of predominantly group play and periods of predominantly solitary play. The results are discussed in relation to the relative maturity of solitary and parallel play and the usefulness of a social participation index at this age range.

Mildred Parten's (Parten, 1932; Parten and Newhall, 1943) study of the social participation of preschool children has become one of the classics of the 1930s era of child psychology. Parten introduced six categories of participation in play behaviour. In particular, she used the term *parallel play* to indicate a limited degree of participation, in which children play near each other, with similar materials, but do not engage in substantial interaction. Parten regarded parallel play as 'more socialized' than solitary or onlooker behaviour but less socialized than associative or cooperative group play. By appropriately weighing her categories, she obtained a composite 'social participation' index, which correlated .61 with age.

The importance and nature of parallel play has been subjected to surprisingly little critical scrutiny, despite the fact that Parten's observations were based on only one nursery school. Nor has the utility of a social participation index been much examined. Particularly puzzling is the nonsignificant correlation of .12 that Parten obtained between social participation and nursery experience. This finding might suggest that a longitudinal study of social participation would give different results from the cross-sectional data she presented.

Parten's own cross-sectional data show some decline in solitary behaviour with age and also some decline in parallel play, with an increase in both associative and cooperative group play. Somewhat similar cross-sectional data were obtained by Barnes (1971), these data also being from one nursery group. However, the trends for solitary and parallel play are small, and for parallel play nonlinear with age, in both studies.

Some support for the utility of a social participation index comes from work by Smith and Connolly (1972) and Smith (1973). These studies employed principal-components analyses to find main dimensions of individual difference in children, based on frequencies of observed behaviours. In both cases a main component of 'social maturity' was obtained. Smith and Connolly (1972) found group play to be loaded positively, parallel play negligibly, and solitary play negatively on this component. Smith (1973) in a separate study found that a social participation index (weighting group play as 1, parallel play as 0, solitary play as −1) correlated .81 with age and was highly loaded on the main social maturity component. These studies were based on 4 day nurseries in England.

Some recent work, however, has suggested that parallel play should not necessarily be regarded as an intermediate form of socialization between solitary and group play; and this in turn would question the use of a social participation index, as used by Parten (1932) and Smith (1973). Moore, Everton and Brophy (1974) suggest that solitary play need not be an indicator of poor social adjustment. This is based on the observation that much solitary play is occupied in goal-directed activities, large muscle play, or educational play; less than 16.5% was classified as onlooking, daydreaming, sulking, or seeking the teacher. However, Moore *et al.* were studying kindergarten rather than nursery school children, and in the latter the proportion of solitary behaviour that is unoccupied is considerably higher (see Table 49.1). Rubin, Maioni, and Hornung (1976) found that about 48% of solitary play in preschool was onlooker or unoccupied behaviour. Nevertheless, Rubin *et al.* also argue that parallel and not solitary play is 'the least mature level of a social cognitive play hierarchy for 3- and 4-year-olds' (p. 418).

The principal-components analysis justification of a social participation index has also been reevaluated in recent work by Roper and Hinde (in press). These authors observed 3- and 4-year-olds in two English nursery classes. Although a principal-components analysis gave a first component somewhat similar to that of Smith (1973), a further rotated factor-analytic solution revealed what these authors interpret as a breakdown of this first component into three subfactors. These were (a) group play versus parallel play, or whether given proximity children were interacting; (b) solitary play, or whether a child was in proximity to others or not; and (c) unoccupied behaviour. These findings cast doubt on the utility of a linear social participation index with parallel play in an intermediate position. However, they do not particularly support the contention of Moore *et al.* (1974) and of Rubin *et al.* (1976) that parallel play is less mature than solitary play. Roper and Hinde's first factor shows no appreciable age correlation, although negative correlations with age were obtained for the second and third factors.

From these contradictory findings, one consensual implication might be drawn. This is that whether a child is occupied at a task or not, is conceptually and empirically largely separate from whether he or she is in proximity or interaction with other children or not. There is no dispute that a preschool child can be engaged alone on a constructive task. However, the fact of being engaged in task activity may not tell us anything about that child's *social* maturity. Indeed, as Jennings (1975) has indicated, people and object orientation may correspond to fairly separate abilities in preschool children. Similarly, the existence of Roper and Hinde's separate third factor (unoccupied or not) contrasts with their first two factors relating to social abilities (proximity to and interaction with others). From this viewpoint, Parten's original scheme can be seen to have compounded purely social participation categories with task-related categories such as 'unoccupied.' It may well be preferable to limit social participation levels to solitary, parallel, and group (and sublevels of these categories). This has been done in the present review and research. With the data in Table 49.1, 'solitary' includes 'unoccupied' and 'onlooker' of Parten's categories, on the assumption that the vast majority of such instances involve neither close proximity with similar materials (parallel) nor substantial interaction (group).

Even given this simplification, the evidence for the intermediate position of parallel play, so far as social abilities are concerned, remains poorly substantiated at best. Critically lacking is any longitudinal evidence that children do in fact proceed through sequential stages of solitary, parallel, and group behaviour, as is suggested in many texts of early childhood education and play. The present report provides longitudinal data on social participation and suggests some reasons for the discrepant findings in the earlier research referred to above.

METHOD

Subjects

Two groups of preschool children were observed over a 9-month period, from October 1971 to June 1972, at a play group in Sheffield, England. Each group met for two mornings each week during school terms. The two groups met in the same premises, with the same play-group staff and equipment, but at different times; subjects for the two groups were from the same population. Thus results for the two groups provide, in Lykken's (1968) terminology, an 'inbuilt' literal replication.

The two groups were started at the end of September 1971 by recruiting children from the local neighbourhood. Social background was varied, mainly from skilled working or middle classes. The great majority of the children had not had any previous nursery experience at other nurseries or play groups.

Each group contained 12 boys and 12 girls, matched for age, with the age range on entry from 28 to 47 months ($M = 35$ months) in the first group (Group 1) and from 28 to 48 months ($M = 36$ months) in the second group (Group 2). Half of the children were over 33 months (older), and half were 33 months or under (younger).

Procedure

Using time-sampling methods, the children's behaviour was observed each morning session through the 9-month period by one observer. The main purpose of the study was to examine the effects of varied amounts of floor space, and play equipment, on the children's behaviour (Smith, 1974; Smith and Connolly, 1977). An independent factor in the design was time through the project. The observational data were obtained in six consecutive time blocks, of about 5 weeks each; each time block contained environmental variations as noted above, but separate time blocks were equivalent in this respect.

At each session, children's behaviour was observed and recorded in short focal-child samples of 40-sec. duration. Four such samples were obtained for each child at each session, with at least a 10-min. separation (usually more) between samples on any one child. Supplementary samples were obtained at the next session in cases of absence (not very frequent; mean attendance was 91% in Group 1 and 90% in Group 2). Each time block contained 10 sessions for each group, which therefore yielded 40 independent samples per child.

At the end of each sample period of 40 sec. the nature of the child's social participation and activity choice for the majority of the sample period was recorded by the observer. The categories relevant to this article are described below.

Nature of Social Behaviour Measures

Group. The focal child has one or more other children who interact substantially with him or her in the nature of the activity, either visually, verbally, through exchanging objects, or in the organization of a game. This category subsumes Parten's categories of associative and cooperative play.

Parallel. The focal child has one or more other children who are in close proximity to him or her and are engaged in similar behaviours. However, these companions do not interact with the focal child or they do so only fleetingly; their presence does not substantially affect his or her behaviour. This category corresponds to Parten's category of parallel play.

Solitary. The child has no companion in group activity or parallel behaviour. The category subsumes Parten's categories of solitary play and onlooker activity and would usually include her category of unoccupied behaviour.

Adult. The child is in group or parallel activity with an adult.

These four categories were comprehensive and mutually exclusive; one category was scored at the end of each sample period.

Nature of Task Activity Measures

Occupied. The child is engaged in active use of some object or apparatus in the environment, or in gross motor activity, or in substantial social interaction.

Unoccupied. The child is not occupied as defined above. Generally, this includes wandering around, just watching other children, just holding, or repetitively fumbling an object.

Interobserver Agreements

Simultaneous recording with a second observer, experienced in child watching and given the above definitions but no specific further training, gave interobserver agreements (no. agreements/ (no. agreements + mean no. disagreements)) of .88 for group, .76 for parallel, .85 for solitary, and .94 for adult. Judgment as to whether a child was occupied or unoccupied gave a concordance of .94.

These concordances were based on 100 simultaneous samples by the two observers. As a check on the time stability of the principal observer, 50 samples were made prior to the start of the main study and another 50 at the midpoint. Concordances were substantially the same at these two occasions.

RESULTS

Table 49.1: Percentages of solitary, parallel, and group activity, and of unoccupied/onlooker as a percentage of solitary, in previous and present studies on nursery-school-aged children

Activity measure	Parten (1932)	Barnes (1971)	Rubin et al. (1976)		Present study	
			MC	LC	Group 1	Group 2
Solitary	29	51	32	35	39	35
Parallel	32	24	29	37	23	27
Group	38	25	39	28	37	38
Unoccupied/solitary	40	47	54	43	37	42

Note. MC = middle class; LC = lower class.

In analysing the results, samples in which the child was with an adult were ignored, as generally this involved some constraint on the child's behaviour. For the remaining samples, the percentages of solitary, parallel and group behaviour are shown in Table 49.1, in comparison with results from Parten (1932), Barnes (1971), and Rubin et al. (1976). The figures are similar, although not supporting Barnes' claim for a decrease in social participation in the 45 years since Parten's data were gathered.

When unoccupied was scored, the child was almost invariably solitary, although a few cases of parallel behaviour did occur. Unoccupied as a percentage of solitary behaviour is also not greatly different from the other nursery school studies, all being much larger than the 16.5% maximum figure that Moore et al. (1974) obtained for kindergarten children.

Table 49.2: Category totals in successive time blocks and significance levels from analysis of variance

Measure and group	Time Sequence						
	T_1	T_2	T_3	T_4	T_5	T_6	p
Group							
1	192	263	294	317	322	390	.001
2	159	183	290	366	432	378	.001
Parallel							
1	197	188	192	157	179	185	ns
2	261	223	199	212	220	198	ns
Solitary							
1	356	342	308	317	318	235	.001
2	360	376	288	243	205	222	.001
Unoccupied							
1	169	132	78	87	99	65	.001
2	184	162	86	74	73	67	.001

Overall Time Changes

The successive totals for each category in each time block are shown for both groups of children in Table 49.2. There is a consistent increase in group behaviour and decrease in solitary and unoccupied behaviour, while parallel behaviour shows no significant variations. However, these overall trends obscure the actual changes in the nature of primary social behaviour in individual children.

Individual Sequences

Results for each child in each time block were considered separately and assigned a code of G (group), P (parallel), or S (solitary), according to which category had the highest total. A few cases of ties (10 out of 288) were resolved in favour of the 'higher' category. Each code thus shows the most common form of social behaviour for a particular child during one 5-week time block.

The child sequences were put into six different types, shown in Table 49.3. Children are coded by group (1 and 2), older or younger age (O or Y), boy or girl (B and G), and a number from 1 to 6.

The types and subtypes are listed in order of age means. Type A children started in G. There is little difference between A1 children who always stayed in G and A2 children who alternated G with some blocks of S.

Type B children started in S (B1 and B2) or P (B3) and made a transition to G at some point. The 11 B1 children went direct from S to G, whereas the 6 B2 children went through from S to G with P as an intermediary stage.

Table 49.3: Types of sequence of predominant social activity for individual children over six successive time blocks

Type and subtype	M age (in mo.)	M unoccupied/ solitary (%)	Children	Time sequence					
				T_1	T_2	T_3	T_4	T_5	T_6
A (n = 13)[a]									
A1	40.6	31.7	1OB2, 1OB4, 1OG1	G	G	G	G	G	G
			1OG4, 1OG6, 2OB1	G	G	G	G	G	G
			2OB4, 2OB5, 2OG1	G	G	G	G	G	G
A2	39.5	33.3	1OG3, 2OB2	G	S	G	G	G	G
			1YG3	G	G	G	S	G	G
			1OG2	G	S	G	S	G	G
B (n = 24)[b]									
B1	34.6	31.3	1YB4, 2YB3	S	S	G	G	G	G
			2OB3	S	S	S	G	G	G
			1OB6, 1OG5	S	S	S	S	G	G
			1OB3, 1YG4	S	S	S	S	S	G
			1YB1	S	G	S	G	G	G
			2OG3	S	S	S	G	G	S
			2OB6	S	S	S	S	G	S
			1YG5	S	S	S	G	G	P
B2	34.3	48.5	2OG2, 2YG4	S	P	G	G	G	G
			1YB5	S	S	P	G	G	G
			1YG2	S	S	S	P	G	G
			2YB4	S	S	S	S	P	G
			1OB5	S	S	P	S	G	G
B3	33.3	67.9	2YG2, 2YG5, 2YG6	P	P	P	G	G	G
			2YB2	P	G	P	G	G	P
			2OG3	P	S	G	G	G	G
			2OG6, 2YG1	P	S	S	S	G	S
C (n = 11)[c]									
C1	33.2	40.8	1OB1, 1YB2, 1YB3	S	S	S	S	S	S
			1YB6, 1YG1, 1YG6	S	S	S	S	S	S
			2OG4, 2YB1, 2YB6	S	S	S	S	S	S
C2	31.0	31.5	2YG3	S	S	P	S	S	S
			2YB5	P	S	P	P	S	P

Note. Children are coded, in order, by group (1 and 2), older or younger (O and Y), boy or girl (B and G), and a number from 1 to 6. Codes to which the children were assigned in successive time blocks on the basis of predominant social behaviour are as follows: G (group), S (solitary), and P (parallel). Children 1OG6 and 2YB3 left shortly before the study ended. Their T_6 data were obtained during T_5.

[a] M age = 40.2 mo.; mean unoccupied/solitary = 32.2%; starts in G.
[b] M age = 34.2 mo.; mean unoccupied/solitary = 46.3%; makes transition to G.
[c] M age = 32.8 mo.; mean unoccupied/solitary = 39.1%; makes no transition to G.

Type C children failed to make a transition to G. They either stayed in S all the time (C1) or varied between S and P (C2).

Type A children are significantly older than Type B children, $U(13, 24) = 56.0, p < .01$, and Type C children, $U(13, 11) = 21.0, p < .01$. Type B and C children do not differ significantly in age, $U(24, 11) = 105.0$, ns.

Unoccupied as a percentage of solitary behaviour does not differ significantly between any of the three main types on Mann-Whitney tests. Individual children showed a lot of variation in this statistic.

Transition Probabilities Between States

Figure 49.1 shows the transition probabilities between S, P, and G, from one time block to the next, summed separately for all 24 older children (34–48 months) and all 24 younger children (28–33 months). The older children most often stay in G, next most often stay in S, and next most often transfer between the two states. Transitions to P are very rare. The younger children most often stay in S, next most often stay in G, and are approximately equally likely to move from S to P, P to G, or S to G.

As parallel is overall the least likely of the three social behaviour categories (see Table 49.1), it is possible that its apparent relative unimportance (see Table 49.3 and Figure 49.1) is exaggerated when coding each time block as S, P, or G. Perhaps even for Type B1 children, for example, there is an increase in parallel before the child shows predominantly group activity, and a decrease afterwards, even though parallel is never the most likely category for a substantial time period. These possibilities were examined for the 11 Type B1 children.

First, the two successive S states before the transition to G were examined to see whether parallel showed an increase. Out of 10 cases, 4 showed an increase and 6 a decrease.

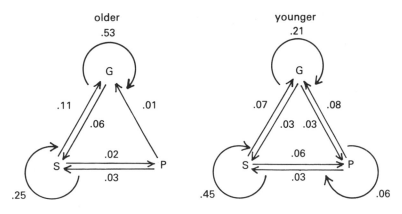

Figure 49.1 Transition probabilities between states of social behaviour for older and younger preschool children.

Second, the two successive G states after the transition from S were examined to see whether parallel showed a decrease. Out of eight cases, 4 showed a decrease and 4 an increase.

In both cases, there is no evidence for any systematic relation between the amount of parallel activity and the transition from S to G.

DISCUSSION

The results point clearly to differences in the sequences of social participation in children over time, only partly attributable to chronological age. Thirteen children, mainly older (11 were over 3 years old) went more or less directly into predominantly group play with companions. Of these, 9 remained this way continuously, but 4 alternated substantial time blocks of predominantly solitary behaviour. These children were no younger than the others, and their solitary play was no more or less occupied. Probably, these bouts of solitary behaviour reflected changing friendship preferences, without indicating immaturity on the part of the children concerned.

Eleven children started predominantly in solitary behaviour, and at some point they changed directly to predominantly group behaviour. No substantial period of predominantly parallel behaviour intervened, nor was there evidence for any nonrandom change in parallel behaviour during the transition period. One sequence for social involvement therefore seems to be to go fairly directly from playing alone to playing with others. This seems to be a preferred sequence for older children (see Figure 49.1). It is also followed by some younger children: 5 of the 11 were under 33 months old on entry.

However, six children did show a transition from solitary, through parallel, to group behaviour. Four of the six were under 33 months old on entry. This seems to be an alternative sequence for the 2-year-olds or younger three-year-olds, and it corresponds to the 'classic' view of social participation, although it is not the most common in this sample.

Five children went directly from parallel to group behaviour, and three more did so with bouts of solitary behaviour intervening. Finally, 11 children either stayed in predominantly solitary behaviour, or (two children) alternated with bouts of parallel behaviour.

Although older children generally showed less solitary behaviour, the percentage of unoccupied activity in solitary behaviour was not significantly different. Variations between individual children outweighed variations between types. This supports the notion that the extent to which a child may occupy him- or herself in an activity is, to some extent at least, independent of his or her social participation level.

In summary, parallel behaviour is found throughout the preschool period, in 2- to 5-year-old children. It does decrease with age, but not very substantially (cf. Barnes, 1971; Parten, 1932). However it is usually only found as a predominant behaviour in 2-year-olds, or younger 3-year-olds, and in such circumstances it does often precede a period of predominantly group behaviour. Most 3- and 4-year-olds move from mainly solitary to mainly group behaviour directly. Thus a phase of predominantly parallel behaviour is a sign of a younger or perhaps a less mature child. To this extent, Rubin et al. (1976) are right to question the social maturity of parallel play.

Solitary behaviour differs in that it does decrease noticeably with age through the preschool period (cf. Barnes, 1971; Parten, 1932). Although less frequent in older children, however, some 3- and 4-year olds do show periods of predominantly solitary behaviour, alternating with predominantly group behaviour. In this sense, solitary play can be seen perhaps as a mature coping behaviour, in children who would not now show predominantly parallel play. However, solitary play seems to be an 'option' for these older children, in a way in which it is not for the younger ones (see Table 49.3).

The results do question the usefulness of a social participation index in which parallel is weighted intermediately between solitary and group. At best, it would be a reasonable approximation for 2-year-olds and younger 3-year-olds. For older 3-year-olds and 4-year-olds, it is a much less good approximation. It is probably not coincidental that the earlier studies using social participation indexes (Parten, 1932; Smith, 1973; Smith and Connolly, 1972) had many 2-year-olds in the sample, whereas in the more critical studies (Moore et al., 1974; Roper and Hinde, in press; Rubin et al., 1976) all the children were 3 years old or over.

It would be worthwhile to investigate further the different sequences shown by children as they become able to play a lot with other children. Why do some 2-year-olds seem to rely on parallel play and others not? This will require more detailed longitudinal studies at this age range as well as further knowledge of factors outside the immediate nursery situation.

Acknowledgements

The facilities on which this research is based were supported financially by Grant 1414/2 from the Social Science Research Council, London.

The author is grateful to Robert Hinde and Rosemary Roper for their comments on an earlier draft of the manuscript.

Requests for reprints should be sent to Peter K. Smith, Department of Psychology, University of Sheffield, Sheffield, S10 2TN, England.

References

Barnes, K. E. (1971) 'Preschool play norms: a replication', Developmental Psychology, 5, 99–103.

Jennings, K. D. (1975) 'People versus object orientation, social behavior, and intellectual abilities in preschool children', Developmental Psychology, 11, 511–19.

Lykken, D. T. (1968) 'Statistical significance in psychological research', Psychological Bulletin, 70, 151–9.

Moore, N. V., Everton, C. M. and Brophy, J. E. (1974) 'Solitary play: some functional reconsiderations', Dev. Psychology, 10, 830–4.

Parten, M. B. (1932) 'Social participation among preschool children', J. Abnorm. Soc. Psychol., 27, 243–69.

Parten, M. and Newhall, S. M. (1943) 'Social behaviour of preschool children' in Barker, R. G., Kounin, J. S. and Wright, H. F. (eds.), Child Behaviour and Development, New York: McGraw-Hill.

Roper, R., and Hinde, R. A. 'Social behavior in a nursery school: consistency and complexity', Child Development.

Rubin, K. H., Maioni, T. L. and Hornung, M. (1976) 'Free play behaviors in middle- and lower-class preschoolers: Parten and Piaget revisited', Child Development, 47, 414–19.

Smith, P. K. (1973) 'Temporal clusters and individual differences in the behaviour of preschool children' in Michael, R. P. and Crook, J. H. (eds.) Comparative Ecology and Behaviour of Primates, New York and London: Academic Press.

Smith, P. K. (1974) 'Social and situational determinants of fear in the playgroup' in Lewis, M. and Rosenblum, L. A. (eds.) The Origins of Fear, New York: Wiley.

Smith, P. K. and Connolly, K. (1972) 'Patterns of play and social interaction in preschool children' in Blurton Jones, N. (ed.) Ethological Studies of Child Behaviour, Cambridge University Press.

Smith, P. K. and Connolly K. J. (1977) 'Social and aggressive behavior in preschool children as a function of crowding', Social Science Information, 16, 601–20.

The development of moral judgement
Joan Tamburrini

Piaget (1932) has stressed the important part played by experience in peer groups in the development of moral judgement. He points out that morality consists in a system of rules, and moral behaviour reflects, in part, the respect an individual has acquired for those rules. He therefore investigated children's understanding and use of the rules of the game of marbles. He chose to study the rules of a game because, on the whole, they are not learned from adults and adults do not impose rewards and punishments which might influence how the game is played. Piaget found that between the ages of two and six children's knowledge of the rules of the game is fragmentary, but they consider them sacred and immutable. They believe the rules have been handed down from adults, or even from God, and that it would be wrong to alter them in any way.

This rigid attitude toward rules on the one hand and the way in which young children actually play the game on the other hand appears somewhat paradoxical. For in their games young children frequently show a disregard for the rules. At this stage each plays the game in his own way and an outcome in which each is the 'winner' is not seen as impossible or contradictory. A young child's playing of the game is egocentric: he does not take into consideration the other children's points of view.

It is not until the age of seven, on the average, that children begin to play the game co-operatively rather than egocentrically. Children then understand that rules are necessary to the game as a social activity. They adhere to the rules and try to make sure that others do so too. However, they still believe rules are sacred and must be obeyed. Gradually the child moves to a stage in which he believes that rules can be generated and changed as long as it is through the common agreement of the players.

Young children's belief that rules are generated by authority and are unalterable is reflected not only in their ideas about the rules of games but equally in contexts involving morality, that is in issues about right and wrong, about punishment and justice, for example. Piaget tested their understanding of such moral issues by asking them to make judgements with respect to pairs of stories involving ostensibly similar behaviour but differing significantly in terms of moral intention. For example, one pair of stories involved a child breaking crockery: in one story a trayful of crockery was broken accidentally by a child who was trying to be helpful; in the other story a child broke one cup but as a result of taking something from the larder after having been forbidden to do so. Young children judge that the child in the first story has been the naughtiest. Their judgements are based on the seriousness of the outcome (a trayful of broken crockery as against only one broken cup), and they ignore the differences in intention. Judgements of this kind are based, in part, on the child's perception of the rules as rigid and therefore not subject to varying interpretation in the light of extenuating circumstances, and, in part, on the child's inability to 'decentre' and take into account intention as well as consequence.

Piaget and other psychologists concerned with moral development, such as Kohlberg and Turiel (1971) and Damon (1977), have emphasized the importance of social interaction in the peer group as a source of moral development. As he interacts socially with other children a child learns increasingly to consider other children's points of view and to reconsider and possibly modify his ideas when they are in conflict with those of others. Rules come to be appreciated as regulators of social interaction and the need for their democratic acceptance is gradually perceived.

The development from egocentricity to increasing co-operation in young children's social interaction is particularly reflected in their play, and is in part a developmental matter as the preceding paper by Smith shows. However, teachers may also facilitate the development of social co-operation through the materials they provide and the kinds of activities they encourage. Tizard (1977) claims that there is a traditional concern in English nursery schools for the development of individuality which is reflected in the materials teachers provide, the activities they encourage and the comments they make. Other materials and activities, she suggests, might encourage the development of more social co-operation. She quotes in a study in which the removal of some table toys led to an increase in co-operative activities.

Different cultures will, of course, facilitate and encourage those kinds of development which they value most. Bronfenbrenner (1971) has shown how the emphasis on co-operation and the collective in the USSR is reflected in

Russian nursery schools and kindergartens:

> From the very beginning stress is placed on teaching children to share and to engage in joint activity. Frequent reference is made to common ownership: 'Mine is ours, ours is mine'. Collective play is emphasized. Not only group games, but special complex toys are designed which require the co-operation of two to three children to make them work.

In Papers 31 and 32 it was pointed out that a teacher's values are inevitably reflected in the materials she provides and the ways she interacts with her pupils. Cross-cultural studies like those of Bronfenbrenner show how the values a teacher holds and transmits are often those of the culture of which she is a member.

References
Bronfenbrenner, U. (1971) *Two Worlds of Childhood: USA and USSR*, Allen & Unwin.
Damon, W. (1977) *The Social World of the Child*, Jossey-Bass.
Kohlberg, L. and Turiel, P. (1971) 'Moral development and moral education' in Lesser, G. (ed.) *Psychology and Educational Practice*, Scott, Forman.
Piaget, J. (1932) *The Moral Judgment of the Child*, Routledge & Kegan Paul.
Tizard, B. (1977) 'Play: the child's way of learning?' in Tizard, B. and Harvey, D. (eds.) *Biology of Play*, Heinemann.

Discussion Guide Y

1 Compare as a group your findings in Activity 52. Which boy, the one who broke one plate or the one who broke more than ten, did the majority of children think the naughtiest? What reasons did they give? Did they, on the whole, ignore the boy's intentions and centre on the consequences? What was the extent, if any, of individual differences? What implications for child rearing and for education would you draw from your findings?

2 Compare as a group your findings in Activity 51 so that you isolate:
   (a) the changes from parallel to social play in relation to size of groups, age of children and length of time the child has attended the school class or playgroup;
   (b) the extent to which single sex or mixed groups predominated, and whether in this respect there were any differences according to age or materials.

3 Compare these findings with those reported by Smith in Paper 49. What similarities are there between Smith's findings and yours? Are there any differences? If so, can you account for them in any way?

Module Eight

Pre-School Provision

Provision for children of pre-school age is of three kinds: care-taking provision, play provision, and provision which is under the aegis of Local Education Authorities in institutions staffed in part by trained teachers, that is in nursery schools and nursery classes. Paper 55 is a glossary listing the various kinds of provision found.

It may seem strange that the reference to nursery schools and classes in the first sentence of this Introduction is so oblique. They could have been referred to simply as 'educational' provision. The reason for such obliqueness lies in the nature of a current debate concerning the kind of service nursery schools are and should be providing. The debate is introduced in Paper 51 by Van der Eyken in which he reports the findings of a survey that nursery school teachers gave greater weighting to the social and emotional development of young children than to their intellectual development.

Van der Eyken suggests that this low priority given to intellectual development may reflect the historical influence of psychoanalysis which emphasized emotional development. This echoes the claim made in Paper 31 that the non-intervening style in relation to children's play may well stem from the psychoanalytic tradition. By contrast, a more recent influence on nursery schools has been 'compensatory' education. Paper 52 by Chazan and Cox gives brief descriptions of various compensatory programmes in the USA and in Britain, and examines their theoretical bases and evidence of their degrees of success.

The advent of compensatory programmes has given a greater focus to the debate concerning the ethos and purposes of nursery schools. Some authorities have claimed that compensatory programmes have a greater concern for intellectual development in general and for language development in particular than do traditional nursery schools with their emphases on social and emotional development. They have suggested that traditional nursery schools would do well to adopt some of the priorities and procedures of compensatory education. Others have maintained that some compensatory programmes stress language in isolation from other aspects of children's development and have made too great a use of materials which are unrelated to children's experiences. They have urged that nursery schools should continue to be concerned with the development of the child in various domains, social, emotional, physical as well as intellectual. The debate is illustrated by the interchange between Blank and Tizard in Papers 53 and 54.

Module Eight

Pre-School Provision

- Read the introduction to the module and then read Paper 51 which introduces the debate concerning pre-school provision
- Complete Activities 53, 54 and 55 which will enable you to compare the provision you find in a nursery school or class with that in a pre-school playgroup
- Complete Activity 56 which asks you to think about the purposes of nursery education. This should help you in the reading of the following papers.
- Read Papers 52, 53 and 54 which focus the debate already introduced in Paper 51
- Complete Activity 57 which is designed to help you organize some of the main points in the controversy discussed in the papers in this module
- Consult Paper 55 to make sure you are aware of the main kinds of pre-school provision
- Work through Discussion Guide Z

Reading	140 mins.
Activities	390 mins.
Discussion	190 mins.
Total	720 mins.
	= 12 hrs.

The ethos of the nursery school
W. Van der Eyken

For most people, the term 'pre-school provision' is closely related in their mind with the idea of a nursery school or a nursery class. Given the history of nursery schooling, that is not surprising. There is a logical connection between the idea of a conventional school, with its specially-trained staff and available equipment, its purpose-built structure and its relationship with the rest of the educational system, and the idea that such provision ought also to be available for younger children. There are, however, also a number of crucial differences between what one might consider a 'conventional' school for the over-fives and a nursery school, and it is these differences which raise questions about the nature of nursery schools, their ethos and their relationship both to the community and to the rest of the educational system.

In the first place, the term 'school' is totally inappropriate for children under five, and while no sensible person — whether he be teacher, parent or administrator — actually sees them as 'schools' in the strict sense, nevertheless the terminology has unfortunate consequences, in particular for the relationship between staff and parents. 'Schools', as we all know, are official centres run by professional people. Generally speaking, they are not seen by the working-class community as centres which are easily accessible to parents, no matter how much individual members of staff may welcome such direct and constant contact. Secondly, 'schools' breed, inevitably, a sense of 'professionalism' in which, in many subtle ways, and for many perfectly good reasons, the parental role is somewhat diminished, and, in its crudest manifestations, undermined. Thirdly, there now exists a long tradition of 'nursery schooling' which lays claim to a certain 'received wisdom' about the practice of nursery schooling; about the curriculum, about the relationship between teachers and children, about the value system of the early years, about the relative merits of aims. These views are often strongly held and defended in 'professional' terms, and they have given the nursery schools a certain ethos which is particularly their own.

To illustrate what I mean, let us consider in some detail the findings of a recent inquiry sponsored by the Schools Council into the views of professional, qualified nursery teachers (Schools Council, 1972). The first question that this inquiry, conducted on a 40 per cent national sample, asked was — who are the nursery teachers?

To those who think that nursery education is in the hands of the unmarried or the childless, the results proved salutary: 64 per cent of the 578 teachers were married, and half of them had children of their own. Most of them were mature, professional people, two-thirds of them having taught in schools for twenty years or more. Nearly all of them possessed teaching certificates, the majority having trained for two years, and for two-thirds of them, nursery education had been included as a major part of their study. Moreover, more than half the teachers suggested that they were allied to an active local branch of the Nursery Schools Association, and gave the impression of being a strongly dedicated and identified professional group while containing only a very small number of graduates (2.4 per cent of the total sample) or of people who felt the need for further qualifications other than those directly related to their own teaching practice. Although the survey evidence might indicate that, as a group, nursery teachers were intellectually rather narrow in their interests, this must be weighed against their probably correct assessment of the value of many theoretical courses or paper qualifications when dealing with young children. Moreover, it is plain from the survey that what these teachers enjoyed most was actually working with the children; a vocationally directed group of people, to whom economic or personal considerations ran very much secondary to their desire to be involved with the young.

When these people were asked about the aims of nursery education, and were asked to differentiate between social, intellectual, aesthetic, physical and home–school relationship factors they tended, as anyone might in their circumstances, to give an overall nod of approval to all of them, but when their detailed replies to questions were analysed, it was striking that the teachers gave a considerably greater weighting to the social and emotional development of children, and considered that intellectual development was, if a choice had to be made, the least important. When their replies were factor-analysed and reordered in the light of this analysis, it transpired that these teachers — and, by implication, most nursery teachers in general — placed greatest emphasis on the development of 'self' and identity in a child, helping the child to understand his own feelings and those of others, to become independent, to control his own emotions and develop confidence. The second set of objectives that the teachers favoured dealt with school-related objectives, such as helping a child to fit in with routines, with easy relationships with adults, with accepting and respecting authority and with following simple directives. The third set of objectives they favoured dealt with physical development, and the fourth with general social behaviour. Once again, intellectual or cognitive development took a low priority.

It is, of course, easy to misread the responses to questionnaires, for so much depends on how the respondents interpret the questions. Perhaps it is easier to consider their own, direct and unstructured replies. Of these, the majority dealt with the social–emotional–moral development of the child, and were in the vein of: 'to provide a friendly, stable, stimulating environment in which a child may be happy', or said things like 'My chief aim is that each individual child in my care should ... become a well-integrated, well-adjusted human being', or 'To help every child reach its full potential'. Words like 'potential', 'mature', 'happy', 'stimulating' are, of course, rich in potential but too imprecise for the modern educational psychometrician; they form, however, the key words in the nursery-school language and they perhaps illustrate the suspicion that many experienced teachers have of elaborating their own linguistic code, or making more explicit their own professional intentions. Only 6 per cent of the statements relating to aims, for example, specifically mentioned a child's progress with language development, despite the fact that this is today regarded as one of the most fundamental areas of pre-school stimulus.

A recent study by Valerie Thomas (1973, pp. 209–16) into the use of language in a nursery class produced a highly critical report on this aspect of nursery provision. Valerie Thomas, who observed a small sample of children for a complete day, recorded every response uttered by and to them, noted their activities and the time spent on each. According to her observation of the staff,

> Children's speech was rarely corrected or enlarged, and adult patterns appeared little more than an elaborated version of the children's. Their sentences were short and simply constructed, containing few adjectives or adverbs. A considerable proportion of their speech was in the form of commands, or emotionally-toned remarks such as 'Naughty' or 'I am surprised at you!' and social phrases such as

> 'Jolly good!' and 'Oh, pretty!' ... Minimum verbalization was accepted by the nursery staff and no child was expected to repeat, clarify or extend a statement. Often a single word, with a gesture formed a request ... The nursery did not try to compensate for any experiential or cultural deficiencies. It appeared self-absorbed and contained and little reference was made to the world beyond its walls. The experiences presented during the day were invariable, the pattern of activities was repetitive and the equipment emphasized gross motor activity.

According to Valerie Thomas,

> The adult's conception of the value of pre-school education and of their role within it, determined the environment and the activities. To the headmistress and the nursery staff, its chief value lay in the social and emotional benefits from a contact with other children. Advantaged children would be encouraged to share, the disadvantaged provided with love and security. Improvements to the nursery would arise from more room and a covered play area. No mention was made of additions that might bring cognitive benefits, such as a higher child–staff ratio, a wider range of equipment, advisory assistance or the provision of relevant courses.

When asked what methods they would use to achieve their stated objectives, teachers in the Schools Council survey very seldom veered away from their favourite belief that a 'rich, stimulating appropriate environment' would do almost any trick. More notably, perhaps, very few, if any, teachers believed in a 'structured' programme of work of which the Engelmann–Bereiter version in the United States is an extreme example and the Peabody Language Development Kit used by Halsey and his teams in their EPA action research a moderate one. Although the project did not specifically question teachers about their views on 'structured learning', it seems reasonable to suppose that, if any teachers had favoured this, they would have said so. What in fact emerged — though, again, one must make allowances for the interpretation of questionnaire responses — is that nursery-school teachers are perhaps oversensitive to their recognition that child development is a complex process, and are therefore timorous about developing any very specific programme within their own nursery schools, over and beyond the conventional divisions into certain forms of activity and the presence of certain accepted play media like sand, water, clay, dough and paint. The historical roots of psycho-analysis, with their emphasis on model-making to release the child's mental inhibitions, have, one feels, grown deep.

Perhaps of even greater concern, however, is the fact that the teachers in the sample, in discussing the relationships between the home and the school, saw the contact between parents and the school very largely in terms of keeping themselves informed about the child's background, rather than of a personal interaction in which the parent played a positive and central role. A professed comment such as the aim 'to create a friendly relationship between school and home, so that both work together for the good of the child, and parents feel free to discuss problems' is an indication of the way teachers perceive such a relationship. Another teacher suggested that the aim should be 'to have good relationship with the parents, as knowledge of the home background helps in the understanding of the child's individual needs'. A third indicated the aim as 'to have daily contact with parents so that the home and school have the mutual purpose of understanding the child'. Another indicated the aim 'to be always available to talk to parents and strive to help with the problems concerning the children'.

Remarks such as these indicate a general belief among nursery school teachers that their centre of operation is within the school, and that the focus of their attention is on the individual child, as an entity in itself, divorced from the context of its family, its culture and its environment; that while they should be available for contact, it is the parents who should approach *them* and that the approach should then be on the professional–client basis, relating to identifiable problems with a child.

This interpretation is, no doubt, a rather harsh one, but as the researchers themselves offered no discussion of these statements other than the banal observation that 'teachers consider that the development of a good relationship between home and school is of ultimate benefit to the child' and 'they establish this link through friendly relationships and through a friendly school atmosphere' one is left with the evidence before one. It is in this area of nursery–school beliefs — that aims must not be specified other than in the most vague terminology, that objectives can very largely be met in terms of 'warm, friendly, stimulating environment' and that the role of parents is intrinsically one of information-giving about the child — that many feel that nursery education, as at present practised in this country, is not equipped by itself to meet the high social and educational expectations placed upon pre-school provision.

There is one further feature of the 1972 Schools Council survey which goes some way towards strengthening that argument. In the survey, the teachers were asked to comment on a list of fifteen categories of children who, it was suggested, might benefit from nursery education. In asking the teachers to indicate which groups they thought would derive most benefit, they were told that 'it is understood that, however you regard the needs of these different groups of children, you would wish to preserve a balanced intake'. This assumption contradicts the question asked, but in the event, the teachers responded by saying that 'children from deprived homes' would benefit most and that other disadvantaged groups, such as 'children from EPAs', 'children from high-rise flats', 'non-

English-speaking immigrant children' and 'children with emotional problems' would also benefit considerably. In fourteenth place, one from the bottom, they placed 'children with normal home backgrounds'. (Last of all were 'mentally handicapped children' presumably because of the difficulty they perceived in dealing with such children in a normal nursery.)

Given these responses, the teachers were asked: 'In your opinion, what proportion of a nursery chool intake should be composed of ordinary children without special problems?' The distribution of replies is given in the following table.

Table 51.1 Percentage of nursery-school intake of children without special problems

	100%	75%	50%	25%	10%	0%
per cent responses	2.3	70.3	22.2	4.0	0.7	0.5
accumulative responses	2.3	72.6	94.8	98.8	99.5	100.0

This table indicates that, while nursery-school teachers regard nursery school desirable, but not essential, for 'children from normal home backgrounds', when it comes to selecting their own school intakes, it is these children they favour above all others. Indeed, having recognized by their previous responses the great need of disadvantaged children to receive pre-school experiences, more than two-thirds of the teachers nevertheless felt that as many as three-quarters of their school intake should be from 'normal homes'.

This bias, towards the conformist, very often middle-class and more malleable child, is another reason why the nursery school, while in many respects admirable for many children who can benefit from it, should not be seen as necessarily a medium of social change, or a radical instrument for intervention in the social processes that affect the pre-school child. That is not to say that nursery schooling, as it is now practised, does not have a lot to offer, or that its basic practices do not contain the roots for a radical programme. But to judge that, one has to leave questionnaires, and go and see the practice itself.

'When you catch a rainbow, can you actually touch it?'
'Please, how quick is time?'
'What makes the chimney pots move sideways past the clouds?'

In a little nursery school in one of London's most affluent areas about thirty children attend for the full day, and another dozen come only for the morning. Two large rooms are filled with all the bric-a-brac of child play — puzzles, Wendy houses, rocking horses, bricks, books, trains, wooden toys, cooking materials, paper and crayons, scissors and paste, water, sand and every conceivable activity to amuse and instruct the small child. Tables and chairs of

child dimensions are scattered informally throughout the rooms and the children are totally free to move from activity to activity, coming together in different groups. A third small room is kept as a 'secret hide-away', a store room that is normally closed to adults and in which children may seek a refuge from the teachers and helpers in the school. In this small room three girls may build themselves a house out of wooden blocks and chairs, and organize an elaborate household. Two boys might work out a secret trap for one of their friends, or a single child, wishing to be alone and undisturbed, may find a haven here.

But it is the garden that is their real delight. To the uninitiated visitor it might at first seem a dangerous place for children, with masonry and uneven paths forming hills and rockeries and flower beds; with a sunken garden, a sandpit, and a clutter of play equipment, including a complex of scaffolding and step ladders that provides an endless source of exercise and inventive play. There are nets for climbing, and an extended net for swinging and bouncing. There are work benches for woodwork and special areas for digging. An outside tap can provide water for puddles or a hose. Planks of wood are available to be turned into pirate ships, tanks or homes. All is ready for instant conversion into the fantasies or realities of the child's mind.

It is an unstructured day that children spend in such a school. Once they have put their coats away and settled down, they are free to turn to anything they wish. This freedom is often a release for those who come from homes which, however 'good' they may be in the socio-economic sense, still act as a restraint on the demands of a rapidly developing child. The initial response will be violent bursts of energy, wild aggression, an uncoordinated exuberance. Sometimes the violence has other origins. Repressive parents, or parents who squabble constantly in front of a child, or a death in the family, all leave their marks on a growing mind. They create an aura of instability, an environment which is unsafe or in which the small child feels insecure and unloved.

It is easy to find the children who face such particular difficulties. If a visitor confines himself to observing the activities of the children and makes no move to communicate with them, they will accept his presence but ignore his personality and carry on with their interests. But if the visitor shows an interest in them, seats himself among them, questions their activities and comments on their performances, he is immediately flooded with a band of children who seek to hold his hand, to cling to him, to sit on his knee, to monopolize his attention, to adopt him as a substitute parent. He is regaled with anecdotes, with unending recollections of past incidents, with stories about their families, with elaborate descriptions of their ventures. These are not children being simply friendly and out-going; their natures demand a thirst for an attention that has not been satisfied in the past. It might take the form of violence, with a child hitting the visitor repeatedly, clinging to his legs, hurling punches at him. One child, who had just knocked two pieces of wood together to make an aeroplane, saw its potential as an axe and lashed out with it at me:

'Do you want to hurt me?'

'I am going to smash you up.'

'Go on, then, knock my fingers off.'

He lashed out, and hit my fingers. I bent the fingers into the palm of my hand.

'Now see if you can knock my hand off.'

He hit out again, catching my hand. I bent my hand at the wrist, and pretended he had knocked it off.

'Are you going to knock my arm off?' I asked, bending it at the elbow. He hesitated, wondering how far he could go. Then he burst out laughing. I laughed too. He put down the rudimentary axe and ran off to play. He had recently lost his father.

One is reminded of a note Susan Isaacs once kept of a child who attended the Malting House School. The boy:

> shows more hatred in his expression than any child I have observed. His opening remarks when coming to the school were: 'I will kill you! I will shoot you! I will hit you in the face! I will kill you blind dead! I will throw you on the roof so that you can't get down!'

This violence needs careful handling. It needs understanding and it needs organization. It must not be repressed, but at the same time, it cannot be allowed to vent itself on other small children. Parents find it incomprehensible that nursery teachers should allow what to them is such violent anti-social behaviour, just as they find it impossible to understand that A. G. Neill, the pioneering headmaster of Summerhill School, Leiston, Suffolk, once went around his school with a disturbed child and the two together threw rocks at the windows until most of them were broken.

Most of the released violence at a nursery school is not so drastic and consists of little more than rushing around, and the occasional fight or knocking down of bricks. The very presence of other children, and the social code that their presence imposes, acts as a restraint. The important feature is that in the environment of a good nursery school repressions have an outlet and that once released the child can be free to divert his attentions away from his own immediate problems and direct them at the world at large.

In a permissive atmosphere such children blossom. At this particular nursery there were some very bright children. One small girl was a balletomane and although she could not yet read she had surrounded herself, at the age of three, with every book on ballet she could find in the school. She recounted in detail the entire story of *The Sleeping Beauty* ballet she had recently seen, and added the scenario of *Puss in Boots* and *Treasure Island* for good measure. More than that, she could open one of the books and point to a particular dancer, giving his name and recalling that she had seen him dance a particular role.

Next to her, another small child recalled, with infinite detail, the range of cars and their makes that her uncle had possessed. Names like Lancia, Cortina and Renault came easily to this child, who had an almost photographic mental record of the specifications of each vehicle.

The development of these children occurs in concert. Even though they may not become close friends, their very presence in the same house creates a social climate that is beneficial to all of them. The school abounds in social opportunities for children to come to terms with others. They can wander into the kitchens and help themselves to milk or simply go and talk to cook. Their teachers and assistants are constantly available for advice, succour or stimulus. Their mothers are free to wander in and stay with the children or come and fetch them home. Visitors are constantly strolling in, either to gain their first impression of nursery life or, as students, to watch more closely the behaviour of young children. At the end of the morning and afternoon sessions, after the bustle and noisiness of free activity, a sudden hush falls on the school as the children quietly gather their chairs together and listen communally to a story.

It is an intense world of incredible activity, raw on the ears of those who believe that children ought to be seen and not heard, but welcome to an increasing number of parents. The Plowden Committee found that not only did 73 per cent of primary school teachers believe that all children whose parents wanted it should be exposed to such experiences, but the Committee's National Survey enquiry into parental attitudes (*Children and their Primary Schools,* vol. 2, appendix 3, tables 41 and 42) showed that a third of the parents would have preferred their children to have started some kind of schooling before the age of five.

Pregnant mothers are known to sidle past doors of another London nursery school and try to engage the headmistress in a spirited conversation that inevitably ends with a query as to whether their unborn child could be put down for attendance. The school, in the heart of the hotel trade and flanking some of the seamier East End areas, refuses. With a population of ever-moving families around it, it wisely waits until children are at least two years old before putting them on the waiting list and does not accept them into the school before the age of three.

The nursery is 'purpose-built' — it was designed as a nursery when the building went up in 1930. Consequently, it has the kind of child-centred architecture that all good schools should have, with wash basins of the right height, a washroom and cloakroom to every playroom, simple access from the playrooms to the play area outside and large windows that allow plenty of light. It could still be better: there are heavy swing doors in the corridor that challenge the strongest five-year-old. They keep out draughts and children at one and the same time. There is not enough light in these corridors, and the paint could be gayer. But despite this and the heavy-jowled, squat exterior of the thirties, the building also has many virtues.

Basically there are three large rooms all equipped in much the same way. In this space some fifty-three children spend most of their day, arriving at quarter past nine in the morning and leaving at quarter to four in the afternoon. In addition a further thirty-three children come just for the morning period, going home at 11.45 a.m. and another thirty-three come just for the afternoon, arriving at 1.20 p.m. At the last count this school had a waiting list of 140 names and was receiving applications at the rate of twenty a month.

All sorts of children come to this nursery school. Many of them live in high blocks of flats. Many others are the victims of the hotel trade. One child was kept sitting in a high chair in the same room in which the central heating plant operated. He arrived at school grossly overweight, scarcely able to move his limbs. Other children are the offspring of university staff and might reflect either good environments or be the subjects of that particularly cold and impersonal neglect that characterizes better educated parents preoccupied with their careers. Many of the children come from overseas, or have parents who are not themselves British, and consequently have difficulty with the language. None of them has to pay to attend this subsidized nursery school, but most make a voluntary contribution of some kind and many parents join a special club to take a personal interest in the affairs of the school.

It is a place that inspires interest. From the brass rubbings hanging on the walls of the entrance hall, to the gay patterns of children's paintings that crowd every space in the playrooms themselves, this is a world dominated by the child, his creations, his discoveries and his needs. There is an abundance of potential experience packed into every corner. A rabbit munches lettuce in the hall. Racks of books stand in every room. Easels, pots of paint, each with its separate brush, and sheets of paper clipped to the boards with clothes-pegs, wait ready for the creation of the artist. Sand trays, woodwork benches, clay, collections of shells, Wendy houses packed with toy dolls, cots, tea sets and model furniture, toy cars and garages, counting material, peg-boards and puzzles, baskets full of fancy dress materials, and masses of paper, pencils, crayons and plasticine wait neatly upon low shelves for the childhood impulse to reach out.

Outside, sandpits and rope ladders, tunnels, hoops and slides, rocking horses and cars stand ready to be clambered upon, swung aloft or shaped into castles or moats.

A trained nursery teacher is in charge of each of these three rooms and a trained assistant helps her look after the children. In addition nursery students and a number of other helpers move about constantly in attendance. But there is no coercion and little actual guidance. Apart from the morning and afternoon drink of milk, the sessions around the piano, the compulsory rest period on camp beds and the morning and afternoon story sessions in the reading corners created next to each room, the adults maintain the discreet role of advisers and friends. 'If we told them what to do, it wouldn't be them doing it, would it?' was the simple, direct philosophy expounded by one assistant. There is a spirit of mutual cooperation and respect between adult and child that is striking to the visitor. One child, slashing away at a piece of paper with a brush loaded with violent colour, announced that the painting was finished. With infinite care, the assistant removed the completed sheet from the board and hung it to dry over a clothes-hanger. It was not crumpled up, or thrown away, or called a mess. It was accepted as a piece of work, an individual act, and treated in exactly the same way as the painting by another girl, done with infinite care and the gritting of small teeth, that turned into a gay and fetching clown.

A stranger who walks into such a school is struck by the mature way in which the children move, by their apparent lack of concern at the approach of visitors.

'That looks very gay, Susan,' I commented on one little girl's work with coloured scraps of paper.

'How do you know my name?' she asked, without looking up.

'It is written down on the top of this sheet.'

'Yes, it is,' she replied. 'And that is Mary and that is Caroline. What is your name?'

This mature approach is also reflected in their social behaviour towards one another. In one room a small girl was curled up asleep in a doll's chair. She had been like that for some time, but the half-dozen other children in the room with her took no notice. There was no attempt to wake her, to shout, or, on the other hand, to muffle the natural noise of their play. She was left to her own devices, with an unconscious respect for her privacy and her personal desires.

The children are governed by few rules, but show a natural respect for those that do exist. While they may occasionally baulk at tidying up materials after they have used them, this takes the form of a diplomatic haggling with the assistants as to how much help they are going to get with the task. All accept readily that they need to wear aprons while painting, and when they occasionally forget to take them off and dash out into the garden to play, they immediately remove them on being reminded.

It is a gay, busy, intense world, to which the children are introduced gradually, with their mothers coming frequently. After a short while — no more than a week — the child is immersed in it, restricting himself at first to the familiar activities, but gradually learning from the others what other possibilities exist and extending his interests until finally he has mastered an enormous range of experiences the variety of which is astounding.

In the hallway two boys with upturned boxes are involved in a mysterious, inexplicable game. A third sits on a large wooden truck which he pushes with his legs. Three girls are holding an involved tea party in a Wendy house. Two boys are pushing pegs into numbers, the number of pegs relating to the value of the number. 'Thirty-eight, thirty-nine, forty . . .' murmurs one boy under his breath. In one corner a boy all alone reaches into two big wicker baskets and pulls out blocks of wood which he carefully arranges into a long railway line. Utterly absorbed, he brings an engine from a shelf and begins to push it along the line. Two girls sit, like old ladies at a bridge party, chatting, while their fingers knead clay into small cakes that are gently placed in a cake mould. Three other girls spread their hands out on sheets of paper and draw the outline of their fingers. Then they fill the tracing with a multitude of coloured pieces of paper.

A small, squat and intensely dark African boy rummages among the games on a shelf, and brings forth a mathematical puzzle. Singing a song under his breath he begins to fit various coloured blocks on to a set of pegs. On a wall, otherwise covered by paintings, there is a notice:

Things we collect: Matchboxes, old magazines, cotton reels, lace or ribbon, string, pieces of balsa wood, assorted boxes, old Christmas cards, unwanted story books.

As a nursery school this one has obvious points to recommend it, but it begs the question whether nursery schools themselves, as separate entities removed from the mainstream of educational thought and work, are desirable. As we have seen, their recommendation sprang originally from the poor quality of work in existing elementary schools which failed to cater for the needs of young children. Nowhere in Britain has education been so thoroughly changed as in the methods of teaching in the primary schools. The Plowden Committee Report paid handsome credit to this advance, which is evident to any visitor at any infant school. Many of the ideas that began with Froebel or Montessori have been adopted by the infant schools, so that they now bear no resemblance to those earlier classes. This being the case, is there still a need to segregate the under-fives from their elders?

Some would argue that there is, but in at least one experimental school in London the reverse is proving the case. At the Eveline Lowe School in Camberwell, children from three-and-a-half to nine come to their new school each morning and move into the same building. The youngest children have their own nursery, but the remainder are split up into family groups with age ranges from four to six and seven to nine. The entire school is one unit separated only by doors that can be opened by the smallest child. Although the costing of this new school was strictly controlled, it has certain obvious design advantages over the standard primary school. The equipment is lavish and of a high quality. There is an abundance of toys, wash basins, toilets for each class, quiet story-telling corners for each group, curtains and carpeting, that gives the school an atmosphere more akin to a modern home than an institution.

The children are drawn from the local neighbourhood and many of them have homes in high flats. For them the school is an oasis of child-centred activity in a harsh world of brick and mortar alien to their needs.

One teacher said:

When they first come to us, they seem overawed by the unexpected freedom they enjoy. They will come up to you and in a hushed voice ask: 'Can I use *all* this paper?' or 'Am I allowed to play with this truck?' or 'May I do that, too?' It is as if they cannot grasp the properties of their freedom. But this soon passes. Sometimes it is only an hour or two before they have found their feet and then they give vent to a sudden burst of exhilaration and hyperactivity that can be deafening.

What is noticeable about the school, however, is the extraordinary social integration that takes place in it. Without any prompting a group of children, led by a potential Sarah Bernhardt, made up a play, used wooden blocks to mark out a stage and acted the whole thing out for their own amusement. It was obviously a vehicle for the leader's considerable histrionic talents, but the others enjoyed it as much and there was no attempt to involve the teacher or impress anyone but themselves. A small boy who had hurt himself outside was being tended with great care by one of the girls. Three girls were having a quiet gossip in a carpeted area intended to act as a sitting-room. They poured each other cups of water and were obviously absorbed in their role as young housewives. A group of boys had used wooden blocks to build themselves a bus, and with a loose steering wheel pretending to drive their friends through the neighbourhood. Two boys and a girl were at the work table, making 'magic pots'. One boy, very much a lone wolf, wandered around with a small screwdriver in his hand. Wherever a screw could be found, this child set to work to undo it. A special box of materials — front-door bells, bits of machines, an old gramophone — was his special

delight. Faced with such opportunities for revealing the hidden secrets of technology, he was happy. And then there were the painters, using either their fingers or brushes, endlessly producing works to be hung up and dried.

Every now and then, these small children wander through to the rooms where their older brothers or sisters or friends are also at work. They share the hall for musical movement and an occasional assembly, but far more important, they are able to gain incentives from the older children and to take an interest in their work. They are not treated as a race apart.

The nursery section of the Eveline Lowe School has a practically unstructured day. Trays of milk bottles are left in the corridor for the children to help themselves. Every morning and every afternoon there is a special story session when the part-time children leave. Beyond this, the day is of their own making.

Unlike the nursery school, however, a much more conscious attempt is made to provide direct intellectual stimulus. At any time, children can demand the attention of the teacher and be directed towards certain goals. A boy who was weighing various materials on a scale was asked: 'Do you think one thing can weigh as much as a lot of things?'

'Let's see. If we put this big stone on this side, and we put a lot of these beads on this side, let's see what happens. Put some more on. What is happening? Now put some more on . . .'

Another group, playing about on a sofa in a special corner reserved for quiet reading and study, demanded a story. They themselves drew the curtains, switched on the light, screened off the area from the rest of the playroom by drawing a curtain across the opening and invited the teacher in. She complied and they got their story. Indeed, books abound throughout the school and any child at any time and any age can find himself with something to read.

No formal reading scheme is adopted by the school. As a child shows an interest in writing or has his name written on a painting or piece of work, he is encouraged to copy it or any other words that are of particular interest. From writing comes reading. Some of the four-year-olds, in addition, insist on being 'given a book' to read, following the example of their older brothers and sisters. Here the academic example of older children is particularly strong and beneficial. By aspiring to emulate their elders, the youngsters demonstrate a maturity and sophistication that is unusual for such an age group.

There is, of course, nothing new in the Eveline Lowe School arrangements. Welsh village schools often took children from two to seven, and the old, all-age schools similarly mixed their intake. The experimental London school was at least partly inspired by the Plowden Committee, which took great interest in its planning.

Unfortunately the Committee's investigations and the opening of the school did not quite coincide, so that the ultimate Report contains little mention of the project. Had the Committee been able to see the school in action, it might well have reconsidered its views about a national provision of separate nursery schools, needing their own sites and a duplication of many facilities that, in an integrated school, can so economically be shared. It is one thing to ask that local authorities set up a separate chain of nursery schools. It is quite another to authorize that new infant schools be so designed and built to cater for children from three-and-a-half years of age.

This change would also have other benefits. It would bring to an end the unhealthy segregation of young children from those only a few years, or months, older. It would bring the — at present — pre-school child firmly within the ambit of the Department of Education and Science and allow infant teaching a wider range. It would do away entirely with the unnecessary anguish that at present accompanies the starting of formal schooling. By introducing small children on a voluntary basis, into the schools from three-and-a-half or even three, and by allowing them either morning or afternoon session, with full-time sessions only for those children whose mothers were out to work or whose home environment demanded it, school would cease to be a dread or a novel experience, and would become, instead, an accepted and normal feature of every child's early years.

Finally, it would place the emphasis where it belongs — on the educational needs of these children, rather than, historically and unfortunately, on the kind of 'social rescue' basis on which so many nursery schools still operate.

Reference
Thomas, V. (1973) 'Children's use of language in the nursery', *Educ. Res.,* NFER, 209–16.

A survey of language programmes for disadvantaged children
M. Chazan and T. Cox

Approaches in the USA

The programmes designed for disadvantaged children in the USA have been so heterogeneous in content and so wide in scope that it is difficult to classify their approaches in any precise way. In general, programmes have been analysed along the following main dimensions (see Bartlett, 1972):

1. *goals:* emphases on particular language structures and functions;
2. *interactional patterns:* the type of teacher–child or child–child interaction encouraged;
3. *amount of preorganisation:* the extent to which the programme is structured or follows a planned sequence of activities.

A variety of categories has been used to indicate differences in emphasis along these dimensions. The Stanford Research Institute has distinguished between 'preacademic', 'cognitive discovery' and 'discovery' approaches in compensatory programmes (Bissell, 1973), while Weikart (1967) differentiates between 'traditional', 'structured' and 'task-orientated' programmes. Bartlett (1972) categorises language schemes in terms of those which emphasise 'pattern repetition', 'instructional dialogue' or 'improvised interaction', and Hammill and Larsen (1974) refer to approaches which stress 'psycholinguistic' training. On the basis of these analyses, the main approaches characterising language programmes in the USA will, for convenience, be categorised here as follows:

1. traditional (informal) enrichment
2. cognitive discovery
3. preacademic
4. psycholinguistic training
5. instructional dialogue.

These categories will be used only to indicate differences in emphasis between programmes. However great the differences between language programmes appear to be, they often have much in common, and, as Bissell (1973) states, the classifying of educational approaches requires detailed analyses of programme content if it is to be meaningful. Further, the orientation claimed by a programme is not always borne out in practice, and some of the more successful projects in the USA, for example, those carried out by the Institute for Developmental Studies in New York (Deutsch *et al.,* 1967) and by Gray and Klaus (1970) in Nashville, Tennessee, have adopted a broad framework for their activities which does not fit neatly into any one of the categories listed above.

1. Traditional (informal) enrichment

This approach, characteristic, for example, of the Bank Street College programmes (Wolotsky, 1967) and those of the Education Development Center in Newton, Massachusetts (see Little and Smith, 1971), is one modelled on the 'traditional' philosophy and practices of the British infant school, where informal help and encouragement from adults is seen as providing the best opportunity for children to increase their linguistic skills (Parry and Archer, 1974). The emphasis is on a flexibility of approach, free play and self-expression, incidental language learning in an appropriate environment rather than on specific language lessons, with highly structured materials or situations, and on unobtrusive guidance rather than direction by the teacher. Language learning is important, but equally important is the development of the child 'as a whole', especially his personal adjustment. So many approaches are subsumed under this heading that it is particularly difficult to evaluate the effects of 'informal' or 'traditional' programmes, but in general these have been found to be less effective with disadvantaged children than the more structured approaches described below (Weikart, 1972; Karnes, 1973). However, most educationists would agree that, for some part at least of their school day, informal approaches and free activity are desirable for young children.

2. Cognitive discovery

The 'cognitive discovery' approach, which is particularly influenced by the theories of Piaget, aims at promoting 'the growth of cognitive processes, such as categorising, differentiating, abstracting, and inferring, by providing continuous verbal accompaniment to children's sequenced exploration' (Bissell, 1973; p. 69). This approach will be illustrated by reference to Weikart's cognitive programmes and the Florida parent–educator model.

Weikart's cognitive programmes. The Perry Preschool project was started in 1962 for three- and four-year-old disadvantaged Negro children at Ypsilanti, Michigan (Sonquist and Kamii, 1967). Inspired by Piagetian theory, the project used techniques of 'verbal bombardment', in which the child was involved in a series of questions designed to help him to move gradually from the sensorimotor stage to the preconceptual stage, from contact with an actual object to verbal symbolisation of it (Laing, 1968).

Following the Perry Project, the Ypsilanti Early Education Programme was put into operation from 1967 to 1970. This programme aimed to develop a preschool curriculum, based on Piaget's theories, for disadvantaged four-year-old children (Kamii and Radin, 1970; Kamii, 1973). In the early stages of the programme, the tendency was to simplify certain Piagetian tasks and to try to help children to go from one stage to the next as quickly as possible; but, as the project proceeded, it was felt that it was important to help the child to develop his total cognitive framework rather than emphasise particular tasks such as seriation or conservation. The general procedure was for the teacher to set up a situation or propose an activity, and to see how the children reacted before deciding what to pick upon in order to extend the child's thinking: 'The teacher does not shape a response, nor transmit or program the input of knowledge (the empiricist approach). She does not go to the other extreme either of passively watching children play while waiting for "readiness" to unfold (a maturationist approach). She structures the environment for children to activate and apply their schemes (i.e. the cognitive structures through which external stimuli are understood). She then intervenes unobtrusively by applying Piaget's exploratory method so that the children will test out their ideas against objects and other people, and build new schemes by differentiation and integration of previously constructed schemes. A curriculum based on this interactionism can, therefore, never be presented in a cookbook fashion' (Kamii, 1973, p. 227). In this programme, language is considered important as a tool for precise communication and as a stimulator of cognitive development, but language is not seen as the source or cause of logical thinking.

A controlled enquiry, comparing the 'cognitive discovery' approach with other models, showed that this approach produced good results, though these were no better than those found in the case of other programmes involving careful planning, expert teaching, and well-defined objectives (Weikart, 1972).

Florida Parent–Educator Programme. One of the main aims of this project was to educate mothers of very young infants, in their own homes, in specific techniques of cognitive and verbal stimulation accompanying a warm interpersonal relationship (Gordon, 1968). The design of the programme was influenced firstly by the Piagetian view of the importance of the sensorimotor period in the intellectual development of the child, and secondly by Bernstein's linguistic theory: the mother was helped to provide a model of a more elaborate language code than she might have used without the guidance given. Specially trained 'home tutors', themselves from disadvantaged backgrounds, used role-playing and demonstration techniques to train the mothers. They taught the mothers to make play materials, and encouraged them to verbalise in a variety of ways interacting with their infants.

The evaluation carried out gave encouraging results, and this home-focused approach is strongly supported by Bronfenbrenner (1974), who, on the basis of a review of early intervention programmes in the USA over the past decade, concluded that programmes actively involving parents, especially those working in the home with parent and child simultaneously, were more effective than approaches where parents were not active participants.

3. *Preacademic*

The emphasis in the academically-orientated early childhood programme, which has its basis in behaviour modification theory, is on promoting language development through direct teaching of specific skills, using a demanding rather than a persuasive approach, and requiring imitative and structured, rather than individual and intuitive, responses from the children. This approach was strongly advocated by Bereiter and Engelmann (1966) and has since been further developed by Engelmann and his associates (Engelmann *et al.,* 1970). It stresses that disadvantaged children are particularly weak in language skills, and that this aspect of development is of paramount importance. The teacher takes on a highly directive role, making use of pattern repetition and extrinsic reinforcement as much as possible, and the child's success is judged in terms of how accurately he imitates the teacher's language model.

The 'preacademic' approach has been much criticised, particularly on the grounds of its lack of flexibility, its reliance on direct teaching and rote repetition, its ignoring of individual differences and its emphasis on teaching materials rather than cognitive processes (Blank, 1973a). However, in spite of the criticisms, the results of evaluation studies of this approach have supported its effectiveness, not only in the USA (Bereiter, 1972; Karnes, 1973), but in other cultures, such as Australia (Nurcombe et al., 1973).

4. Psycholinguistic training

A number of language programmes have been developed on the basis of Osgood's (1957) linguistic theory and the Illinois Test of Psycholinguistic Abilities (ITPA: Kirk et al., 1968) associated with his formulation. While there are many different psycholinguistic theories, Hammill and Larsen (1974), in a review of the effectiveness of what they call 'psycholinguistic training', use this term to refer to those programmes which have been inspired by the Osgood model. Psycholinguistic programmes of this kind, which are based upon the assumption that discrete elements of language behaviour are identifiable, measurable and, if defective, remediable, will be exemplified here by reference to a language handbook prepared by Merle Karnes and colleagues in 1968, and to the Peabody Language Development Kit (Dunn and Smith, 1964).

Activities for Developing Psycholinguistic Skills (Karnes et al, 1968). This is the title of a manual containing varied suggestions for activities for improving the skills of communication and information-processing of four-year-old culturally disadvantaged children. Largely following the ITPA model, the manual suggests activities to help these children in auditory and visual decoding (understanding), auditory vocal and visual motor association, vocal and motor encoding (expression), grammatical and visual closure (integration) and auditory vocal and visual motor memory. It is stressed that the manual is intended as a guide, not a curriculum, and that a number of different communication processes will often be involved simultaneously in the activities listed in the handbook.

Peabody Language Development Kit (PLDK). The PLDK is designed, through a series of 180 carefully sequenced daily lessons, to stimulate the receptive, associative and expressive components of oral language development. It provides a variety of teaching aids, including pictorial material, puppets, life-sized plastic fruits and vegetables, magnetic shapes and strips, and recordings of different sounds. The Teacher's Manual is very detailed and gives explicit instructions for using the kit.

According to the devisers of the programme, which is influenced not only by Osgood but also by Skinner (1957), Torrance (1962) and Guilford (1967), the PLDK stresses overall oral language and verbal intelligence training rather than specific training in selected psycholinguistic processes. It aims to encourage divergent as well as convergent and associative thinking. The kit is broad in coverage, offering varied types of activities and embracing general vocabulary enrichment, the teaching of key sentence patterns and the use of language to serve many functions, ranging from logical and mathematical to social and emotional.

Evaluation of psycholinguistic training. Hammill and Larsen (1974) have reviewed thirty-nine studies between 1964 and 1974, including work with retarded children, which have attempted to evaluate psycholinguistic approaches. Although some studies reported success with disadvantaged children, most of the skills identified in the ITPA (particularly visual and grammatic closure, and visual and auditory reception skills) were not responsive to intervention. However, the review suggested that at least one of the skills tapped by the ITPA (i.e. verbal expression) could be improved by direct training. Hammill and Larsen concluded that the idea that psycholinguistic constructs, as measured by the ITPA, can be trained by existing techniques remains invalidated. Although better results may be obtained with improved techniques, they consider that without further research caution is needed in making claims for the trainability of psycholinguistic processes.

5. Instructional dialogue

In this approach, the emphasis is on discussion between the teacher and the individual child. The task of the child is not to imitate the teacher, but rather to use language to convey and organise information accurately. The teacher provides structured learning situations and guides the child's thinking by asking leading questions and making suggestions, but the child has greater freedom of action and response than, for example, in the 'preacademic' approach. The 'instructional dialogue' approach will be illustrated here by reference to the work of Blank and Solomon (1968, 1969; see also Blank, 1973b).

A tutorial language programme. Blank and Solomon (1968) have developed an approach which is based on dialogue between teacher and child for about fifteen to twenty minutes each day. They emphasise that the most effective teaching is carried out through individual tutoring. The child should not be allowed to leave a task unfinished: if necessary, the task can be simplified, but the child should still be required to meet the demands set by the teacher. The main aim of the programme is to help the child to progress towards abstract thinking. During the teaching session, the teacher uses no gestures, but helps the child to use language to complete the task set. The child is encouraged to extend his thinking beyond the concrete situation, for example, by discussing alternative courses of action or attempting explanations of events. Errors made by the child in his verbal responses are used by the teacher as a basis for developing the child's thinking skills. Common and inexpensive objects readily available in the child's environment (e.g. paper, crayons, blocks, toys, simple books) are all that is needed for the programme.

A small-scale evaluation of this approach showed a marked gain in IQ for three- and four-year-old children who received the specialised tutoring for four months, and no significant gains in the case of children not receiving any special programme, or given individual attention without the specialised training.

While it is more satisfactory to use measures of specific aspects of language development rather than intelligence tests to assess the effectiveness of language programmes, the results of this evaluation are encouraging.

Language programmes in Britain

As compared with the USA, very few language programmes have been developed in Britain. Consequently, with insufficient resources to embark on the construction of their own programmes, some projects for disadvantaged children in Britain have been forced to use American-based materials in at least a part of their work. In particular, the Peabody Language Development Kit has been found useful, perhaps mainly because its explicitness, while not arousing as much hostility as the Bereiter and Engelmann approach, makes evaluation somewhat less difficult than is the case with other programmes. However, several language programmes or handbooks have been, or are being, specifically devised for use in nursery or infant schools in Britain, for example those by Gahagan and Gahagan (1970), Shiach (1972), Downes (to be published) and Tough (1973a). These approaches will be described below, after a discussion of the language programmes forming part of, firstly, the Educational Priority Area (EPA) projects and, secondly, the action research undertaken by the National Foundation for Education Research (NFER). Little work has been carried out in Britain along the lines of the Florida Parent–Educator Programme described above, but mention will be made of a small-scale mother–child interaction project in Scotland (Donachy, 1973).

The EPA projects

Projects in England. In the national EPA action-research project which began in 1968, the Peabody Language Development Kit (Level P) was selected as one of the instruments for intervention experiments in a number of nursery schools, there being 'no British pre-school language programme available' (Halsey, 1972). Although nearly all the children involved enjoyed the programme, the teachers and assistants using the kit reacted in a wide variety of ways (Quigley, 1971). Some were very hostile, some were highly enthusiastic, while others had mixed feelings about the kit. Most of the criticisms arose

because the materials, although robust and attractive, had been designed for use with American children. In general, although the structure of the course was not considered altogether unsuitable, it was clear that many teachers in Britain were not happy with the idea of having a specific and regular session of language activities.

Controlled comparisons were made between the groups of children using the PLDK and children not receiving any special programme. Most of the experimental groups did show an improvement in language development over a period of a year, but very few of the differences between the experimental and control groups were statistically significant.

In addition to the use of the Peabody Kit, project teams in different parts of England also developed language programmes of their own. In Liverpool, twenty-four stories were written, each accompanied by a large wall picture and a puppet presenter (a popular feature in the PLDK). In London, the emphasis was put on directing the attention of nursery school staff to 'language-producing situations' and on helping them to increase the quality of their own verbal interactions with the children, by a greater concentration on one-to-one contact. The West Riding project developed an individual language programme based on Marion Blank's tutorial method described above. These small-scale experiments indicated that it would be worthwhile developing a variety of language programmes that would be of direct help to disadvantaged children and yet would be acceptable to British teaching traditions.

Dundee Project. As part of an EPA research project in Dundee, Scotland, an experimental study of educational compensation was carried out, initially involving over five hundred children from nine pre-school establishments (Harvey and Lee, 1974). In this project, there was no specific language programme, but language growth was encouraged in the framework of an integrated scheme designed to enhance general cognitive development. 'Themes' were planned, usually lasting for a full week and maintaining continuity of emphasis on a single cognitive concept. Each theme was introduced by an activity or experience, and then the selected concept was dealt with from different points of view, i.e. through different senses, using varied play material, differently contrived situations and a wide range of songs, nursery rhymes and stories. As in the English EPA project, the analysis of the results of the experiments showed that, while there was evidence of the value of the programme, many of the comparisons between experimental and control groups being in the expected direction, few of the differences between the groups were statistically significant.

NFER Pre-School Project

This action-research project, which began in 1968, aimed to introduce and evaluate a compensatory programme of language, perceptual and general cognitive training for disadvantaged children attending nursery schools (H. L. Williams, 1973). The Peabody Language Development Kit, radically revised to suit the needs of the children participating in the project, was used as one of the main procedures to enhance language development. In addition, verbal exchange between adult and child in the classroom was encouraged in a variety of other ways, including the use of a graded series of games. The results of the evaluation of the programme are not yet available.

'Talk Reform' (Gahagan–Bernstein)

The main aim of this programme, developed for infant school children by Gahagan and Gahagan (1970) and inspired largely by the work of Bernstein, was to elaborate and broaden the spoken language of children who live in an environment where language is seen as serving rather limited functions. Based on situations occurring continually during the normal infant school day, the programme sets up tasks in which a 'restricted' mode of speech would not be adequate: it combines 'intensive, formal training' with an enriching environment, and encourages the child to give greater attention to oral language and to use language more explicitly. A variety of activities and techniques, including some advocated by Bereiter and Engelmann, are suggested for daily twenty-minute lessons over the three infant school years. The materials, which are not elaborate or expensive, are frequently changed and the level of difficulty is increased gradually.

An evaluation of the programme showed improvement in the children's ability to generate sentences, to make and code finer discriminations among objects presented visually or tactually, and to master the more difficult problems on a verbal concept sorting test. Cazden (1972) comments that, with such an imaginative programme and such initially promising results, the Gahagan–Bernstein programme provides an important base for further curriculum work. As a visitor from the United States, she was surprised to find that compensatory education programmes in Britain were operating largely independently of this work and depending instead on less interesting ideas imported from the USA.

'Teach Them to Speak' (Shiach)

Shiach (1972) presents a language development programme in 200 lessons. Influenced by Luria, Vygotsky and Bernstein, he aims to help teachers of children within the age range four to seven years to develop the oral language skills of all their pupils. No special kit is provided, and the materials recommended can be easily collected or bought by the class teacher, e.g. picture cards, posters, colour cubes, hand puppets and various objects. The lessons, one for each day, last for about half an hour, and are designed to give a feeling of success through graded steps. There is constant revision, drill and repetition, with the emphasis on descriptions and explanations in well-structured, grammatically complete and correct sentences.

No evaluation study or even details of pilot work are mentioned in Shiach's book. Cox (1973) considers that the programme is potentially useful, especially for inexperienced teachers, in its emphasis on structured language activities. However, there is no clear grading in the level of difficulty of the lessons, and the emphasis is on class teaching rather than on teaching individuals or small groups. Some of the activities, too, are rather stereotyped and could be dull for young children. Further, great stress is laid on 'expansion' by the teacher; that is, modifying and extending the child's oral responses to achieve a desired sentence form. This approach is less stimulating, and likely to be less successful, than 'modelling' as suggested by Cazden (1965), in which the adult responds to the child's utterance not by expanding it but by making a fresh statement logically related to it, or the 'dialogue' approach evolved by Blank and Solomon (1968).

Communication Skills in Early Childhood Project

Following a Pre-School Language Project lasting eighteen months, the Communication Skills in Early Childhood Project is currently being developed at Leeds under the direction of Joan Tough (1973b). In these projects, the emphasis has been put on formulating ideas about what might be the best way of discovering what children can do with their language, and how the teacher can stimulate the child to use language for his own purposes and for extending his thinking. In the Communication Skills project, the main objective is to develop a guide to the fostering of language skills in the nursery and infant classroom that will be useful for teachers.

This project is concerned with language in early childhood in general rather than specifically with disadvantaged children, but has clear implications for work with children from a restricted linguistic environment. Tough (1973a) emphasises that such children need skills in using language as a means of examining the detail, the relationships and the structure of the world around them: the development of these skills in school is dependent upon a particular kind of relationship between the teacher and the child, one which encourages flexible ways of thinking. A different kind of learning environment for disadvantaged children is not called for, but the content of the dialogue between teacher and child will differ in the case of the disadvantaged, because of the need to stimulate his interest. The teacher will use the child's response as a starting point from which talk might lead into deeper and more complex thinking. For the disadvantaged child, the teacher may be the only person who can provide the development of new uses of language and who can help him to see that communicating his ideas is worth while.

With the aid of teachers' groups, the Communication Skills project is developing along lines of its own, but its 'instructional dialogue' approach has much in common with that of Marion Blank mentioned above.

Schools Council Project in Compensatory Education

The Programme Development Unit (PDU) of the Schools Council Project in Compensatory Education has produced a handbook of suggestions for teachers of disadvantaged children in their first year in the infant school (Downes, to be published). The PDU adopts a rationale similar to that of Blank and Solomon in that it focuses upon the vocabulary and language structures associated with logical thinking and reasoning. The main aim is to help the disadvantaged children to develop more elaborated speech — accurate descriptions and explanations, and the use of questions to elicit information. The handbook contains a set of guidelines and suggested activities from which the teacher can select and adapt as required, rather than a detailed, pre-sequenced 'package' of language activities. The normal resources of the infant classroom can be used to provide the enrichment which the deprived child needs: for example, some of the teachers' groups operating in the project analysed the familiar activity corners of the infant classroom in order to see how these could be used to enhance language development. Language games, too, are suggested as a useful way of helping the child to acquire appropriate concepts and structures. Audio-visual materials have also much potential in the infant school (see Chazan and Downes, 1971), but the PDU puts the emphasis on the teacher using her own ingenuity to produce these materials rather than relying on a set of materials being widely available (P. Williams, 1973).

The activities suggested in the handbook have been tried out by a number of infant school teachers in various parts of the country, and the results of a preliminary controlled evaluation study of the 'programme', involving eighty-eight children (mean age 4 years 10 months) from five schools have been encouraging (Downes, 1975).

Home-based programmes

As previously mentioned, experiments in the United States suggest that home-based programmes are of value, and should be tried out on a wide scale. This view is supported by a small-scale enquiry carried out in Renfrewshire, Scotland (Donachy, 1973), in which an experimental group of nine pre-school culturally deprived children was exposed to six months of weekly home sessions during which health visitors used toys and books to stimulate verbal interaction between mother and child. The experimental group made significantly greater gains in IQ, though not in language, than either of two control groups, one of which received weekly visits and non-educational gifts from health visitors, the other receiving no intervention between pre- and post-tests. Following this pilot study, a project focusing on mother–child interaction has been organised through schools in deprived areas, with encouraging results, including the incidental benefits of the better motivation of the parents and teachers, a diffusion effect on siblings, and improved parent–teacher relations.

The influence of Piaget

Ever since his book on *The Language and Thought of the Child* (1923, revised 1959), a pioneering contribution to the understanding of language development, Piaget has illuminated the relationship between language and thinking in many of his works. However, it cannot be said that his theoretical formulation has had a substantial influence on the development of language programmes for disadvantaged children in Britain, although Piaget's general theory of cognitive growth has widely influenced other aspects of the school curriculum, particularly mathematics and science. As shown above, some programmes in the USA have been inspired by Piagetian theory, but there is little evidence of Piaget's influence in other programmes. Since the work of Piaget is widely disseminated in courses in education and psychology at all levels, it is of interest to speculate why it has, apparently at least, had so little impact on those concerned with the construction of language programmes.

Several possible reasons may be suggested for this ostensible lack of influence. Firstly, while language is important to Piaget, and is seen by him as the vehicle by which thought is socialised, he does not consider it to be the original basis of, or the whole of, logical thinking (Phillips, 1969). For Piaget, the ability to use language to express logic is an outcome of activity, and attempts to improve the child's logic solely through instructing him in the use of language are not likely to be very successful (Almy, 1966).

Secondly, Piaget has not explicitly put forward a theory of *language* acquisition, although Sinclair-de-Zwart (1969) has speculated on the general form that such a theory might take. The latter writer points out that in the relatively few works that he has written on language, Piaget has been concerned with language as a factor in the child's cognitive development and not with the content and structure of the child's language as such. Piaget's writings, therefore, provide little guidance as to how children's linguistic skills might be enhanced.

Thirdly, Piaget's writings, which are not always easy to understand, have not been addressed to educators. It is not surprising, therefore, if work on the educational applications of his theories is not far advanced.

Finally, Piaget has not been enthusiastic about the acceleration of mental development, even if he admits the possibility of such acceleration (Phillips, 1969).

However, it is probable that Piaget has had a much wider influence on approaches to language learning than would superficially appear to be the case. As Beard (1969) observes, Piaget's work provides support for the varied and stimulating environment provided by British nursery and infant schools, but also stresses that attention from adults, especially in answering questions and in conversation, is immensely important to development in early childhood. It also implies the need for increasingly structured activities for children as they grow older, so that they can move from complete dependence on concrete materials to partial dependence on these, and then gradually to dispensing with concrete aids altogether. Piaget has also emphasised the need to understand how the child sees things, and to realise that the limitations of the child's thinking are sometimes masked by language. For example, as Almy (1966) points out, in the case of socially disadvantaged children, no adequate comparison of quantities can be made by a child who does not understand the terms 'more' and 'less' or 'most' and 'least', but comprehension of these terms may not be developed through words alone or even associations of word and picture, but rather through a combination of manipulation and verbalisation. Further, Piaget's work indicates that a wide range of activities in teaching any concept is particularly valuable, and that, where children are introduced too soon to any kind of activity, they are likely to become confused and develop a distaste for learning (Beard, 1969). Even at the nursery or infant school stage, the teacher will be dealing with several 'levels' of cognitive development and must, therefore, adopt a predominantly individual approach.

Kamii (1971) has described in what ways a pre-school based on Piagetian principles differs from other pre-schools. She asserts that Piaget's theory gives a unique developmental perspective to early childhood education, encompassing all the activities that have been developed by the traditional nursery school as well as adding a great deal of depth to these activities. Piaget's work, in her view, helps the teacher to delineate and teach the broad basic abilities that are necessary for all the subjects that the child has to cope with in later school life. In the Ypsilanti projects described above, Kamii, who feels that the teaching of broad basic abilities is more fruitful than sequencing teaching goals by subject matter, has demonstrated how the Piagetian perspective can be translated into an educational programme. However, teachers are likely to need much expert guidance if they are to put such a programme into operation.

Conclusion

In general, controlled comparisons of different experimental approaches in early childhood intervention programmes (including those concerned with language) in the USA have not shown any one approach to be markedly superior to others. However, children involved in programmes that were carefully planned and expertly directed have recorded somewhat greater gains in cognitive performance and academic achievement than children exposed to less well-designed programmes or those following the normal curriculum. In Britain, no large-scale evaluation of language programmes for disadvantaged children has been undertaken: the more recent programmes have not been evaluated, and those evaluation studies which have been carried out (see above) have been on a very limited scale, involving small samples of children over relatively short periods.

Thus, from the work completed to date, it is not feasible to suggest clear guidelines for the future development of language programmes. However, the American experience indicates that particular attention should be paid to increasing the awareness on the part of teachers of the language problems of disadvantaged children, and to cultivating the skills of teachers in dealing with these problems. Further, while the teacher will find it helpful to have varied resources to meet a wide range of individual needs — and all the programmes so far developed have something to offer — it is important that she should have reasonably well-defined objectives if her methods are to be effective. It is likely that, in the British context, a judicious combination of structured activities in small groups and the individual 'instructional dialogue' approach will help disadvantaged children to improve their language skills, but much further experimental work is needed before clearer indications can be given about the best direction in which to go. Certainly the evidence so far available, while disappointing in some respects, suggests that the language of disadvantaged children does need special attention within the nursery and infant school, and that such attention should be sustained over a substantial period, supplemented as much as possible by work in the home.

References

Almy, M. (1966) *Studies of Young Children's Thinking,* New York: Teachers College Press.

Bartlett, E. J. (1972) 'Selecting preschool language programs' in Cazden, C. B. (ed.) *Language in Early Childhood Education,* Washington, D.C.: National Association for the Education of Young Children.

Beard, R. M. (1969) *An Outline of Piaget's Developmental Psychology,* Routledge & Kegan Paul.

Bereiter, C. E. (1972) 'An academic preschool for disadvantaged children: conclusions from evaluation studies' in Stanley, J. C. (ed.) *Preschool Programs for the Disadvantaged,* Baltimore: Johns Hopkins University Press.

Bereiter, C. E. and Engelmann, S. (1966) *Teaching Disadvantaged Children in the Preschool,* Englewood Cliffs, N.J.: Prentice-Hall.

Bissell, J. S. (1973) 'Planned variation in head start and follow through' in Stanley, J. C. (ed.) *Compensatory Education for Children, Ages 2 to 8,* Baltimore: Johns Hopkins University Press.

Blank, M. (1973a) 'Implicit assumptions underlying preschool intervention programs' in Spodek, B. (ed.) *Early Childhood Education,* Englewood Cliffs, N. J.: Prentice-Hall.

Blank, M. (1973b) *Teaching Learning in the Pre-school: A Dialogue Approach,* Columbus, Ohio: Charles E. Merrill.

Blank, M. and Solomon, F. (1968) 'A tutorial language program to develop abstract thinking in socially disadvantaged preschool children', *Child Development,* 39, 379–89.

Blank, M. and Solomon, F. (1969) 'How shall the disadvantaged child be taught?' *Child Development,* 40, 47–61.

Bronfenbrenner, U. (1974) 'Children, families and social policy: an American perspective' in Department of Health and Social Security, *The Family in Society: Dimensions of Parenthood,* HMSO.

Cazden, C. B. (1965) 'Environmental assistance to the child's acquisition of grammar', unpublished doctoral dissertation, Graduate School of Education, Harvard University.

Cazden, C. B. (1972) (ed.) *Language in Early Childhood Education,* Washington, D.C.: National Association for the Education of Young Children.

Chazan, M. and Downes, G. (1971) (eds.) *Compensatory Education and the New Media,* Occasional Publication No. 3, Schools Council Research Project in Compensatory Education, Department of Education, University College of Swansea.

Cox, T. (1973) 'Review of Shiach, G. M, *Teach Them to Speak', Brit. J. Educ. Psychol.,* 43, 217–18.

Deutsch, M. *et al.* (1967) *The Disadvantaged Child,* New York: Basic Books.

Donachy, W. (1973) 'Promoting cognitive growth in culturally deprived preschool children', paper given at B.P.S. Education Section Annual Conference, Royal Holloway College, London.

Downes, G. (1975) 'An evaluation of a language programme', personal communication.

Downes, G. (to be published) *Language Development and the Disadvantaged Child,* Schools Council Project in Compensatory Education.

Dunn, L. M. and Smith, L. O. (1964) *Peabody Language Development Kit,* Nashville, Tenn.: Institute for Mental Retardation and Intellectual Development, George Peabody College for Teachers.

Engelmann, S., Osborn, J. and Engelmann, T. (1970) *Distar Language I and II,* Chicago: Science Research Associates.

Gahagan, D. M. and Gahagan, G. A. (1970) *Talk Reform,* Routledge & Kegan Paul.

Gordon, I. J. (1968) *Parental Involvement in Compensatory Education,* University of Illinois Press (for Eric Clearinghouse on Early Childhood Education).

Gray, S. W. and Klaus, R. A. (1970) 'The Early Training Project: a seventh year report', *Child Development,* 41, 4, 909–24.

Guilford, J. P. (1967) *The Nature of Human Intelligence,* New York: McGraw-Hill.

Halsey, A. H. (ed.) (1972) *Educational Priority, Vol. I: E.P.A. Problems and Policies,* HMSO.

Hammill, D. D. and Larsen, S. C. (1974) 'The effectiveness of psycholinguistic training', *Exceptional Children,* 41, 1, 5–15.

Harvey, S. and Lee, T. R. (1974) 'An experimental study of educational compensation' in *Educational Priority, Vol. 5: E.P.A. – A Scottish Study,* HMSO.

Kamii, C. K. (1971) 'Evaluation of learning in preschool education: socio-emotional, perceptual-motor and cognitive development' in Bloom, B. S., Hastings, J. T. and Madaus, G. F. (eds.) *Handbook on Formative and Summative Evaluation of Student Learning,* New York: McGraw-Hill.

Kamii, C. (1973) 'A sketch of the Piaget-derived preschool curriculum developed by the Ypsilanti Early Education Program' in Spodek, B. (ed.) *Early Childhood Education,* Englewood Cliffs, N.J.: Prentice-Hall.

Kamii, C. and Radin, N. (1970) 'A framework for a preschool curriculum based on some Piagetian concepts' in Athey, I. J. and Rubadeau, D. O. (eds.) *Educational Implications of Piaget's Theory,* New York: Wiley.

Karnes, M. B. (1973) 'Evaluation and implications of research with young handicapped and low-income children' in Stanley, J. C. (ed.) *Compensatory Education for Children Ages 2 to 8,* Baltimore: Johns Hopkins University Press.

Karnes, M. B. *et al.* (1968) *Activities for Developing Psycholinguistic Skills with Preschool Culturally Disadvantaged Children,* Washington, D.C.: Council for Exceptional Children.

Kirk, S. A., McCarthy, J. J. and Kirk, W. D. (1968) *The Illinois Test of Psycholinguistic Abilities* (rev. edn), Urbana: University of Illinois Press.

Laing, A. F. (1968) 'Compensatory education for young children' in *Compensatory Education: An Introduction.* Occasional Publication No. 1, Schools Council Research Project in Compensatory Education, Department of Education, University College of Swansea.

Little, A. and Smith, G. (1971) *Strategies of Compensation: a Review of Educational Projects for the Disadvantaged in the United States,* Paris: Centre for Educational Research and Innovation, Organisation for Economic Co-operation Development.

Nurcombe, B., De Lacey, P., Moffitt, P. and Taylor, L. (1973) 'The question of aboriginal intelligence: the first three years of the Bourke preschool experiment', *Med. J., Aust.,* 2, 625–30.

Osgood, C. E. (1957) 'Motivational dynamics of language behaviour' in Jones, M. R. (ed.) *Nebraska Symposium on Motivation,* Lincoln: University of Nebraska Press.

Parry, M. and Archer, H. (1974) *Pre-school Education,* London: Macmillan (Schools Council Research Studies).

Piaget, J. (1959) *The Language and Thought of the Child* (3rd rev. edn), Routledge & Kegan Paul (original French edn, 1923).

Phillips, J. L. (1969) *The Origins of Intellect: Piaget's Theory,* San Francisco: W. H. Freeman.

Quigley, H. (1971) 'Nursery teachers' reaction to the Peabody Language Development Kit', *Brit. J. Educ. Psychol,* 41, 2, 155–62.

Shiach, G. M. (1972) *Teach Them to Speak,* Ward Lock Educational.

Sinclair-De-Zwart, H. (1969) 'Developmental psycholinguistics' in Elkind, D. and Flavell, J. (eds.) *Studies in Cognitive Development,* Oxford University Press.

Skinner, B. F. (1957) *Verbal Behaviour,* New York: Appleton-Century-Crofts.

Sonquist, H. and Kamii, C. (1967) 'Applying some Piagetian concepts in the classroom for the disadvantaged', *Young Children,* 22, 231–45.

Torrance, E. P. (1962) *Guiding Creative Talent,* Englewood Cliffs, N.J.: Prentice-Hall.

Tough, J. (1973a) *Focus on Meaning: talking to some purpose with young children,* Allen & Unwin.

Tough, J. (1973b) 'Communication skills in early childhood project', *Dialogue,* 14, 12–13.

Weikart, D. P. (1967) 'Results of preschool intervention programs', Ypsilanti, Michigan (mimeo).

Weikart, D. P. (1972) 'Relationship of curriculum, teaching and learning in preschool education' in Stanley, J. C. (ed.) *Preschool Programs for the Disadvantaged,* Baltimore: Johns Hopkins University Press.

Williams, H. L. (1973) 'Compensatory education in the nursery school' in Chazan, M. (ed.) *Compensatory Education,* Butterworths.

Williams, P. (1973) 'The Schools Council Research and Development Project in Compensatory Education' in Chazan, M. (ed.) *Compensatory Education,* Butterworths.

Wolotsky, H. (1967) 'The Early Childhood Center' in Klopf, G. J. and Hohman, W. A. (eds.) *Perspectives on Learning* (Papers from the Bank Street Fiftieth Anniversary Invitational Symposium), New York: Bank Street College of Education.

Pre-school and/or education: a comment
Marion Blank

There are two major, but separate, forces responsible for the expansion of pre-school services. One force stems from the desire of women to have support services in the rearing of their children; the other derives from the use of pre-schools as a possible means of preventing future academic failure. For purposes of simplifying communication, I will henceforth refer to the former as 'shared rearing pre-schools' and to the latter as 'academic pre-schools'. There are, of course, a number of points of convergence between these two types of pre-schools, e.g. the use of materials that are attractive to children; the possible provision of preventative medical services, etc. Nevertheless, I believe these forces, and the structures they lead to, are so different that any attempt to merge them at this time will only obscure already complex and controversial issues.

The general failure to separate forces as diverse as these is by no means unique to the pre-school situation. It is characteristic of almost any analysis relating to children. For example, the fields of both psychology and education typically group children, and those who work with children, along the parameter of age rather than topic. Thus, in psychology, no one will think it is at all unusual to hear a professional refer to himself as a 'child psychologist'. But many an eyebrow would be raised if a comparable professional referred to himself as an 'adult psychologist'. Rather than using the dimension of age, the person concerned with adult functioning defines himself according to a problem area so that his self-description is in such terms as 'clinical psychologist', 'neuropsychologist', and 'industrial psychologist'. Many of these divisions are applicable to the study of children and therefore a person interested in children could easily define himself in these terms. But he, or she, rarely does so.

It is this failure to differentiate that has led us all too easily to consider the variety of pre-school services as a single entity. Just because the same age-range children are involved, however, it does not mean that the same issues or problems are present. It is as if we decided to combine a factory and a university together under the name 'adult activity centre' simply because they both contain persons over 18 years of age for prolonged stretches of time during traditional working hours. There are points of similarity between the two institutions and a case could be made for the unification. Nevertheless, in exclusively focusing on the similarity, a great deal of information is lost about crucial differences. I believe a similar point holds for the two types of pre-school education. In emphasizing this point, I do not wish to imply that the study of the child will be enhanced if the child is 'dissected' into as many subparts as possible. Rather, I believe that the care of 'the whole child' in any setting will be much more effective if, beforehand, one has analysed the uniqueness of the situation as fully as possible.

The differences between the two pre-school forces are evident in almost any aspects of the problem that one might wish to consider. This includes the question of goals, curriculum, the role of the teacher, methods of evaluation, structure and timing of the instruction, and the role of experimental findings. In order to gain a clearer picture of the differences it seems valuable to consider briefly each of these points relative to the two pre-school forces. First I will consider the 'shared rearing pre-school' which, as noted above, is designed to provide the parents of young children with services to aid them in the responsibilities of child care. As such, the major purpose of programmes within the framework is to offer a service that will help the parents and the entire family to function in a more effective and more enjoyable manner. I believe this goal to be of inestimable value. Frequently, however, it is not recognized as such. In part, the lack of recognition may stem from the fact that this sort of service is seen primarily as a support to mothers. Accordingly, as with so many other issues concerning the needs of women, it has not been awarded a high priority by society. All those familiar with the extraordinary amount of care required by young children will, however, recognize the crucial help that such a service can provide to the people in question.

There are, however, other forces which have led us to neglect the value of 'shared rearing pre-schools'. We live in a society that places tremendous value on formal education while simultaneously rarely considering the support of widespread services to enhance the ease of living. As a result any group requesting support, in particular, government support, for the expansion of 'shared rearing' services will downplay the ease aspect and emphasize the educational aspect in the hope that the picture so drawn will make the programmes more attractive. (Given that the bulk of my experience has been in the United States, my comments may be more valid for that situation. Nevertheless, my observations in other technologically advanced nations lead me to think that similar conditions pertain in many other countries as well.) The political wisdom of an approach which upgrades 'education' and downplays 'shared rearing' remains to be determined, i.e. perhaps it may lead to more readily obtaining support for pre-school programmes. But it seems clear that this approach has also been a factor in forcing 'shared rearing pre-schools' to take on educational purposes which they were never intended to serve and which they may well not be suited to fulfill.

An acknowledgement of 'shared rearing' as the key function of one type of pre-school in no way lessens the complexities of what must be known to design and operate an effective pre-school. But the 'priorities' are quite different from that commonly associated with the word 'school'. The major goal now is not to change, educate, alter or modify the child along particular lines, although this may occur. Rather it is to provide, during the hours of the day when the children are in the schools, a secure benign environment that is compatible with the interests and predispositions of the young child. This somewhat 'indirect' provision of services is by no means unique to the 'shared rearing preschool'. For instance, the primary function of a hospital is not to feed people. However, given the needs of the human organism, it is sensible and desirable to offer them food as nutritious as possible during their stay.

The provision of a humane and interesting environment for young children might have been a problem some generations back — before the work of pioneers such as Montessori, Froebel and Dewey. Even now, our care of children can be improved in many areas, e.g. more flexible hours not so tightly tied to the working day; centres closer to the children's homes, etc. Nevertheless, it seems clear that with our present knowledge — and adequate funding — one could provide an appealing, supportive environment for most young children if one chose to do so — and if the parents wanted them to be in such a setting.

Given these loose constraints and the great adaptability of the human organism, the actual structure of any programme in a 'shared rearing preschool' could vary considerably. For example, major dimension of variability might be the degree of structured activity, i.e. some programmes could be quite structured, others could consist much more of free-play. Regardless of the variability in the programmes, however, the role of the 'curriculum' would be minimal — if one uses the term 'curriculum' according to the common meaning of offering a body of knowledge and information to the learner that would not readily be available in his usual environment. The issue will perhaps become clearer if we examine it with reference to the measurable effects of having attended school. Thus, we can say with a reasonable degree of assurance that the average child is much less likely to be literate if he does not have some sort of formal schooling. In that sense, failure to experience the curricula of formal education will have marked and measurable effects on the child's functioning. One would be hard-pressed, however, to identify a comparable set of skills that would fail to emerge if the child did not attend pre-school. In this sense, failure to be exposed to the 'curricula' of pre-school education will not

have the same sort of measurable effects on his behaviour. In this context, if one wished to retain the term 'curriculum' for the pre-school then it would seem most appropriate to have it take on the meaning of making available to the child materials that are appealing so that he may employ or rehearse his skills — skills that he is acquiring at a particular age regardless of whether he is in a 'shared rearing school' or not.

Pursuit of this line of reasoning leads one to conclude that the training of teachers for this setting would not focus on curriculum transmission, but on the observation of normal behaviour, on understanding the breadth and limitations of young children's skills, on dealing with the needs and concerns of parents, and most important, on understanding the dynamics of group interaction and on developing ways to effect good interchange among members of a group. With the exception of the family and group dynamic emphasis, the current training of most pre-school personnel is well suited to the demands they will meet in the work situation.

Methods of evaluating 'shared rearing pre-school' programmes also do not seem to pose insuperable problems. It seems reasonable to ask that the evaluation focus on the goals of the programme, namely on the provision of services to ease the burdens on the parents. Therefore, if the parents were pleased and if the children were content, then such a programme would, and should, be considered successful.

Once established, 'shared rearing pre-schools' could function not only as a service to the families involved. They could also be valuable centres for research on young children's behaviour and on the types of organizations most suitable for encouraging healthy development in children. In this context, many of the suggestions raised by the investigators interviewed by Dr Tizard (1974) could serve as catalysts for research. In particular, studies could be carried out on children's interests in art and music, children's spontaneous use of language with adults and peers, the optimal physical organization of a room, etc. Such research findings could then provide the basis for improving the 'shared rearing pre-school' centres. But the establishment and expansion of such centres need not wait for these research findings. Enough expertise is currently available to set up reasonably effective centres at present if society sees this as a valuable goal.

The question of 'academic pre-schools' presents a totally different picture. Here the central goal is not

day-care, but education. As such these programmes belong not to the area of the pre-school age per se, but to the area of specialized education which runs the gamut of ages — from preschool to university level. Perhaps the major difference between 'academic pre-schools' and other specialized educational efforts is that the educational demands placed on the former are so extensive as to go beyond the demands placed upon any other educational unit. For example, in other areas of schooling, as noted above, the academic goal is to transmit a curriculum covering a limited and specified subject matter, e.g. a particular section of mathematics, a beginning set of reading skills, a section of European history, etc. The goal of the 'academic pre-school', however, is not the transmission of a limited subject matter. Rather it is a basic alteration in the child's level of functioning so that not only all present academic learning, but all future academic learning will be enhanced. It is only such an ambitious goal that allows one to conclude that a programme has 'failed' — not because it has failed to achieve immediate gains, but because the gains were not sustained after the children left the programme. It is probably also such an ambitious goal that has focused us almost exclusively on the maintenance of gains and has led us to ignore other, equally important, issues. For instance, one rarely hears the question of whether specialized programmes can be initiated as effectively at later ages if there have been no special efforts to foster change when the child was in an earlier stage of development. In asking this question, the criterion of success of an 'academic pre-school' becomes not 'self-maintenance of gain', but rather the school's role in permitting the child to remain open to later specialized instruction if and when it is made available to him.

Regardless of the criterion of success, it may well prove to be the case that the goals of an 'academic pre-school' are unattainable, in that excessive and unique demands have been placed upon this type of education unit. But equally, it must be said that our efforts until now have hardly been of a nature sufficient to yield a definite answer to the problem. In fact, partly because of the failure to differentiate between 'shared rearing' and 'academic pre-schools', many initial efforts at the latter were merely the implementation of the former with the exception that the population involved mainly children from lower socio-economic backgrounds. Given the fact that 'shared rearing' programmes were not designed with educational goals in the forefront, it is not surprising that such programmes often failed to achieve the hoped-for change.

With the problem formulated in this manner, it seems evident that such issues as curriculum, evaluation, and implementation take on a radically different colouring than they did for the 'shared rearing' programmes. First of all, the curriculum and its method of presentation become crucial. The issue now is no longer one of solely presenting material that is age-appropriate and appealing. Instead, the material becomes the chief source for effecting basic changes in the way the child deals with demands related to the academic setting. Co-existing with this increase in demand for precise curricula is the rather dismaying absence of information necessary for the design of such curricula. Instead, the field is strewn with controversy and confusion. For example as Dr Tizard's report indicates, there is evidence from a variety of sources that the area of language may be a particularly crucial one for children who are likely to experience difficulty at school. However, the issue of what, if anything, needs changing is hotly debated as we have all witnessed in the well known 'difference-deficit' controversy (see Bernstein, 1972; Ginsburg, 1972; Labov, 1970).

It may be instructive at this point to elaborate somewhat on the gap between what is known from the experimental laboratory and what is needed for the teaching situation. Because my own work has been in the area of language, I will use this area to illustrate the points I wish to make. However, comparable difficulties hold for other areas relevant to the development of effective 'academic pre-school' programmes, i.e. motivation, attention, etc. Specifically, for many years in the area of language research, words were viewed primarily as a tool in concept formation, e.g. through the use of a word such as *animal*, it was felt that we could meaningfully group, in a single category, such diverse creatures as a snail, elephant and sparrow. Language in its other roles, in particular in its role as a means of communication, was barely touched upon. In other words, language was seen almost exclusively as a skill *within* a person, and not as a medium of exchange *between* persons. The absence of techniques and models from the latter perspective is particularly crucial for the school, for it represents a situation that relies heavily upon linguistic interchange for both assessing and altering a child's functioning.

Once the communication aspects of language are fully recognized it may well help us broaden our understanding of the school situation. For example, Dr Tizard (1974) states that 'the curriculum of the nursery school can hardly be distinguished from that of the home' (p. viii). As long as the study of language is confined to units such as words and sentences uttered by a single person, then this generalization appears to have validity. For example, a mother at home might well say, 'Oh it's nearly time to go. Let's put these things away', and a teacher in school might say the same thing. Similarly a child at home and at school could easily be heard to utter nearly identical statements in the two settings. Once the linguistic analysis goes beyond the sentence uttered by one person and considers the communication network, the picture changes considerably. Then the crucial measure is not the type of sentence, but such measures as 'who initiated the exchange?', 'over how many interchanges was the exchange maintained?', and 'how relevant was the utterance to the content and to what the other person just said or did?'. As the communication functions of language have become to be recognized, work has begun to grow in interactional analyses of language behaviour (Allen, 1973; Olson, 1974; Sinclair and Coulthard, 1975). As it develops further, I believe that it will show that there are dramatic differences between the language of the home and the pre-school class.

Even if such data are obtained, however, they will not automatically offer ways in which the language of the classroom can be made to be more like the language of the home (even if that is a desirable goal). In addition, such data will not automatically offer a solution to the problem of how to facilitate productive exchanges in children who enter the school with limited mastery in this sphere (Tough, 1973). In this connection, it is unimportant whether the behaviour that one wishes to foster is in the sphere of language, of perception, or attraction or motivation. Regardless of the area, the same problem holds: specifically, the documentation of the normative acquisition of a skill by no means indicates the method that must be employed to foster those skills in children who are experiencing difficulty. For example, as Dr Tizard (1974) points out, the children most in need of attention usually are the ones least likely to receive such attention. I do not believe that this state of affairs stems from lack of awareness or prejudice on the part of the teacher. Rather, it seems to reflect the fact that most people feel more comfortable in speaking with others who speak freely in return and, conversely, feel less comfortable in speaking with others who are likely to be taciturn. A resolution to this problem will not come from simply telling teachers to 'speak more' because as any smoker knows, people do not readily change long-ingrained dispositions by a simple statement that they should do so. Instead, if a solution is to be found, it will depend upon the development of well-delineated techniques that will enable a teacher to overcome the obstacles inherent in this type of exchange.

From this vantage point, it seems clear that the problem of teacher education in an 'academic pre-school' is very different from that for a 'shared rearing pre-school'. The teachers' role must go beyond that of providing an effective, pleasant environment in which to live. Instead, they must structure the material, information, and language in extremely precise ways if they are to achieve the ambitious goal of altering the children's manner of functioning in the entire academic sphere (see Blank, 1973; and Frankenstein, 1972, for illustrations of the type of care that the teacher must exert). Needless to say, the burden on the teacher in such a setting is much greater than it has been until now and furthermore the information necessary to enable the teacher to cope with such demands is not as yet even available.

As a result of all these factors, in contrast to 'shared rearing' programmes, 'academic pre-school' programmes cannot at present be meaningfully initiated on a large scale. This is not to say that no programmes should be initiated. Rather, I believe it essential that the programmes be initiated on a small, carefully controlled scale which can answer specific questions, such as: 'What material and interchange is most effective in altering specific behaviours?' 'At what age is it easiest to effect changes?' 'How should the group be organized to obtain maximal gains?' 'Should parents be trained?' If so, 'should their training be directed to getting them to serve as "teachers" to their own children?'. It seems that only through projects directed at questions such as these will we be able to gradually piece together the information needed, if we are to know whether effective 'academic pre-school' programmes can be established. The investment, however, is more in terms of a long-term commitment in time and involvement rather than in massive infusions of money for short periods of time. The absence of ready solutions at the moment, moreover, should not serve as a major deterrent to work in this area, for the problems are not unique to the 'academic pre-school'. Many of the central problems in our society — for example, the treatment of the aged — require a similar long-term commitment with no immediate pay-off necessarily forthcoming. I believe that should we fail to make the effort to reach and help members of our community, society will be far poorer for all its citizens.

References
Allen, D. (1973) *The development of prediction in child language*, unpublished doctoral dissertation, New York: Teachers College Columbia University.

Bernstein, B. (1972) *Class, Codes and Control*, Routledge & Kegan Paul.

Blank, M. (1973) *Teaching Learning in the Pre-school: A Dialogue Approach*, Columbus, Ohio: Charles Merrill.

Frankenstein, C. (1972) *They think again: Summary of an educational experiment with disadvantaged adolescents*, Jerusalem, Israel: Report from the School of Education, Hebrew University.

Ginsburg, H. (1972) *The myth of the deprived child*, Englewood Cliffs, N. J.: Prentice-Hall.

Labov, W. (1970) *The logic of non-standard English in Language and Poverty*, F. Williams (ed.), Chicago: Markham.

Olson, D. R. (1974) *From utterance to text: The bias of language in speech and writing*, paper presented at the Epistemics meeting, Nashville, Tenn.: Vanderbilt University.

Sinclair, J. and Coulthard, R. M. (1975) *Towards an analysis of discourse: The English used by teachers and pupils*, Oxford University Press.

Tizard, B. (1974) *Early Childhood Education*, NFER.

Tough, J. (1973) *The language of young children in education, in the early years*, M. Chazan (ed.), University College of Swansea, Aberfan Disaster Fund.

Reply to Marion Blank
B. Tizard

I want to comment on the issue raised by Marion Blank,* that is, the distinction between child-rearing, or upbringing, and education, and the question of the relative contribution which families and formal institutions make to the educational process.

There are real disagreements on this issue, which have important implications for practice, and these disagreements are associated with different meanings given to the term education. Joan Tough defines education as a process 'entrusted to schools . . . through which society intervenes in the life of an individual in order to transmit values, attitudes, skills and knowledge'. In the case of a young child the goals of such a process might include 'moving towards self-control and self-discipline, becoming responsible and reflective, capable of communicating his thinking to others, and having an impetus towards knowing about and understanding the world in which he lives'. Upbringing, on the other hand, is a process which goes on in the home, and which may be more or less compatible with education, since many parents do not accept an 'educational' role, and many of those who do are unsuccessful in achieving it. The implication of this view is that early childhood education is a job for professionals, and that most young children will not be adequately educated unless they attend nursery school.

To confine the term education to a process that occurs in schools seems, however, very unrealistic, just as it seems very unlikely that the qualities of an 'educated' three-year-old described above could be the outcome of attendance at a morning nursery school. If instead one defines education as any directed effort on the part of one person with the aim that another should acquire skills, bodies of knowledge, attitudes or values, then it is clear that both upbringing and edu-

cation go on at home and at school. Certainly, much of what a child learns at home is not the result of an educational process, that is, much of his learning results from experiences which have not been planned by an educating adult, or which are the unintended product of planned experiences. This, however, is equally true of school. What the child may learn from an arithmetic lesson is as likely to be a sense of inadequacy or confusion as a numerical skill. Whilst an adult believes he is teaching one thing, the child may well be learning something quite different, and many of the child's basic attitudes and values, for example his concepts of self-identity, class, and sex-role probably result from incidental or unintended learning, rather than from an educational process.

Equally clearly, education is not a process which is confined to school. Much education nowadays occurs through the medium of television; every day large numbers of children watch programmes like *Blue Peter* which have a deliberate educational intent, and are devised not only to impart knowledge but to develop thinking skills. In some families the child's whole environment is arranged with an educational intent — his books, toys, outings, clothes, even his room decorations are chosen with an overt instructional purpose.

It is true the 'invisible curriculum' of families differ. What the mother sees as important to teach her child varies enormously across, and within, social classes, so that many children arrive at primary school ill-prepared for the tasks which confront them. It is not that the child has received no education at home, but rather that some kinds of home education are more appropriate than others for preparing the child for the demands of the primary school. For these children the 'curriculum' of the early years may have to be altered, either by influencing the mother's conception of what she should transmit to the child or by offering supplementary learning experi-

ences outside the home. There is, however, considerable doubt whether the traditional nursery school effectively fulfils this latter function, and a great deal more investigation is needed into what children learn, and what they don't learn, at nursery school. However, the main implication of the broader definition of education is that educationalists need to concern themselves with all the settings in which children are learning. A major concern must be a study of transmission within the home, and the very complex factors which influence this transmission process.

It is because of the implications for practice that I am also unwilling to accept Marion Blank's sharp distinction between upbringing and education. She restricts the term education to attempts by the school to make basic alterations in the child's level of functioning. At the pre-school level she argues that such efforts are only needed for those children in risk of subsequent school failure; for other children, play groups and nursery school need provide only a benign, secure, and interesting environment. All upbringing is likely to involve education in Marion Blank's sense, e.g. any attempt to get a child to see another's point of view, or to assume responsibility for dressing himself, is an attempt to alter his level of functioning.

There are, of course, big differences between families and between different kinds of pre-school institution in the kind of change they try to effect in the child, and the kind of functions they consider important to develop. At the present time, most substitute-care arrangements accept little responsibility for the intellectual development of their charges — at their best, they provide only the secure benign environment described by Marion Blank, and their educational efforts are largely directed to social development, or to achieving a certain standard of obedience, and hygiene. If the home is acting as an effective edu-

*See Paper 53.

cational agent in other directions, this deficiency in group care need not be important. But for the children of working mothers — and the number of these is increasing — for five days a week parent–child interaction is likely to be brief and limited to a period when both are tired and probably irritable.

For these children the educational component of the upbringing which they receive in substitute care may be crucial. We have to find ways to bring up children away from their families in such a way that the educational goals which we consider important can be attained. This may be difficult, if only because of the relatively poor ratio of adults to children in most group settings, but a recognition that the process of child-rearing involves education is more likely to lead to better practice than the separation of these roles. If education is seen as a specialized activity, then most adult–child contacts are down-graded to 'child-rearing'. But if education is seen as a pervasive process, then all adult–child contacts are potentially important and fruitful, and nurses, play-group leaders and childminders should be seen by themselves and by others as offering not only care but education to their charges.

The logic of this argument may seem to deprive the nursery school teacher of her professional role. This should, however, surely be that of a specialist, who because of her greater knowledge of child development and educational techniques is able to help the non-specialists to make their aims explicit, to work out the best methods of attaining them, to help them to assess the success of their attempts, and to innovate new aims herself, and theories and methods. The pedagogy of the early years is as yet relatively undeveloped. We have very little idea of how, by planning, to achieve our educational goals, or how to achieve a better relationship between what the adult teaches and what the child learns. For these reasons it seems to me important at a time of expansion of services for under-fives to emphasize the need for innovation, both in the kind of services provided and in educational thinking.

Glossary
W. Van der Eyken

Adventure Playground   As the name implies, this is a play area that has not been planned, but where materials like wood, sand, bricks, old tyres, ropes and 'junk' are arranged to form climbing areas as well as the resource for constantly changing structures. Adventure playgrounds are found in a number of London housing estates and near some parks, with supervisory staff who use the playground as a centre for many other social activities.

Bewahranstalten   A German form of nursery, accepting children mainly from working mothers, and taking them into care.

Child Minder   A person who looks after children, usually in her own home and for a fee, while their mothers are out to work. Child minders now have to be registered under the Nurseries and Child Minders Regulation Act, 1948, which was amended by S.60, of the Health Services and Public Health Act, 1968.

Crèche   Originally a French concept, a *crèche* accepts babies of working mothers for the full day, providing health and care but not essentially concerned with educational needs.

Day Nursery   This is basically for older pre-school children whose mothers are away or at work. It has a welfare rather than an educational orientation, and is often provided by industry to help female staff.

École Maternelle   The French equivalent of the kindergarten, which enrols children as young as two years of age and takes them until they move, at six, to the *école primaire.* It sets out to provide a rich educational environment, and is staffed by trained teachers.

Foster Homes   The provision of substitute homes for children whose mothers find themselves in circumstances where they can no longer look after children themselves. Most fostering is arranged through local authorities, and run by them, but there is also a considerable element of private fostering.

Hospital Day Nursery   These are special facilities for hospital staff, and often give preference to the children of unsupported mothers. They are usually on or near hospital premises, and are staffed by qualified nurses assisted by auxiliaries, as recommended in the Ministry of Health Circular HM(66)/46: 'Day Nurseries in hospitals for children of nursing staff'.

Industrial or company nurseries   Usually set up and run by industry or commerce for the benefit of women employees. Often provided as an incentive to attract female labour in areas of labour shortage. A small survey some years ago indicated that their standards were high on the health side, and met the regulations laid down by the Ministry of Health. But the sample was small, and national statistics do not exist.

Jardins des Enfants   The Belgian equivalent of the kindergarten.

Kindergarten   The creation of Friedrich Froebel, it originally was a place which embodied his mystic philosophy that childhood is not simply a preparation for adulthood but an essential aspect of the Divine Unity. Now commonly used as a generic term for any school taking pre-school children and giving them a 'child-orientated' learning environment.

Krippe   The German equivalent of the *crèche*, often sponsored by industry.

Nursery   An ambivalent term, which might be applied to any place where young children are looked after. More usually it is an abbreviation for a day nursery.

Nursery classes   These are special classes attached to infant schools where children of pre-school age are introduced to the existing educational environment. Many local authorities see nursery classes as the most immediate way of providing the extra pre-school places available under Circular 2/73.*

Nursery school   The word 'school' is misleading. Fundamentally these are centres for the three to five year olds, with no formal lessons, but where children are supervised by trained staff and given an educationally stimulating environment in which, through a mixture of 'self-discovery' and socializing with other children and adults, they can broaden their range of experiences and develop their skills.

*See Appendix 2 of original source.

One o'Clock Clubs Mostly found around London situated in public parks, these clubs, staffed by a trained playleader and assistants, provide places where mothers and their small children can meet and play. They are open during the week from 1 p.m. (hence the name) until about 4.30, and are often run in conjunction with either a playpark or adventure playground, in areas of dense housing. Other city centres have similar schemes, but the Greater London Council's Playleadership Scheme, with its own training system, is unique in the extent and quality of its provision.

Playgroup A group of usually between six and twenty children and their mothers meeting regularly during the week to play together for a morning or afternoon session in — usually — a church hall or similar local venue. The emphasis is on parental involvement and do-it-yourself, on harnessing the considerable enthusiasm and energy of mothers to provide a stimulating environment for their own children. A small charge has usually to be made to cover overhead expenses.

Discussion Guide Z

1 Compare and discuss your findings as a group for the activities in this unit as follows:

  (a) What provision did you find at the nursery schools (classes) but not at the pre-school playgroups?

  (b) What provision did you find at the pre-school playgroups but not at the nursery schools (classes)?

  (c) To what extent do you think these differences indicated differences in emphases and purposes between the nursery schools (classes) and pre-school playgroups?

2 Examine as a group the purposes of nursery education as you perceive them (Activity 56). To what extent is there agreement among you regarding the two most and two least important purposes? To what extent could the purposes you set out have been categorized in terms of Blank's categories?

3 In Activity 57 you isolated the differences among Blank's Tizard's and Van der Eyken's recommendations concerning pre-school education. To what extent do you agree/disagree with these various positions?

  In discussing this issue you should give reasons, and you should try to refer to material covered in previous modules. For example, one issue which would seem to be connected to the claims variously made by Blank, Tizard and Van der Eyken is that of the professional skills required by a nursery school teacher if she is to achieve some of the goals and to carry out some of the strategies for which papers in previous modules have argued, for example, to facilitate children's language development, to adopt appropriate styles in relation to children's play and to diagnose children's cognitive levels. In this way this discussion should, as far as possible, summarize some of the issues covered in the last four modules.

Reading List

Module One
Pre-Natal Development

Ashley Montagu, M. F. *Life Before Birth.* New York: New American Library. 1964.
What happens and what can happen between conception and birth of a person. Documented with clinical studies and the results of medical research. A general book for everyone interested in human beings.

Butler, N. R., Goldstein, H. and Ross, E. M. 'Cigarette smoking in pregnancy: its influence on birth weight and perinatal mortality'. *Brit. Med. Journal,* 1, 127, 1972.

Drillien, C. M. *The Growth and Development of the Prematurely Born Infant.* Livingston. 1964.

Flanagan, G. L. *The First Nine Months of Life.* Heinemann. 1963.
An illustrated description for the general reader of the course of development from a single cell to the birth of the individual.

Gesell, A. *The Embryology of Human Behaviour.* New York: Harper Brothers. 1945.
A descriptive record using photographs and diagrams.

Lewin, R. (ed.) *Child Alive.* Temple Smith. 1975.
New insights into the development of young babies from research and clinical studies.

Nilsson, L., Ingelman-Sundberg, A. and Wirsen, C. *The Everyday Miracle. A Child is Born.* Allen Lane: Penguin. 1967.
Historic photographs used as a basis for the story of the week by week development life before birth.

Nilsson, L. et al. *A Child is Born.* Faber & Faber. 1977.
Completely revised edition. New photographs of life before birth.

Tanner, J. M. et al. *Growth.* Life Science Library, Time-Life International. 1966.
An illustrated story of the complex, intricate process of human growth.

Tanner, J. M. 'Variability of growth and maturity in new-born infants'. Lewis, M. and Rosenblum, L. A. (eds.) *The Effect of the Infant on its Care-Giver.* Wiley. 1974.

Tanner, J. M. *Foetus into Man.* London: Open Books. 1978.
Physical growth from conception to maturity.

Module Two
Perceptual Discrimination and the Growth of Sociability

Bower, T. G. R. *The Perceptual World of the Child.* Fontana/Open Books Original. 1977.
A brief summary of the work of the author based on his experimental studies of very young babies. Emphasizing their ability to pick up social information from those around them.

Carpenter, G. 'Mother's face and the newborn' in Lewin, R. (ed.). *Child Alive.* Temple Smith. 1975.

Fantz, R. L. *The Origin of Form Perception.* Scientific American Reprint No. 459. May 1961.
A report of the now classic research by Fantz dealing with the question: Is man's ability to perceive the form of objects inborn or must it be learned?

Haber, R. N. and Hershenson, M. *The Psychology of Visual Perception.* Holt Rinehart & Winston. 1973.
A useful reference book on the role of the perceiver in processing information. Chapter 15, 'The development of visual space perception', is particularly relevant for Module 2.

Leach, P. *Babyhood.* Penguin. 1975.
This book deals in a most 'readable' way with how babies are handled and how they react. About development in the first two years of life – a distillation of the 'mountain of recent research' in the field of early child development.

McGurk, H. 'Visual perception in young infants' in Foss, B. (ed). *New Perspectives in Child Development.* Penguin. 1974.
This first chapter is about visual perception in young babies based on recent investigations; the section, 'Vision and other sensory modalities', is particularly important. Chapter 5, on 'Infant attachments', by C. Corter, is also relevant for this module.

Schaffer, H. R. *The Growth of Sociability.* Penguin. 1971.
A valuable, brief guide to a mass of data on infant behaviour concerned with basic questions of the baby's innate equipment and learning ability in relation to other human beings.

Wolff, P. H. 'Observations on the early development of smiling' in Foss, B. M. (ed.) *Determinants of Infant Behaviour* Vol. 2. Methuen. 1963.

Module Three
Social/Cognitive and Motor Development

Ainsworth, M. D. S., Bell, S. M. and Stayron, D. J. Infant–mother attachment and social development: 'socialisation' as a product of reciprocal responsiveness to signals, in Richards, M. P. M. (ed.) *The Integration of a Child into a Social World.* Cambridge University Press. 1974.

Bower, T. G. R. *Development in Infancy.* W. H. Freeman. 1974.
A study of perceptual, motor and cognitive development in infancy.

Bower, T. G. R. *The Perceptual World of the Child.* Fontana/Open Books Original. 1977.
The view that humans are born with a surprisingly rich and well-organized perceptual system which includes the ability to pick up and use social information from those around them.

Bowlby, J. *Attachment and Loss. Vol. 1 Attachment.* Hogarth Press. 1969.

Bruner, J. S. *Beyond the Information Given.* Allen & Unwin. 1974.
Bruner's major papers on the 'psychology of knowing', chapters 15 and 17.

Bruner, J. and Garton, A. (eds.). *Human Growth and Development.* (Wolfson College Lectures. 1976.) Clarendon Press, Oxford. 1978.

Corter, C. 'Infant attachments' in *New Perspectives in Child Development.* Penguin. 1974.

Gesell, A. and Thompson, H. *Learning and Growth in Identical Twins: an experimental study by the method of twin control.* Genetic Psychology Monograph 6, pages 1–124.

Leach, P. *Babyhood.* Penguin. 1975.

Lewin, R. (ed.) *Child Alive.* Temple Smith. 1975.
New insights into the development of young children. Chapter 7 'Early attempts at Speech' by Trevarthen, is particularly important.

McGurk, H. 'Visual perception in young infants' in *New Perspectives in Child Development.* Foss, B. (ed.). Penguin. 1974.

McGurk, H. (ed.) *Issues in Childhood Social Development.* Methuen. 1978.
Social development seen as an interaction process to which the baby makes his own dynamic contribution.

Phillips, J. L. Jr. *The Origins of Intellect – Piaget's Theory.* W. H. Freeman. 1969.
Chapter 1 is a brief overview of Piaget's theory; Chapter 11 is concerned with the sensory-motor period.

Piaget, J. *The Construction of Reality in the Child.* Routledge & Kegan Paul. 1955. (Original French Edition, 1937.)
Introduction and Chapter 1 are concerned with the development of 'object concept' in six stages – an aspect of the evolution of sensory-motor intelligence.

Richards, M. P. M. (ed.) *The Integration of a Child into a Social World.* Cambridge University Press. 1974.
Chapter 5, 'First steps in becoming social', an introduction to various aspects of the child's relationships with adults.

Rutter, M. *Maternal Deprivation Reassessed.* Penguin. 1975.
An examination of factors that make possible the realization of human potential and defeat it.

Schaffer, H. R. *The Growth of Sociability.* Penguin. 1971.

Schaffer, H. R. *Mothering,* in the Developing Child Series. Bruner, J., Cole, M. and Lloyd, B. (eds.). Fontana/Open Books Original. 1977.

Schaffer, H. R. and Emerson, P. E. 'The development of social attachments in infancy', Monograph Social Research, *Child Development,* vol. 29, no. 3.

Sheridan, M. *Children's Developmental Progress from birth to five years: The Stycar Sequences.* NFER Publishing Company Ltd. 1975.
Illustrated charts of children's developmental progress from one month to five years under four headings: (1) Posture and Large Movements; (2) Vision and Fine Movements; (3) Hearing and Speech; (4) Social Behaviour and Play.

Stern, D. *The First Relationship: Infant and Mother,* in the Developing Child Series. Bruner, J., Cole, M. and Lloyd, B. (eds.). Fontana/Open Books Original. 1977.

Trevarthen, C. 'Early attempts at speech' in Lewin, R. (ed.) *Child Alive.* Temple Smith. 1975.

Module Four

Factors affecting early development and learning

Bowlby, J. *Attachment and Loss, Vol. 1 Attachment.* Penguin Books. 1971.
The first of three volumes on human attachment and separation dealing with the nature of the child's tie to his mother.

Brown, R. *A First Language: The Early Stage.* Penguin Books. 1976.
The child's first step towards communicating with his fellow human beings.

Bruner, J. 'Learning how to do things with words' in *Human Growth and Development.* Bruner, J. S. and Garton, A. (eds.). Clarendon Press, Oxford. 1978.
How the infant learns to use language in a fashion that meets the requirements of social living.

Bruner, J., Jolly, A. and Sylva, K. (eds.) *Play: Its Role in Development and Evolution.* Penguin Books. 1976.
A range of material including philosophical, scientific and literary studies of play.

Clarke, A. M. and Clarke, A. D. B. *Early Experiences: Myth and Evidence.* Open Books, London. 1976.
This book challenges the belief that the child's early social experience extends a disproportionate influence on later development.

Erikson, E. *Childhood and Society.* Penguin. 1964.
A case-study approach to a theoretical discussion of the formative years of childhood.

Garvey, G. *Play,* in series The Developing Child. Fontana/Open Books Original. 1977.
The author describes the various manifestations of playfulness among young children.

Lowe, M. 'Trends in the development of representational play in infants from one to three years', *Journal of Child Psychology and Psychiatry,* 1975, 16, 33–48.

Millar, S. *The Psychology of Play.* Penguin Books. 1968.
A readable account of present knowledge about games and play.

Piaget, J. *Plays, Dreams and Imitation in Childhood.* Tavistock Publications. 1971.
The third in a series devoted to the first years of the child's development.

Robertson, J. and Robertson, J. *Young Children in Brief Separation.* Tavistock Institute of Human Relations, London, 1967, 1968 and 1969.
A series of films and guides.

Ryan, J. 'Early language development: towards a communication analysis' in *The Integration of a Child into a Social World,* Richards, M. P. M. (ed.). Cambridge University Press. 1974.
An attempt to find a framework for the analysis and description of the communication skills that a child acquires in the first two years of life.

Ryan, J. 'The development of language' in *Child Alive,* Lewin, R. (ed.). Temple Smith. 1975.

Smilansky, S. *The Effects of Sociodramatic Play on Disadvantaged Pre-School Children.* John Wiley and Sons. 1968.
A report of research into imaginative play with disadvantaged pre-school children in Israel.

Spitz, R. A. 'Anxiety in Infancy: a study of its manifestations in the first year of life', *Int. J. Psycho-Anal.,* 31, 138–43. 1950.
An early study of the effects of separation.

Stern, D. *The First Relationship: Infant and Mother.* Fontana/Open Books. 1977.
Describes the processes of social interaction: the behaviour of parent and baby that make them up and also their structure, goals, and importance for development.

Tizard, J., Moss, P. and Perry, J. *All Our Children. Pre-school services in a changing society.* Temple Smith/New Society. 1976.
This book examines the situation of working mothers and the various types of provision made for their children.

Tizard, B. and Harvey, D. (eds.) *Biology of Play.* Spastics International Medical Pub. 1977.
A selective range of current thinking observational work and experiments on play.

Trevarthen, C. 'Early attempts at speech' in *Child Alive.* Temple Smith. 1975.
Modern recording techniques reveal indications that infants of a few weeks of age show signs of intentions to speak. Five babies were filmed once a week from birth until they were six months old. Their behaviour indicated that they perceived things and people differently.

Winnicott, D. W. *Playing and Reality.* Tavistock Publications. 1971.
Winnicott explores the intermediate area between internal and external reality and the nature of symbolism in childhood games.

Module Five

Representation and Cognitive Development

Bruner, J. S., Jolly, A. and Sylva, K. (eds.) *Play: Its Role in Development and Evolution.* Penguin. 1976.
A selection of papers including psychological studies of play and philosophical accounts.

Butterworth, G. (ed.) *Piaget, Education and Teaching.* Harvester Press. 1977.
A relatively introductory text.

Donaldson, M. *Children's Minds.* Fontana/Open Books. 1978.
A lucidly presented case drawing on relevant evidence for claiming that in situations that are most meaningful to them young children's intellectual functioning is at a higher level than it is in standard Piagetian tests.

Elkind, D. *Child Development and Education: a Piagetian Perspective.* New York: Oxford University Press. 1977.
A slightly more difficult text than McNally's. (Both McNally's and Elkind's texts deal with the stages of middle childhood and adolescence as well as early childhood. It should also be noted that these are only two among many accounts of Piaget's theory.)

Goodnow, J. *Children's Drawing.* Fontana/Open Books. 1977.
An account of how children solve problems in their drawings and of how their strategies, when they do so, are developmental and relate to intellectual development.

Light, P. *The Development of Social Sensitivity.* Cambridge University Press. 1979.
An important study of egocentricity in a group of four-year-old children, exploring individual differences and their association with social experience.

Millar, S. *The Psychology of Play.* Penguin. 1968.
An introductory text on kinds of play and various psychological explanations for it.

Tizard, B. and Harvey, D. (eds.) *Biology of Play.* Heinemann. 1978.
A selection of papers including investigations which concern some of the most important issues about play.

Winnicott, D. W. *Playing and Reality.* Penguin. 1980.
An interpretation of play mainly in terms of psycho-analytical theory.

Winnicott, D. W. *The Piggle.* Penguin. 1980.
A psycho-analytical study of a young child as reflected in her play.

Module Six

Language Development

Derrick, J. *The Child's Acquisition of Language.* NFER. 1977.
A simple introductory text dealing with language development in young children and the ways in which the mother and pre-school education may foster it.

Francis, H. *Language in Childhood.* Elek. 1975.
This book explores conceptions of how children acquire language, and looks at language learning between the ages of three and seven years. It includes a study of the speech of the author's son at three years of age.

Herriot, P. *An Introduction to the Psychology of Language.* Methuen. 1970.
In spite of its title this is a more advanced text.

McShane, J. *Learning to Talk.* Cambridge University Press. 1980.
This is an important book not only for its observational study of language development in the second year of life, but also for the thesis presented that learning to name objects is the direct route to the acquisition of language structure.

Tough, J. *Listening to Children Talking.* Ward Lock Educational in association with Drake Educational Associates. 1976.
Part of the Schools Council Communication Skills in Early Childhood Project, this volume is a guide to help teachers appraise and categorize children's language.

Tough, J. *Talking and Learning.* Ward Lock Educational in association with Drake Educational Associates. 1977.
A companion volume to the above, this book is a guide to fostering communication skills in nursery and infant schools.

Module Seven

Social Development

Bronfenbrenner, U. *Two Worlds of Childhood: USA and USSR.* Allen & Unwin. 1970.
A comparative study of children's social and moral behaviour in the two countries. The differences are related to differences in child rearing and education.

McGurk, H. (ed.) *Issues in Childhood Social Development.* Methuen. 1978.
A collection of papers on various aspects of children's social development.

Module Eight

Pre-School Provision

Pilling, D. and Pringle, M. K. *Controversial Issues in Child Development.* Elek. 1978.
One of the five issues thoroughly examined is the effectiveness of various pre-school intervention programmes.

Webb, L. *The Purpose and Practice in Nursery Education.* Blackwell. 1974.
An examination of what the purpose and practice appear to be and a discussion of what the author thinks they should be.

Oxford Pre-school Research Project. Grant McIntyre. 1980.
There are six volumes, listed below, reporting the results of this research. The first volume by Bruner presents an overview of the findings; the content of the other volumes is clear from the titles.

Bruner, J. S. Vol. 1 *Under Five in Britain.*

Sylva, K., Roy, C. and Painter, M. Vol. 2 *Childwatching at Playgroup and Nursery School.*

Bryant, B., Harris, M. and Newton, D. Vol. 3 *Children and Minders.*

Garland, C. and White, S. Vol. 4 *Children and Day Nurseries.*

Wood, D., McMahon, L. and Cranstoun, Y. Vol. 5 *Working with Under Fives.*

Smith, T. Vol. 6 *Parents' Pre-school Involvement.*

Glossary

Aberrant Irregular, deviation from norm.

Accommodation Adjustment, adaptation, modification as a result of new experiences.

Adaptive significance Significance for learning and adjustment.

Adipose Pertaining to fat, fatty.

Aesthetic values Concerned with the appreciation of beauty.

Amnion Innermost membrane enclosing foetus before birth.

Antibodies Kinds of substances in the blood tending to neutralize others that are harmful.

Autonomous Independent.

Binocular depth perception Two eyes operating conjointly giving impression of depth at short range.

Cartilage Firm elastic tissue; gristle changing later to bone.

Chromosome Rod-like or thread-like structure occurring in the nucleus of animal and plant cells, carrying genetic material.

Cloze method A method for assessing the readability of written material which involves masking some of the words which the reader then has to guess from the text.

Cognitive processes Mental processes concerned with knowing, such as, perception, imagery, reasoning etc.

Coitus Sexual connection; copulation.

Configuration Form, pattern, structure; an integrated whole.

Congenital Present in an individual at birth.

Connotation Implied consequence; meaning.

Conservation This is one of the most important concepts investigated by Piaget and is the understanding that the quantity of a continuous substance, such as plasticine or water, of discrete objects, such as counters, of length, area or weight, remain the same across a transformation, for example, when the plasticine is transformed from a ball to a sausage-like shape, when a liquid is poured from one container into another of different dimensions, or when the configuration of a number of objects is changed.

Contour Outline.

Control group If an experimenter wants to know whether a certain characteristic or condition is significant or effective one of the most common experimental designs used involves comparing an experimental and control group. The experimental group possesses the characteristic or is subject to the condition whereas the control goup does not or is not. Similarly, if an experimenter wants to compare the effectiveness of various conditions he will use several experimental groups, each of which is characterised by one of the conditions, and a control group.

Convergent Turning towards meeting point.

Cornea Transparent horny part of anterior covering of the eyeball.

Correlation A statistical procedure for finding the relationship between two variables. If an increase in one variable is related to an increase in the other the correlation is positive. If the increase in one variable is related to a decrease in the other the correlation is negative.

Decoding (see also **encoding**) The psychological process by which a person derives meaning from a verbal message.

Developmental quotient Ratio between chronological age and assessed level of behaviour.

Difference/deficit controversy The controversy as to whether the language codes called by Bernstein 'restricted' and 'elaborated' are merely different or whether the restricted code is deficient as compared with the elaborated code. Bernstein objects to the deficit view and attacks the concept of 'compensatory' education in part because it implies a deficit.

Displacement Transfer of an object from one place to another.

Dorsum (of foot) Underneath of foot.

Ego-centricism Interpretation from own personal viewpoint.

Embryo Offspring of animal before birth: hence human embryo.

Empirical Based on experience; in psychology based on systematic observation and experiment.

Encoding (see also **decoding**) The psychological process by which a person converts meaning into a verbal message.

Endocrine Ductless glands secreting internally.

En face (positive) In front of face, face to face.

Exigent Exacting, demanding.

Experimental group See **Control group**.

Ex post facto Acting retrospectively.

Extensor movements Straightening out.

Fertilized egg Ovum that has been fertilized by sperm.

Fixation The directing and focusing of both eyes (or one eye) on an object or point so that the image falls on the fovea(s).

Foci Points of convergence.

Foetus Fully developed embryo in the womb.

Form perception Discrimination of visual pattern.

Fovea the area of clearest vision in the centre of the retina upon which the image falls when an object is fixated.

Functor A form that marks grammatical structures and carries modulatory meanings.

Gene The carrier of a hereditary factor in the chromosomes in the germ cell.

Generative grammar A description of a language which consists of a set of rules from which all and only the sentences considered grammatical by a native speaker of that language can be generated.

Habituation (method) Accustoming subject (of an experiment) to an experience.

Homogeneous Of the same kind.

Hormone Kinds of internal secretion that pass into the blood and stimulate organs to action.

Identical twins Developed from a single fertilized ovum.

Inanimate Not endowed with animal life.

Indicator Person or thing that points out.

Indicative Stating a thing as a fact.

Inherent Existing in.

Inhomogeneity Lack of similarity.

Immunity Being proof against contagion.

Innate Present in the individual at birth; inborn.

Innate potential Inborn ability.

Instrumental Serving as an instrument or means.

Intentional On purpose, with intent.

Interactional synchrony Moving in precise rhythm with the segments of human speech.

Interlocutor One who takes part in dialogue or conversation.

Lango (hairs) The soft downy hair which develops before birth all over the body, most of which is shed at birth.

Lens Transparent surface of the eye.

Lexical Of the words of a language.

Lexicon All the words and morphemes in the language of an individual or a community.

Locus Exact place of something.

Luminosity Throwing light.

Maturation The process of growth and development itself, as contrasting with the learning process.

Median Situated in the middle; the middle point of a rank ordered list of scores.

Menstruation Monthly flow of blood from the mucous coat or uterus.

Metamorphosis Change of form.

Molecule Small particle.

Morpheme Smallest meaningful unit of a language.

Naive/naively In a childlike, simple or unsophisticated way.

Nativist One who emphasizes the inborn rather than the acquired character of certain factors in experience, e.g. space perception.

Neurological theory Theory related to the structure and function of the central nervous system.

Nidation Nesting.

Nominal of, as, like, a noun; existing in name only.

Nucleus Centre of life of a cell consisting of specialized material.

Object concept Piagetian notion of the continued existence of an object no longer in the visual field.

257

Orientation   Determination of one's position, how one stands.

Ossification   Turning into bone, hardening.

Ova   Plural of ovum, the female germ cell.

Ovulation   Release of ovum from the ovary.

Pedagogical   Implying teaching.

Perception   The process of becoming immediately aware of something.

Perceiver   The person perceiving.

Peripheral vision   The opposite of central; away from the fovea.

Permeable   Capable of being diffused through.

Phenomenal appearance   Immediate experience.

Phoneme   A unit of significant sound in a given language.

Placenta   Flattened, circular, spongy, vascular organ helping to nourish foetus which is attached to it by the umbilical cord.

Presuppositional   Before supposition or hypothesis.

Primordial (cell)   Existing from the beginning.

Psycholinguistics   Study of the psychological processes underlying speech.

Reflex   Automatic response, unlearned.

Reinforcement   Strengthen or support: technique (psychological) to obtain desired repetition of behaviour.

Representation (mental)   Mental image of likeness.

Retina   Layer at the back of the eye, sensitive to light, on which the images of external objects in the field of vision are formed by the lens system, containing rods and cones.

Scanning   Looking intently at all parts successively.

Segregation   Separation or isolation.

Semantic   Related to meaning in language.

Sensory excitation   Stimulation of sensory nerves.

Startle measure   Measurement of startle response, e.g. by means of monitoring pattern of heart beat.

Supine   Lying face upwards.

Syntactical (classes)   According to syntax.

Syntax   Sentence construction, the grammatical arrangement of words in speech or writing.

T unit   A measure derived by Kellogg Hunt involving one main clause and all its subordinate clauses.

Tracking   Eye movements when following a moving object.

Trophoblasts   Nutrition cells.

Umbilical cord   Rope-like structure passing from foetus to placenta.

Utterance   Emitted audibly; expressing in words.

Ventral suspension   Suspended by belly.

Vernix (cream)   Baby brings vernix cream in skin folds from womb.

Vertex   Meeting points of lines.

Video-recording   Recording with video camera.

Virus   Morbid poison; poison of contagious disease.

Visual acuity   The degree of discrimination of which the eye is capable.

Vocalization   The forming of sound patterns, the uttering of words.

Vocative   Case used in addressing person or thing.

Acknowledgements

The compilers and publishers are indebted to the following for permission to reprint the material specified.

The publishers have made every effort to trace copyright holders, but if they have inadvertently overlooked any, they will be pleased to make the necessary arrangements at the first opportunity.

Paper 3: from *The Seventh, Eighth and Ninth Month* by Geraldine Lux Flanagan.
Reprinted by permission of William Heinemann Medical Books Ltd.

Paper 9: from *The Psychology of Visual Perception* by Ralph Norman Haber and Maurice Hershenson.
Copyright © 1973 by Holt, Rinehart & Winston, Inc.
Reprinted by permission of Holt, Rinehart & Winston.

Paper 13: from *Babyhood* by Penelope Leach, pp. 82–88.
Copyright © Penelope Leach, 1975.
Reprinted by permission of Penguin Books Ltd.

Paper 20: from *Children's Developmental Progress from Birth to Five Years (The Stycar Sequences)* by Mary Sheridan, 1975.
Reprinted by permission of the National Foundation for Educational Research in England and Wales.

Paper 23: from *Human Growth and Development: Wolfson College Lectures 1976,* edited by Jerome S. Bruner and Alison Garton.
Copyright © Wolfson College, Oxford 1978.
Reprinted by permission of Oxford University Press.

Paper 29: from *The Biology of Play,* edited by B. Tizard and D. Harvey.
Copyright © Spastics International Medical Publications, 1977.

Paper 33: from *Beyond the Information Given* by J. S. Bruner.
Copyright © George Allen & Unwin, 1974.

Paper 34: from *Piaget, Education and Teaching* by D. W. McNally (pp. 26–31).
Copyright © The Harvester Press Ltd., 1974.

Papers 36 and **42**: from *Children's Minds* by Margaret Donaldson (pp. 19–25 and 32–39 respectively).
Copyright © Fontana Paperbacks, 1978.

Paper 38: from the publication *The New Era,* May/June 1978 (vol. 50).
Reprinted by permission of The World Education Fellowship.

Paper 40: from *Language and Education* by Andrew Wilkinson.
Copyright © Oxford University Press, 1975.
Reprinted by permission of Oxford University Press.

Paper 45: from *Language in Teaching and Learning* by H. Francis.
Copyright © George Allen & Unwin, 1977.

Paper 46: from *Cognitive Development: Research Based on a Neo-Piagetian Approach* edited by J. A. Keats, K. F. Collis *et al.*
Copyright © John Wiley & Sons, Ltd., 1978.
Reprinted by permission of John Wiley & Sons, Ltd.

Paper 47: from *Development in Human Learning* by E. A. Lunzer and J. F. Morris.
Copyright © Granada Publishing Ltd., 1968.

Paper 48: from *Language and Social Behaviour* by W. P. Robinson (Penguin, 1972).
Copyright © W. P. Robinson.

Paper 49: reprinted from *Developmental Psychology,* 1978, vol. 14, no. 5, 517–522.
Copyright © (1978) by the American Psychological Association.
Reprinted by permission.

Papers 51 and **55**: from *The Pre-School Years* by W. Van der Eyken. Penguin Education, Fourth Edition, 1977, pp. 128–145 and 9–11 respectively.
Copyright © Willem Van der Eyken, 1967, 1969, 1974, 1977.
Reprinted by permission of Penguin Books Ltd.

Paper 52: from *Piaget, Psychology and Education* edited by V. P. Varma and P. Williams (Hodder & Stoughton, 1976).
Copyright © Maurice Chazan and Theo Cox.

Papers 53 and **54**: from *Early Childhood Education* by B. Tizard (National Foundation for Educational Research, 1974).
Copyright © National Foundation for Educational Research in England and Wales.

Cover photographs: by kind permission of Charing Cross Hospital Medical School.

Activity Guides

Module 1   Pre-Natal Development
Unit   1   Birth – the impact of change

Allow at least 20 minutes for this activity.

This activity can be carried out with a partner or individually. Check your answers to the questions on photograph 1 with Part A of Paper 2, which should be used as a commentary.

The first photograph shows a new-born baby being held firmly by the doctor who has supervised his birth. The baby has not yet been cleaned up from his journey through the birth passage of his mother, and his life-line cord from the placenta is still attached.

1. What emotions would you expect the parents to experience as they view their new-born baby for the first time (assuming that this is their first-born)? Try to imagine your own emotions. Tick the likely emotions.

apprehension		
anxiety		
curiosity		
relief		
delight		
fear		
disappointment		
disgust		

2. Suggest other emotions likely to be experienced by parents at this time:

(a) in relation to the sex of the child;
(b) in the case of an apparently handicapped child.

3. How is the baby likely to behave?

smile   cry   scream   laugh

4. What must be done soon after birth?

5. What is involved in this action?

6. What is still to come?

Check your answers with Part A of Paper 2.

Module 1   Pre-Natal Development
Unit   1   Birth – the impact of change

Changes in Environment

You should allow at least 10 minutes for the completion of this activity.

This activity should be carried out alone. From the warm closeness of the womb out into the world: which of the following experiences are changes which will affect the baby?

	yes	no
change of temperature		
pull of gravity		
effort of breathing		
sensation of light		
sensation of hunger		
effort of sucking		
head lag		
sound of voices		
random movements of limbs		
clinging with reflex grasp		

Check your answers with Paper 2 (Part B).

Module 1   Pre-Natal Development
Unit   1   Birth – the impact of change

You should allow at least 10 minutes for the completion of this activity.

This activity should be carried out on an individual basis.
Full-term at nine months most babies can make the necessary adjustments to their changed environment **but** could the baby survive at seven months?

What do you think he would be capable of doing at seven months?

	yes	no
kicking		
grasping		
sucking		
breathing		
crying		

Could the baby **survive** if born two months early?

yes   no

Check your answers with Paper 3 'The seventh, eighth and ninth months'.

Some further questions to think about:
    How and when does the miracle start?
    What part does heredity play in pre-natal development?
    How is the sex of the baby determined?
    When does the heart begin to beat?
    When do the small arms and legs begin to move?

Read Paper 4 to find the answers to some of the questions posed above. Further material on pre-natal development will be found in Unit 2.
Take your records of Activities 1–3 to the discussion group.

Module 1 Pre-Natal Development
Unit   2 The Embryo

Allow at least 10 minutes for completion of this activity.

This activity can be carried out in a group or individually. Study photographs 2–4 with care; use Paper 5 to assist you in answering the questions.

Photograph 2 (magnification × 1400)

What is this?	
What can it become?	
What must happen first?	

Photograph 3 (magnification × 440)

What are these?	
Where are they going?	

Photograph 4 (magnification × 400)

What is happening here?	
What important process will happen next?	

After studying photographs 2–4 write down your answers and check them with Paper 5.

Module 1 Pre-Natal Development
Unit   2 The Embryo

Allow at least 10 minutes for this activity.

This activity can be carried out with a partner or individually.
Study photographs 5–7 with care (magnification × 280).
What is happening in this series of slides:

(a) to the number of cells?	
(b) to the size of the cells?	
(c) to the size of the envelope?	

After studying photographs 5–7 write down your answers and check with Paper 5. View photographs 5–7 a second time, making rough labelled sketches of what you see and writing your own commentary to remind you of the sequence of events and processes involved, and to use later in your discussion group.

Module 1   Pre-Natal Development
Unit   2   The Embryo

Allow at least 10 minutes for this activity.

Refer to Paper 5 during this activity. This activity can
be carried out in a group or individually. Study
photographs 8 and 9 with care; use Paper 5 to help
you with the questions.

Photograph 8   (magnification × 96)
The fertilized ovum travels from the oviduct to the
uterus.

(a) Can you identify the fertilized ovum?
    Draw what you can see and label the ovum.

(b) What is happening to the ovum during this journey?

Photograph 9   (magnification × 112)
The vital process of embedding in the uterus is depic-
ted. Notice the change in structure of the fertilized
ovum.

 (a) Why is the process of vital importance to the new life?

 (b) Why is the process described as hazardous?

After studying photographs 8 and 9 write down your
answers and check them with Paper 5.

Module 1   Pre-Natal Development
Unit   2   The Embryo

Allow at least 10 minutes for this activity.

This activity can be carried out in a group or individually. Study photograph 10 – the embryo at thirty-
three days (6mm).

*Draw a rough sketch of the embryo as you see it on
photograph 10 and label the parts as below:*

1. the blunt head end consisting of the forehead
   with the foremost part of the brain;
2. the developing eye: a faint oval on the head just
   visible on the surface;
3. the primitive mouth cavity lying just below the
   forehead;
4. horizontal segments along the back gradually
   decreasing in size toward the tail – the future
   spine (faintly indicated);
5. the embryonic limb buds;
6. the surrounding placenta.

Remember the actual size is 6mm.

Module 1   Pre-Natal Development
Unit   2   The Embryo

Allow at least 10 minutes for this activity.

This activity can be carried out alone or in a group. Study photograph 11 – the embryo at 6 weeks. Focus your attention on the environment of the baby. Note the amniotic sac has been split open. Attempt the following questions; if you need assistance in answering them refer to the relevant section of Paper 5.

1. What surrounds the baby?	
2. Where is he?	
3. What is he doing?	
4. Why does he not drown?	
5. How is he secured?	

6. Can you see:	yes	no
(a) the lidless eye?		
(b) the enormous forehead?		
(c) the very short arms and legs?		

Study photograph 11 a second time and check your answers after reading Paper 5 (section headed 'The Placenta').
Make a rough sketch of what you see. Label the parts you can identify.

Read Paper 6: 'The placenta – life-line for a precious parasite'.

Module 1 Pre-Natal Development
Unit   3 Embryo to Foetus

Allow at least 30 minutes for this activity.

This activity can be carried out either in a group or individually. Refer to Paper 7. Study photographs 12–17 with care; use Paper 7 to assist you in answering the questions.

Circle the appropriate response:

Photograph 12 7 weeks 22 mm	1.	Note: (a) proportions of head to trunk (b) faint indication of ear (c) severed cord
	2.	Will the eyelids: close? remain open?
Photograph 13 8 weeks 30 mm (approx.)	3.	Note the amniotic sac and size of the placenta.
	4.	What is the dark bulge? eye heart liver
	5.	Is the heart already beating?
Photograph 14 10 weeks 44 mm	6.	Note the position of the ear.
	7.	Can the baby open his eyes at this stage? yes no
Photograph 15 16 weeks 100 mm (approx.)	8.	Can you identify the following: (a) the amniotic sac; (b) the placenta; (c) the umbilical cord; (d) the eye (dark shadow); (e) the ear (note position).
	9.	Make a sketch and label the above parts.
	10.	Compare with photograph 13 at 8 weeks.
Photograph 16 20 weeks 150 mm	11.	(a) What causes the eyelids to fuse? (b) What is the reason for this? (c) Can the baby open his eyes again before birth? yes no
Photograph 17 36 weeks (full-term) 340 mm (approx.)	12.	Note: the change in proportions; the curve of the spine; the flexed limbs; the position of the head; the more rounded chubby appearance of this full-term baby. Ready for life? But he did not live. What might be the reasons for this?

Check your answers with Paper 7.

Module 1   Pre-Natal Development
Unit   3   Embryo to Foetus

Allow at least 45 minutes for this activity.

This activity can be carried out either in a group or individually. Refer to Paper 7. Study photographs 18-27 with care noting the development of the hands and feet; use Paper 7 to assist you in answering the questions.

Circle the appropriate response:

Photograph 18 5–6 weeks 17 mm	1.	Which grow first? fingers arms hands
	2.	Are there any joints yet? yes no Note the amniotic sac has been opened.
Photograph 19 7 weeks 22 mm	3.	Can the baby touch its face yet? yes no
	4.	Can the hands reach each other? yes no
Photograph 20 10 weeks 43 mm	5.	Note the lengthening and flexing of the arms, the shaping of the fingers and the beginning of the nails.
	6.	The hands can meet but can the fingers grasp anything? yes no
Photograph 21 18 weeks 124 mm	7.	What is the baby holding?
	8.	How does this happen?
Photograph 22 20 weeks 150 mm	9.	Is he sucking his thumb? yes no
Photograph 23 20 weeks 150 mm	10.	What is involved in this behaviour? (a) eye–hand co-ordination; (b) reflex action; (c) sensitive areas.
Photograph 24 20 weeks 150 mm	11.	Note the general shape of the hand and the position of the thumb in relation to the fingers for later functioning. Note the finger joints, finger tips and nails.

Module 1 Pre-Natal Development
Unit   3 Embryo to Foetus

Photograph 25 5–6 weeks 17 mm (approx.)	12.	Can you see the lower limb buds? yes no
	13.	What shape are they? oval round square
	14.	Draw what you can see indicating the future toes.
	15.	Note the dominating umbilical cord in relation to the undeveloped trunk.
Photograph 26 20 weeks 150 mm	16.	Note the size of the head in relation to the rest of the body especially the lower trunk. Note the flexion at thigh, knee and ankle.
Photograph 27 24 weeks 220 mm	17.	What is the baby doing with his legs?
	18.	What results from this activity?
	19.	What can happen to the mother as a result of this activity?
Photograph 1 36 weeks 340 mm (approx.) full-term new-born	20.	Consider the hazards of his journey through the birth canal and the equipment he brings with him to cope with immediate changes in his environment after birth.

	21.	Think of adjustments related to:
		   breathing;
		   feeding;
		   moving in space;
		   sleeping and waking up;
		   light and dark;
		   day and night;
		   contact with others
		which must be made by the baby in the first weeks after birth.

Visit to a new-born baby

Allow at least 1½ hours for this activity.

This activity should be carried out individually. Read the introduction to Module 2. Arrange to visit a mother, preferably a relative or friend who has a new-born baby. If possible arrange to see the baby being fed, or bathed, rather than when asleep. Observe the baby carefully noticing his behaviour. Watch the baby's eyes, his hands and feet; notice any sounds he makes.

Over a ten-minute period check the following:

	yes	no
Does the baby look at the mother?		
Does he look away and then look back?		
Does he move his hands and arms?		
Does he kick with his feet?		
Does he move hands, arms and feet together?		
Does he cry during this period?		
Does he make any other noises?		

Ask the mother to tell you about her baby.

His name	Age:	
Weight at birth		
Breast-fed	yes	no
Bottle-fed		
Is he still fed during the night?		
Does he cry during the night?		
Does this disturb the parents' rest?		

Ask the mother to tell you anything she has noticed specially about her baby.

Note: If the father is present draw him into the conversation and notice his response to the baby (indicate this below).

warm   interested   uninterested

Note any activities he undertakes with the baby. If there are any other young children present notice how they react to the baby. Note the ages of any other children in the family.
Keep your observation records for use in your discussion group.

Module 2 Perceptual Discrimination and the Growth of Sociability
Unit   1 Seeing is Believing

Allow at least 10 minutes for this activity.

Consider the statement:

seeing is believing

Do you accept or reject this statement?
Tick your choice:

accept	
reject	

Spend five minutes recording your reasons.

After discussion with your group add any further
reasons and comments you wish to make regarding
this question.

Module 2   Perceptual Discrimination and the Growth of Sociability
Unit   1   Seeing is Believing

Perceptual experience — making sense of what we see

Allow at least 10 minutes for this activity.

Look at the picture below.

What do you see? Record your answers to the following questions.

1.   What do you see when you look at the picture?

2.   Look again. Can you see anything else?   yes/no

3.   If your answer is yes, what do you see now?

4.   Can you shift easily from one view to the other?   yes/no

5.   Which is the dominant view for you?

Solution in Discussion Guide D

Module 2 Perceptual Discrimination and the Growth of Sociability
Unit   1 Seeing is Believing

What do you see?

Allow at least 10 minutes for this activity.

Look at the picture.

What do you see? Record your answers to the following questions.

1. What kind of person do you see when you look
    at the picture?

2. Look again. Can you see another kind of   yes/no
    person?

3. If your answer is yes, what do you see now?

4. Can you shift easily from one view to the   yes/no
    other?

5. Which is the dominant view for you?

Solution in Discussion Guide D.
Note: Do not be unduly worried if you cannot see
        two pictures.

Module 2   Perceptual Discrimination and the Growth of Sociability
Unit   2   Early Stages of Perceptual Development

Allow at least 25 minutes for this activity.

A. What do very young babies attend to?

This activity should be carried out individually.
Visual scanning: When a young baby is awake his eyes are engaged in scanning his surroundings for visual interest.
Fixating: When his eyes alight on something stimulating they fixate, that is, they stop moving; he appears to be gazing at the person or object that interests him.
Length of fixation time: What affects the length of time he gazes (fixates) on a particular visual stimulus?

Circle answer:	novelty	shape	colour	complexity

Would you expect to find any difference in fixation time on the following pairs of visual patterns in very young babies (one to fifteen weeks)? Material presented in random groups.

	◉	☰	a bull's-eye design and horizontal stripes	
▦	☐	▫	a checker-board and two sizes of plain square	
	✚	◯	a cross and a circle	
	▲	▲	two identical triangles	

1. Number the pairs of test patterns in order 1–4 on the basis of what you think would provide preferential interest for these very young babies.
2. Indicate which of the pairs would obtain the longest period of attention.

Read Paper 10 for results obtained by Fantz.

B. What about the human face?

What type of response do you think a baby would make to these drawings?
Would you expect any difference in attention shown by a young baby to these three representations?

1   2   3

Fantz showed the three objects, paired in all possible combinations, to 49 infants aged from 4 days to 6 months old.
Number the above figures in order of attention preference of babies.
Check your answers with Paper 10.

Smiling response
1. When does a baby first smile in response to a human face?
   Circle the age you select.

6 weeks	3 months	2 months

2. What part of the face interests the infant?

hair	mouth	eyes	nose

See Paper 12 for the results of further research.

Module 2   Perceptual Discrimination and the Growth of Sociability
Unit   3   To Smile or not to Smile?

First-hand observations of babies at four to eight weeks

Allow at least one hour for this activity.

See the paper entitled 'General guidance for first-hand observations of young children' in Module 2.
Note: Make yourself familiar with the observation checklist below before arranging your visit.
When arranging your visit tell the mother you would like to observe the baby when he is in her arms and preferably awake! A sitting-up position with necessary support is more suitable than lying down. Tell her the kind of behaviour you hope to observe (see checklist).
When mother and baby are comfortably settled: *make the following observations over a period of 10 minutes.*

Tick either yes or no column

Observation checklist	yes	no
1. Does the baby look into his mother's face:		
(a) when mother is silent?		
(b) when she 'talks' to him?		
2. Does he look at her and then look away?		
3. Does he fixate on a bright object, such as your wrist-watch, held about eight inches from his eyes?		
4. Can he follow a moving object? Move your watch in an arc of about forty-five degrees; do the baby's eyes follow the object?		
5. Notice the baby's hands. Are they clenched?		
unclenched?		
6. Are the baby's hands moving?		
just the hands and fingers?		
arms and hands?		
7. Does the baby move his hands towards the moving object?		
8. What happens if you put a rattle into the baby's clenched fist?		
Does he look at it?		
9. Ask the mother whether the baby has smiled at her: in response to her smile;		
spontaneously.		

After this ten-minute period make a note of any further behaviour that you find interesting, and also any comments from the mother.

Module 2 Perceptual Discrimination and the Growth of Sociability
Unit   3 To Smile or not to Smile?

Obtain the following information from the mother:

Basic data:		
First name:		Sex:
Age: Months Weeks Days		
Position in family: 1 2 3 4 5 (circle)		
Date of visit:		

Note whether the baby has experienced brief or
longer separation from the mother since birth:

Keep your observations, comments and basic data for
the follow-up discussion with your colleagues.

Module 2   Perceptual Discrimination and the Growth of Sociability
Unit   3   To Smile or not to Smile?

A second visit to a very young baby

Allow at least one hour for this activity.

Arrange to make a second visit (alone) to the baby
about four weeks after your first visit.
Repeat the observations and experiments made in
the first visit.
Spend a period of ten minutes or so on these activities
when mother and baby are relaxed.
Make a list of any **changes** in the baby's behaviour
since the last time you saw him.

Changes in behaviour

Extend your observations to include the baby's
response to **sounds**, especially human voices.
Make the following observations over a period of ten
minutes.

	yes	no
1. Does the baby make any sounds spontaneously?		
Immediately after his mother finished 'talking' to him?		
2. Does he smile spontaneously?		
Immediately after his mother 'talks' to him?		
While she 'talks' to him?		
3. If the father is present ask him if he will 'talk' to the baby. Notice how the baby responds to the father.		
Does he look at him?		
Does he smile at him?		
Does he respond with sounds?		
4. Add any further observations or comments, such as whether the baby sucks his fingers or his thumb.		

Make a note of any comments on the baby's
behaviour from the parents.

Keep your observations and comments for the
follow-up discussion with your colleagues.

Module 3   Social/Cognitive and Motor Development
Unit   1   Mother–Child Interaction

First-hand observations of babies aged three to six months

Allow at least one hour for this activity.

Arrange a visit to a mother with a young baby as
proposed in Paper 14. Ask the mother to talk and play
with the baby for about ten to fifteen minutes, first
without a toy and later to introduce one toy followed
by a choice from two or three toys.
Ask her to attempt to include you in the play after the
baby has become used to your presence.
Note the contextual situation and atmosphere of the
home.

Study the checklist before your visit.
Tick behaviour as and when it occurs during the
fifteen minutes (except when you are involved with
the baby, in which case tick after the fifteen minutes
is over).

Baby sitting on mother's lap.	
Baby sitting on floor near mother.	
Mother observes baby's activity.	
Mother attracts baby's attention – smiles.	
talks.	
Baby watches mother's face.	
Baby watches mother's face – smiles.	
turns away.	
Baby touches mother's face.	
Baby makes sounds, e.g. 'ad – dah'.	
Mother repeats baby's sounds.	
Baby imitates mother.	
Mother makes different sounds.	
Baby imitates mother.	
Baby moves arms up and down.	
Baby kicks moving legs and feet.	
Mother gives baby toy to hold.	
Baby grasps toy, sucks toy, bangs toy, looks at toy, drops toy, looks for toy in direction of fall. (circle)	
Mother shows baby toy and talks to baby about it.	
Baby talks back.	
Baby looks at observer when mother talks to observer.	
Baby happy to be nursed by observer.	

Module 3   Social/Cognitive and Motor Development
Unit   1   Mother–Child Interaction

Baby cries to be returned to mother.	
Mother offers baby choice of toys.	
Baby chooses toy, looks at it, sucks it, offers toy to mother, offers it to observer, takes it back.	
Baby grasps toy when offered by observer.	
Further observations.	

Comments from mother.

Additional comments from observer.
Note if you are able to see the baby fed and/or bathed.

Make a brief note of communications between mother and baby in terms of exchange of particular sounds or baby 'talk'.

Is the baby happy to be left for a short time (about half an hour) with another familiar adult?   yes/no

Basic data

First name:	Sex:		
Age:	Months	Weeks	Days
Position in family:	1 2 3 4 5 6 (circle)		
Date of visit:			

Note whether baby has experienced brief or longer separation from mother since birth.

Keep your observations and comments for discussion group.

Module 3 Social/Cognitive and Motor Development
Unit   2 Behaviour with Objects and Persons

Replication of Piaget's hidden object experiment

Allow at least 1 hour for this activity.

Make yourself familiar with the checklist before
arranging your visit.
Arrange a visit to a mother with a baby between six
and nine months; explain to the mother what you
would like her to do and that the visit would be short,
that is, between 30 and 45 minutes.

Method
When the baby is sitting comfortably, with support,
playing with a familiar toy, ask the mother to **place the
toy under a cover** in front of the child.
Note: the baby's attention must be directed to the toy
and he must **see** it hidden under the cover.
Record your observations on the checklist.
Checklist for behaviour towards toy that baby has
seen hidden.

Does the baby:	6/7 mths	8/9 mths
look at the spot where the toy was?		
look away from the spot?		
begin to look upset (start to cry)?		
start to play with something else?		
search for the toy under the cover?		
remove the cover from the toy?		
express emotion (positive or negative) at the reappearance of the toy?	pos:	neg:

Variation on above
If the baby behaves as if the toy no longer exists
expose a small part of the toy to see if this leads to his
re-discovering it.   yes/no

Displacement test
If the baby finds the toy try Piaget's displacement test:
pretend to hide the toy under the first cover but actually hide it under a second cover nearby.
Does the baby find the toy under the second
cover?   yes/no

Additional data
Comments made by the mother or other care-giver
regarding the situation.

Repeat sequence noting any changes of behaviour.

Module 3 Social/Cognitive and Motor Development
Unit   2 Behaviour with Objects and Persons

Complete personal data after each observation
record to assist recall for discussion purposes.

First name:	Sex:
Age at date of visit:	Date of birth:
Position in family:	1 2 3 4 5 6 (ring)
Other children present: yes/no	
Baby appears upset at presence of observer: yes/no	
Other comments, e.g. note toys available, books etc.	
Brief note of any difficulties encountered.	

Module 3   Social/Cognitive and Motor Development
Unit   2   Behaviour with Objects and Persons

Bower's experiments with moving objects

Allow at least one hour for this activity.

Make yourself familiar with the checklist before
arranging your visit.
Arrange a visit to a mother with a baby aged six to
nine months; if possible re-visit a mother and baby
already known to you.
Ask the mother to settle the baby happily and then to
interest him in a familiar toy. Sit where you can watch
unobtrusively the baby's eye movements.

Task 1
Ask the mother to play a game with the baby moving
the toy from a point A to point B about two feet away.
Repeat this several times then move toy to point C
about the same distance on the other side of A.

Watch the baby's eye movements	6/7 mths	8/9 mths
Does the baby: look where the toy goes first, that is, point B?		
look at point C where the toy is now standing?		

Task 2
Provide a piece of cardboard or book to serve as a screen.
Ask the mother to move the toy behind the screen, when the
baby is watching her, and bring it out the other side.

Watch the baby's eye movements	6/7 mths	8/9 mths
Does the baby: track the moving toy with his eyes and link up with it as it emerges from behind the screen?		
continue to look at the screen?		
look at his mother's face?		

Module 3 Social/Cognitive and Motor Development
Unit   2 Behaviour with Objects and Persons

Task 3
Ask the mother to wait for the baby to watch her and then to
move the toy behind the screen and leave it there.

Watch the baby's eye movements	6/7 mths	8/9 mths
Does the baby: continue his tracking to the other side of the screen?		
try to remove the screen to get to the toy?		
become interested in something else?		

Task 4
Ask the mother to move the toy behind the screen and bring it
out at a different level (higher).

Watch the baby's eye movements	6/7 mths	8/9 mths
Does the baby: track along the original line of movement?		
shift his tracking to the new line of movement?		
appear upset by the change of movement?		

Task 5
Ask the mother to have a different toy in readiness behind the screen.
Move the first toy behind the screen and bring out the second different
toy on the same line of movement.

Watch the baby's eye movements	6/7 mths	8/9 mths
Does the baby: track the new toy without apparent upset?		
seem upset by the change and look back at the screen?		
look for the first toy behind the screen?		

Additional notes
Add notes of any other responses by the baby to
these activities.

Add mother's comments and any additional information she may offer.

Module 3   Social/Cognitive and Motor Development
Unit   2   Behaviour with Objects and Persons

**Complete personal data after each observation
record to assist recall for discussion purposes.**

First name:	Sex:
Age at date of visit:	Date of birth:
Position in family: 1 2 3 4 5 6 (ring)	
Other children present: yes/no	
Baby appears upset by presence of observer: yes/no	
Other comments, e.g., note toys available, books etc.	
Brief notes of any difficulties encountered.	

Module 3 Social/Cognitive and Motor Development
Unit   3 Learning to Walk

Posture and Large Movements at one month

Allow at least 10 minutes for this activity.

In order to begin to understand the culmination of one year's growth and development in the achievement of **walking** we need to consider earlier motor development and behaviour.

Consider your response to the following right/ wrong statements referring to a baby's behaviour at **one month.**

Behaviour at one month	yes	no
1. When lifted from cot:		
baby's head falls loosely.		
baby's head is held up firmly.		
2. When held sitting:		
baby's back is straight.		
baby's back is one complete curve.		
3. When held standing on a hard surface:		
baby presses down feet.		
baby straightens body.		
baby usually makes a forward reflex 'walking' movement.		

Check your answers with Sheridan's Scale for Posture and Large Movements at **one month** (Paper 20).
Study the line drawings.

Module 3   Social/Cognitive and Motor Development
Unit   3   Learning to Walk

First-hand observations of behaviour relevant to the development of walking at six months

Allow at least 30 minutes for this activity.

Checklist for observation at **six months**, or as near as possible to this age (from M. Sheridan's Developmental Scale).
Note: Only tick behaviour you observe.

Posture and large movements

Sits with support in cot or pram and turns head from side to side to look around him.	
When lying down lifts legs into vertical and grasps one foot or (later) two feet.	
When hands grasped braces shoulders and pulls himself to sit.	

Social behaviour and play

Offered rattle, reaches for it immediately; shakes deliberately to make it sound, often regarding it closely at the same time.	
Friendly with strangers but occasionally shows some shyness or even slight anxiety when approached too near or abruptly, especially if mother is out of sight.	

Complete personal data after each observation record.

First Name:	Sex:
Age at date of visit:	Date of birth:
Position in family: 1 2 3 4 5 6 (ring)	
Other children present: yes/no	
Child appears upset by presence of observer: yes/no	
Other comments, e.g., note toys available.	

Module 3   Social/Cognitive and Motor Development
Unit   3   Learning to Walk

First-hand observations of behaviour relevant to the development of walking at twelve months

Allow at least 30 minutes for this activity.

Checklist for observations at twelve months, or as near as possible to this age (from M. Sheridan's Development Scale).
Note: Only tick behaviour you observe.

Posture and large movements

Sits well on the floor and for indefinite time.	
Can rise to sitting position from lying down.	
Crawls on hands and knees, shuffles on buttocks or bear-walks rapidly about the floor.	
Pulls to standing and lets himself down again holding on to furniture.	
Walks forward and sideways with only one hand held.	
May stand alone for a few moments.	
May walk alone.	
May crawl upstairs (average 13 to 14 months).	

Social behaviour and play

Enjoys putting small objects in and out of containers.	
Emotionally still very dependent upon familiar adult especially mother.	
Gives toys to adult on request and sometimes spontaneously.	
Demonstrates affection to familiar adults.	

Complete personal data after each observation record.

First name: Sex:	
Age at date of visit: Date of birth:	
Position in family: 1 2 3 4 5 6 (ring)	
Other children present: yes/no	
Child appears upset by presence of observer: yes/no	
Other comments, e.g., note toys available.	

Module 3   Social/Cognitive and Motor Development
Unit   3   Learning to Walk

First-hand observations of behaviour relevant to the development of walking at eighteen months

Allow at least 30 minutes for this activity.

Checklist for observations at eighteen months, or as
near as possible to this age (from M. Sheridan's
Developmental Scale).
Note: Only tick behaviour you observe.

Posture and large movements

Walks well with feet only slightly apart.	
Starts and stops safely.	
No longer needs to hold upper arms in extension to balance.	
Runs carefully, head held erect in midline, eyes fixed on ground one or two yards ahead, usually cannot continue round obstacles.	
Pushes and pulls large toys, boxes etc. round floor.	
Kneels upright on flat surface without support.	
Squats to pick up fallen toy.	

Social behaviour and play

Briefly imitates simple, everyday activities, e.g. feeding doll, reading book, brushing floor, washing clothes, etc. (circle)	
Emotionally still very dependent upon familiar adult, especially mother.	
Alternates between clinging and resistance.	

Complete personal data after each observation record.

First name: Sex:
Age at date of visit: Date of birth:
Position in family: 1 2 3 4 5 6   (ring)
Other children present: yes/no
Child appears upset by presence of observer: yes/no
Other comments, e.g. note toys available.
Note any spontaneous imaginative play.

D.—J

Module 3   Social/Cognitive and Motor Development
Unit   3   Learning to Walk

Comparative Summary Chart indicating changes in posture and large movements at six, twelve and eighteen months.

Allow at least 15 minutes for this activity.

Name/age	Posture and large movements	yes	no
Six months			
First name: Age: months weeks Position in family 1 2 3 4 5 6	Sits with support.		
	Turns head from side to side.		
	Reaches for object within reach.		
Twelve months First name: Age: months weeks Position in family 1 2 3 4 5 6	Crawls/bear-walks:		
	about floor; upstairs.		
	Walks alone arms extended.		
Eighteen months First name: Age: months weeks Position in family 1 2 3 4 5 6	Walks well (without arms extended).		
	Carries toy.		
	Pushes/pulls large toys.		
	Cannot cope with obstacles.		
	Squats to pick up fallen toy.		

Note: Bring this chart with observation records to discussion group.

Module 4   Factors affecting early Development and Learning
Unit   1   Communication before words

Allow at least 40 minutes for this activity.

Make yourself familiar with these guidance notes and checklist *before* arranging your visit.
Tell the mother you would like to see her playing with her child, aged between twelve and eighteen months. Ask her to provide a choice of familiar toys placed just beyond the baby's reach and to indicate them to the baby by pointing and later to talk about them and give the baby the toy he seems to want to play with. Ask her to try to get the baby interested in playing with one of the toys.
Observe mother and baby for a period of fifteen minutes or so.

1. Focus on the 'shared field of attention' of the mother and baby.
2. Note how the mother or the baby gets the other to 'share the field of attention', that is, to 'zero in on a topic' as Bruner puts it.
3. Notice whether the mother follows the baby's line of regard or the baby the mother's.
4. Note how the mother responds to the baby's vocalizing and the baby responds to the mother.

Tape-recording
Load a blank cassette into the recorder.
Put the recorder in a safe place, away from the baby, and locate the microphone behind the baby's head and quite close. The microphone and recorder should be separated by at least two feet. Start the recorder, and switch on the microphone before beginning.

Time check
Check numbers at five-minute intervals if you have a counter, otherwise identify with a spoken check every five minutes. This will assist identification on tape in later discussion.
Note: It is possible that a young child may be so absorbed with the mother and/or toy that vocalization is minimal. In this situation concentrate on observing behaviour of the baby and the mother's contribution, vocal or otherwise.

Complete basic data and comments from mother.

During your fifteen minutes of observation complete the following checklist.

Tick over periods of 5 mins	3 periods of 5 mins		
	1st	2nd	3rd
1. Baby follows mother's pointing finger with his eyes.			
2. Baby points at object.			
3. Baby vocalizes while pointing.			
Sounds repeated.			

(continued)

Module 4   Factors affecting early Development and Learning
Unit   1   Communication before words

---

4. Mother responds by: pointing;
 	
            reaching for object;
 	
            vocalizing;
 	
            using words.

5. Mother gives desired toy to baby.
6. Variety of sounds vocalized by baby in relation to play; repeated (R).
7. Baby's sounds: repeated by mother;   expanded by mother.
8. Baby gives toy to mother.
9. Recognized word used by baby.
10. Recognized two-word sentence by baby e.g. 'all gone', 'bye-bye, teddy', 'car gone'.
11. Mother repeats word(s);   expands two-word sentence.
12. Expressions of emotion by smiling, pouting, frowning, arm-waving, crying, shrieking etc. (circle)

Stop tape after fifteen minutes (5 × 3).

Basic data

First name:	Sex:
Age at date of visit:	Date of birth:
Position in family:	1 2 3 4 5 6 (ring)

Whether baby cries
  (a) at being left on his own;
  (b) at strangers.
	yes/no
	yes/no

Comments from mother:	
Further observations and/or comments:	

Module 4 Factors affecting early Development and Learning
Unit 2 Social Basis of Language Development

Listening to and analysing the tape-recording

Allow at least 50 minutes for this activity.

After making your tape-recording you will want to
listen to it. This will not be easy to start with; we all
have to learn to listen consciously to tape-recordings
of language especially the early stages of language
development. This activity is concerned with the pre-
linguistic stage of language.

The aim is to note the sounds and the context in which
they are embedded. To do this we need to become
familiar with the sequence of sounds and to relate this
sequence to the sequence of activities noted by you
on the checklist.

Transcription
Position the tape-recorder so that the loudspeaker
faces you.

Note the time of starting and time of completing the
tape and five-minute intervals.

Listen at least twice to the tape before beginning to
transcribe.

The third time:

Make a list of sounds in sequence noting the
baby's and the mother's contributions.

Number the sequence of sounds, e.g.

1. baby's high pitched shriek;
2. baby: 'dad-dad';
3. baby: 'ad-da'.

Note repetitive sounds by adding (R).

Note sequence of repeated sounds (SR);
pauses (P); long pauses (PP).

Note imitation by baby of mother (I. b. of m.).

Note imitation by mother of baby (I. m. of b.).

Note any identifiable words.

Mark five-minute intervals against your numbered
sequence. If your recorder has a counter note the
number at five-minute intervals. (This will aid
retrieval of examples during discussion.)

Mark the most interesting three- to five-minute
sequence on your transcript and check that you can
retrieve it for use in discussion.

Check on the following materials and bring them with
you to your discussion group.
1. Observation checklist.
2. Personal data records.
3. Additional comments and notes on situation.
4. Cassette tape and transcription sequence.
5. Cassette tape-recorder.

Module 4   Factors affecting early Development and Learning
Unit   2   Social Basis of Language Development

Social interaction: words and people

Allow at least 50 minutes for this activity.

Mother–child and observer–child interaction in play situation, preferably in child's own home. Age: fifteen/eighteen months to two years.

Arrangements for visit to child's home.
See the general guidance paper in Module 2. Try to work with a mother and baby already known to you. Aim to record observations of behaviour *and* to tape-record child's speech with mother and with observer. Make yourself familiar with the following schedule *before* your visit.

1. Arrange with mother, or other care-giver to play with child, sharing toys or a picture-book, talking to him naturally about his toys and encouraging him to talk (emphasize this aspect). Tell her you will **not** join in during the first five minutes.
2. Ask the mother to bring you into the play with the child after about five minutes and then let you take over the 'conversation' with the child for the next ten minutes. This is, of course, assuming that the child is not upset by your presence!
3. Request permission to use your tape-recorder. On the occasion of your observation visit:
   Set up the tape-recorder **out of sight and out of reach** of the child. If using a separate microphone fix it firmly behind the child's head. A battery-powered recorder can be put inside a shopping bag. The microphone can be fixed so that it just peeps out of the top. But remember to place bag out of reach of the child: he is likely to be mobile at this age.
   Ask the mother where she will be playing with the child.

When mother and child are comfortably settled:
switch on tape-recorder **and** microphone;
sit quietly where you can see both mother and child without being too obtrusive;
make your observations of the child's behaviour on the checklist;
note five-minute intervals verbally on the tape.

Module 4   Factors affecting early Development and Learning
Unit   2   Social Basis of Language Development

Task 1: Mother involves the child with toy(s) or picture book	yes	no
Mother points and names toy/picture.		
Mother points and speaks about toy/picture.		
Child grasps toy without speaking.		
Child points to picture without speaking.		
Child grasps toy and vocalizes.		
Child points to picture and vocalizes.		
Child names toy.		
Child names picture.		
Child uses two-word sentence with toy.		
Child uses two-word sentence with book.		
Mother expands two-word sentence.		
Child repeats mother's expanded two-word sentence.		
Child repeats own two-word sentence.		
Child vocalizes using jargon not interpretable.		

Task 2: Mother brings observer into play
Sit near to the child but wait for signs that he has accepted your move. When the child is used to your presence take part in a 'conversation' about the toy/book.
Follow the child's lead. Let him start the 'conversation'. Keep your contribution to encouraging or imitative sounds. Reflect back his words without expansion.
Continue for about five minutes. Give signal on the tape for second five minutes.

Task 3: Observer changes role
If child seems happy with you **change your role**; take the initiative in talking to the child about his toy or book. Use his name and speak in simple sentences describing actions with the toy.
Example: 'Here comes Teddy' or 'Where's it gone?'
Give the child time to speak in between your comments. When he is speaking let him finish — wait for a pause.
Reply to his contributions. Make a guess at what he means if you are not sure.

(continued)

Module 4   Factors affecting early Development and Learning
Unit   2   Social Basis of Language Development

Task 4: Two-word sentences

Note carefully the context of any two-word sentences
used by the child. Expand these in relation to the
child's intended framework of meaning:

      Example: 'Car broke.'
      Expansion: 'Yes, the car is broken.'

Wait to see if the child repeats your expanded
sentence or repeats his own two-word sentence.
Continue with this changed role for five minutes or so.
Give signal for third five minutes.
Switch off the tape-recorder.

Task 5: Talk with the mother

Before you begin to talk to the mother provide the
child with some fresh play materials, from his own
toys if possible.
Ask the mother if she enjoys talking to her child about
his toys and/or his books.
Do they look at picture books together? yes/no
Ask her if she can recall any further examples of the
child's speech.
Obtain the following information from her to use in
discussion.

Basic data
First name: Sex:
Age at date of visit: Date of birth:
Position of family: 1 2 3 4 5 6 (ring)
Child cries (a) on being left on own;   yes/no   (b) at strangers.   yes/no

Module 4 Factors affecting early Development and Learning
Unit   2 Social Basis of Language Development

Transcript of tape-recording

Allow at least 50 minutes for this activity.

In order to make full use of your recorded material you will need to *transcribe* this ready for use when you engage in discussion.
Note: it is a good idea to do the transcription with the help of a colleague in order to check for accuracy.
Method
Listen to the replay of each five-minute section before transcribing, to familiarize yourself with the sequence.
Next record each utterance on the schedule stopping the recorder to do so. Complete speaker column.
Replay each five-minute section to check for accuracy.
You will be surprised how difficult it is to be accurate in the early stages of transcribing from tape-recorded material!

Task 1	Time in 5 mins	No.	*Utterances*	*Speaker*
Mother and child	0 mins	1	Look, Mummie	child
		2	Yes, it's a car	mother
		3	car – car	child
		4		
		5		
		6		
		7		
		8		
		9		
Replay/Check		10		
Task 2	5 mins	11		
Observer and child – observer passive		12		
		13		
		14		
		15		
		16		
		17		
		18		
		19		
Replay/Check		20		

Module 4   Factors affecting early Development and Learning
Unit   2   Social Basis of Language Development

Tasks 3 and 4 Observer changes role; initiates and expands child's two-word sentences	10 mins	21		
		22		
		23		
		24		
		25		
		26		
		27		
		28		
		29		
		30		
Replay/Check				

Number of utterances
Compare number of utterances by child:
1. when mother was playing and talking to him;
2. when observer was playing and talking in a passive role;
3. when observer was taking the initiative extending conversation and expanded two-word sentences.
Discuss differences found with group.

Expansion by adults of child's two-word sentences:
Underline in red any examples of two-word expansions by adults either by mother or observer for easy identification in discussion group.
Re-read Paper 26, the summary of Brown and Bellugi's research, to check whether your records illustrate any further points raised by them.

Module 4 Factors affecting early Development and Learning
Unit   3 Development of Imaginative Play — play with objects and 'pretend play'

Observations of play from fifteen months to two years

Allow at least one hour for this activity.

Arrange with a mother, if possible well-known to you, with a toddler of fifteen months to two years, to visit their home when the mother can be free to play with the child and you can be permitted to join in the play when the child is happily settled. If there are older children one of them might be willing to play with the child initially instead of the mother.
Study the observation schedule *before* arranging your visit.
Ask for the normal play situation with toys familiar to the child such as bricks/blocks, small miniature toys, containers, teddy/dolls, imaginative toys/equipment, dressing up clothes etc.

During the visit: Task 1
When you have established a friendly relationship with the mother and child sit quietly in the background and make a list of toys available.
Note how the mother interests the child in toys etc.

Task 2
After about five minutes show an interest in the child's play and in the toys *but* don't take over from the mother or older child. The young child may give you toys to hold but will probably take them back from you almost immediately.

Task 3
Observation record
When a suitable opportunity occurs withdraw from interacting with the child and observe his play for about ten minutes. Tick the type of play activity as it occurs. Indicate intense concentration by circling your tick.

A.	Manipulating objects			
	Putting objects in and out of containers.			
	Putting objects together.			
	Banging objects together.			
	Throwing objects.			
B.	Constructional			
	Placing blocks one on top of the other.			
	Building tower, note number of blocks.			
	Knocking it down.			
	Re-building.			

Module 4 Factors affecting early Development and Learning

Unit 3 Development of Imaginative Play — play with objects and 'pretend play'

C.	Imitative			
	Imitating tower building.			
	Imitating action of another child or of mother:			
	immediately;			
	after an interval of time (deferred imitation).			
D.	Make-believe play with objects			
	Representing one thing by another:			
	Examples: putting bricks or other objects in line;			
	pushing along with accompanying train noises;			
	using brick as car or aeroplane;			
	feeding teddy/doll with or without utensils.			
E.	Make-believe role play			
	Driving car/bus.			
	Being the milkman with/without objects.			
	Being a doctor, listening to heart beat, using a stethoscope:			
	with objects;			
	without objects.			
	Being mother dressing dolls, pouring tea, etc.			
	Being father smoking, reading the paper, etc.			
	Joining in make-believe play with another child.			
F.	Language accompanying play			
	Unidentifiable sounds accompanying play.			
	Naming words (things and actions).			
	Two-word sentences.			
	Sentences of three/four or more words.			
	Questions to self, to mother or to other child.			
	Sentences accompanying play activity.			

Module 4   Factors affecting early Development and Learning
Unit   3   Development of Imaginative Play — play with objects and 'pretend play'

Task 4
After play session of fifteen to twenty minutes ask mother:

child's favourite toy(s);

his favourite play activity;

whether he plays alone happily; always / sometimes / never
whether he talks to himself while he plays; always / sometimes / never
if she can remember when he began to engage in make-believe play;

whether she encourages or discourages this;

whether she actually joins in the make-believe play; yes/no

any other comments about the child's play.

Basic data

First name: Date of birth: Age at date of visit: Position in family: 1   2   3   4   5   6   (ring) Plays with older siblings: Looks for mother, wants to be with her

Bring records to discussion group.

Module 5 Representation and Cognitive Development
Unit   1 Symbolic Play

You should take about 10 minutes to complete this activity.

Below are three statements that have been made frequently concerning children's play. Examine each one and then tick in the appropriate column according to whether you think it is always, often, sometimes or seldom a characteristic of play.

Play is . . .	always	often	sometimes	seldom
1. a spontaneous activity;				
2. voluntary;				
3. pleasurable;				
4. a non-serious activity.				

Now read Paper 30 and compare your answers with the argument contained in it.

Module 5   Representation and Cognitive Development
Unit   1   Symbolic Play

Allow at least 30 minutes for this activity.

The following six descriptions of young children's activities with sand and water are taken from Manning and Sharp (1977).* Read each one carefully and tick in the appropriate section according to whether you consider it an example of play or of exploration.

1. Elsie was observed playing with sand in a shallow individual sand tray. She made small piles of sand in different parts of the tray, traced paths with her fingers and kept moving a small pile of sand around. When the teacher asked her what she was doing Elsie said, 'A little girl lives here.' She pointed to one pile of sand saying, 'She's got a kitten that plays with her in the garden, but it got out when the little girl wasn't looking, and ran away and got lost. The little girl is looking for her kitten; she's going to the police station.'

   exploration / play

2. A boy was playing with small plastic animals in the sand tray. He buried the animals, then indicated the base of the tray which he had scraped clean and informed his companion: 'This is the sea; these are the caves and the crocodile is hiding. You hold this one. You say "come out there".'

   exploration / play

3. Two boys were using a fine meshed sieve over a bucket. First they held it high and low and watched the flow of sand. Kevin said, 'Look now it's coming out fast, now it's filling my bucket, quickly, oooh, it's going all over the sides of my bucket, hold it lower, then it'll go in. Let me have it now. You pour now.'

   exploration / play

   Next they poured different amounts of sand into the sieve and Martin said, 'Put more in now – a lot, a lot, look it's coming fast – now it's slow – it's finished – yes, it's empty.'

   exploration / play

4. A group of five-year-olds, three girls and two boys, had taken the water wheel from the water to the sand. They had never played with it before. One boy struggled to make the wheel work with wet sand. When asked why it wasn't working he said there was too much sand at the top and he would have to take a little out to make it work. When this failed, the second boy emptied the top, used a spoon to drop the sand through on to the wheel and then poked the sand through the hole with his finger.

   exploration / play

5. Ronald and Fred, playing in the paddling pool, noticed that they were making footprints; they immediately started a stalking game. Fred said, 'I'm an Indian and I'm following your footprints – I'm crawling along.' Ronald ran in and out of the pool making footprints, but when the stalker was upon him he jumped into the pool, and announced, 'You can't follow me now because I'm not making footprints in the water. I'm in a lake, I've got to the other side and you can't find me.'

   exploration / play

6. Five-year-olds Stephen and Richard were filling different-sized yoghurt cartons. When they went for more, Stephen discovered that they floated as he put them in the water. Richard, pouring from a small watering can, said, 'Oh, this one's still floating, and I've put some water in it.' Stephen suggested, 'See if you can sink it with more water.'

   exploration / play

* Manning, K. and Sharp, A. (1977) *Structuring Play in the Early Years at School,* Ward Lock Educational.

Module 5   Representation and Cognitive Development
Unit   1   Symbolic Play

You should take about 30 minutes to complete this activity.

List below factors in the human and material environment which it would appear from the evidence
discussed in Paper 31 might influence the development of young children's symbolic play (a) favourably
and (b) unfavourably. Under each factor write a brief
statement of the relevant evidence.

(a) **Favourably**
    1.

    2.

    3.

(b) **Unfavourably**
    1.

    2.

    3.

Module 5 Representation and Cognitive Development
Unit   1 Symbolic Play

Allow at least 1¾ hours for this activity.

For this activity you should visit a nursery school. You will probably need a morning's visit to carry out the following observations. This activity may be carried out individually or in pairs if this is more convenient.

1. Make four ten-minute observations of children's play, recording in detail what materials they were using, what themes they were pursuing in their play and what they said. Note the age of the children.

2. Make notes of occasions where you might have been able to extend children's play, giving details of how you would have done this.

3. Make notes of any occasions where you would think it appropriate (a) not to intervene in any way, and (b) to redirect children's play. Give your reasons.

Module 5 Representation and Cognitive Development
Unit 2 Young Children's Drawings and Paintings

Allow at least 2 hours for this activity.

For this activity you should select two children, one of about four and one of about five years of age, and administer to them the following tasks.* You should give each child the task separately. Record the children's responses in detail. If preferred you may work in pairs for this activity, one of you working with the four-year-old and the other with the five-year-old child. If you work in pairs you may be able to carry out this activy and Activity 36 on a single morning's visit using the same children. If you work individually you will probably need a morning's visit for this activity.

Purpose of tasks
To examine young children's concepts of topological and Euclidean shapes.

Materials
You will need eight cards on which you have reproduced the topological and Euclidean drawings below, several pieces of paper and pencils or felt-tipped pens.

topological drawings

Euclidean drawings

Procedure
You should show the child the cards one at a time, starting with the topological shapes, and ask him to draw a picture 'just like this one on the card'. When the child has finished a drawing ask him whether it is the same as the one on the card. Record his answer.

Expected levels of performance
As stated in Paper 32 children discriminate topological before Euclidean features, and they do not produce accurate Euclidean representations until seven years of age on the average. The average four-year-old child will reproduce the topological features correctly, that is he will draw closed figures and will place the dot correctly inside, outside or on the boundary of the closed figures as on the cards. The Euclidean figures will not normally be reproduced accurately at this age: typically all the Euclidean shapes are reproduced as irregular closed figures. At about five years of age, on average, children are able to represent circles and squares. A rhombus and shapes with acute and obtuse angles are not differentiated until an average age of six years.

* Taken from Piaget, J. and Inhelder, B. (1963) *The Child's Conception of Space,* Routledge & Kegan Paul.

Module 5   Representation and Cognitive Development
Unit   2   Young Children's Drawings and Paintings

Allow at least 2 hours for this activity.

For this activity you should again select two children, one of about four and one of about five years of age. If you worked in pairs for Activity 35 you may prefer to do so again for this activity, in which case you may be able to complete Activities 35 and 36 on the same visit and with the same children.

Purpose of task
This task is adapted from one used by Goodnow and discussed in Paper 32. It tests the hypothesis that young children avoid overlapping in their drawings.

Materials
You will need drawings as below and pencils or felt-tipped pens.

Procedure
Give each child, one at a time, the drawing and say, 'Another little boy (girl) drew this. He (she) didn't finish it. Would you finish it for me. First put some hair on the head.' When the child has done so, say, 'Now you can put anything else you like in the drawing.'

Results
You should keep the drawings the children complete and record the following:
1. Do the children avoid overlapping the hair and arms?
2. Examine carefully any other features the children have added to see whether they can be interpreted in terms of what you read in Paper 32. For example, did a child add hands and, if so, are there the correct number of fingers? Are there any examples of mandala or radial forms? Are there any examples of synthetic incapacity?

Module 5   Representation and Cognitive Development
Unit   3   Young Children's Thinking

Allow at least 1½ hours for this activity.

You should visit a nursery school or class and administer the following two tasks to two children, one of about four and one of about five years of age. Both children should have at least two siblings. (This is necessary for Task 2; the teacher should have this information.) Both tasks are Piagetian tests for egocentricity. You will need the same children for Activity 38. It may be possible for you to carry this out on the same visit, but young children quickly tire and lose concentration. It is important that you do not try to coerce them if they appear reluctant to co-operate, and if this is the case you should arrange a second visit. In each case administer the tasks to the children separately. You may again work in pairs if you wish, one of you working with each child.

Task 1

1. Sit opposite the child and show him first your right and then your left hand, saying 'This is my right hand', 'This is my left hand'. (Note that it is extremely important that you sit opposite the child not beside him.)

2. Then hold out first one hand and then the other each time getting the child to tell you which hand it is. If he does not answer correctly tell him which hand it is.

3. Repeat this until the child can identify your right and left hand correctly.

4. When he can do this ask him to show you his right hand, then his left hand. Record each child's response.

Expected level of performance. Most children under the age of five are unable to decentre to the experimenter's point of view and will show him the wrong hand.

Task 2

1. Ask the child, 'Have you any brothers?' If he says he has, ask him, 'What are their names?'

2. Ask the child, 'Have you any sisters?' If he says he has, ask him, 'What are their names?'

3. When you have obtained this information ask the child how many brothers (sisters or brothers and sisters) he has. For example, if a child replies to 1 and 2 that he has two brothers, John and Peter you should ask, 'How many brothers has John?' 'How many brothers has Peter?' If a child replies that she has a brother and a sister, Robert and Sharon, you should ask, 'How many brothers and sisters has Robert?' 'How many brothers and sisters has Sharon?'

Expected level of performance. Usually a child under the age of five is unable to decentre to the point of view of his or her siblings and will respond to question 3 without taking himself or herself into account.

Activity 38

Module 5   Representation and Cognitive Development
Unit   3   Young Children's Thinking

Allow at least one hour for this activity.

Visit a nursery school or class and give the following task to three children, one of three-and-a-half, one of four to four-and-a-half and one of five, or the nearest approximations you can get to these ages. This task is a test for egocentricity devised by Martin Hughes which you will have read about in Paper 36. If preferred, three of you may work together, each working with one child.

You will need two cardboard 'walls' and three small dolls, two representing policemen and the other a little boy, as in the illustrations in Paper 36.

Place the child, 'walls' and dolls as in the second illustration in Paper 36. Give each child the task separately. Tell the child, 'This little boy has been naughty and wants to hide from the policemen. Put him behind one of these walls (pointing) so that this policeman (pointing) and this policeman (pointing) can't see him.'

Record each child's response carefully.

As you will have read in Donaldson's paper, 90 per cent of the children could perform this task correctly, that is they were able to decentre and thus to give a non-egocentric response.

Activity 39

Module 5   Representation and Cognitive Development
Unit   4   Learning, Teaching and Cognitive Development

Allow at least one hour for this activity.

List below the equipment you think might be appropriate for use in the water tray in a nursery school or class; do this in the left-hand column. Beside each piece of equipment list in the right-hand column the concept or concepts which children might develop by using it. Then do this in a similar way with any other common area of provision in early childhood education.

Equipment	Concepts
1. With water tray	

Module 6 Language Development
Unit   1   The Child's Acquisition of Language and the Role of the Adult

Allow at least 15 minutes for this activity.

Now that you have read Paper 39, read the following extracts from books on children's language development. Mark in the appropriate box according to whether you think the extract deals primarily with phonological, morphological, syntactic or semantic aspects of language.

'Brown . . . traced the development of . . . the pre-positions "in" and "on". When Brown listed all occurrences of these along with the nouns with which they were used by the children a . . . principle motivating their differential use was revealed. The nouns used with "in" were objects which could contain other objects, i.e. they were objects having cavities or containing internal spaces such as "bag", "box" and "briefcase". The nouns used with "on" were all objects which had flat surfaces which could support other objects, such as "floor", "shelf" and "table". In addition one of the children had a meaning for "in" which was used to denote intermingling . . . as in "in my hair" and "in the snow".' (Cromer, R. F. (1974) 'The development of language and cognition' in Foss, B. (ed.) *New Perspectives in Child Development*, Penguin.)

phonological	morphological	syntactic	semantic

'. . . children between two and four years of age tend first to adopt a limited set of separately acquired plural forms and then systematically to apply particular marking rules across all plurals, sometimes extending them inappropriately . . . "s" can be added to nouns with no plural form, e.g. "peoples"; vowel-change plurals in both singular and plural forms, e.g.

"mans" and "mens"; mass nouns, e.g. "milks"; and pronouns and adjectives, e.g. "twos", "somes" and "pinks" ' (Francis, H. (1975) *Language in Childhood*, Elek.)

phonological	morphological	syntactic	semantic

'When my own son was just beginning to speak I decided that . . . I ought to study how he progressed and see what order the different sounds and combination of sounds appeared in . . . At first . . . *light* was pronounced *dight, lady* was pronounced *dady*' (Smith, N. 'How children learn to speak', *The Listener* (2 December 1971).)

phonological	morphological	syntactic	semantic

'One test situation that even two-year-old children can understand is a request to imitate. During period C . . . when Adam was inverting AUX [auxiliary verb] and N.P. [noun phrase] in yes–no questions . . . [he was given] such an imitation test:
    Adult: Adam say what I say: 'Where can he put them?'
    Adam: Where he can put them?
This evidence strengthens the assertion that Adam's language system could not cope with the inversion transformation in this linguistic context' (Cazden, C. (1972) *Child Language and Education,* Holt, Rinehart and Winston.)

phonological	morphological	syntactic	semantic

Module 6   Language Development
Unit   1   The Child's Acquisition of Language and the Role of the Adult

Allow at least 15 minutes with each child in this activity.

In Paper 41 reference is made to a test in the form of a game which Bellugi gave to a three-year-old, Adam. Try out this test/game with three or four children aged between two-and-a-half and three years. You should ask the children, one at a time, to play a game with you and then to 'Say what I say'. The test is designed to find out whether the children can imitate correctly the structure for 'wh' questions in which the auxiliary verb precedes the noun or pronoun. Examples are:

'Where **can he** put them?'
'Why **can't we** play?'
'What **will the lady** eat for tea?'

You should compose more similar questions of your own. Record each child's response and note whether he or she is able to imitate each sentence correctly or whether instead the auxiliary verb and noun or pronoun are in the wrong order, for example:

Where he can put them?
Why we can't play?

Remember that for this activity, as for all that involve working with young children, you will need considerable time first to get to know the children and to make a relationship with them so that they are happy to play the 'game' with you. Do not try to persuade an unwilling child to co-operate.

You may, if you prefer, work in groups of three or four, each of you working with one child. The time taken for the activity will clearly depend on whether you work individually or in groups.

Module 6   Language Development
Unit   1   The Child's Acquisition of Language and the Role of the Adult

You should allow about 2 hours for this activity.

Arrange to work with three children aged 2, 3 and 4 years. You should have two sets of test materials. One set should consist of a toy car, a model garage, tree, gate and bridge. These could be simple and if you cannot find manufactured models you could make them from cardboard, for example. The second set of materials should consist of a stick, a ring and a tube. Test the children's understanding of the words below firstly by asking them to manipulate the toys appropriately, for example, 'make the car go under the bridge', 'make the car go into the garage', 'put the car beside the bridge'. Then you should repeat the test using the stick, ring and tube, for example, 'put the tube beside the stick', 'make the stick go through the ring'. Work with one child at a time. Discontinue the activity if the child tires.

words tested	2-year-old model toys	2-year-old stick etc.	3-year-old model toys	3-year-old stick etc.	4-year-old model toys	4-year-old stick etc.
in						
into						
on						
beside						
behind						
under						
over						
around						
along						
through						
below						
backward						

Module 6   Language Development
Unit   1   The Child's Acquisition of Language and the Role of the Adult

Allow at least 15 minutes for this activity.

Below are three examples of alternative ways, A
and B, that an adult might respond when a child's
statement includes a grammatical error. Examine the
alternative responses in each example. Make notes
on which response, A or B, you think most
appropriate and why.

Example 1

Child:	'The bird flied away.'
Adult response A:	'No, the bird **flew** away.'
Adult response B:	'Yes, the bird flew **away**.'

Example 2

Child:	'Janey gived me her dolly to play with.'
Adult response A:	'No. Janey **gave** you her dolly to play with.'
Adult response B:	'Yes, Janey gave you her **dolly** to play with.'

Example 3

Child:	'Mummy, Ann said she's going to learn me skipping.'
Adult response A:	'Not **learn**, darling, **teach**. Ann is going to **teach** you to skip.'
Adult response B:	'Yes? She's going to teach you to **skip**? How nice.'

Module 6   Language Development
Unit   1   The Child's Acquisition of Language and the Role of the Adult

Allow about 30 minutes for this activity.

Below are some more examples of adults' responses to children's statements. Make notes on how appropriate/inappropriate you think each response is and why. Note which responses involve extension and which do not. Where you think a more appropriate response could have been given note what you think it should have been.

Example 1
A four-year-old girl was on the beach with her father. Balancing carefully she walked along a drainage pipe until she came to its outlet. She then became interested in the water that was streaming from it onto the beach, turned round, surveyed the length of the pipe along which she had just walked and asked her father what it was. Holding his arms out to catch her he answered, 'It's for nice little girls to jump off.'

Example 2
Walking with his parents in a park a five-year-old boy looked up at a very tall metasequoia tree, remarking, 'Look at this tree.' His mother replied, 'Yes, it's touching the sky'.

Example 3
A four-year-old girl picked up a pine-cone on a walk in the woods and showing it to her father said, 'Look, it's sort of broken.' Her father replied, 'Yes, it looks as though it might have been chewed. Perhaps it was a squirrel. Squirrels do chew pine-cones.'

Example 4
A three-year-old boy waiting with his mother at a bus stop saw an excavator pass and asked what it was. His mother replied, 'Oh do stop asking questions. Here comes the bus.'

Example 5
A three-year-old girl stared for some time at an aquarium in a pet-shop window and then commented, 'The fishes keep opening their mouths.' Her mother answered, 'Yes, darling, aren't they lovely?'

Example 6
A five-year-old girl watched intently as her mother rolled some pastry and said, 'It's squashing.' Her mother answered, 'Yes, I'm rolling it out thinner to make it fit on that dish. As it gets bigger this way [pointing out the circumference] it gets thinner here, doesn't it' [pointing to its thickness].

Module 6   Language Development
Unit   2   Language and the Development of Thinking

This activity should take between one and two hours.

List below some of the ways in which language can
facilitate the development of thinking discussed in
Paper 45.

Module 6   Language Development
Unit   2   Language and the Development of Thinking

Allow at least 1½ hours for this activity.

Visit a nursery school or pre-school playgroup and collect four or five fifteen-minute observations of the language used by children playing and exploring in different contexts. These contexts might include, for example, home-corner play, play and exploration with sand and/or water, constructional activities. However, what you select must clearly be determined in part by what is available. Make sure the children cover the age-range three to five years. Record as many examples of speech as you can in each

fifteen-minute period noting the age of the speaker in each case. Examine these samples for any examples of a restricted code as given by Keats and Keats in Paper 46. State which characteristics of a restricted code are exemplified in each sample.

It would be preferable if the schools visited by you as a group included a high proportion whose intake was largely from a working-class background.

The following kind of response guide might be helpful.

First 15 minutes Context	Speech of younger children	Speech of older children
Second 15 minutes		
Third 15 minutes		
Fourth 15 minutes		
Fifth 15 minutes		

Module 7   Social Development
Unit   1   The Child, the Adult and the Culture

You should complete this activity in 30–60 minutes.

From your reading of Paper 47:

1. List below what you understand to be the three most important factors influencing identification.

   (a)

   (b)

   (c)

2. In what ways have psychologists distinguished between identification and imitation.

Module 7   Social Development
Unit   1   The Child, the Adult and the Culture

Allow at least 1¾ hours for this activity.

Visit a nursery school, class or pre-school playgroup. Observe for approximately 10 minutes for each activity children engaged in the following:
(a) domestic play, (b) play with dressing-up clothes, (c) play with large construction equipment.

If some of these activities are not available substitute others of your own choosing.

Record in detail what the children do and say and what materials they use. You should also record the age and sex of each child.

When you get home analyse your observations for examples of behaviour which are clearly modelled on adult behaviour. List these below in the left-hand column. In the middle column list beside each item of behaviour the model on which it is based if it is clear, for example, adult male, adult female, television character (specify). In the right-hand column list the category of behaviour modelled including examples of aggression and same-sex role identification.

You may, if you prefer, work in pairs for this activity. You should keep these observations for further analysis (in Activities 49 and 50) and for discussion. It would be useful to look at what is required for Activities 49 and 50 so that you are aware of the need to collect sufficient relevant data.

Behaviour	Model	Category

Module 7   Social Development
Unit   1   The Child, the Adult and the Culture

Allow at least 30 minutes for this activity.

Re-examine your observations collected for Activity 48. Select two examples of behaviour which you think it might be desirable to elaborate or modify. Give your reasons below. For each item of behaviour list the strategies you would adopt in order to elaborate or modify the behaviour in question.

1.
   (a)

   (b)

   (c)

2.
   (a)

   (b)

   (c)

Module 7   Social Development
Unit   1   The Child, the Adult and the Culture

Allow at least 30 minutes for this activity.

Re-examine your observations carried out for Activity 49. List below:
   (a) examples of girls selecting materials and adopting roles which match a female stereotype;
   (b) examples of boys selecting materials and adopting roles which match a male stereotype;
   (c) examples of girls selecting materials and adopting roles which conflict with a female stereotype;
   (d) examples of boys selecting materials and adopting roles which conflict with a male stereotype.

Module 7   Social Development
Unit   2   Peer-Group Relationships

Allow at least 1¼ hours for this activity.

You should visit a nursery school, class or pre-school playgroup. Make as many observations, each lasting about 5 minutes, as you can of children playing in groups of two or more. Analyse your samples for examples of (a) parallel play and (b) social (co-operative) play. List these in the left-hand column below. Beside these list, in column 2, the size of each group and, in column 3, the sex and ages of the children involved. You should also find out how long each child has attended the nursery school, class or playgroup.

	Size of groups	Age of children
(a) Parallel play		
(b) Social play		

.D.—K

Module 7   Social Development
Unit   2   Peer-Group Relationships

Allow at least one hour for this activity.

The following test for moral judgement should be given to two five-year-old children (separately). The test is a modified form of a pair of Piaget's stories (Paper 50) and is also adapted by the use of illustrations to make it a little easier for young children to hold the details in mind.

Show the child the picture and tell the stories as follows pointing to the relevant illustration:

Story 1
Picture 1: Here is a little boy. His name is John. He wanted to help his mother by washing up the plates for her. Here is John at the sink washing up the plates.
Picture 2: When he had washed and dried the plates he put them on a tray to take them to the cupboard. Here is John carrying the tray full of plates.
Picture 3: On his way to the cupboard John tripped and dropped the tray. All the plates were broken. There were more than ten plates. Here are the broken plates.

Story 2
Picture 1: Here is another little boy. His name is Peter. Peter's mother made some cakes and put them in a cupboard. She told Peter he wasn't to touch them.
Picture 2: When his mother wasn't looking Peter climbed on a chair to reach the shelf in the cupboard where the cakes were. Here is Peter standing on the chair. He wanted to take a cake, but as he tried to get it he knocked a plate down, one plate, and it broke. Here is the broken plate on the floor.

When you have told the stories first make sure the child has understood by getting him to repeat them. Then ask him, 'Is one of the boys naughtier than the other?' If the child says, 'Yes', ask him, 'Which one, Peter or John, who was the naughtiest?' When he replies ask, 'Why was John (or Peter) the naughtiest?'

If the child replies to the first question, 'No, they are both naughty', ask him, 'If you were their mother would you punish them both the same?' If the child says, 'No', ask him which boy should be punished the most and why.

Record each child's response in detail.

Module 7   Social Development
Unit   2   Peer-Group Relationships

Story 1

1   2

3

Module 7   Social Development
Unit   2   Peer-Group Relationships

Story 2

1   2

Module 8   Pre-School Provision

Allow at least 2 hours for this activity.

Visit a nursery school or nursery class and make a detailed list of the provision made for the children. List the areas of provision in the left-hand column and the material within each area in the right-hand column. For example, home-corner play would be entered in the left-hand column, and the list set out next to it in the right-hand column might include telephone, cups and saucers, small table, shopping basket and so on. Keep this list as you will need to consult it for Activity 55 and Discussion Z.

Areas of provision	Materials provided within areas

Module 8   Pre-School Provision

Allow at least 2 hours for this activity.

Visit a pre-school playgroup. Make a detailed list of provision made for the children as you did for Activity 53. You should keep this list as it will be needed for Activity 55 and for Discussion Z.

Areas of provision	Materials provided within areas

Module 8   Pre-School Provision

Allow at least one hour for this activity.

Compare the provision you observed at a nursery
school or nursery class (Activity 53) and at a
pre-school playgroup (Activity 54). List the
differences as follows:

1. Provision found at nursery school but not at pre-school playgroup.

2. Provision found at pre-school playgroup but not at nursery school.

Module 8   Pre-School Provision

Allow at least 30 minutes for this activity.

Make a list of what you think should be the purposes
of a modern nursery school. When you have completed your list examine it and mark appropriately
what you consider to be your two most important and
two least important purposes.

   You should keep the list as you will need it in
connection with the discussion in this unit.

Module 8   Pre-School Provision

Allow at least one hour for this activity.

You are asked to complete this activity before engaging in Discussion Z.

Compare the recommendations of Blank (Paper 53), Tizard (Paper 54) and Van der Eyken (Paper 51) as follows:

1. What are the differences between the recommendations of Blank and of Tizard?

2. What are the differences between the recommendations of Blank and of Van der Eyken?

3. What are the differences between the recommendations of Tizard and of Van der Eyken?